Robert Kudielka on Bridget Riley

Essays and interviews 1972–2003

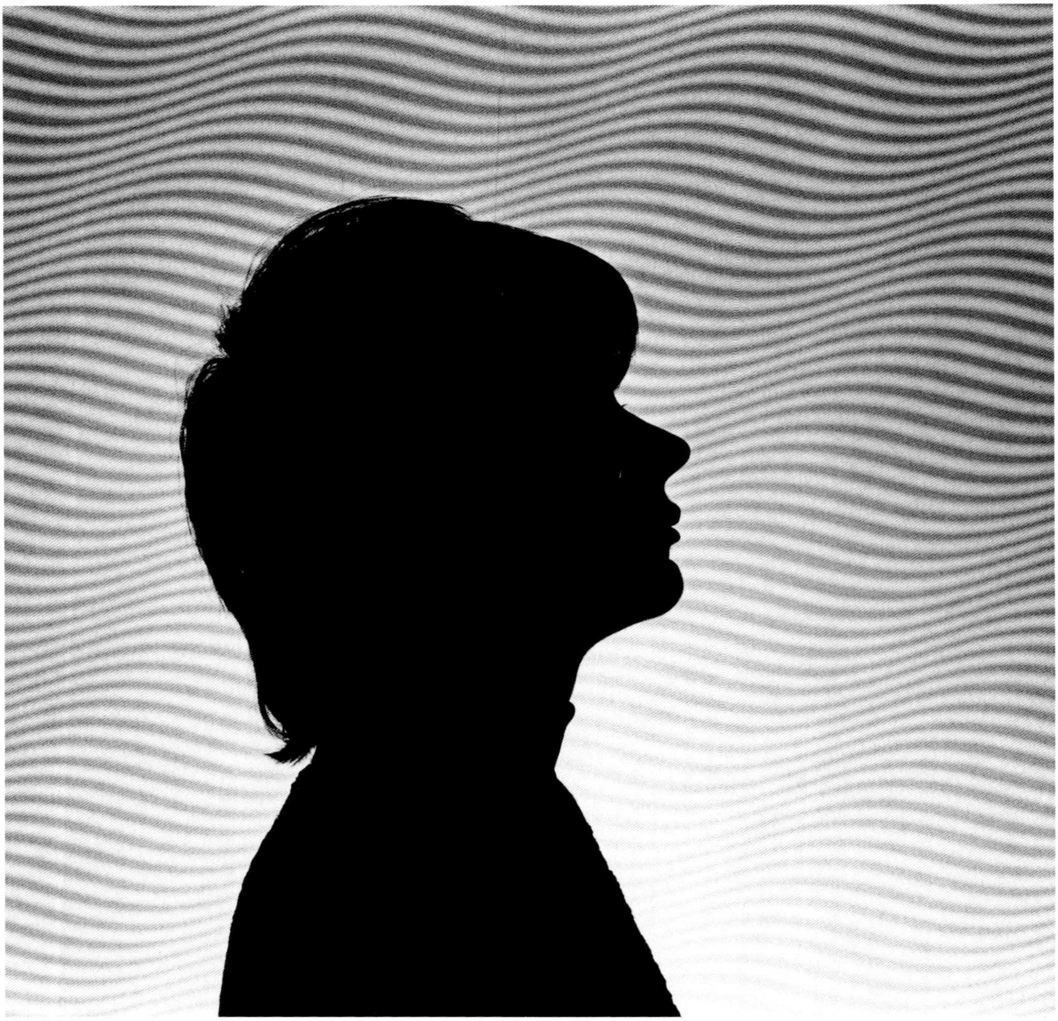

Robert Kudielka on Bridget Riley

Essays and interviews 1972–2003

Ridinghouse

First published in the United Kingdom in 2005 by
Ridinghouse
47 Lexington Street, London W1R 3LG
Distributed by Cornerhouse
70 Oxford Street Manchester M15 5NH
Telephone +44 (0) 161 2001501

Photographic credits
Photographs: Prudence Cuming Associates, London
With the following exceptions:
Bridget Riley portrait: © 2005 Jack Mitchell (p. 2)
Bridget Riley and Robert Kudielka photograph © 2005 Manfred Mayer (p. 6)
Bridget Riley portrait © 2005 Andrew Lamb (p. 236)
Mondrian: © 2005 Mondrian/ Holtzman Trust c/o HCR International, Warrenton Virginia USA (p. 93)
Pollock: The Metropolitan Museum of Art, George A. Hearn Fund, 1957 (57.92). Photograph © 2005 The Metropolitan Museum of Art and © 2005 ARS, NY and DACS, London (p. 100)
Ballet Rambert: © 2005 V&A Images, Theatre Museum (p. 126)

British Library Cataloguing-in-Publication Data
A catalogue record of this book is available from the British Library

ISBN 0 9541710 9 8

Designed and typeset by Tim Harvey

Printed and bound in the United Kingdom by St Ives Westerham Press

Contents

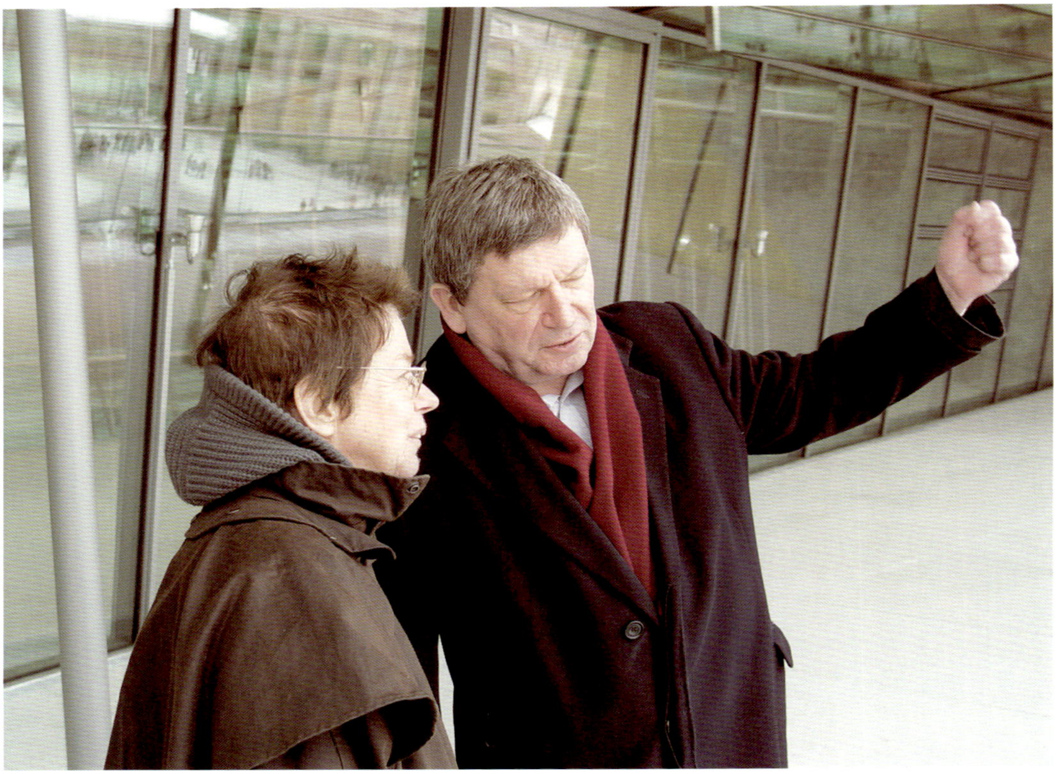

Bridget Riley and Robert Kudielka 2005

Foreword

Robert Kudielka

Following the work of a living artist for almost forty years is a rare occurrence in itself. Apart from Bridget Riley I cannot count many among my artist friends whose work I have observed for such a long time. But preserving a friendship and an interest is quite different from the fascination and tenacity with which I have followed, analysed and discussed almost every turn of her development as an artist. This steady curiosity and eagerness to communicate was surprising even to me when I re-read the texts collected in this book. A sympathetic critic once described me as "professional Riley-watcher", and this is probably a fair description. Only a small elaboration is needed about what turned looking at Riley's work into a professional obsession.

I first met the artist in December 1967 in her London studio in Holland Park, where she still works today. She had just finished the painting *Deny 2*, which was leaning against the wall, along with two other paintings, *Breathe* and *Disturbance*. As I looked around we began to talk

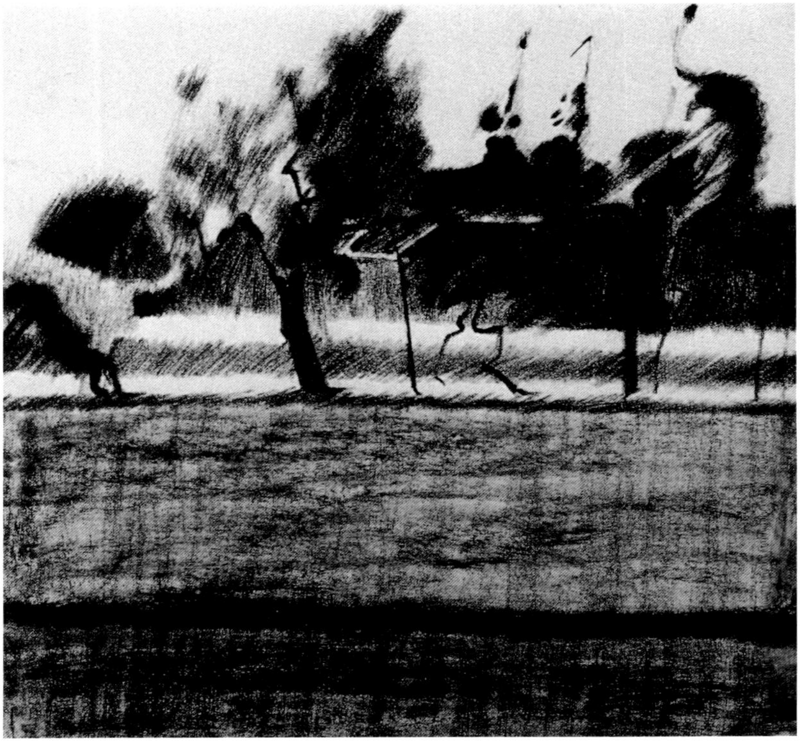

Tonal Landscape Study 1959

about the work and it quickly dawned on me that I had found my match: an uncompromising visual intelligence pursuing an art free of assumed significance and loaded ambition. This was just the right challenge for a young German philosopher deep in Phenomenology and the History of Metaphysics, who was preparing his Ph.D thesis on Kant's Aesthetics. The title of my first extensive essay on Riley, "Nothing but Appearance", still has a ring of this initial, truly liberating excitement: Imagine – an art with neither reserve nor pretence!

This first, straightforward recognition held good through all the subsequent development of Riley's art. Writing on her work became partly a way of clarifying this excitement, partly an attempt to share it with others. I simply did not understand, and do not to this day, how people could feel hurt, dizzy or blinded by these paintings. So I set myself a certain critical purpose: Instead of explaining how important or meaningful the work is, I wanted to make people *look* by describing the means and considerations that brought the work into existence. In short, I concentrated on what Paul Valéry called the "poietics" of art, refraining from any explicit claims on content. As a result the reader may miss a due historical and social assessment of Riley's work in my writings. But this restriction is deliberate. I wanted to achieve something more simple and elementary than a full-scale interpretation: a guidance that could be relinquished once the reader felt confident and curious enough to look at the work itself.

This of course leaves an obvious contradiction: Why collect and reprint these texts if it was their purpose to eventually become dispensable? Indeed as a running comment on the artist's development they have served their purpose by helping to clear away the smokescreen of hype, prejudice and slander that for a long time clouded the access to Riley's art. But there is another aspect that made me accept Karsten Schubert's proposal to publish this record of forty years of "Riley-watching". Collectively these occasional essays, introductions and interviews add up to a document that is at once personal and objective. It tells the story of a privileged visual education. To this, many people have contributed, not least those who helped me articulate my perceptions in a foreign language either by translating, correcting or editing my efforts: David Britt, David Thompson, Frank Whitford, Andrew Dempsey, and more recently Leigh Markopolous. Their relative contributions are not specifically credited because all final versions are re-worked by me. I am greatly indebted to Bridget Riley for lending her discriminating ear to this task of finishing. The rest is beyond personal gratitude. Thanks to her work my life changed. I began to trust and enjoy, as I hope this book proves, the pleasures of sight.

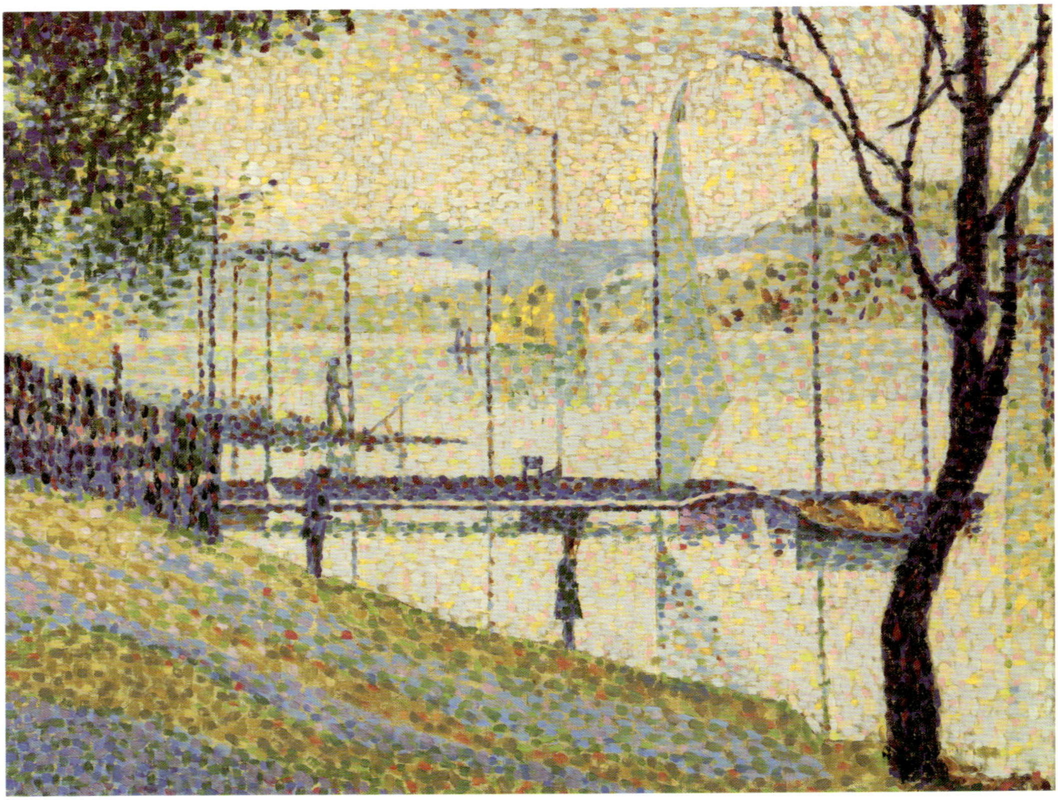

Copy after *Le Pont de Courbevoie* by Georges Seurat 1959

Introduction

Bridget Riley

I first met Robert Kudielka in 1967. He was just finishing his philosophy studies at Tübingen University in Germany. He took a great interest in Contemporary Art, following developments in the art world, visiting New York and attending international events such as Documenta and the Venice Biennale. He came twice a year to London to see exhibitions, meet artists and visit their studios. I had already heard about this young German critic (he wrote for the magazine *Das Kunstwerk*) before we met. Robert knew all the British abstract artists, both sculptors and painters, prominent in the sixties. He enjoyed their company and his visits were very much looked forward to. He did not come with any theoretical baggage nor was he a card-carrying member of some fashionable intellectual circle. Robert listened and looked carefully at what he was shown. He was always courteous and never arrogant.

We soon discovered that we both loved some of the great works of the past and in particular the French nineteenth-century painters; at that time they were still very much out of fashion, their contributions seen as long overtaken by recent developments. Robert and I would meet somewhere on the continent and spend a few days looking at the collection of one of the major museums. These were joyous occasions and laid up a rich store of powerful memories. We sometimes travelled by car and visited such architectural strongholds as the Romanesque churches in Burgundy or the white Baroque churches of Bavaria. Robert showed me treasures particular to Germany such as the beautiful carved screens of Riemenschnieder or what remained of the winding white roads of the Troubadours.

Robert was already a formidable scholar with an astonishing memory, always eager for intellectual experience and insight. He has a way of relating ideas and observations, finding correspondences across a wide range of thought – some unlikely area might reveal a small, but useful nugget, which in juxtaposition with other more familiar areas of enquiry could perhaps throw light on some aspect of human experience. All this was very exciting and our discussions became a vital part of our time together. We never knew quite where our conversations would take us, but the bedrock was always a fascination with visual experience.

I remember one particular occasion which was a turning point – we were looking at a Rubens in the Dahlem Museum in Berlin. It was not a particularly great Rubens and perhaps even that was a help, because we were looking hard to find interest and merit. Almost idly, at first, we began to trace the colour movement, noticing how one colour flowed through the painting performing a number of different functions, both as purely pictorial means and in terms of subject matter. This led on to discovering the roles of the other colours in the painting and slowly the matrix of the colour structure emerged – quite literally before our eyes. It was astonishing! This incident was the start of a great adventure, a work entailing much travelling, endless note taking, research, and above all looking at paintings. The huge labour of this task fell on Robert. I had my work in the studio, which was pressing. But Robert was always generous and as he went along he shared his findings with me.

By this time, Robert was teaching Philosophy of Art at the Universität der Künste in Berlin. He began to work on the preparation of a series of lectures on colour and as these developed he dictated them to me. I remember especially the Van Gogh lecture. We had already visited many of the sites in the south of France where Van Gogh painted, and even though some of them had changed almost beyond recognition, the whole area around St Remy and Arles – in its scale, its light, its trees and fields, its little buildings and its skies – remained unmistakably Vincent's country. Robert and I were down in Provence. It was December and bitterly cold. Robert always moved around when he dictated, whenever I looked up he would be some different place or some different pose – a roving figure in the shadowy perimeters of the room. There was no heating. I was swathed in blankets, scotch to hand, and work often finished in the early hours of the morning. Through these journeys and lectures, Robert and I came to appreciate and understand more deeply a wealth of artistic achievement. And, of course, all this fuelled endless discussions. The colour lectures, delivered in German, were a great success. But I was always very attached to the first smaller series, which he had dictated to me in English.

As time went by Robert and I spread our wings, travelling more and more extensively. We also went what he called 'phenomena hunting' – looking at nature with an analytical eye. Quite aside from such frequent delights as the blue sparkle of the sky glimpsed through the foliage of trees – so much more brilliant than the same sky seen in the open – there were 'the perceptual classics' to recognise. Leonardo's irradiation phenomena which can be frequently seen between different planes of contrasting colours or tones. Also evidence of Delacroix's observations, although these need very special conditions, and so are much more rarely found. The Impressionist experience with colour of light and its complimentary colour of shadow was another huge field. But possibly the most exciting of all is the continual shift in time of depth and space in any given aspect of nature. This phenomenon, which is dependent on the changing light, is one so beloved by Cezanne. It modulates distance, making near and far, void and solid, virtually interchangeable. And as Cezanne noted, 'If I move my head a little to the left or right a whole new subject appears.' Inevitably we became aware not only of what was being seen, but of how one looked. Watching oneself looking is a useful exercise, but if it is to prove of lasting value for either an artist or a spectator it needs some form of practice or pictorial realisation.

Throughout this time Robert continued to make visits to the studio. He was and has remained an excellent critic of my work. He conducted a number of interviews with me for various publications. He has compared these to games of table tennis, but to me they seemed much more like an amiable tug of war, each side trying to win the other over. For a living artist being written about, even by the most sympathetic and closest of individuals, poses certain problems. One is always flattered and pleased if a critic whom one respects shows an interest in one's work and takes the

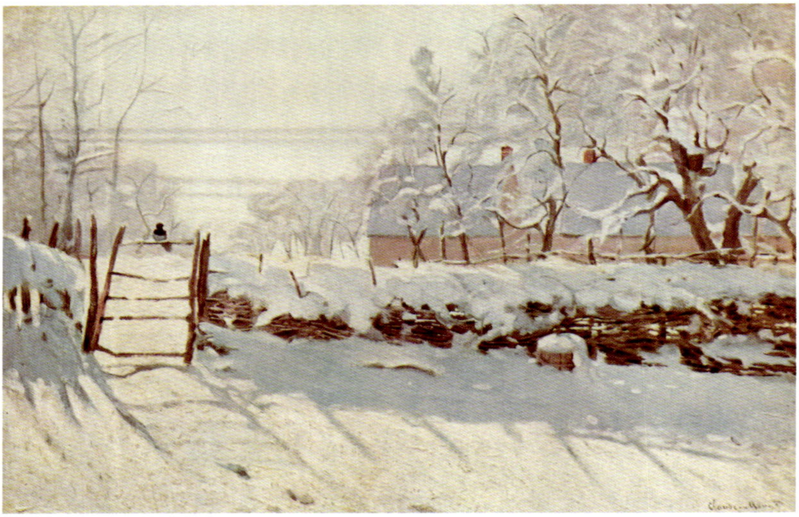

Claude Monet **The Magpie (*La Pie*)** 1868–69

time and trouble to write about it. The principal anxiety may be obvious but it is also complex. Will the critic – can the critic – understand what one is trying to do? One is forced to guard what one believes, correctly or incorrectly, to be the mainspring of one's work. Help is longed for, as Francis Bacon said, 'I wish someone would tell me what to do!', but when help is offered one finds oneself resisting. I have often tried to provide what information I can, agreeing with Mondrian when he said, 'Words are always inadequate, but nevertheless one must try to use them.' Sometimes discourse emerges through a series of rejections. Ad Reinhardt's famous writings called "Art as Art" try, through brilliant satire, to discredit the clichés, the lazy habits, the hypocrisies, and downright stupidities, which obscure the issues of Contemporary Art. I am very fond of a story about Picasso who, when irritated by questions about Cubism whilst he was on a ferry crossing the Seine in Paris, pointed to the sign above the boatman's head which read 'défense de parler au pilot.' This became a battle cry in Picasso's circle. And sometimes more can be conveyed by analogy and deflection as Barnet Newman knew when he said to me, 'If they want me to talk about my painting, I talk about Chartres' – and, indeed, the awe-inspiring grandeur of that great cathedral has a relevance to Newman's aspirations.

In this spirit Robert would sometimes relate anecdotes which threw light on particular artists. I remember one about Monet, who, in the early days of *plein air* painting, was realising the importance of light. It was evident that in general daylight was warm and shadow cool, but more was far from clear. In observing nature, the local colour of vegetation on which the light and shadow was falling, confused the issue. Then one day in winter, there was a heavy fall of snow, the world was white, and there, unmistakably, the precise colour of the sunlight and the shadow was clearly shown as on an *alla prima* canvas. Monet painted these colours as pure, luminous hues, thus generating a light effect through colour.

As the eighties and nineties wore on Robert increasingly devoted himself to the Berlin institution in which he taught. He invited English sculptors and painters to set up workshops or to do a semester's teaching. He was always very generous in his support and appreciation of artistic endeavours, cherishing and encouraging all that was positive. He is the most loyal of friends. It is more true to say of Robert than of anyone else I know that he lives in his mind, and from the insights I have had into that place, it is wonderfully rich and well-stocked. One day when we were in France, Robert was sitting at his writing table looking across the terrace at the old evergreen oak outside, he suddenly said, 'You are like an oak tree!' I was so surprised as I certainly didn't feel in the slightest bit like an oak tree! I said, 'If that is so, what are you?' He replied, 'Me – oh, I'm a dandelion. I shake my head and things fly about.'

To a Summer's Day 2 1980 (detail, overleaf)

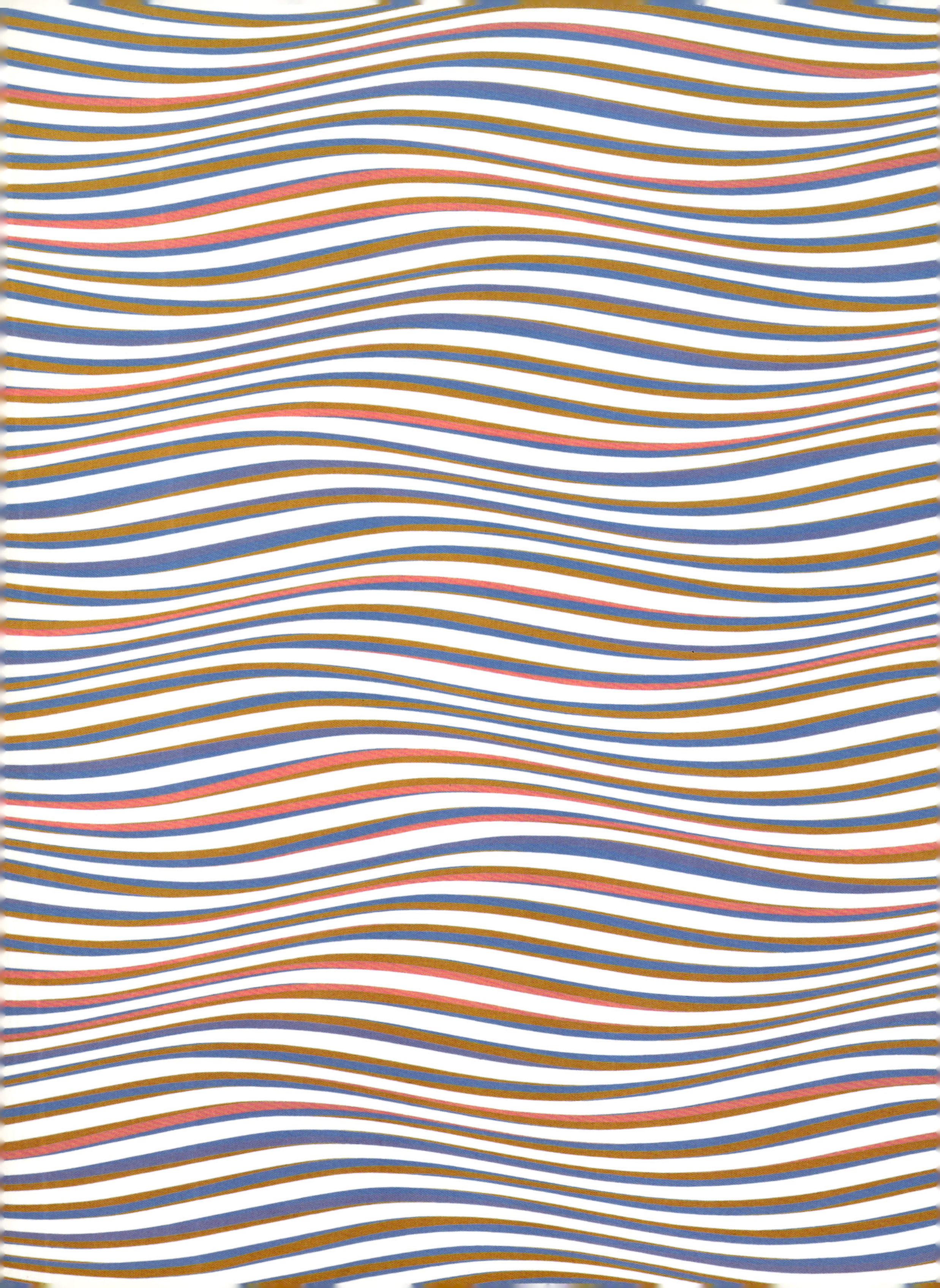

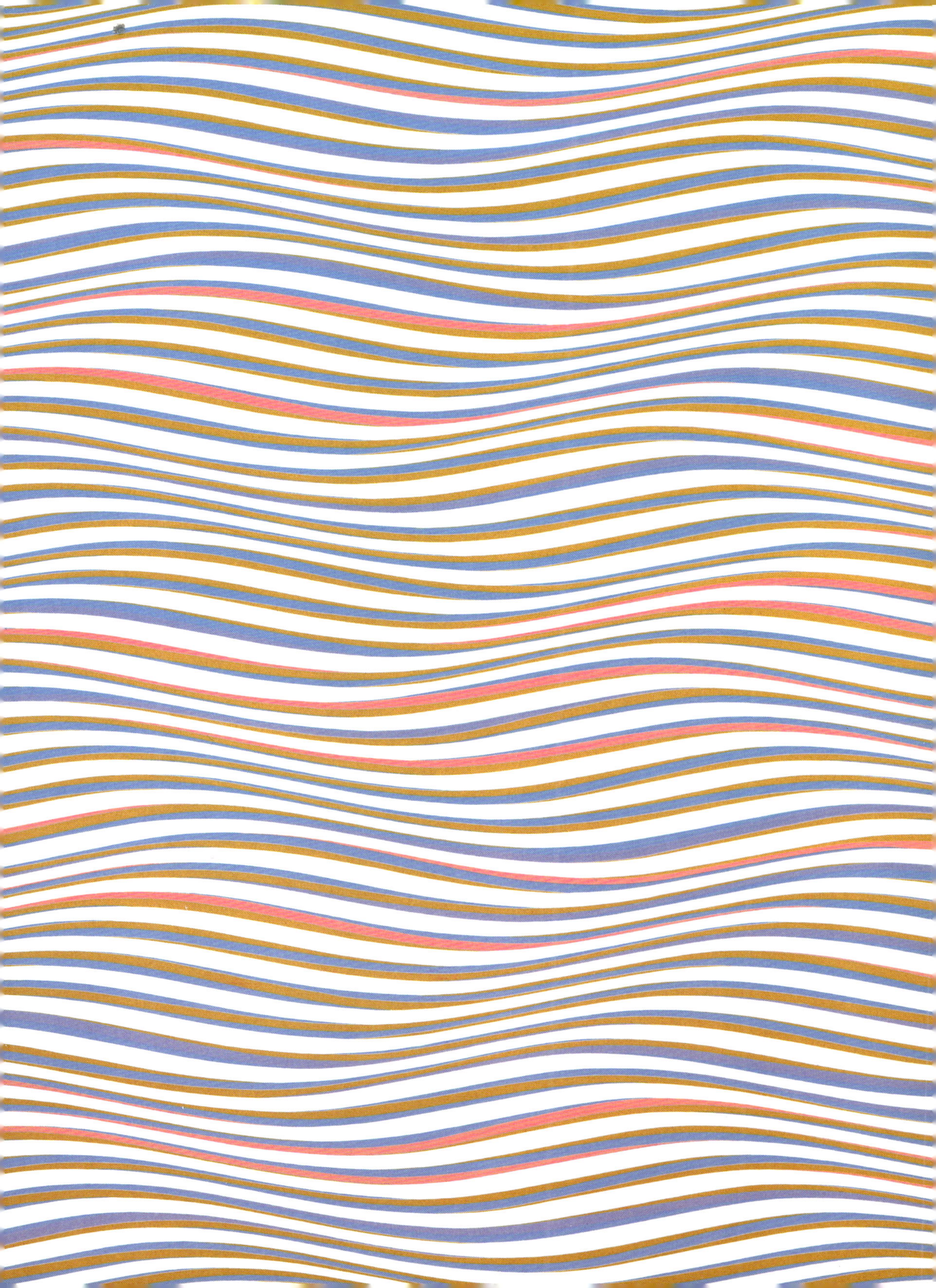

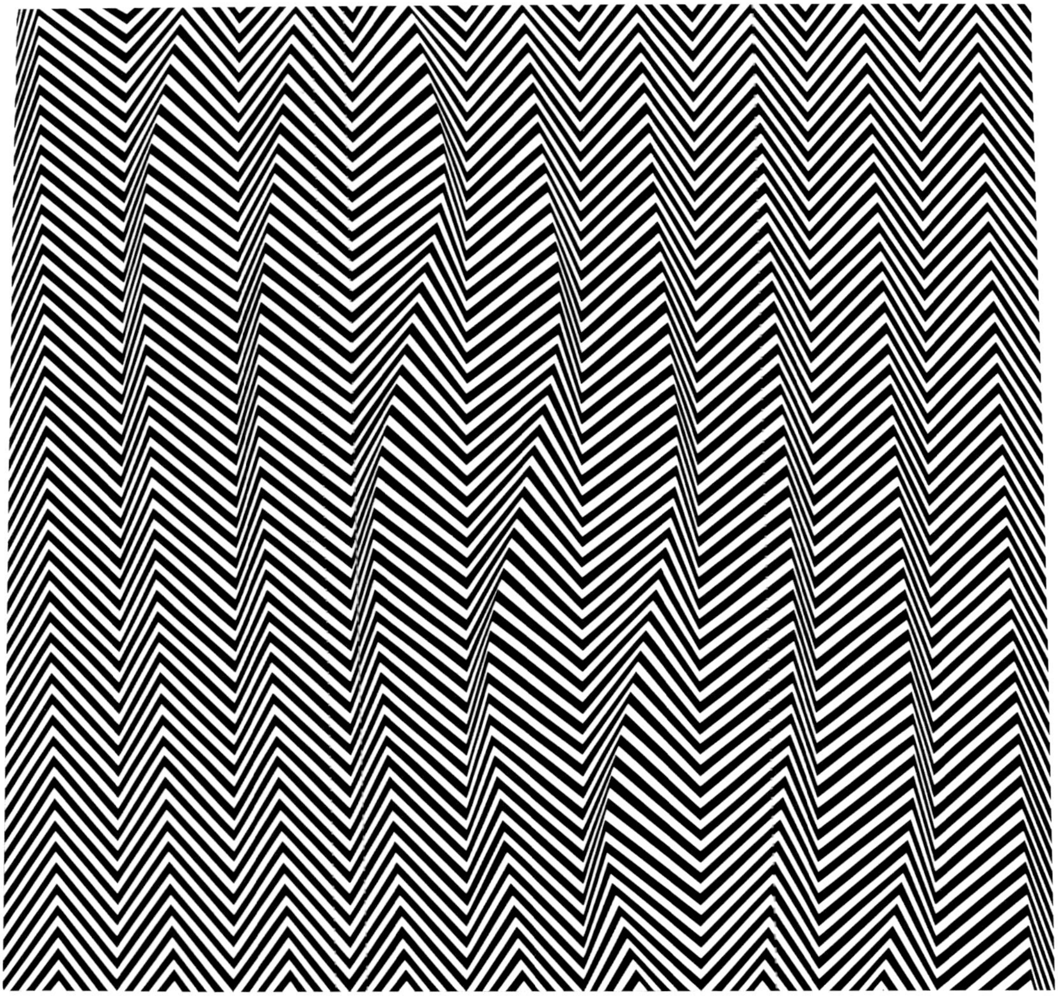

Descending 1965

Conversation

1972

ROBERT KUDIELKA: *You are one of the few artists today who make preparatory studies. Why don't you work on the canvas directly?*

BRIDGET RILEY: Well, that would be impossible for me because the structure of my paintings has to be precisely balanced. They need immaculate execution. I have to build up a bank of visual information first – about colours, forms, proportions, directions, etc. This is the essential basis to my work.

RK: *What returns are there from this 'bank'?*

BR: The studies I make have different purposes. At the beginning I try to be as unselective as possible – to allow things to happen, later gradually tightening up until all aspects have been drawn together.

RK: *How do you find your direction in this process?*

BR: I proceed by trial and error – exploring and slowly establishing a particular situation. Obviously many studies will be discarded *en route* to a painting, though they may still be interesting as visual statements.

RK: *And yet, there is a difference between a study and a painting ...*

BR: There are several differences. The studies deal with aspects, the paintings with totality. The studies are flexible and malleable, whereas the paintings are decisive and finite. And, of course, there is the obvious difference of scale.

RK: *What does scale mean to you?*

BR: Maybe scale could be compared to a key in music. Scale is not simply size, although size is a factor of scale. Changing the size of an image always means recreating its scale. I have to readjust and rebalance the factors involved. It is an act of perceptual equation. Sitting at your table and working on a study is quite different from your response to a painting which is hanging on the wall. There is no possibility of enlarging it automatically.

RK: *If scale is the key in which your work is notated, what theme you are playing? Is it in the air or do you invent it?*

BR: No – I take something – a colour – say yellow. What is yellow? Merely a name, an inert notion. But if you put a yellow with other colours, in different proportions and positions, it starts to show a certain potential. It may appear lighter or darker, expand or flow into other colours, changing them. It could glow, advance or recede and so on. None of this behaviour you would know until you try. So right at the beginning I think ... well, I just see what yellow can do.

RK: *What about the forms you use?*

BR: When I started, around 1960, forms such as triangles, squares, circles, rhomboids, etc. were no longer burdened by the heavy load of associations and symbolic overtones which they had carried in the '20s and '30s as Constructivist motifs. They were simple forms without any pretensions, in a condition for working with. Just 'to hand'.

RK: *Yet there has been a change. The more you got involved with colour, the less distinctive the forms became.*

BR: In my recent colour work I have been using stripes, either parallel or twisting around each other, because they are unassertive forms. Form and colour seem to be fundamentally incompatible – they destroy each other. In my earlier work, when I was developing complex forms, the energies of the medium could only be fully released by simplifying colour to a black-and-white constant (with occasional grey sequences). Conversely colour energies need a virtually neutral vehicle if they are to develop uninhibitedly. The repeated stripe seems to meet these conditions.

RK: *You think that a more elaborate shape would not be suitable?*

BR: No. Take a green triangle – it has three points, three conflicting

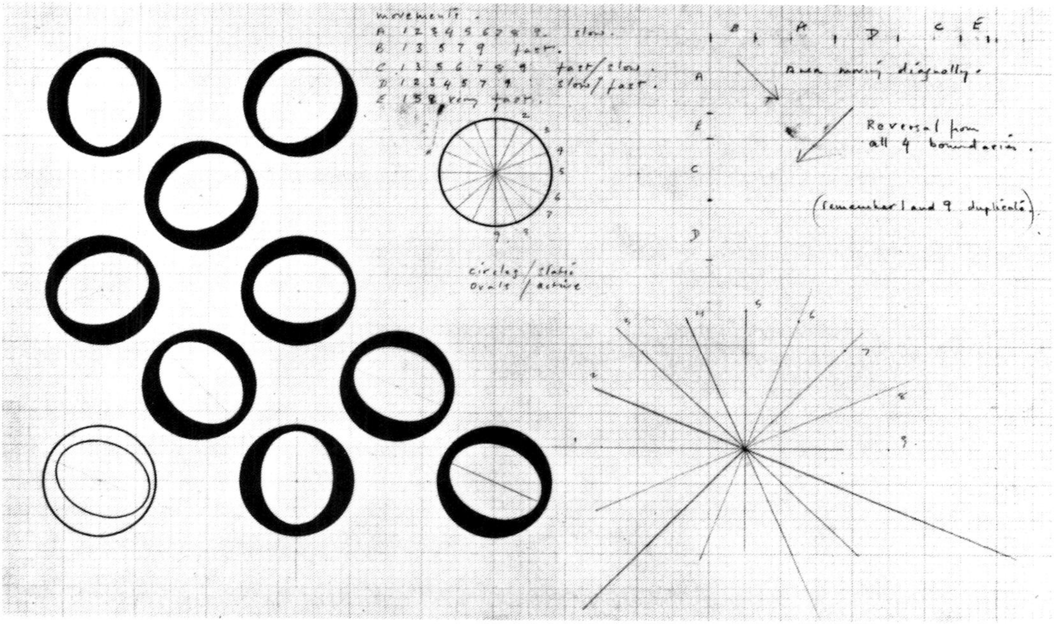

Untitled study related to *Disturbance* 1964

directions, there is a central volume in the form and an active edge exposure: all these factors add up to complexities which would effectively inhibit the green's expansion and mutability. I have always tried to avoid 'colouring forms'. I want to create a colour-form, not coloured forms.

RK: *Are you concerned with perceptual principles?*

BR: Well, look at the paintings. I'm not demonstrating any scientific principle, nor perceptual, arithmetical or geometrical. That doesn't interest me at all.

RK: *I wonder what the context is within which you work?*

BR: Relationships such as constancy and change – contrast and harmony – identity and contradiction – directions – rhythm – pace – repetition – accumulating and dispersing density.

RK: *Let's take an example. What does the oval mean to you?*

BR: In a sense the oval is a directional circle. Its range lies between the emphasis on direction on one hand (at the expense of its circularity), and emphasis on circularity (at the expense of direction) on the other. An oval is very different in character at each extreme. When it is highly directional it is a light, fast form. As the directional aspect decreases the oval becomes heavy and static.

RK: *But surely these dynamic relationships are not confined to single forms?*

BR: Of course not. It is very important that each form finally relinquishes its separateness in the whole. It must be fully absorbed. So while it is necessary in the early stages to analyse each unit, my aim is to enable it to release sufficient energy to precipitate its dissolution in totality.

RK: *So the single forms are the means to create a total situation?*

BR: They are part of the medium with which I am working.

RK: *Well, what is the medium?*

BR: Superficially the medium seems to be identical with the means. And obviously this is true in a sense that, for the composer, actual notes or particular instruments are part of his medium. But the medium as a whole is the relationship of this sort of means between themselves and me. I am, like the musician, a kind of 'listener-in' – overhearing potential activities.

RK: *'Listener' – that's a beautiful description, and a paradox, too. Because in this case the listener is also the speaker. After all, you make the paintings.*

BR: Yes – for quite a long time I was embarrassed by using the word 'I', the first person, in relation to my work – I much preferred to say 'one', because I felt that this thing, the medium, was so strong and rich, that I was just an agent who caught these various inflections and allowed them to play their own thing – freely.

RK: *What do you mean, to allow things to 'play freely'?*

BR: When these elements are *not* asked to do something which is against their nature – (not asked to serve concepts or to represent) – *then* I think that they are allowed to 'play freely' – to show their vitality. But there are hazards, for instance, of merely recording automatically in a random kind of way. These energies are, in a proper sense, 'wild' – one can easily be overwhelmed, carried away. This results in images which are virtually inaccessible, beyond perception, in fact. And yet this is the *core* of the medium and it is in this area that fruitful dialogue takes place. It is not only a one-way relationship of taming the wild, but can also be the reverse. I am supported by the medium but at the risk of being overwhelmed by it – the medium both carries you and threatens to carry you away. I don't trust a painting unless it has had this period – it is the only route by which to avoid the decorative or the academic.

RK: *The opposite of the wild would be the decorative?*

BR: Yes, the known, which is easy to handle, easy to arrange, because you are completely familiar with the relationships. Their vitality has been sapped – their energy used up – their teeth, so to speak, have been drawn.

RK: *I wonder how far this polarity of the medium affects the spectator. The subject of your earlier black-and-white work for instance, is movement …*

BR: There are at least two forms of movement. The 'one-dimensional' movement, which has to do with progression. Movement described on the picture plane itself.

RK: *It's readable –*

BR: Yes – but as you look at the painting you become involved in another kind of movement as a total experience which happens in time, successively, *between* you and the canvas – the graphic movement anticipates this kind of experience.

RK: *So in one case it is traditional, descriptive movement, like* Futurism, *movement opposed to stability. The other is movement not opposed to stability but occurring simultaneously – in a sense, even provoked by stability, as in* Descending.

BR: That's perfectly true. And this interplay between movement and stability is paralleled in my recent work by the interplay of light and colour. The colours painted on the canvas can be identified as certain hues – but as one looks at the painting one sees a luminous disembodied light, variously coloured.[1]

RK: I *see, you don't 'describe' light by colour.*

BR: No, I don't paint light. I present a colour situation which releases light as you look at it.

RK: *That means that the painting doesn't exist factually.*

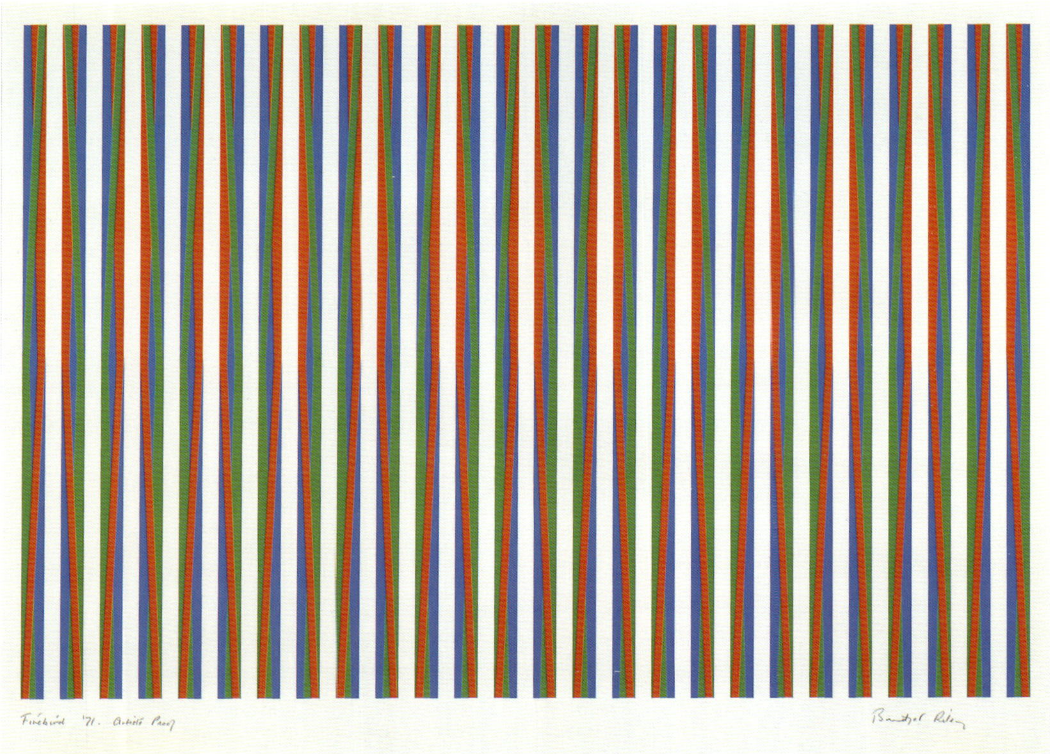

Firebird 1971

BR: No, in a way, it only comes to life when looked at from a certain distance.
RK: *If you stand close to the canvas you just see the colour –*
BR: Yes – objective hues, say cerise, olive, turquoise...
RK: *But if you stand too far away from the painting?*
BR: You only see a nebulous grey. The painting has eluded you.
RK: *And between these two extremes – the experience you intend?*
BR: The area of activity – of light.
RK: *So light is also something which happens between two polarities: the stable body of colour...*
BR: And its absolute dissolution. When grey eclipses the light, the painting is unable to offer anything.
RK: *Is that how the spectator experiences the medium?*
BR: Well, he is probably caught in a dialogue similar to my own. It is interesting to watch people looking at a painting because without any prompting they try to relate to it – they try to find a position in which the thing works for them. A point from which they can experience it. People vary a little – as to how much or how little they can be involved – they unconsciously choose their own relationship to the painting.
RK: *Do they choose? They listen.*
BR: Yes – to let the painting speak.

1 The following references to the 'disembodied light' brought about by periodic colour structures are related to paintings like *Late Morning* (1967–68) and *Orient 4* (1970).

First published in German in the exhibition catalogue *Bridget Riley*, Kunstverein Göttingen, 1972, pp. 4–10. The original English version appeared one year later in *Bridget Riley: Paintings and Drawings 1961–1973*, exhibition catalogue, Arts Council of Great Britain, 1973, pp. 9–13. Reprinted in *The Eye's Mind: Bridget Riley. Collected Writings 1965–1999*, ed. Robert Kudielka, London: Thames & Hudson in association with the Serpentine Gallery and De Montfort University, 1999, pp. 80–86.

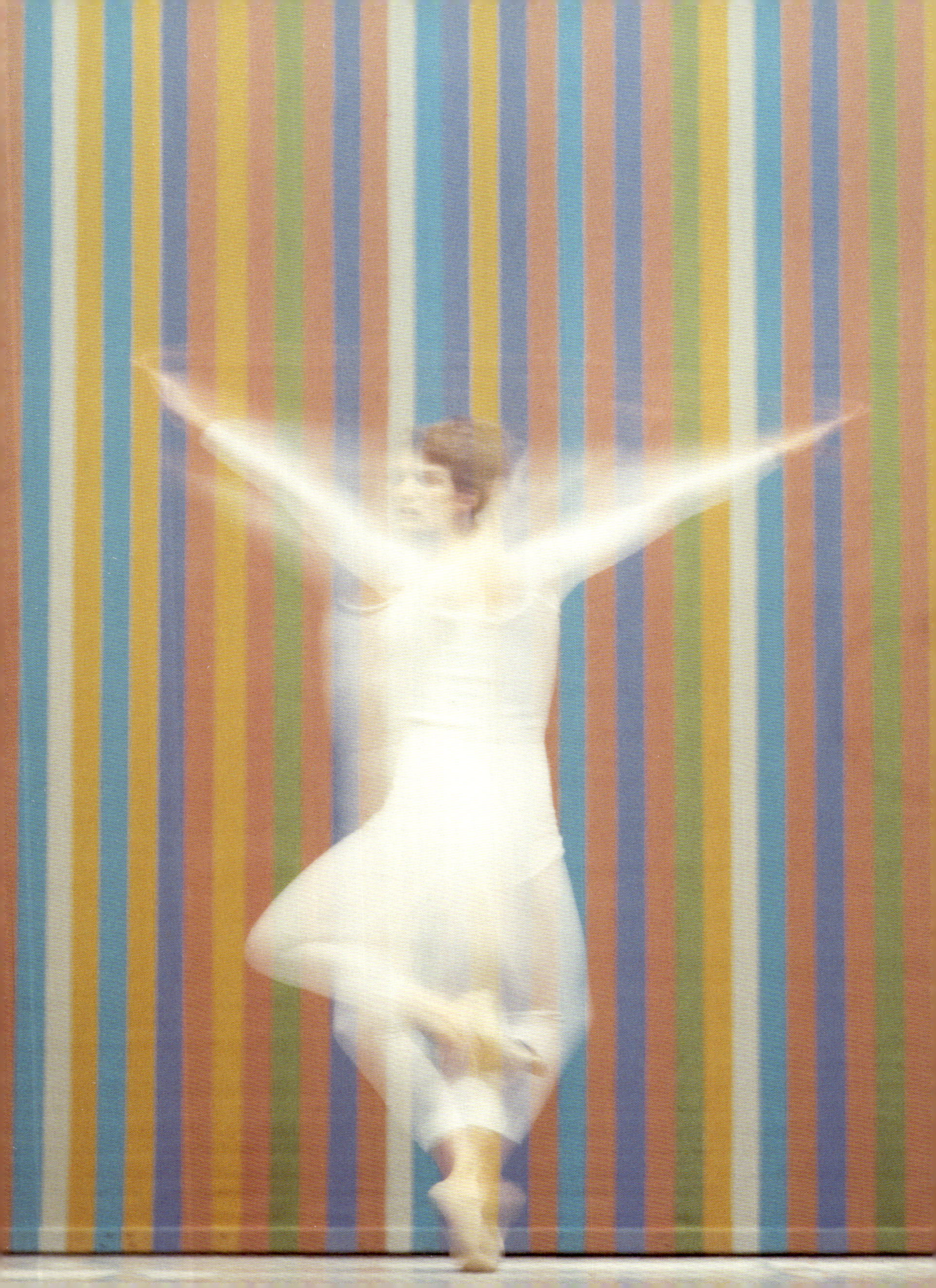

Nothing but Appearance
1978

'Lose the object, and draw nigh, obliquely.'
William Shenstone, *Unconnected Thoughts on Gardening* (1764) [1]

1 A Common Incident

(opposite)
Ballet Rambert / Colour Moves 1983

Sometimes it happens in passing by. Somebody walks in front of the painting. Anyone who has been to an exhibition has had the experience. Just as the view seemed to be clear, so that one could really see the work one wanted to see, someone cuts across the field of vision. Damn it, we think, in a flash of indignation at the ubiquitous presence of our own kind ... other people are always getting in the way. But gently. We are other people, too. What occasions the inconvenience is not its actual cause. It would never happen if we were not obliged, whenever and wherever we want to grasp anything *as such*, to take a step back – to begin with. Every time we consciously direct our attention to something, we start, without thinking twice, by disassociating ourselves from the object in view. The operation is all the more remarkable, as it doesn't seem to be restricted to our physical behaviour only. No matter whether we are actually stepping back, in the presence of the painting, or taking a breath, afterwards, to evaluate an experience, the principle seems to be the same.

Distance is obviously the primary condition of any conscious approach. Only by establishing some sort of space between us and the particular aim of our intention, can we assert the specifically human premise: to relate *freely* to what we want to relate to. And yet, this capacity seems to be inseparably linked with a grave disadvantage. The moment we step back, to get on top of our consciousness, the fundamental weakness is brought out into the open, that we are no more part of things than their self-sufficient reality is part of us. The break becomes painfully conspicuous. Not only that we permanently cross each other's intentions; we also have great difficulty in keeping to the point we chose to concentrate upon, without becoming side-tracked by the unceasing flow of ideas and sensations which cross our mind. It can be absolutely tantalising, in the true sense of the word: nothing seems to be more prone to elude us than the objects on which we turn our attention.

But the World of Day is not the Underworld into which we are tempted to convert it, judging everything we touch and see according to the uneasy flicker that governs our inner universe. Our lack of certainty is only one side of the coin: man's very personal problem, not necessarily an artistic one; and certainly not Bridget Riley's. If somebody unexpectedly walks in front of one of her paintings, before our eyes, he is not, *eo ipso*, upsetting the delicacy of the approach. On the contrary, this fleeting distraction can be a moment of truth: a portent, full of promise, like the billowing of the curtain in the theatre before the performance starts.

For observational distance is an ambivalent thing – more ambivalent than we can usually assume from our own end, adopting as we do the very viewpoint that constitutes it. From our position, a wall in front of the eyes is always a threat. In order to attain and assert the freedom of recognition, the mind requires the advantage of an overall view, the ability to grasp a thing in its totality and situate it in space. The almost instinctive act of stepping back to the position of a beholder signifies first of all, with regard to its release mechanism, a reinforcement of the sovereignty of the conscious mind. Yet that same distance which gives us power over what we are observing, contrives simultaneously to prevent our abusing such power. Although one may not notice it immediately, the object of our predatory attention has slipped out of our grasp. The comfortable atmosphere of familiarity vanishes as it acquires space to unfold in its own right. Thus the result of stepping back is often, contrary to one's intentions, to awake the thing seen from its slumber; and visual appearances are by no means as passive and docile as the observing eye would like them to be. They rebel if one tries to dominate them.

In everyday matters we seldom embark on this conquest. The slight reproach, which might be noticeable on the face of many things that surround us, is usually overlooked in the hurried and heedless pursuit of our own daily affairs; and, the most surprising aspect of this is that it seems to be quite possible to do so. The overt surface of the world shows incredible patience with the way we treat it – as long as we do not consciously face up to it. The plain availability of something, just waiting faithfully, it seems, to be called upon by us, is echoed by the casual and many-coloured use of the word 'matter'. Something seems really matter to us only, when we make a point out of it; otherwise it remains oblique. But there is also, preserved by the age-old memory of language, an explicit indication, that this latent premise, upon which we build our claims, as if entitled to do so, is in fact not nearly as passive and resilient as it appears to be most of the time. Everyone knows that the English term 'matter' is also used in courts of law: it can mean, and most significantly so, a matter of dispute and conflict. This connotation is not pure convention, nor of recent origin. The Latin word *res* and the German word *Sache* fall into the same bracket, being commonly used as global denominations of 'something', but in certain connections also with reference to their original meaning 'something contentious'. There obviously is, then, beneath the bland surface of human self-assurance, a general intimation that any matter, when it comes to the crunch, can be something quite explosive.

This hidden force would have been barely appreciated, however, in its life-giving splendour (threatening for any consolidation of life as it is), if works of art occasionally, and in various degrees, had not honoured it. In contradistinction to all other human activities, to daily work in general (and to the sciences in particular) the vocation of art appears to be that of responding to what is at the *other* end of this distance that we maintain. From very early days, works of visual art have not only given shape and form to their particular materials, as the methodological predilections of art history make us believe; they have, in difference to other object-making endeavours, released the suppressed power of appearance, by letting it play and shine in manifold colours. Moreover, artists have been aware of the earth's internal stirrings, those continual shifts in perception, and instead of imposing decrees upon them, they have coaxed them into the gentle pulse of a constant rhythm.

Bridget Riley's art is, in this respect, of the most ancient descent. It re-establishes the act of relinquishing man's imposition on Nature, a function, which once was fulfilled by thanksgiving rituals, and other celebrational rejoicings. What is initially puzzling is simply its acute modernity. In front of a Riley painting one tends to go 'hot and cold' for a moment – as if suddenly reminded of an unpardonable omission. For in contrast to the predominant tradition in visual art (at least in the Christian era), the inherent potential of that distinctly other end of our conscious approach is not secretly brought home, discreetly suggested, as it were, to the controlling mind – but turned abruptly, in a momentary upheaval, into the mind's eye.

Initially, though, there is no trace of such an event. The paintings open up without resistance. To get his bearings the beholder does not really need to establish observational distance. The step back is more the result of a vague feeling that all this perfection, the high finish, the transparency of the means employed, cannot be all there is to it. You wonder if the first glance has not exhausted all the painting has to give. Should the first glance have been the last as well? At the beginning, the end cannot yet be envisaged. But sometimes, when a third party walks across in front of the painting the curtain flicks up prematurely, as if pulled by invisible hand; and what then shows itself, however fleetingly, is something to remember.

One's attention instantly turns to the intruder; for in spite of one's first feelings of indignation the distraction is secretly welcome. Keeping still is always an effort. Something within us seems to rebel against having to look long in any one direction. We sense that the object of our staring might elude us. The eye can never be certain of the things it focuses upon; least of all when confronted with anything bland and motionless. But the converse is probable, indeed may be the rule. Where objects themselves are in restless and constant motion, the faculty of sight is relieved of the challenge of confrontation; and the detached human gaze can survey the scene from the vantage point of passive stimulation. Nothing captures attention so much as a thing in motion. Successive movement stabilises the viewpoint of the beholder by reducing the presence of the object to a minimum, to a mere point in transition. Action! The scene progresses – the gaze becomes lazy and vacant.

But in Bridget Riley's world, and especially in the coloured band and curve paintings, one is not permitted this passive attitude. The passer-by, who intrudes betwixt us and the canvas, unwittingly acts on her behalf. When the eye clings to this moving distraction, a curious excitation is set up on the fringes of the visual field, which advances frontally towards the spectator. The straight lines begin to buckle, a rustling goes through the well-ordered ranks, the smooth surface swells, breaking into a spring tide. An undreamt-of fire springs from the slender groves; iridescent rivers burst their banks. For a brief, incalculable moment the world as we know it, the world as projected from our viewpoint, literally falls apart. But this is not all. Hardly has the first surprise subsided, when on the periphery of our vision there begin to emerge strange hues, rainbow colours. Where, a second ago, the waves surged, an unexpected cloud now floats into view, laden with ethereal essences: citron, rose, and lilac... The space, which before seemed vacant, is now a cornucopia; time streaks backwards. This, unless all is an illusion, is how it must have looked that day when the step before the first step was taken: out into the untouched garden of appearance.

But then, before one can take a second look, the lines are stilled, the waves subside into curves again. The apparition is past: gone without trace, like the stranger who passed by and stole our viewpoint away. It all looks just as it did at the beginning; only a little more *apparently* so. The surface quivers; there is a tremor in the air. This is the point at which the Imperfect tense of Knowing-it-all, the bite of the serpent, recoils on the spectator. Wasn't the whole magical experience a mere mirage, an optical illusion, subtly contrived and cunningly staged – but scientifically perfectly comprehensible and explicable?

The reality of this experience is in fact beyond doubt. It can be repeated and recaptured. The result will not be the same for everyone, nor the same every time, but a certain variability does not detract from the general applicability of insight. In physiological terms, the phenomenon can be characterised as 'strobic', although to fence it round with science is to shut out the glimpse of Eden that it affords. Indeed, every attempt to trace the source of the event at its origins remains, in the same way, a makeshift expedient – an afterthought. The fact is that no one, however used to these works he may be, can interpret them wholly out of his own resources. For what happens is not, as people like to think, that we are aiming *towards* an end-product, which is Riley's painting. The painting aims us into the unforeseeable.

Some third party, who cuts across our first encounter with the painting, can therefore do more for us than our own intentions. Such an incident brings into play various factors that are special to the art of Bridget Riley.

For one almost hallucinatory moment the beholder sees his own role acted out on an imaginary stage – except for an ultimately decisive difference. He experiences the great eerie silence of the opening act, the formal introduction and confirmation of the protagonist: his own viewpoint. There follows a forceful *peripeteia*, the reversal of the second act: the entrance of the stranger who captures the eye, and the consequent insurrection of nameless forces. But, just at the point when an Arcadian radiance directs all the senses towards the finale, the play breaks off. The third act is not performed. Not because it doesn't exist: it is there. The titles of the paintings – *Late Morning*, *Rise*, *Pæan*, *Attar*, *Song of Orpheus*, etc. – indicate it. No, the play ends as abruptly as it began, because it is not a play at all.

Bridget Riley's art is not theatrical. The hallucination which chance precipitates simply reveals the dramatic disposition of the painting: namely the central function of the reversal, and the fact that the spectator-space becomes the true arena of the action. But the hallucination simultaneously conceals the full truth of the event, which is something far more magical and at the same time more challenging. The cause of what actually takes place is due neither to outside intervention nor to some sleight of hand on the part of the artist. The more clearly the paintings reveal themselves, the more undeniable becomes the mysterious fact that the dramatic reversal springs from the nature of the observer's detachment, which is quite different from his role in the theatre. It is a self-created precipitation of vision. The event set in train by a Riley painting requires that the actor and the spectator be one and the same person.

Why, then, in the course of experiencing this event, has attention been drawn to a third element, an intermediary between the painting and ourselves, as though the intervention of some neutral medium of transmission were inevitable before the dialogue began? Of course it is not necessary: strictly speaking, it is superfluous. The third party has long since moved away from the painting. But by now it is possible to identify the need for such an intermediary, and who that presence was. It was Bridget Riley herself. 'For quite a long time I was embarrassed by using the word "I", the first person, in relation to my work – I much preferred to say "one", because I felt that this thing, the medium, was so strong and rich that I was just an agent who caught these various inflections and allowed them to play their own thing – freely.'[2]

In the end, whenever this last presence has vacated the picture, there remains a pure triadic chord: 'so it seems' – the free play of appearance. Initially, and subsequently, all may appear as it has always appeared since people first started to be obsessed by the reality of things – much too

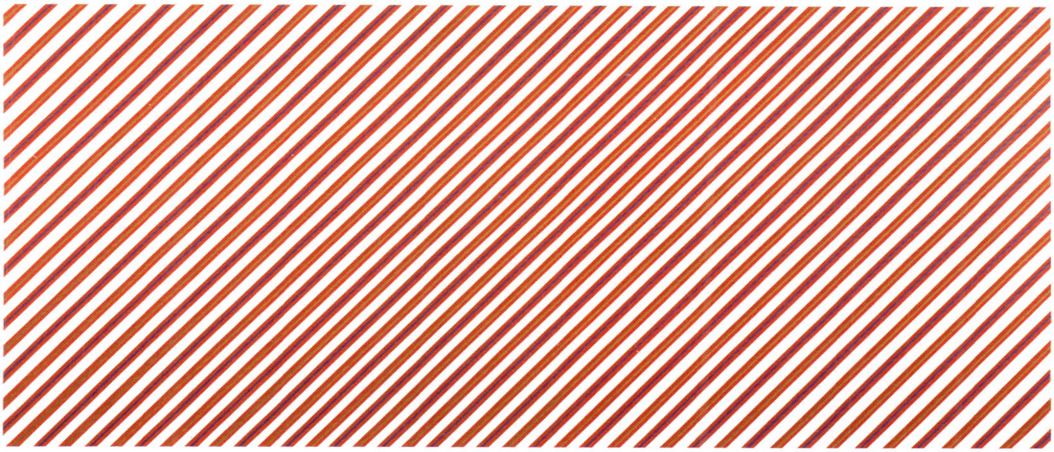

Byzantium 1969 (detail, overleaf)

little; *mere* appearance; nothing but *appearance*. Or, for occasional astounding instants, it will continue to be as it can be from the very beginning – annihilating; far too much; *sheer* appearance; *nothing* but appearance. But from time to time, between an all too easily manageable 'too little' and an utterly unmanageable 'too much', the spectator will feel a gentle nudge, an unexpected eye-opener: nothing *but* appearance. He is allowed to see, as any human being is naturally capable of seeing: like someone passing by.

2 The Elusive Theme

> *'With all its eyes the creature-world beholds*
> *the open. But our eyes, as though reversed,*
> *encircle it on every side, like traps*
> *set round its unobstructed path to freedom.'*
> Rainer Maria Rilke, The Eighth Duino Elegy. [3]

The first glance at a Riley painting would certainly be different if any perceptual experience started from scratch. To step back, *away* from things, does not reveal the whole truth. One might even imagine (if this be madness, then there's method in't) that the eye is only an optical centre, and that the step back is taken just to get a better view of the object. But in vain; the light of day is familiar – our eye anticipates what it sees. Nothing strikes us completely unprepared; and we never start where we begin. The apple has long been eaten when we see the trees in bloom. Our judgement is formed, 'in principle', before we start to look. Our eye does not *see*, it looks *at* things, processing the outer world towards a given centre.

There's no conceiving what would happen if our vision behaved like a flower: opening to the sun, containing the light between the eyelids. Who knows, in that case Bridget Riley could perhaps paint the things she likes: the cool of the morning over the Cornish cliffs, the shamelessly smug swagger of each little flower as it comes out, or high noon, the hour of Pan, in the valley of Vaucluse; and above all, the abrupt reversals in which life renews itself. But there is a painful point, upon which any total experience is fragmented. When our eye turns fully into the direction from which these sensations come, virtually nothing is gained by staring directly; nothing that might, when it came 'to the point', look like a Thing. Worse still: if we force on, our observations become minute, labouring that point, and a febrile excitement overpowers our senses. Does the cool of the morning depend on the dew, like dew drops hanging from the blades of the grass? Or does it come from the light which glistens in the drops on the grass? Or – more problematic still – does the magic simply come from the fact that we, still close to sleep, cannot yet focus on the point, and fall prey, for one chill moment, to a chance illusion? The morning sensation is gone before we can find the answer. Many mornings may disappear in the same way. At best all we can retain is a trail of fragments; and should any painter patch these together and try to force them into a painting, towards that crucial point – even then what results never regains the life which eluded it from the beginning.

Whatever her own start may be *this* is certainly not the end that Bridget Riley is aiming for – never, under any circumstances. Matricide in art, the *crime passionel* against Nature, is unendurable to her. 'Look what he does with his palette-knife!' (Courbet was the offender.) Her final abandonment of direct representation of the things she loves, after years of intensive, often pleasurable effort – this overcoming of her own inclination can ultimately be explained only in terms of an almost religious awe in the face of the primal urgency of life; and, closely linked with this, a near infallible instinct for it. *Sed de persona ipsa silemus.* Explicitly, her rejection of art 'from life' is directed against the over-evaluation of the point occupied by man in the universe. 'Our bearings still suffer from the concept or supposition of Renaissance theory, which is "man as the measure of all things". But man is only part of a bigger whole, and this whole is neither centripetal nor centrifugal. It is much more open and egalitarian.'[4]

Nothing characterises Bridget Riley's artistic stature better than her aversion to every form of pretentiousness, and especially to the wilful exaggerations that distort the light of day: the glitter of lofty aspiration and the turgid tone of futility. 'Pure self-indulgence', is the verdict. The widespread myopia which sees in every beginning the end of man, is something she definitely does not suffer from.

Hers is a very different problem. Obviously she does not paint what everyone sees. But, more than that, in distinction to the masters whom she cherishes – Rubens, for instance, Constable, Cézanne, and above all Monet and Matisse – she does not attempt either to make visible what may be *made* visible, revealed or realised by a human hand. Rather, Bridget Riley embarks on the near impossible endeavour to let things be seen which only *let* themselves be seen. For her subject does not belong to the category of aims or motifs postulated by the human mind. It resides rather in the opposite direction – in an original premise so primordial, in fact, that is doubtful whether it can ever be traced back to

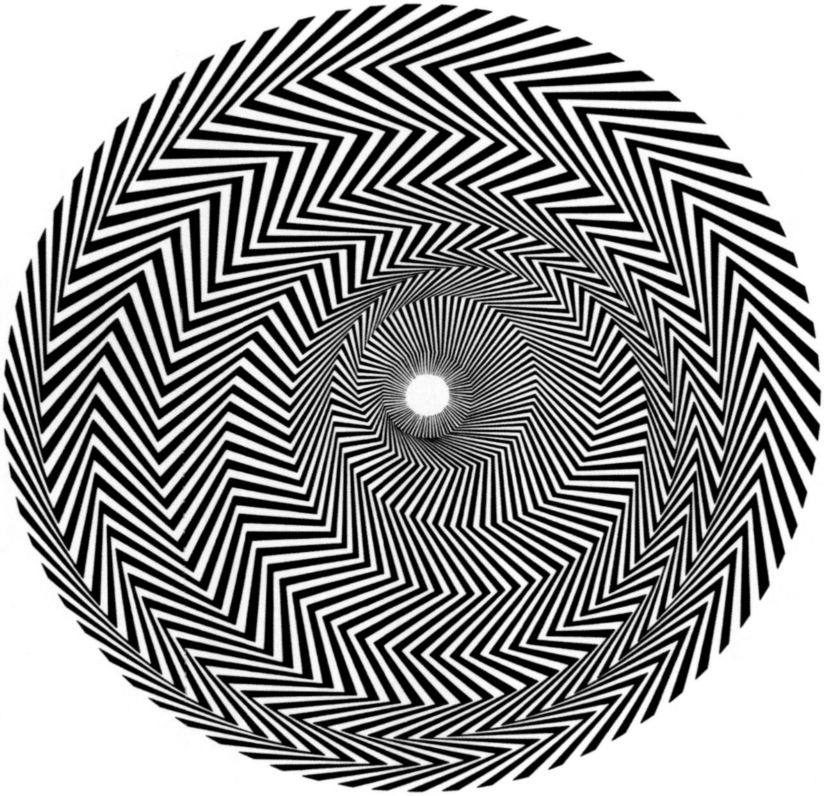

Blaze 1 1962

an inception, a cause or a principle. No wonder that the sheer scale of the challenge often seems menacing to her. 'Sometimes, especially in my recent work', she says, 'I feel it right up almost against my face' – putting her hand in front of her eyes, quite close, but not defensively – 'the thing that refuses to be thought'.

There is nothing indeed to be grasped, let alone to hang on to. In Riley's art the 'hand of the artist' (all too often over-emphasised in criticism) has no place. To display it would be tantamount to retouching. All the handling is carried out by assistants (and this, incidentally, has been the case ever since the days when she had to do a part-time job herself in order to afford a pair of disengaged hands). She involves herself in the execution of the work only occasionally, and then at all stages, from the priming to the final stretching and cleaning of the canvas, primarily in order to keep the various stages of the work better in view, and moreover because exclusive concentration on looking, essential though the eye may be, would contradict its very purpose. For the actual work – the judgement, the decision-making – demands a highly delicate engagement fluctuating between stringent control and an almost throw-away lightness: a kind of seeing that is so radically different from the normal staring at a single point that she prefers to describe it in terms of another mode of perception altogether: as a 'listening-in' to the flux of primal beginnings. Where does the cool of the morning come from? Of what does the silence of a Mediterranean noon consist? What is the power that made a mountain burst apart before Cézanne's eyes, so that his hand almost failed him? Any reply that went beyond pure perception would be foolhardy. Even a bunch of flowers, already cut – who could arrange them in a vase without letting the gathered splendour spread loose around its unknown centre? To maintain this unapproachability, the unique intimacy of the matter, Bridget Riley purged nearly twenty years ago – when she 'started', as she says – all ingratiating handling from her work. Since that time she has established a basis that seems, if isolated, to contradict her very aim. It appears to be so intransigent and resolved that it perplexes even some of her closest friends. For it bears, at first glance, a deceptive resemblance to a full stop before anything has begun.

3 The Arrival of the Great Pan

It is not until later when the event is over that it dawns on one that from the very first moment it was later than one thought. At first, however, all that is apparent is that the start seems in no way burgeoning or promising. On the contrary, it is high noon. The appointment is on the dot. Work does not start any-old-how. The shadows are crisp, the colours clear. 'I take *something*', says Bridget Riley.[5] Not anything, but something. The emphasis is deliberate, rejecting the miasma of artistic fancy, the waiting for the immaculate conception, etc. (no feminine caprice...). But not only the tone, the thing itself is decisive; and more definitively so than one would initially think. Bridget Riley does not dream the Dream of Creation from Nothing (that all too masculine dream...). She works from distinct elements and relationships. In the first phase of her work, from 1960 to 1966, she employed triangles and squares, circles and ovals, straight lines and curves; at first exclusively in black and white, then with occasional sequences of grey. After that the basis shifted. From 1967 onwards the primacy goes to colour. At first two, later three colours form the basis; mainly, until 1973, in the form of bands. Since then curves have served as vehicle, most recently for not only three but five colours.

That's all. To begin with. Nothing rustles or stirs, at the very beginning. As one mentally reviews the individual decisions, they glide past the mind's eye in a spectral parade, and fade into each other at an undefined vanishing point. Twenty years of work – to be instantly surveyed, at least intellectually. And no one, turning that thought over in the thin light of reason, would ever hit upon the punchline. It is only in daylight, in the light of actuality, within the restrictions of space and time, in front of a single painting – that a flame darts out from the apparently cold ashes in the grate. The particular point, towards which everything seems to gravitate, when emerging materially before one's eyes, appears to be far less sure (to say the least) than one might expect. For the experience does not develop in the way which we are used to. As a rule we never adhere to the immediate presence of something, but refer to it, transcending it provisionally in order to understand it from behind, as it were: from a background of overriding ideas and past experiences. A Riley painting, however, bars this habitual process, establishing direct encounter. It is hard to think of another modern artist (certainly not of Vasarely, so often enlisted as an analogy) who has dared to expose the perceptual fabric so manifestly, so completely without any padding or embroidery. 'When I started around 1960, forms such as triangles, squares, circles, rhomboids, etc. were no longer burdened by the heavy load of associations and symbolic overtones which they had carried in the '20s and '30s as Constructivist motifs. They were simple forms without any pretensions, in a condition for working with. Just "to hand".'[6]

That is the point exactly. The elements are naked in essence and Bridget Riley refuses to 'reclothe' them in the process of working. Thus the instinct for interpretation – that ominous appeal to a different kind of authority – falls literally flat. Behind the sheer appearance of the paintings no principle looms, no message lurks, no meaning plays hide-and-seek with the spectator. None of those elevated secondary 'things' step out of the shade to offer comfort. Nor, it seems, does the categorical imperative of Order, the backbone of any upright constructivist, determine the building of the work. The use of ruler, compasses and templates obviously does not serve to impose a formula on experience. The vivacious spirit of Riley's art refuses the worthy proposal of science. 'I'm not demonstrating any scientific principle, nor perceptual, arithmetical or geometrical. That doesn't interest me at all.'[7] The mathematical elements are presented, purely and simply according to laws of art. 'Relationships such as constancy and change – contrast and harmony – identity and contradiction – directions – rhythm – pace – repetition – accumulating and dispersing density'[8] – these form the structure of the paintings: sometimes with almost diagrammatic clarity, in black and white, sometimes in rank and file, with exactly as many colours as anyone can count off on the fingers of one hand.

Such clarity can be disquieting indeed. The more impenetrable the pure surface seems, the more uneasy the senses become. Is there really nothing *else* there, behind it? From the sheer wall of the paintings there always echoes the same laconic answer: nothing else, there is nothing else behind it, *nothing*. Bridget Riley's art contains – in the strict sense of the word – no content. And yet, having lost its main prerogative, our yearning for understanding, far from being disappointed, is rewarded in an unforeseen way. The startling event that suddenly irrupts into the apparent vacuum, like a shout in the stillness of noon, reverses the charge. It throws up, in one instant, a challenge which, at the moment of experience, is more radical in its implications than all conventional objections levelled afterwards against the paintings from recollection. For the power that surprises the beholder, as if from an ambush, is evidently no hollow echo of representations. True, from an objective point of view nothing has changed; there is still nothing else there, behind the surface. But this 'nothing' has become irremediably ambiguous. What if, for an incommensurable instant in time, that mute and patient Something, which is normally suppressed by our way of seeing, had got loose?

The point is too subtle and precise to be struck by the blunted hatchet of outraged common sense. Obviously, the phenomenon as such is as adverse critics describe it. But the sheer scale of it is usually underestimated, and it is only with the capacity to appreciate its full complexity that a profoundly different response emerges. To dismiss Bridget Riley's work as superficial, as having no depth, misses the precise nature of this 'superficiality': during a short, deeply perplexing encounter, the *literal* surface recedes behind the foreground of perception. In the same way the thoughtless view that Riley's art is a typical example of the ominous 'formalist impasse' compromises itself. The problem does not consist at any time in the imperviousness as such, but in its uncanny attraction. Why in the face of these paintings, are we solicited to look in a direction which, by all rational criteria, offers no further prospect? Every time we try to penetrate the hermetic surface, the wall shifts closer and closer. Although the mind quickly becomes aware of the precipitating process, the clash seems to be unavoidable. A strange mixture of freedom and compulsion indeed. There is only one explanation, if it be not sorcery: the paintings of Bridget Riley actually yield themselves to us along that very same sight-line by which we try to distance them.

No mere calculation could pose such a situation – it is too pure and too simple. The origin of the criticism under which Bridget Riley still labours can be fairly accurately pinpointed. In the first century of the Christian era, in the reign of Tiberius, the historian Plutarch tells us that a ship's company, sailing past a small island close to Corfu, heard, in the depths of the forest, a strange lament: 'Great Pan is dead!' The light of a great age of European history seemed extinguished. The Christian literature of the ensuing centuries pounced avidly on this tale; not only because it seemed to symbolise the death of the ancient gods but above all because the capricious ruler of Arcadia presided over the most threatening of all earthly revelations: the unmanning terror of 'There's nothing behind it', the terrible laughter of the noonday which paralyses the narrow self-assured inquisitiveness and debunks it – only to let life flow back, with strength renewed, into its old forms. This mysterious and perilous aspect of Nature had at all costs to be suppressed and officially nullified if the new gospel was to prevail. The result of this massive denial can be seen in the negative connotations that the idea of 'panic' terror has to this day.

Bridget Riley does not have the intention, as some people suspect, of imposing an 'inhuman' way of seeing on the beholder. But equally she does not close her eyes to the curse with which, before he bowed out of history, the pagan god barred the way to Arcadia. When the mind rejects the spirit of noonday stillness, the beauty of things wears threadbare and

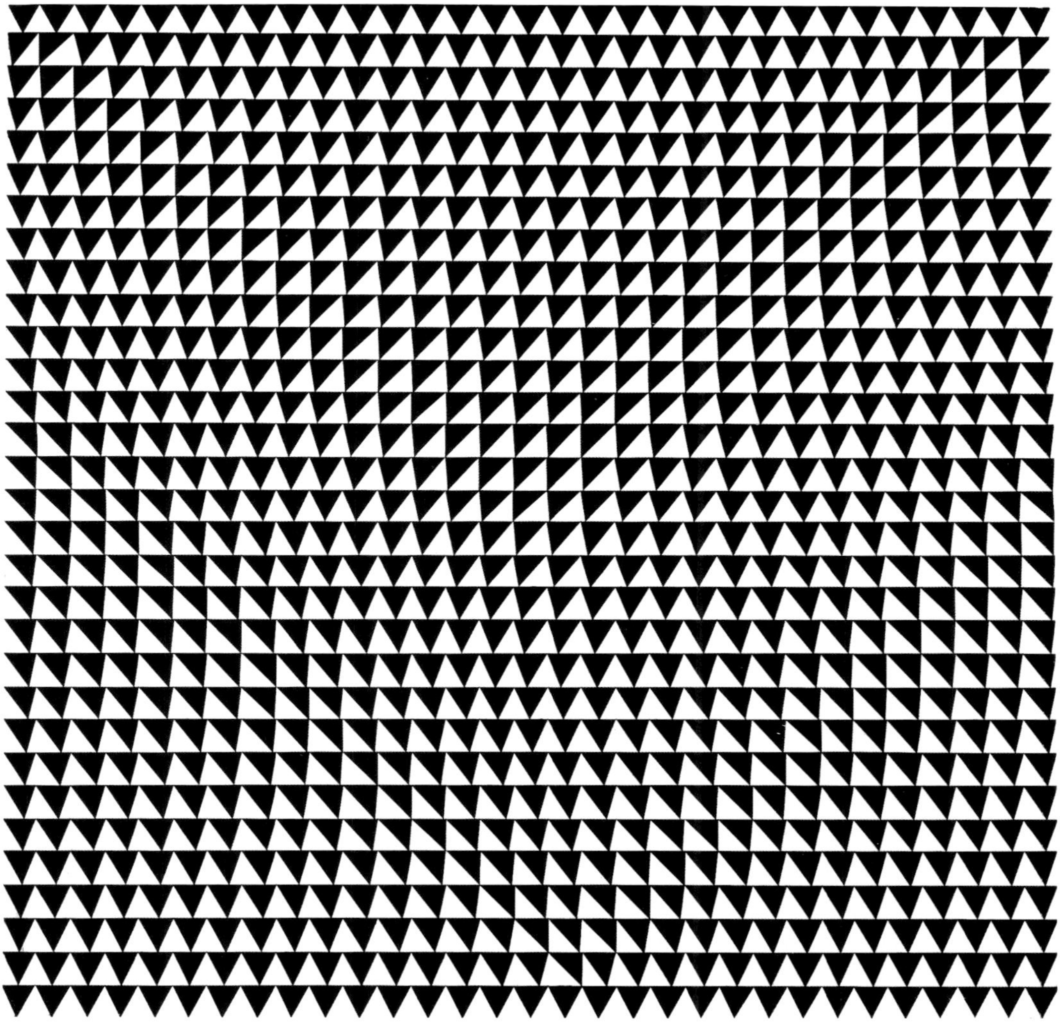

Shiver 1964

a spectral background looms up in which Heaven bears down with a heavy weight of values and principles, and Hell in the form of anxiety and suspicion exerts a constant pressure. Man's world becomes involuntarily his exile. For no one can look beyond the human viewpoint unaided – and thus, Great Pan was worshipped once as a god.

It is this fading of the world of appearances that Bridget Riley passionately objects to. However, having no presiding deity to call upon she is left with those seemingly 'scientific' means to outwit, at least momentarily, the spell that mystifies the entrance to Arcadia. '1 + 1 Equals One', was the statement she made for the catalogue of the 1964 'New Generation' show at the Whitechapel Art Gallery, London – a bit too smart and snappy, she now thinks. Inured to misunderstandings, she perhaps would not again let fall so casually the secret of the catalytic action which yields the gold of appearance. For the bright effrontery of the formula reveals the alchemy of the conjunction: the inner structure of the process that leaps to the critical start.

4 The Self-Precipitating Structure

Many discussions of Riley's work, above all the argument over 'vertigo' and 'optical aggression', would be superfluous if it were first understood just what the overpowering initial clarity itself is all about. From the desert island of order that Bridget Riley seems to inhabit, a long-unheard sound of laughter would reach the ears of passers-by preoccupied only with the predicament of their own viewpoint. The spirit of Arcadia peers round every corner, flickers between the lines, and dances, sparkling, over the still waves: how blind the eye can be, when it thinks itself sure of its gaze! This one blazing high noon, in the full glare of utmost clarity, at the same time is the darkest depth of night.

At first when the beholder is tempted to think that he has grasped the content of the paintings, he has actually not even started to see at all; certainly not in that primal sense that Bridget Riley aims at. For whatever springs to the eye at the outset – 'forms such as triangles, squares, circles, rhomboids, etc.' – are simply expedients of the autonomous power of representation. The eye initially sees only what it already knows and could remain sure of, if it was never actually exposed to the experience of this knowledge. Mathematical figures and proportions are best assessed with eyes half closed; and, surprisingly enough, a similar procedure occurs when one tries to estimate colours objectively.

'1 + 1 Equals One' – this formula starts out as a statement about the primacy of projective synthesis in perception. A purely additive structure of triangles, as in *Shift* (1963) or *Shiver* (1964), for example, is in practice not analytically grasped, as a sum of discrete single units, but synthetically conceived *a priori*: as a totality of one and the same mathematical concept, the idea of 'triangle', represented by an indefinite number of manifestations. The apparently impervious surfaces therefore are less inaccessible to perception than the first impression may suggest. Their generic unity facilitates a cognitive contact. Two colours and three angles and three colours and four angles and five colours ... The objective organisation of the paintings, when analysed, converges conceptually upon one initial inception. All the elements in the paintings originate in the free spontaneity of consciousness – whether they are projected by the inward eye of geometry or conceived from the absolute centre of the colour circle. 'I take *something*', that means to Bridget Riley: something quite *definite* – i.e. the nearest thing to *nothing*.

The subliminal lack of objective substance – in contrast to the overt structural density of the paintings – is however only one, although the ultimately decisive factor in the visual catalysis. Night is imminent long before it falls. But the paradox would perhaps never become manifest, the 'panic' awareness would not happen, nor would the life-giving return, if Bridget Riley contented herself with its bald statement alone. For, as soon as the spirit has assured itself of its own presence through its most specific images – the discarnate intuitions of geometry – it withdraws instantly from the perceptual front to enjoy the certainty of remote and tranquil contemplation. The knife-edge on which Riley's art is poised shows itself perhaps most clearly by accepting, and even flaunting, the inherent curse of mathematical form: the infinite boredom of clarity. No attempt is made at concealing or dispelling by some sort of respectable content. The switch, the total reversal of the situation, takes place solely through the beholder being held by all the means of art to actually perceive the evident, definitive clarity of what appears. The tendency of attention to fade away into apathetic self-contemplation, comparable to mirror-gazing, is prevented by a simple device. Bridget Riley makes, to some extent, perception obligatory through an even distribution of focus by means of repetitive structures. Thus the eye cannot distance itself, for it cannot focus on one particular point; it's always being called upon, from every part of the visual field, to master its own projections. Centre or periphery – every point is present with equal immediacy. And there, right on the threshold of absolute presence, comes the switch.

'1 + 1 Equals One' – the way in which Bridget Riley poses this equation it has a totally different solution from that found in rational terms. The synoptic grasp which recognises one and the same concept in two geometrical forms, takes for granted, as a matter of course, a stratum which permits the empirical distinction. This inconspicuous layer is extremely reliable and patient as long as the checkpoint of observation floats free – being in itself unperceived, though the basic condition of all perception. The eye can then, relying on this fundamental advantage, range easily over the field of perception, and gather the sensory data without being seduced by them. But when this reference point becomes sensitive, as in Riley's work, the hitherto malleable stuff of sight, exposed to attention, flares like a raw nerve. For the phenomenal world seems to have two sides: one, easily available to our awareness, the other, usually hidden from our eyes; withholding a latent potential. Thus when our viewpoint seems to gain total command over perception, as in a painting like *Blaze 1* (1962), this potential is released – and explodes. We can never encompass absolute clarity, because any appearance, even the sun in the zenith of the day, inevitably includes its own opposite. No light without darkness. '1 + 1 Equals One': the unity of day and night.

The event would be wholly lucid in itself, if the one obstinate prejudice that clings to Bridget Riley (and has even furnished a label for her work) could be relinquished: the prejudice that seeing is a purely optical process. The entire dramaturgy of the pictorial event is based on the fact that human seeing is essentially conceptual: a contraction of sensations towards one projective point; and only via this representation, the correlative of human consciousness, do we perceive what we perceive. *Omnis perceptio concipitur via repraesentationis; aut non concipitur.* Bridget Riley turns this fundamental law of perception on its head, by making the formative centre of the visual field perceptible in itself. The vanishing-point itself becomes evanescent, and the substratum of sensation, unrepressed, impinges directly upon the senses.

Nevertheless the switchover does not result in some kind of chaotic upheaval. On the contrary, the 'scopeoclasm' – as the transitory collapse of the view-point might be called (in analogy to the term 'iconoclasm') – is only a prelude to the artistic experience.[9] The time-scale of revelation runs against the logic of analysis. So-called perceptual principles are relevant only in so far as Bridget Riley is tackling a fundamental reality, the innate formalism of human seeing. The visual catharsis provides a dividing line which is as fine as it is sharp: nothing afterwards looks as it was before – although factually everything stays the same. When the convulsive tension has discharged itself, the two conditions of the climax show themselves to be apprehensible and limited in their role:

Firstly, the faculty of representation is articulated by mathematical elements. The eye confronts pure conceptual forms. Recognition is instant and certain, the threshold of perception low: appearance – but without substantiation.

Secondly, the identity of representation is dismantled by repetition. Cognitive attention is weakened by continuous affirmation. The eye runs out of control and as a result the power of the medium breaks loose.

The whole chain of events ultimately rests upon the fact that two potentially equivalent but actually incompatible intentions – objective certainty and perceptual presence – come into conflict on the same terrain. But far from explaining the origin of the paintings, the lucidity of the principles involved simply serves to demonstrate the immense delicacy of the endeavour. The problem, as Bridget Riley has often emphasised, consists not so much in just releasing the latent energy as in harnessing it, without sacrificing its vitality, thus providing the possibility of experience. For the aim of the momentary disturbance is not a break-down of the sensory system, but the removal of a barrier which obstructs the access to a vital experience.

The widespread view that Bridget Riley 'assails' the optic nerve falsifies this achievement even by the way it is formulated. No element in the paintings is deliberately manipulated as a weapon or as a gimmick. Riley's art exerts compulsion on the visual sense only by promoting its innermost aspiration: the longing for clarity. The powerful effect of seeing is essentially self-generated, and like all self-recognition a little painful at first. The overt impersonal character of the means employed is therefore not a sign of lack of imagination, but an indispensable requirement of creative integrity. The vehicle employed must be as generalised, unspecific and downright commonplace as the mathematical agents are by their very nature. The psychology of perception generally underestimates this condition in that it ascribes the effect of the paintings merely to some form of overstimulation. This fails to take the dual nature of human perception – that it is always *perceptio repraesentativa* – into consideration sufficiently. If Bridget Riley were only concerned with subjecting the perceptual mechanism to what might be called (in the jargon of thermodynamics) a heat death, then she could achieve her objective equally well with any repeatable basic form. But she cannot. Again and again she has attempted, often against her own better judgement, to remedy what she has called the 'fairly boring' character of her elements by making the individual forms more particular and 'interesting'. The result has always been unsatisfactory. Even a minute increase in the specificity of the forms leads to a disagreeable congestion of the visual field: the eye anchors itself in the formal pattern, and the effort of recognition sets up friction. The repetitive structures consequently fail to shift into a weightless free-floating rhythm; instead of which they exhaust themselves in a heavy and strangely spasmodic twitching. In short, the result misses the essence of the alchemy: the pure gold of appearance.

The artist's hands are therefore tied, so to speak, by the nature of the enterprise itself. The process of metamorphosis allows of no complications beyond the two constituent factors. The creative work is limited to a subtle and barely detectable modification of the chosen elements, with the aim of dissociating perceptual content from conceptual form: along the narrow ridge, reserved for works of art, where the utmost artificiality in the inception coincides with an elemental, archetypal power in the outcome.

Although not apparent in the final painting, there are two essential directives the artist seems to follow in her working process:

1 The pictorial elements must be 'mathematical', in the original sense of the Greek word *mathémata*: primary forms of that type of knowledge which precedes experience, independent of the empirical world and universally applicable.[10] Only elements of this particular character can be effectively disassociated from the visual energy they help to bring into being.
2 The repetitive structure must be pitched to a precise degree of *frequency* and *saturation* to fulfil a dual function. On one hand, rhythm and contrast should reach such an intensity that the inner dichotomy of perception is opened up; and, on the other hand, the metrical and plastic coherence has to be durable enough to prevent a loss of the energy to be released. Scale is therefore of vital importance.

The best example for the function of these criteria has been given by Bridget Riley herself. In an interview in 1972 she was asked why the formal elements in her black-and-white work were more diverse and complex than those in her colour-work. She replied: 'In my earlier work, when I was developing complex forms, the energies of the medium could only be fully released by simplifying colour to a black-and-white constant (with occasional grey sequences). Conversely, colour energies need a virtually neutral vehicle if they are to develop uninhibitedly. The repeated stripe seems to meet these conditions.'[11]

The expression 'fully released' in this context surely leaves very little room for misapprehension. Her words confirm that the nature of the participation assigned to the beholder is precisely judged. The basis of the paintings seems in each case to stand in inverse proportion to its elaboration. And so the simplicity of the black-white contrast permitted the development of extremely complex structures, whereas the inherent complexities of colours demanded formal simplification. The overriding consideration seems to be that of striking a balance between immediacy and saturation in the perceptual process. – And yet, however well this argument may prove the inner logic of Riley's work, the evidence doesn't seem to be conclusive. *What of colour itself*? Does not the introduction of this new factor overthrow the whole interpretation based on the 'mathematical' nature of Riley's creative premise?

5 The Emergence of Colour

The move to colour in 1967 represents the crucial test of any interpretation of Bridget Riley's work. It was at this point that her artistic self-awareness seems to have developed fully. She realised the paradoxical fact that, to attain her actual objective, she had to start from the opposite end. For a long time she thought what everyone initially thinks: colour, that evanescent, ultimately incalculable phenomenon, oscillating on the borderline between something and nothing – colour is surely not a mathematical thing ... It was in this belief that, in the years when she received international recognition for her rigorous black-and-white work, she was secretly trying to find a footing in colour. These attempts however never left the studio, because they consistently disappointed her. Introduced into the evolved contrast-structure of the early work, mostly in the guise of tonal modulation or chromatic sequence, colour always remained a gratuitous, irremediably external accessory. Later she described this false start disparagingly as 'colouring form', and dismissed it as being incompatible with her true intentions: 'I want to create a colour-form, not coloured forms.'[12] But where to start in order to move colour from being a peripheral attribute into holding a central position?

Others faced with the same dilemma for an equally long time might easily have lost faith in the basis of their work and simply changed their direction altogether. Not so Bridget Riley. The peculiar genius of her work is a wide-awake, unerring confidence in the meaning of experience; and the power of this commitment never appears more compellingly than in an instant of apparent failure. 'You have to accept it in order to

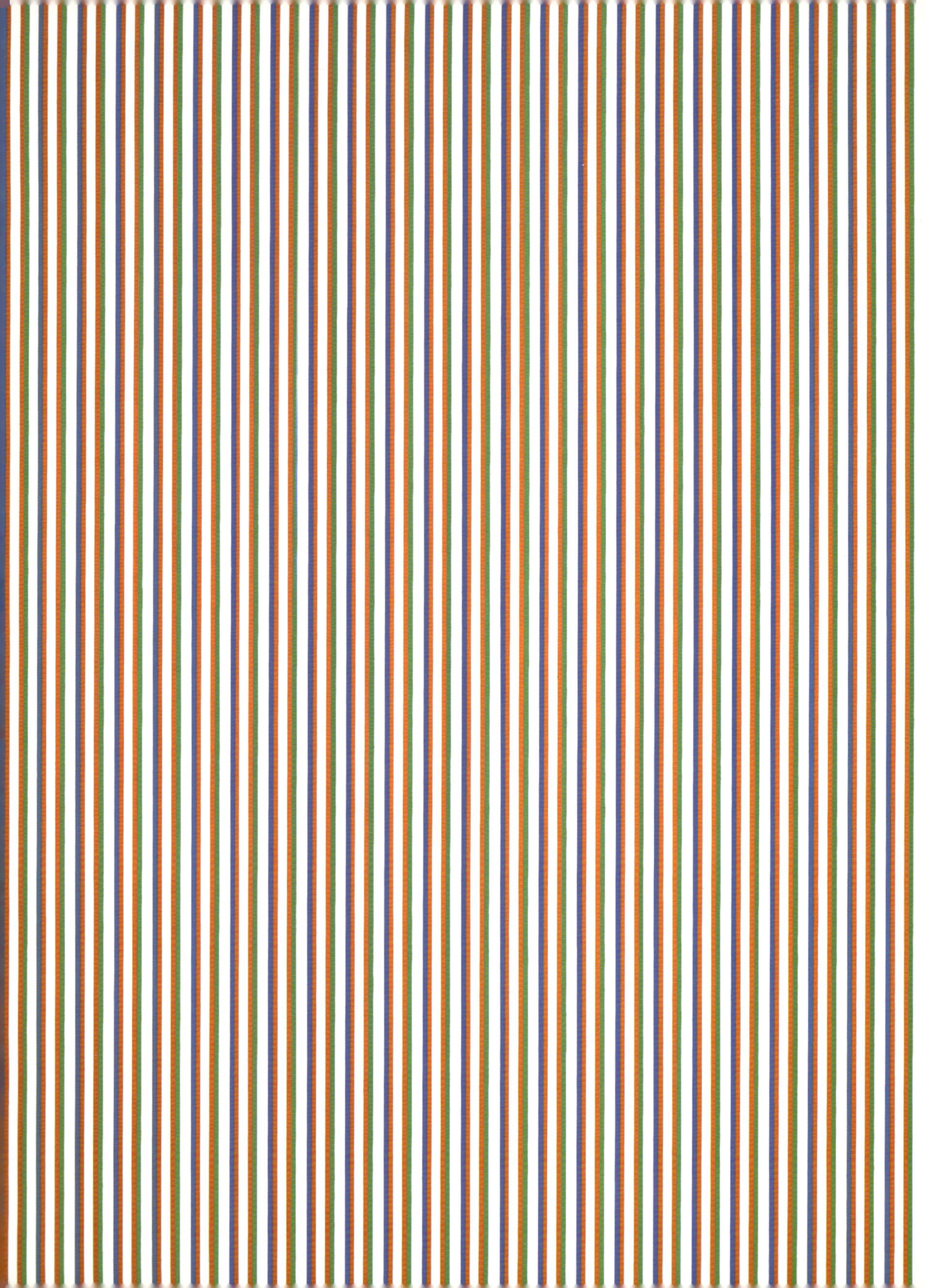

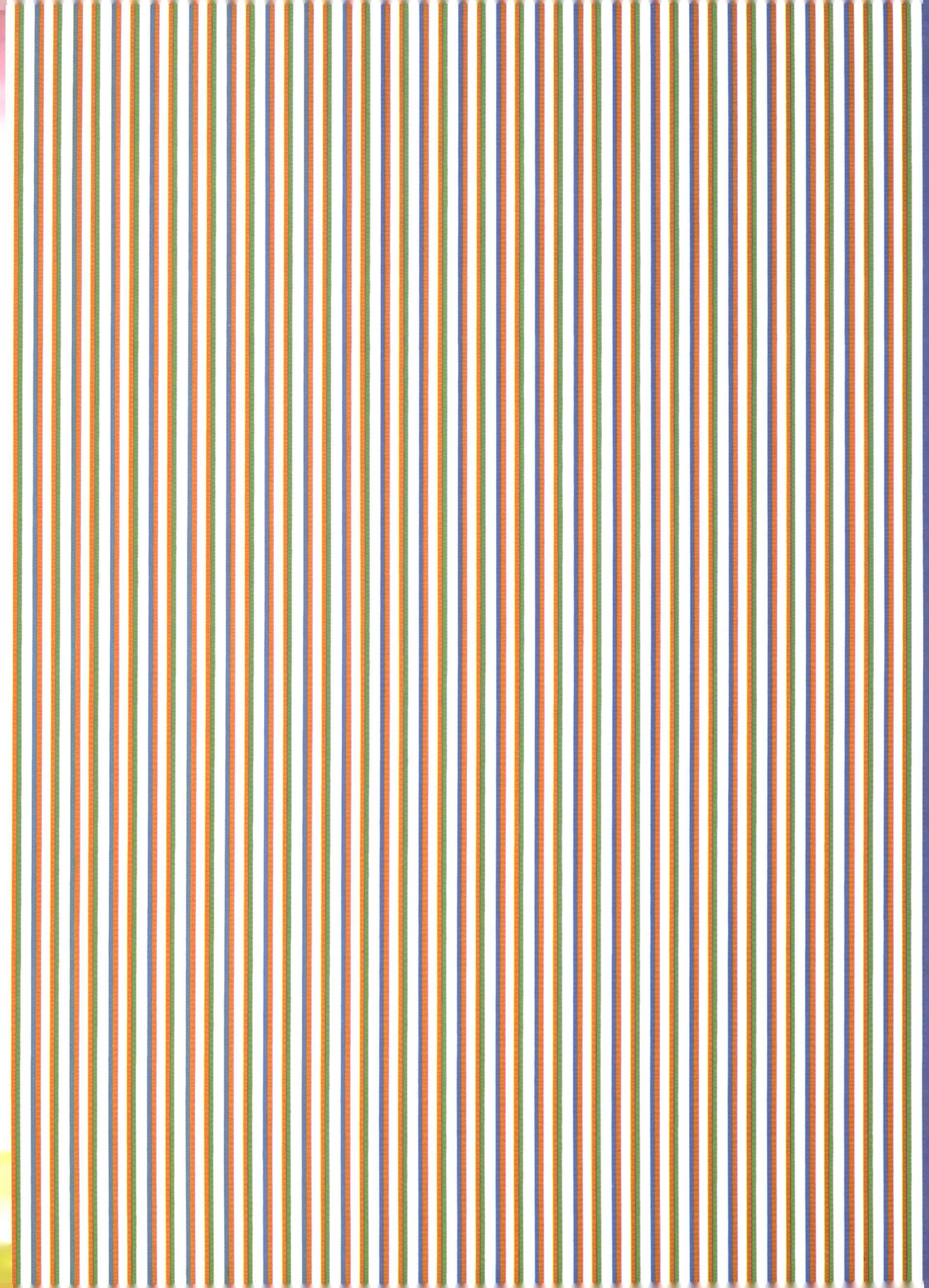

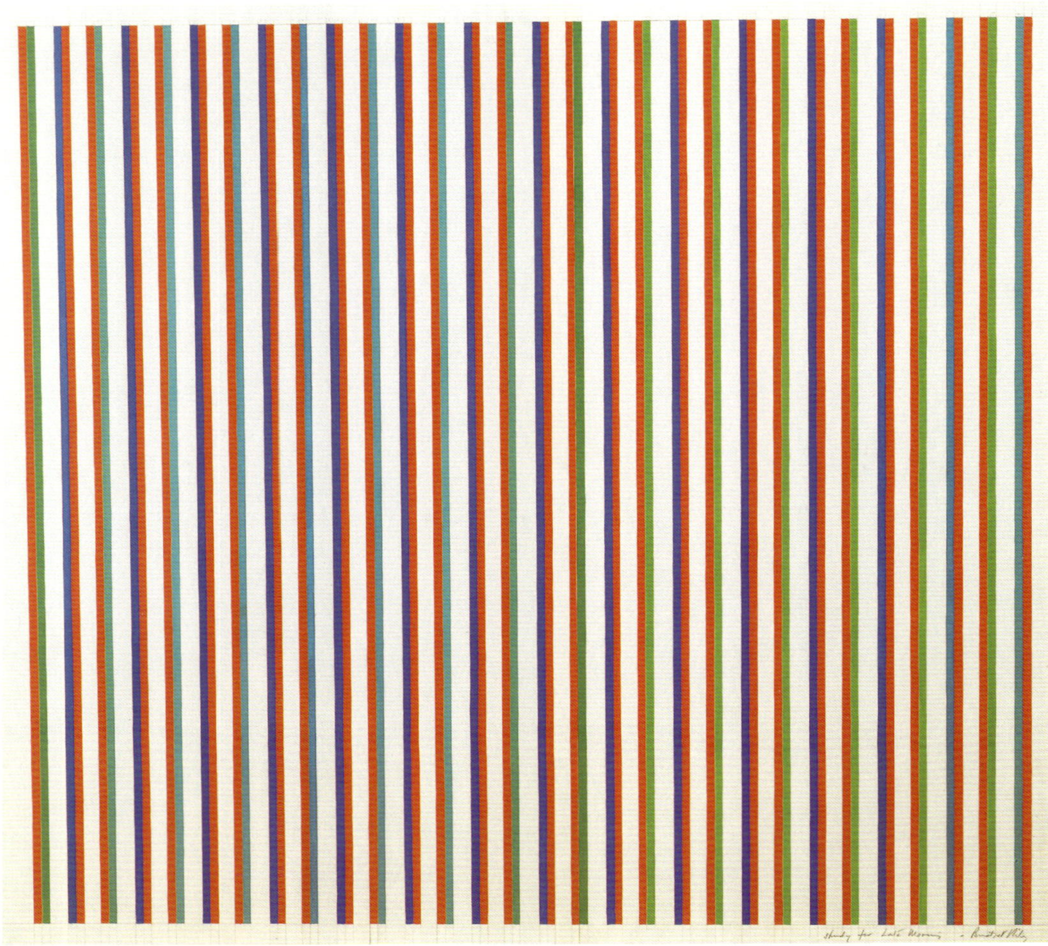

Study for Late Morning 1967

Late Morning 1967–8 (detail, previous page)

come out right at the other end,' is her principle. And so the mathematical basis of her work, which had so long and so obstinately barred her access to colour, ultimately became, in the great, festive unfolding of *Late Morning* (1967), the point of departure for an understanding of colour which makes it possible to speak of Bridget Riley today as a legitimate heir of the pioneer colourists of modern art. In the process of constantly running up against the same barrier, that of the isolation of colour as a superficial coating, the seeming validity of the common prejudice was dispelled. She was prepared to accept a simple but unexpected truth: that colour represents to a certain degree a *mathématon* too, even if not quite in the same sense as measure and form.

'I take *something* – a colour – say yellow', is the full wording of the proposition, which already has been quoted in part. The rightness of applying this statement to the mathematical basis of her whole work is confirmed by the words that immediately follow: 'What is yellow? Merely a name, an inert notion.'[13] 'Yellow' is an abstract concept, taking precedence over actual experience, in the same way as the notion of a triangle, a square, a circle etc. The basic concepts of colour have a similar synthetic universality as geometrical intuitions: although precisely defined in themselves, they do not imply the complexity of their empirical realisation. In experience there exists no such thing as *the* 'yellow', any more than there is the 'circle as such' (let alone *colour*, that mysterious singular). The important distinction consists, however, in the fact that mathematical ideas are clear *and* distinct, whereas the concepts of colour can be represented in logical terms only to a certain degree of clarity.[14] The concept 'yellow' and the idea 'circle' are both sufficiently clear to be recognized by anyone. But the mathematical definition of a circle – that it is the totality of those points which are equidistant from a given centre – contains moreover an exact definition of the characteristics by which anyone can *with certainty* reproduce the same concept. This is obviously not so with colour. However precisely the term 'yellow' may be qualified, as sulphur-yellow, lemon-yellow, saffron-yellow, etc., the things evoked remain no more than approximations which eventually dissolve in a well-nigh unlimited range of possible interpretation.

The fundamental analogy between a colour concept and a mathematical one is nevertheless strong enough to remain valid. In both cases perception is controlled by preconception. Once acknowledged, this connection permits the building of structures which involve the phenomenon of colour in a similar process of dissociation to that of geometrical form. 'What is yellow? Merely a name, an inert notion. But if you put a yellow with other colours, in different proportions and positions, it starts to show a certain potential.'[15]

The easing of the dramatic climax reveals, of course, the different potential of the premise. The essentially indistinct character of colour makes the point of departure less evident, and as the degree of immediate recognition is lowered, the catalytic reversal becomes less acute. Thus 'panic' awareness has been replaced over the years, if one may judge by a number of recent titles of paintings, by the ravishing strains of the Orphean lyre: harmonies that charm the insistent mind, and disarm the piercing gaze.

The transformation shows the subordinate, functional role played by the 'scopeoclasm' in Riley's art. To say that the impact has lessened with the progress of the work, is to misunderstand the dependence of each painting on the premise from which it has been drawn. The confrontation of the colour-work is less pointed in experience simply because it happens on a wider front. Whereas the constituents of the black-and-white work are rooted in human consciousness, colour, even in its conceptual form, seems to be a sort of bridge-head to the outside world. The eye reaches very quickly the apex of exposure and is alerted to the revelation 'There is nothing else there, beyond it'. If one tries to objectively look at the colours of a painting like *Song of Orpheus I* (1978), what does one see? The evanescence of the painting itself. All five colours – yellow, pink, violet, blue and green – are returned to the very light they embody.

The switch is, however, as acute as it was earlier and, for our modes of thinking, even more fundamental. For Bridget Riley reveals the core of true colour painting – that *to see colour is not to look for colour*. The moment we direct our attention at, say, blue or green, we mostly see the reflection of our representations: the sky is blue, the grass green, etc. Moreover, if we stare too enquiringly at it, colour altogether eludes our comprehension and we emasculate the object of observation by reducing it to the bare bones of extension, mass, form. In this way, European thinking has approached phenomena in principle: obviating colour altogether, retaining a world of intellectual chiaroscuro.

Impressionism seems to have been the first explicit challenge to this predicament. Far from obeying the dictates of the 'motif' in objective terms, painters like Pissarro or Monet have deliberately withheld the preconceptions of cognitive vision in order to see – out of the corner of the eye, so to speak – the play of appearance: the fleeting sequences within which the enigma of identity is preserved.[16] In this peripheral vision the green hue of vegetation, for example, lost its objective value and became an instant

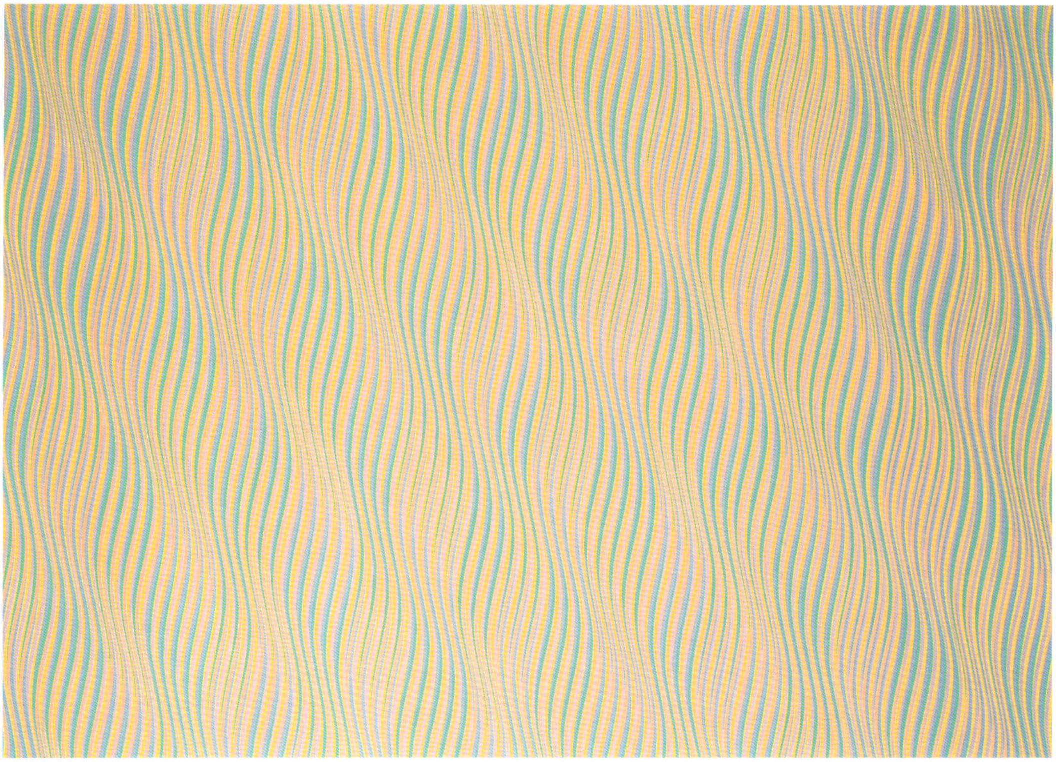

Song of Orpheus 5 1978 (detail, overleaf)

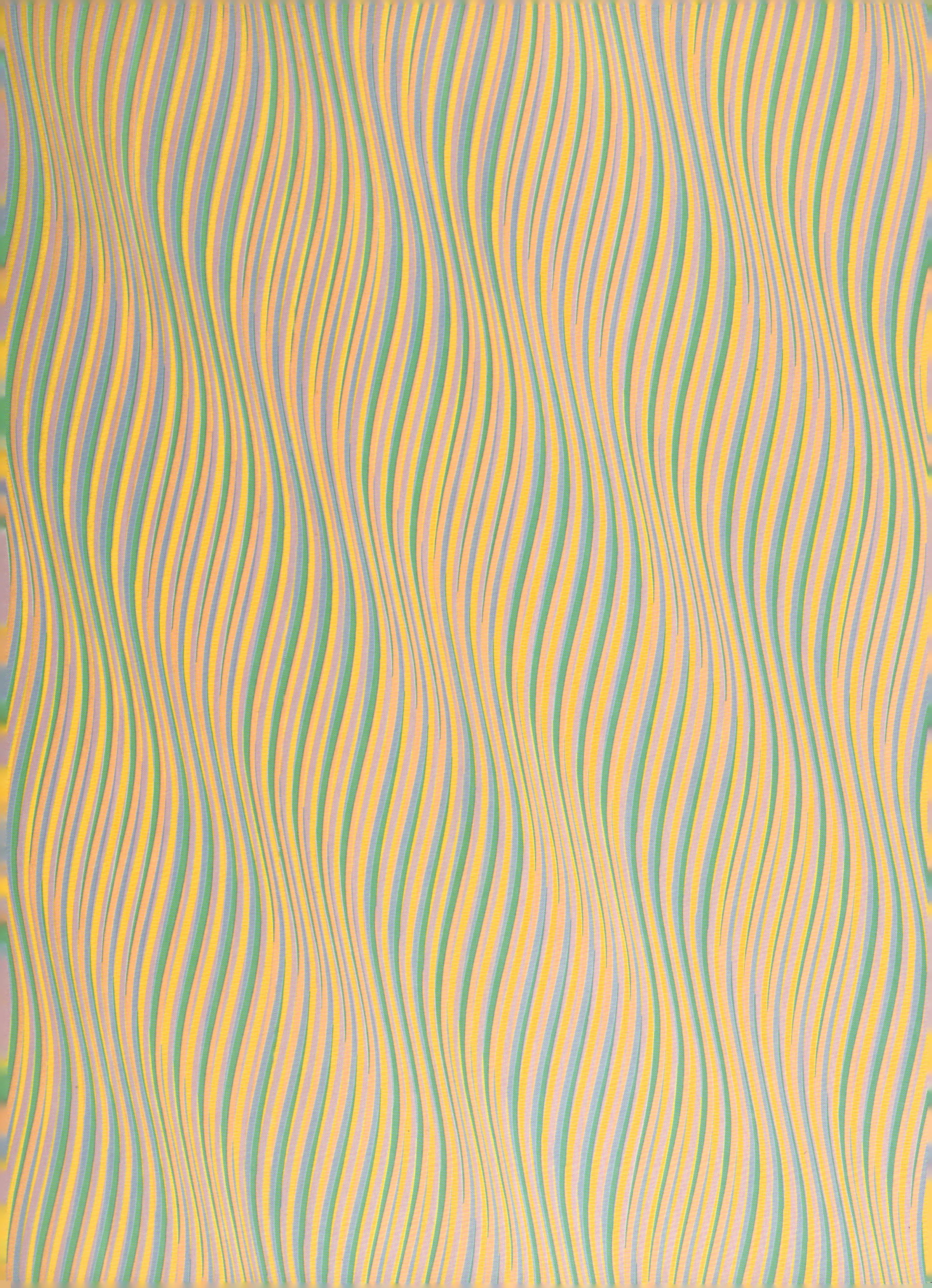

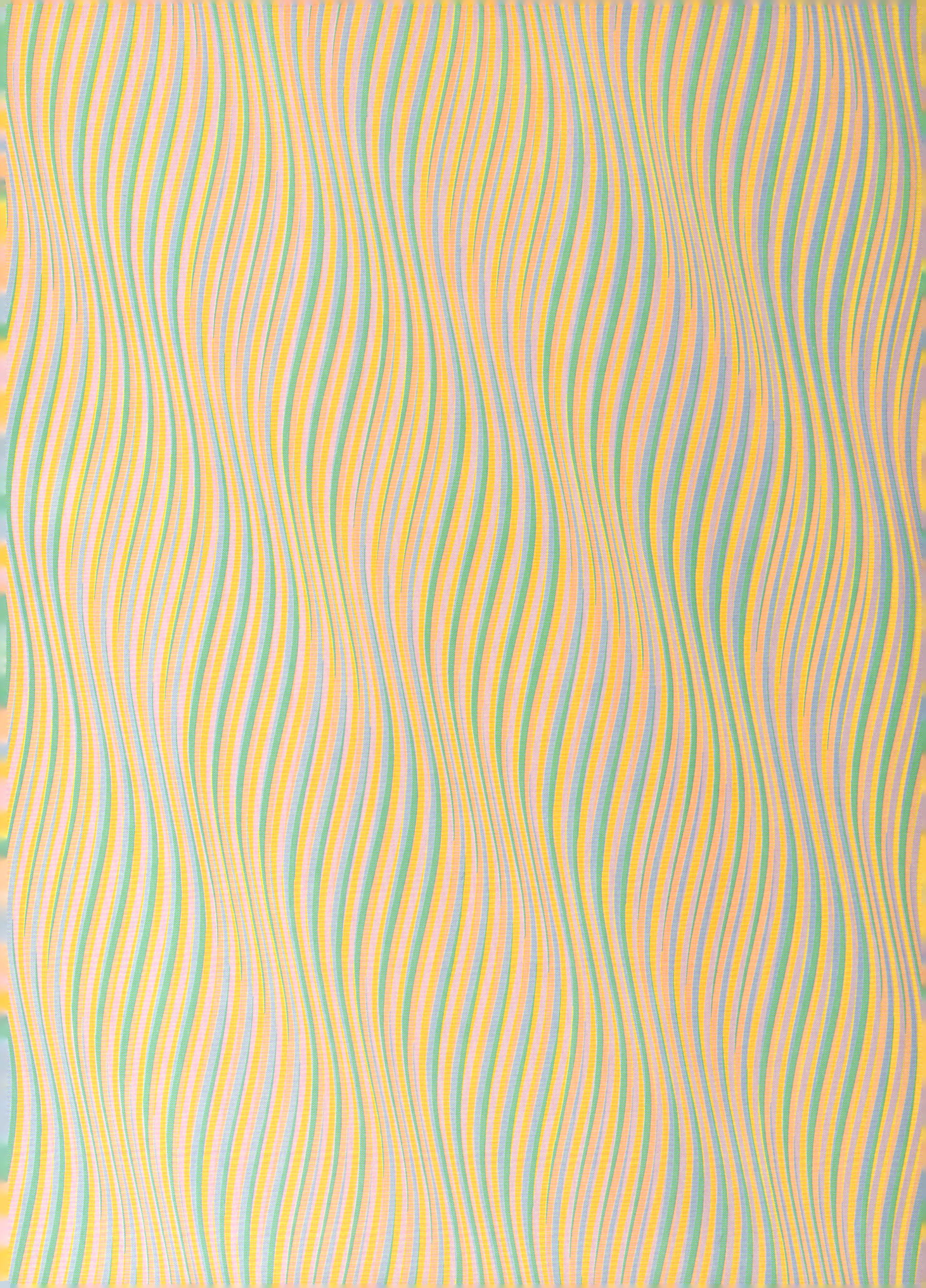

of an overall sensation, precipitating interchange with lilac and blue.

Bridget Riley's understanding of colour draws on this precedent. In difference to the Impressionists, however, she does not exclude the conceptual insinuations of the eye, but incorporates them into her works, as agents of their own dissolution. This approach via the counter-argument eventually enabled her to go beyond even the Impressionist realisation of colour. In *Late Morning* (1967), one instantly recognises a rhythmic red-constant, buttressed by sequences of blue to green. But this schematic structure is only the provisional condition of the painting: the pretext, without which it could not come into existence. For the succession of the colours employed is not self-reliant, recording an actual sequence of sensation. The very attempt to look *for* something calls into action the elusive potential of appearance, buried in the plain actuality of the painting. The highly finished canvas gives way to a beginning, a morning as never before: slowly, in the centre of the painting, a glow of golden light is discharged.

The unique access to the authenticity of appearance Bridget Riley has found in this way shows itself best in comparison with Seurat whose work once introduced her to methodical thinking. Both are centrally involved with colour and light; and both with highly preconceived ideas. In this sense their medium might be considered the same. But the difference between the approach of the two artists is striking as it reveals the crucial issue at stake. For Seurat, notwithstanding his immense knowledge of the medium, did not see the problem of *knowing* it. He constructs a thoroughly coherent equivalent to the world of external appearances without questioning the predicament of sight. The crucial difference between conceptual form and the matter of perception, essential to every phenomenon, doesn't come into play. As a result a complete internalisation envelops the painting. Nature emerges still and airless, strangely petrified, and without a flicker of light. Great Pan is absent.

The contrast to Riley's work could not be greater. Although there are undoubtedly those *mathémata*, which initiate her process of working, they never safeguard, let alone dictate, the final outcome. On the contrary, all conceptual assertions are essentially destined to yield to the perception to which they give rise. For Bridget Riley aims at opening up the very difference which Seurat methodically ignored. It is interesting to note that this divergence is already apparent in her very early work (before 1960), when she was still under the influence of this master. In *Pink Landscape* (1960), for instance, the heat blaze of a Mediterranean noon is not simply captured, absorbed and neutralised by conceptual encroachment. It is rendered perceptible, in its disintegrating power, through an exceptionally agitated surface.

With her colour paintings since *Late Morning* Bridget Riley has fulfilled this early promise – drawing on the experience and understanding provided by the black-and-white work. Unlike Seurat, she does not *contain* the phenomenon of light *within* a colour structure, but *releases* it *through* the agency of colour. Correspondingly, colour acts as an *incentive* of light, instead of being a mere *representation*.

In the course of her development this specific articulation of the split between colour and light, the fundamental distinction of every appearance, has led into a new dimension of working which she refers to as 'the plasticity of the medium'. For the array of her activity is no longer determined by that critical reference-point of recognition alone, as in the black-and-white period. The objective correlative of human consciousness has been transcended towards an identity in its own right: the overt mystery of the day.

Thus the introduction of colour has opened up a prospect of near-overwhelming richness. 'The only failure', she says, 'would be my inability to realise it – *it itself is there*'. But it is not only the potential that is confirmed. The assertion of Riley's artistic confidence, gained through colour, throws also – and almost literally so – a light on the contradiction which underlies all her work since the avowed 'start' in 1960: Why, when the ultimate issue is the realisation of a primal naturalness – why then, this pronounced artificiality of the beginning? What is the sense of starting at high noon, when the appointment is with the freshness of the morning hour? The answer gains now its full weight: Bridget Riley approaches her subject in this paradoxical way, because it seems to be denied to us, by the very nature of human sensibility, to grasp anything original in the way we, and artists in particular, long to grasp it: *immediately* – 'at source', so to speak.

6 The Reversal

> *'Who's turned us round like this, so that we always,*
> *do what we may, retain the attitude*
> *of someone who's departing?'*
> *Rainer Maria Rilke, The Eighth Duino Elegy*[17]

The deflection which makes us unfaithful to what we see, is more deeply rooted than it initially seems. Like a ubiquitous shadow it accompanies us wherever we go, changing its form in relation to its circumstances. Although it throws into relief varying empirical manifestations – modes of perception, recurrent associations, conventions of education, etc. – the nature of this deflection is not expressed through its self-same manifestations. Any bid for 'freedom', which breaks only with these superficial cultural conventions is therefore doomed to failure. The basic condition remains: we are not in line with the course that Nature herself takes.

The human mind, unlike the song of the birds, does not rise with the sun; it is alerted by the awareness that time is finite, and that every day has a close. Whatever we start, starts with an end. In this way the distant horizon is closer to us than our immediate existence; and we come back to the present only in order to make our own kind of start: a beginning towards the particular objectives in view.

The way of looking, which Bridget Riley articulates, is rooted in the pattern of our existence. The eye, as she employs it, is not the simple soul of the 'formalist impasse'. It includes the intellectual perspective within which all our conceptual responses operate: the immediate identification of the object of attention; the transgression of its presence through interpretation; and on top of it all – in the far distance, so to speak – the assertion of principles, to which the interpreting activity itself succumbs. No wonder, that the mind of the beholder is deeply disquieted by the arrival of the Great Pan ...

Nevertheless, the intervention of the mythological apparition shows in this context a profound legitimacy. For the dramatic reversal of projective vision enacts the circular rhythm underlying our vision itself. Bridget Riley emphasises the other side, as it were, of man's principal advantage: the indispensable condition that any concept has to relate to the same sensory basis, which it essentially surpasses, in order to become even perceptible – let alone *real*.

The significance of this cyclic momentum shows itself most clearly through the opposition it encounters. The dominance of finite destination, this strange deflection of man, has perhaps always lent itself to the temptation of indulging in the bland gaze, which takes nothing else into account than its own immovable aim. But this distorting preference did not become historically effective, before the straight sight-line was officially established. Thus, as Bridget Riley herself has suggested, the Renaissance concept of centralised perspective might have been the first step towards profanation of Nature. The critical phase, however, was not reached until the impertinence of the enquiring eye started to contradict its very aim – the insight into the magic of appearance.

The historical moment, when this contradiction came out into the open, can be identified as clearly as the disappearance of the Great Pan. It was in the nineteenth century that the cul-de-sac of representation became the main road, and the mere sight of changing inflections prompted the most fierce reactions. A simple homage to the daylight appeared as an act of aggression. 'I may cause something of an outcry among the enemies of blue and pink through this radiance, this magical light, that I set out to represent', wrote Monet, with the wisdom of experience, to his dealer Durand-Ruel in March 1884.[18] The 'outcry' provoked by the Impressionists came from the same quarter as the accusation of aggressiveness against Bridget Riley's paintings. They both betray a loss of conceptual certainty. And even the rationalisation is the same: namely, that this 'magical light' is no more than a superficial phenomenon – in Monet's case a fleeting 'impression' (as if the celebrated blue and pink were obvious to everybody), and in Bridget Riley's an 'optical effect' (as if her catalytic process were based solely on the physical organ).

The adverse judgement undermines itself. The devaluation of the phenomenal aspect of the world implies that the 'true, genuine and profound' apprehension of objects is not to be formed by perception but by conceptual generalisations. And yet, the opposite does not guarantee authenticity either. Even Monet's 'impressions' are not so available that they could be realised without a highly sophisticated human way of looking. His art centralises around his famous 'peripheral vision'. Bridget Riley's visual events are conceived in an area in which the attention is, so to speak, turned away from the matter in hand. The surprisingly widespread view that there is such a thing as purely passive perception, open to the charms of the world like a window open to the sun, is manifestly fallacious. This oversimplification is the exact counterpart of the verdict that appearance is purely superficial: its origin lies in the same dismissal of natural complexity, now transferred to the human sensory apparatus itself.

Thus even the utmost rejection betrays a ray of truth. Appearance and human sensibility are inseparably linked. We see only so far as we exert our capacity for sight. Any intention to render available the world of appearances therefore requires our activity: the effort of letting them – *be*. This work, which cannot be compared with any other work, because it is directed against the very intention of 'work', has acquired since the end of the eighteenth century a specific name. Art – without any further embellishment: work *against* work.

Riley's exceptional position within the contemporary art scene is decisively affected by the fact that she has consistently subscribed more to the tendencies of 'classic' modernism than to those of immediate contemporaneity. Her preferences and her criteria may have changed since the first, tentative encounter with Seurat. But the general orientation has remained the same. The work she does continues a way of 'working' that has been primarily established by Cézanne and Monet, especially in the late paintings of both artists.

In the presence of the *motif*, the *Montagne Sainte-Victoire*, Cézanne witnessed the dramatic failure of the attempt to endow the dimensions of nature with form on a human scale; and it has become apparent that to have endured this defeat, to the very point where the power of nature became manifest as such, is an achievement without precedent: a victory over the projective process, which has given a second meaning to the name that happens to be borne by the *motif* itself.[19] The solution that Monet offers in his late works is less tragic, in the true sense of the word, than Cézanne's, but not less significant. (And it is clearly closer to Riley's own preoccupations.) The structure of the *Nymphéas* is frequently determined by a drift of pictorial incident towards the periphery; and in the middle (where for Cézanne the centre of the conflict opened up), a curious, blind spot emerges. It might be described as an emptiness or void – the bottomless reflection of the ark of the sky on the surface of the water. The objective correlative X is thus invalidated, neutralised by a perfect sensual anticipation, and appearance slips in through the corner of our eye.

Leaving aside any question of artistic stature, there seems to be a common interest in loosening the grip of the precocious viewpoint over perception. The signs indicate a departure from a departure that has lost the momentum of exclusive orientation. But unlike her predecessors, Bridget Riley does not confront the beholder with the *result* of this change, she sets the transformation itself in train – for him.

The resources on which she draws are evidently common property. The significant shift is slight, basically one of emphasis within the ambivalent framework of our visual world; but the upshot is explosive. Our view is turned the other way. We are no longer drawn in the direction we are familiar with: towards the horizon of pressing aspirations and incessant queries – 'What is the sense, the meaning, the purpose of it all?' The gentle humanity of Riley's art is perhaps most evident in the way it undermines flabby profundities – and does so by making the beholder look just a little further. Her whole *oeuvre* is a triumphant affirmation of one subtle distinction: the perspective of finite reality would not be a finite perspective (rather a terrifying Fate) if it were to run to an ultimately definable objective.

'I am sometimes asked "What is your objective?" and this I cannot truthfully answer.'[20] The statement is not at all frivolous or naïve. It shows, rather, a sober honesty. Who could ever truthfully say more? The refusal to answer conveys simply that the question was wrongly conceived. For whatever could have been found out in this perspective has been settled at the very outset. Bridget Riley does not work for the sake of a particular objective or towards an end. She starts by asserting an ultimate position: the preconceptions inherent in the human mind. They are the precise formal functions of finite consciousness – as certain in principle, and as inexplicit in empirical terms, as the end of existence itself. In short: dead knowledge, as against the flow of life.

However, once this position has been staked out and insistently brought to the spectator's attention, the latent momentum of circularity comes into action. The 'point' vanishes, the leaves rustle, Great Pan appears. Does our route seem so pointless only because our eye insists on staring straight ahead? What if the significance of departure were found, not in some remote objective, but in a return to the present? The finite outlook remains. But the coercion of necessity is relieved by the sudden reaffirmation of a life-giving pulse. We inevitably adopt the 'attitude of someone who's departing' – but we could never maintain it if we were not, thanks to a vital, endlessly tolerant origin, renewed and redeemed. 'I work "from" something rather than "towards" something', is Bridget Riley's positive answer.[21] Not the riddle of the end, but the secret of the beginning is her theme.

The problem of interpretation is that the art of Bridget Riley is directed against the very nature of discourse. The paintings are not products to be endlessly 'pointed out', assessed and probed with questions, but initiations into an old ritual – naturally with modern rules. Every work can be understood as an offering, in the primeval sense: a gift most beautifully wrought to do just one thing – to be rendered back to the light of the day from which it was taken; and to gather, with the gift, the mind of the spectator. The burden of knowing is an essential part of the ceremony. Bridget Riley distributes the apples of knowledge generously. But when one tries to devour the fruit, the mind falters, for a moment. Not because the apples were poisoned. What an idea! Not at all. The momentary faltering springs from a vivid, never previously experienced desire. A request that is richer than any satiation: to have eaten the apple of knowledge – and yet, to feel no other wish than to see the trees bloom. '1 + 1 Equals One'.

1 William Shenstone, *Essays on Men and Manners* (1764), reprinted in Harrison's British Classics 8, 1787, Essay XXII, p. 38. The principle of the 'oblique approach' concerns in this context the interplay of paths and views in the English Garden: 'When a building, or other object, has been once viewed from its proper point, the foot should never travel to it by the same path which the eye has travelled over before' (ibid).

2 *Conversation* 1972, p. 22 [in this volume]

3 Rainer Maria Rilke, *Duino Elegies* (1922). Engl. translation with an introduction and commentary by J. B. Leishman and Stephen Spender. 2nd Ed., London: Chatto & Windus 1977, p. 77. – The last line of the quotation is slightly misleading in English. Disregarding the flow of the words, the original wording is 'set around its free outgoing'. The connection of' Nature with 'freedom' could suggest a Romantic reading – which Rilke, partly through his encounter with Cézanne's work in 1907, has long surpassed in the *Elegies*. His problem is precisely the difference between 'freedom' as man's specific determination, and Nature's 'free unfolding'.

4 Quoted after Bryan Robertson, "Introduction" to *Bridget Riley. Paintings and Drawings 1951–1971*, catalogue of the Hayward Gallery retrospective exhibition, London: The Arts Council of Great Britain, 1971, p. 14.

5 *Conversation* 1972, p. 20 [in this volume]

6 Ibid.

7 Op. cit., p. 22.

8 Ibid.

9 The honour of having recognised this cyclic momentum for the first time goes to Anton Ehrenzweig (1908–1966), author of many books on the relationship between art and the creative unconscious, and an early critical champion of Riley's art. He met the artist in 1963, and his major essay on her work, "The Pictorial Space of Bridget Riley" (published in *Art International*, Feb. 1965, Vol. IX, no. 1, pp. 20–24), remains fundamental to any interpretation. For Ehrenzweig's psycho-analytical training enabled him to see the limits of our habitual predilection for order and comfort, and to feel free to appreciate the life-giving return of the work. 'One can distinguish two contrasting phases in the subjective experience of Bridget Riley's paintings – the first phase can be called cold, hard, aggressive, "devouring"; the second warm, expansive, reassuring' (ibid., p. 21).

10 The interpretation and criticism of the 'mathematical' principles of human understanding has been a life-long concern of the philosopher Martin Heidegger. I owe him the important distinction that 'mathematics', as we all learn them, are only the most overt and complete manifestation of an operational condition which is effective in all human curiosity: we approach the unknown always along the lines of what we know for certain already. (For the historical context see Heidegger's essay "Die Zeit des Weltbildes", in: M. H., *Holzwege*, 4th ed., Frankfurt a. M. 1963, pp. 69–104.)

11 *Conversation* 1972, p. 20 [in this volume]

12 Op. cit., p. 22.

13 Op. cit., p. 20.

14 The distinction between clear and distinct concepts marked an important step in the evolution of European logic in the 17th century; and on this unique occasion, colour, if only because a perfect example, seemed to have played a significant role in Western thinking. It was Leibniz, who argued that Descartes' definition of truth (as certitude)

through the criterion *clare et distincte* was not sufficiently founded, because we do have clear ideas such as the notions of colour which cannot be substantiated by logical distinction. The argument was first raised in an essay in 1684, "Meditationes de cognitione, veritate et ideis" (cf. C. J. Gerhardt (ed.), *Die philosophischen Schriften von G. W. Leibniz*, vol. IV, Berlin 1875 sq., pp. 422–426).

15 *Conversation*, p. 20 [in this volume]

16 This phenomenological way of looking has been excellently described and discussed by Andrew Forge in *Monet at Giverny*, London: Mathews Miller & Dunbar, 1975, pp. 7–14). – The same author has written a perceptive article on Riley's colour work: "On looking at Paintings by Bridget Riley", *Art International*, vol. XV, no. 3, 20 March 1971, pp. 16–21.

17 R. M. Rilke, *Duino Elegies*, p. 81.

18 Letter to Paul Durand-Ruel, 11 March 1884 (from Bordighera). In: Lionello Venturi, *Les Archives de l'Impressionisme*, Vol. I. Paris – New York: Durand-Ruel Editeurs 1939, p. 273. – The French original reads: 'Cela fera peut-être on peu crier les ennemis du bleue et du rose, car c'est justement cet éclat, cette lumière féerique que je m'attache à rendre.'

19 Bridget Riley saw in November 1977 the exhibition *Cézanne. The Late Work* at the Museum of Modern Art, New York, and was overwhelmed by the 'primal, archaic earliness of nature' which breaks through the structure of paintings.

20 Maurice de Sausmarez, *Bridget Riley*, London: Studio Vista 1970, p. 91. Reprinted in *The Eye's Mind* (1999), p. 79.

21 Ibid.

Introduction to the catalogue of the retrospective exhibition *Bridget Riley: Works 1959–78*, London: The British Council in association with The Illustrated London News, 1978, pp. 7–39. The incident described in the first chapter of this piece inspired the American choreographer Robert North to create a ballet on the basis of five backcloths which he asked Riley to design in advance. It was called *Colour Moves* and first performed by the Ballet Rambert at the Edinburgh Festival in 1983.

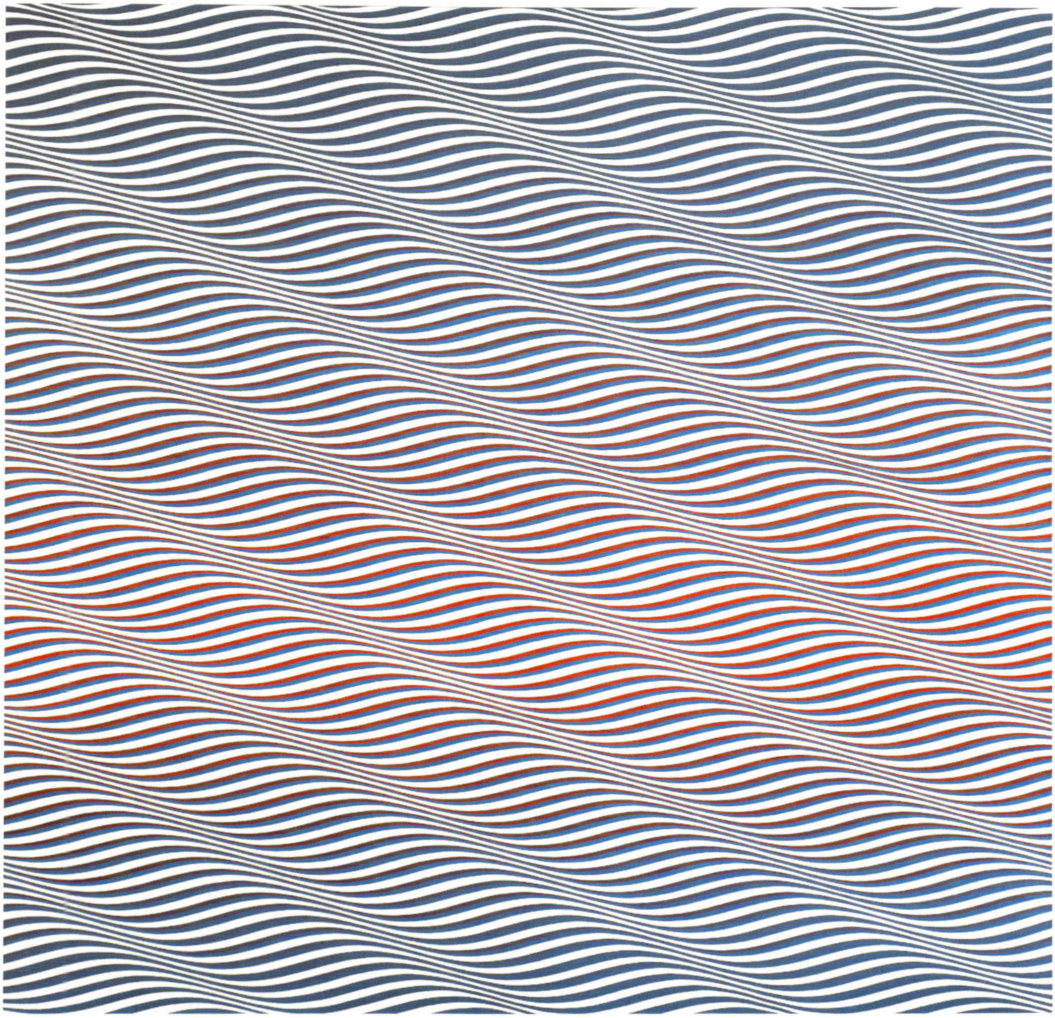

Cataract 3 1967

Into Colour

Conversation

1978

ROBERT KUDIELKA: *In 1965 you wrote about your black-and-white work: 'The basis of my paintings is this: that in each of them a particular situation is stated. Certain elements within that situation remain constant. Others precipitate the destruction of themselves by themselves. Recurrently, as a result of the cyclic movement of repose, disturbance and repose, the original situation is restated.'*[1] *Is this also true for the colour work you have been doing since 1967?*

BRIDGET RILEY: Yes, in a way. I still start by establishing a particular situation. All my work is one thing, as it were, it may appear different but it is essentially the same. As I used to choose a particular form in my black-and-white work as a point of departure, I now choose a particular group of colours. For several years I used only three colours in each painting, though more recently I have used five – and with those colours, say, yellow, pink, violet, blue and green, I build up a structure which does two different things at the same time: the individual colours change their identity through juxtaposition and by re-relating these juxtapositions the collective colour of the group is changed.

RK: *But there doesn't seem to be a cyclic momentum now. As a spectator you can't rely upon a stable point of departure because the shifts and changes are already taking effect from the very first glance at the painting.*

BR: That's because you cannot establish a clearly recognisable constant in colour, as you can in form. Colour, and especially the coloured light it generates, is naturally not as distinct as the black and white contrast was.

RK: *So could one say that change itself has become the constant in your recent work?*

BR: You could say that change is a consistent characteristic of colour, but in perception these changes do not take place as ruptures, nor are they in any sense rapid. They are shifts within a particular envelope. Every painting has its own character – its own 'light'; it may be a fresh shining sparkle or a saturated yellow glow, or even a dusky mid-tone. But none of these qualities can be precisely nailed down any more than those of real daylight. They are unavoidably elusive.

RK: *This makes the work very susceptible to changing conditions of light, doesn't it?*

BR: Very much so. In fact, one of the problems I have to deal with is that these recent paintings come across in startlingly different ways in any given light.

RK: *I suppose it is this uncertainty that makes them difficult to grasp or penetrate. The grey paintings which you did around 1966, like* Deny, Drift, Cataract *and others, still approached the issue of light and colour according to the binary principle of the black and white contrast.*

BR: Those paintings are not so much about contrast, or colour for that matter, as about tone – tone in its purest sense. *Deny* and *Drift*, for instance, were built on an inversion of colour and tone. When the tonal values are equal you can clearly see the colour opposition between the dull red and blue. Conversely, when the tonal contrast is at its strongest the difference in hue is overpowered by the opposition of light against dark.

RK: *Explained like this, in this technical way, it sounds rather close to a perceptual demonstration.*

BR: Good heavens, those are only the mechanics of the painting – not the actual experience. Most people are not even aware of them; and they need not be either. I didn't choose the title *Deny* by chance. That whole group of paintings grew out of, and away from, the absolute opposition of black and white. I wanted something which operated on more levels, was capable of more development, had a more 'grey'd' quality, like the

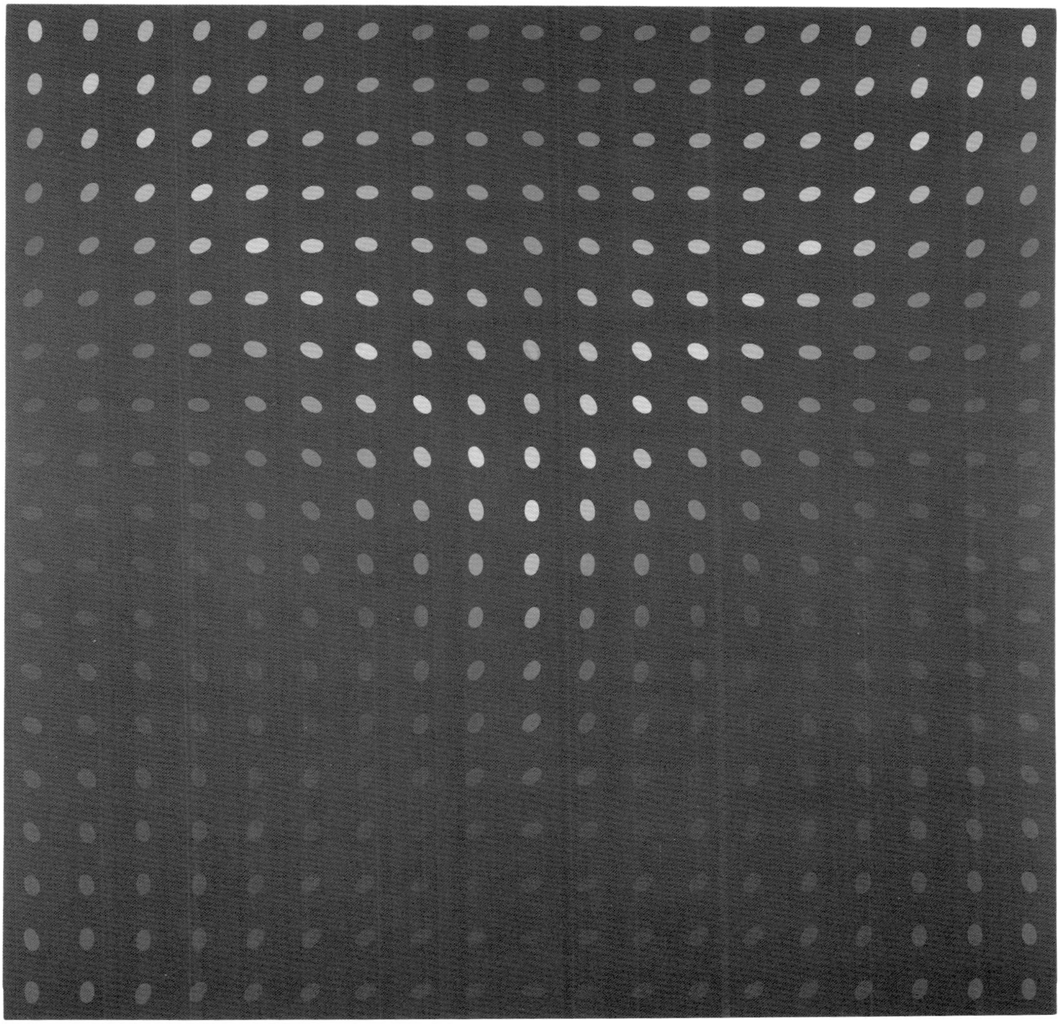

Deny 2 1967

indeterminate nature of reality.

RK: *It's very interesting that Cataract, which already anticipates your final step into colour painting, despite its firm tonal structure shows a loose spread of bright luminous colour in the area where the dominant grey curves split into red and turquoise.*

BR: Those colours spread from the edge, the curve has a long edge-exposure. The stripe paintings that I did afterwards also depend very much on this quality. The ovals in *Deny* still contain visual energy, as separate entities, rather like the Pointillist marks of Seurat did. But a long thin line of colour, essentially 'edge', without a large volume to carry, is the ideal element to work with this elusive relationship between colour and light.

RK: *This means that it was not a stylistic choice that stripes became the dominant formal element in your work from 1967 to 1973?*

BR: No, not at all – nor for that matter was my using of larger areas. The reasons lay in the necessity of building up a fluctuating colour field. In the same way that I had to sacrifice distinctive forms in order to release the energy of colour-light, it was necessary to increase the scale of the event in order to prevent focused looking.

RK: *You mean that the visual 'grip' had to be loosened? In* Late Morning *or* Rise*, for instance, I feel it impossible to encompass so large a field because the eye is foiled in its attempt to penetrate the repetitive structure. This rebuff, however, does not lead to perceptual inertia. Paradoxically, it seems to be the beginning of the spectator's engagement with the painting.*

BR: That is true. Technically *Late Morning* consists of a repeated red constant right across the canvas, paired with sequences from blue to green. *Rise* is a three-colour painting, only magenta, turquoise and olive, used in different juxtapositions. But what actually makes the paintings alive is the discharge of coloured light. In the centre of *Late Morning* it is a golden-tinted haze, and in *Rise* disembodied colours spread over the entire surface.

RK: *The simplicity of the constituents is astounding. Most of your colour work before 1977 is based on three colours plus white and the structural device seems to be similar in each case: two colours are nearly opposites (like red and green in* Late Morning*, or magenta and turquoise in* Rise 1*), while the third colour is an adjacent which shifts the emphasis. It reminds me very much of the aesthetic principle which underlies the Zen gardens of Japan: main stone – counter stone – adjacent stones.*

BR: That's interesting. From *Rise* onwards I realised that it was very important not to have a direct opposition. If there were, the colour energy would be locked up in the complementary contrast, as though in a

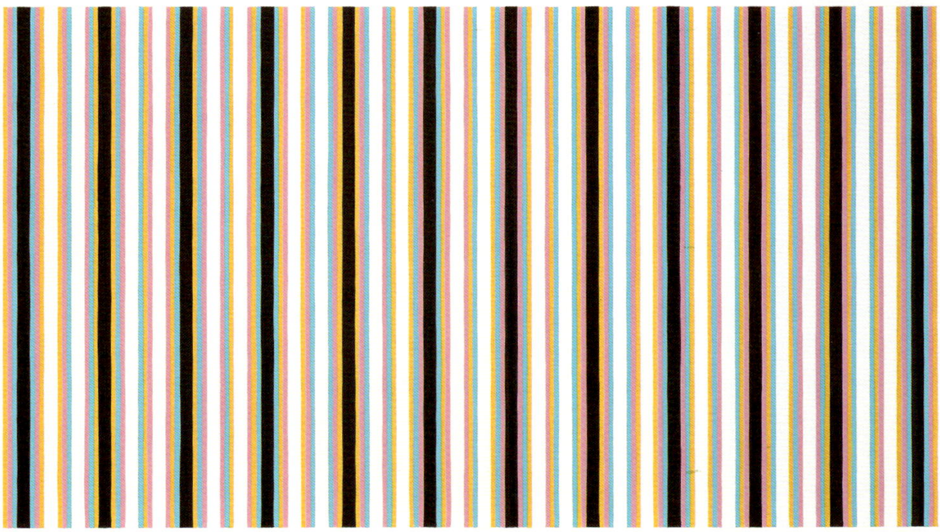

Study '72 – Three Colours in Different Orders, with Black 1972

straightjacket. It is released by instability, a freely floating flux. Each colour has to be balanced so that the slightest influence from a neighbouring colour will throw it off that very balance – and this is true for all of them in turn, whether there are three or five colours, so that they continually shift this way and that. But there also has to be an overall colour-bias which governs the entire canvas. Otherwise the sheer amount of coloured light released will lead to iridescence, light energy running right around the spectrum. But I was only able to bring about such a general emphasis after a while – at first it was confined to certain areas and patches.

RK: *I also see a structural bias of colour, going against the actual direction of the bands. If you look at* Late Morning, *and in particular* Veld, *the colour activity seems to rebound against the linear thrust. It can be so intense that – in the strong light you prefer for these paintings – the lines momentarily seem to twist, and I wonder whether this led to those twisted bands which you have been using since 1970?*

BR: I had found out quite early that perceptual activity takes place in opposition to the graphic field. In *Orient 4* and *Vapour* I made deliberate use of this. In those paintings I crossed one line diagonally over the other two and mirrored this configuration. These 'cross-overs' eventually became 'twists' of all three colours. What happens then you can see most clearly in *Zing*. Green, red and blue twist around each other in turn four times within a continuous band; and by mirroring these vertical bands a series of colour zones appears, travelling horizontally across the canvas. The colour of each of these zones is not *literal* colour – it is not actually painted. It emerges solely through visual fusion.

RK: *The paintings around and following* Zing *form one of the most coherent groups in your work. However, the final paintings,* Fade *and* Clandestine, *show a return of grey and black sequences. Did you feel the need to reintroduce a more plastic pictorial space?*

BR: You may be right, but I never consciously thought in such terms. I wanted to give more substance to the colour zones through those grey and black sequences. Perhaps you can see the sort of things I was involved with best in a big painting I did at that time, *Cantus Firmus*. In this canvas each side is visually pinned flat by equalising tone and colour, and a layered space opens up towards the centre. It's rather like being in a Gothic cathedral where light filters through the throng of the columns and gives the sensation of a space which seems to be both open and closed at the same time.

RK: *However, this density was achieved by recreating the tonal momentum of your*

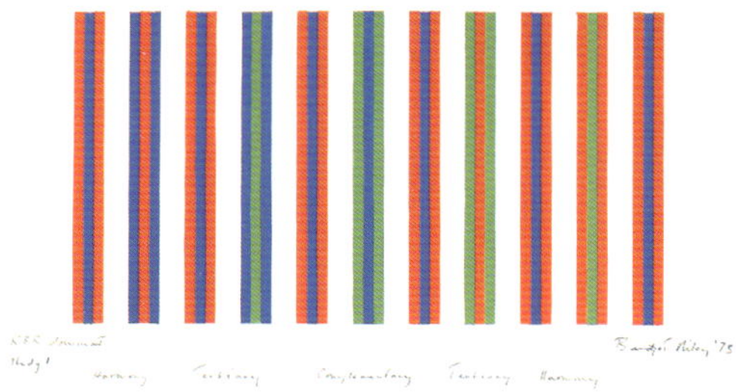

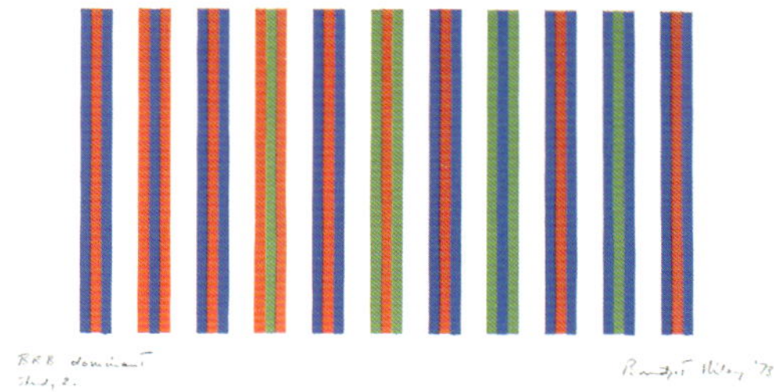

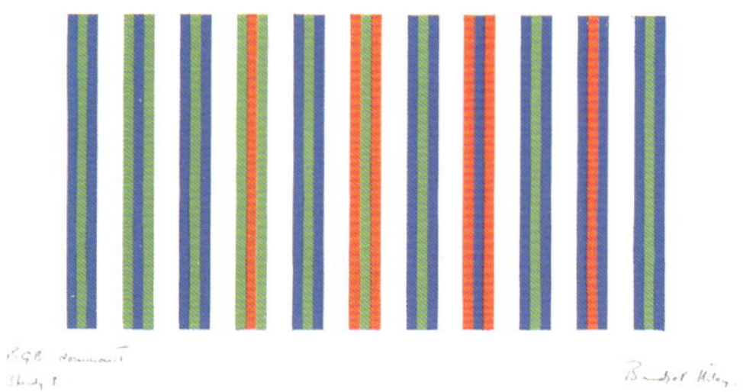

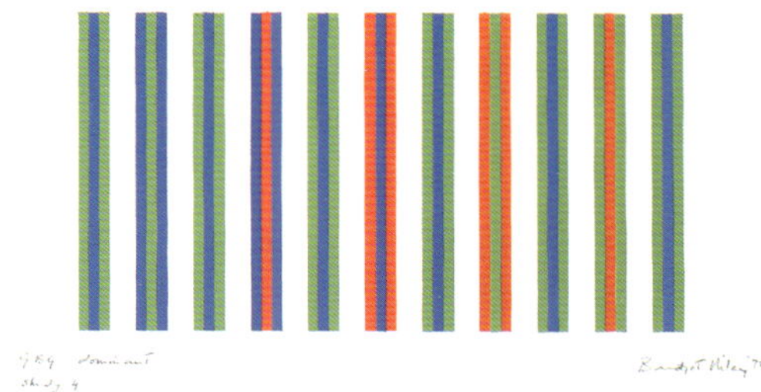

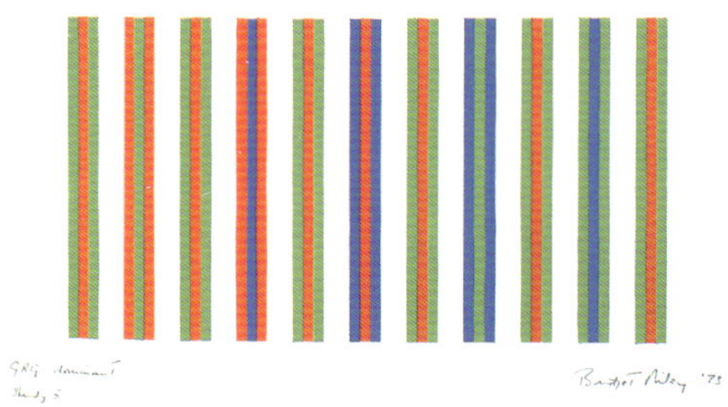

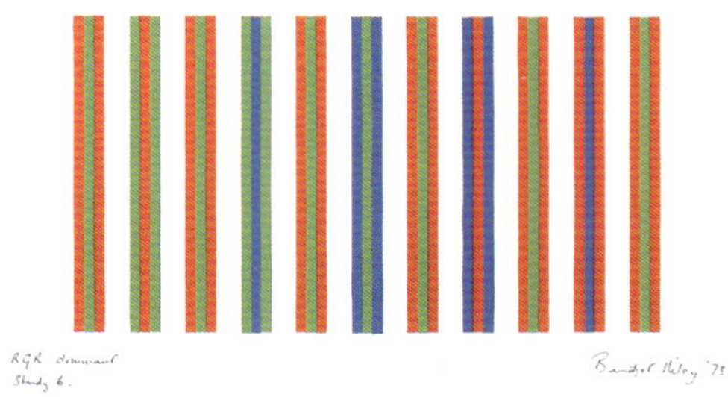

Six colour studies for *Pæan* 1973

grey work in the late 1960s. Pæan, being about the same problem, seems to me a more developed work. There you have introduced a similar 'substance' without employing a tonal movement – simply through the grouping of three clear and strong colours – red, blue and green – in different juxtapositions.

BR: I painted *Pœan* about the same time as Cantus Firmus in fact, and they are related through their titles. *Pœan* is like a powerful chant gathering momentum through assembling blocks of colour bands in an apparently random way. But there is an underpinning of order based on the different spatial sensations of these blocks. The greatest depth is in the centre of the canvas whereas towards each side this space is reduced to support the central event.

RK: *I remember in about 1974, shortly after you had completed these two paintings that you started to use the term 'plasticity of the medium' in talking about your work.[2] Yet there was still a problem of organisation, if I remember correctly. After years of strict formal structuring, you had touched very closely, especially with Pæan, on the fringes of free painterly organisation.*

BR: It was a double-edged experience. On one hand, I liked the rougher visual texture which I was able to bring off by grouping blocks of colour solely according to their perceptual presence; and I saw a whole new area opening up. On the other hand, one cannot tackle the instability and infinite variety of colour relationships without relying on some sort of formal backbone. You can see in Matisse just how essential drawing is if one is going to be involved with colour.

RK: *I would like to take this point further. It seems that this 'formal backbone', which, I agree, colourists seem to need, became in your work the gentle, flowing curve – rather like the arabesque was for Matisse.*

BR: Maybe. At any rate, in the mid-1970s I started to use the curve again, this time as a rhythmic vehicle for colour. This was different from the earlier paintings like Cataract. By using twisted curves I could bunch up colour sensations in a way that went further than the lateral groupings in *Pœan*. When colours are twisted along the rise and fall of a curve their juxtapositions change continually. There are innumerable sequences each of which throws up a different sensation. From these I build up clusters which then flow one into another almost imperceptibly.

RK: *The result reminds me somewhat of Pollock's work, in sensation at least. Paintings like* Aurulum *and* Reef *have the same sort of open rhythm.*

BR: Pollock has always been a hero of mine. But if there is any similarity whatsoever, I have arrived at it by a very different route. It's almost the opposite approach. The unexpected thing in his free structure is the immense control, whereas the unexpected thing in my controlled structure is the free play of visual forces. In effect, my formal scaffolding is buried to such an extent that it becomes subservient to the 'action' of the colour.

RK: *More than that, I think. In this group of paintings you also started to eliminate the white ground which had been an amplifier of the colour interaction for a long time. The use of plain grey and later of tinted greys has added a new plastic density to your work.*

BR: It was the need for an overall envelope. Having stepped up the colour activity through those clusters provided by the twisted curve structure, I had to re-establish a colour dominance. The coloured grey grounds – a violet grey in *Reef*, a yellow grey in *Aurulum* – were a straightforward way of doing this.

RK: *But not for long, it seems. The next step, basic to the* Song of Orpheus *series and also to the* Orphean Elegies*, led in the opposite direction. You increased the colour activity even more.*

BR: You mean by my substituting two more colours for the grey and so making five colours altogether and an entire field of twisted curves at the same time?

RK: *Yes. It appears to me that your work tends to evolve through a kind of exchange between past and present: you sometimes paint out what you have set up perceptually in earlier paintings which in turn gives rise to fresh perceptual activity and so a growing complexity is brought about.*

BR: It's certainly never a one-way movement. I try to keep the constituents of any complexity simple. There is a tremendous range of colour inflections in the *Song of Orpheus* canvases. But the origin of this profusion is a simple structure. All five colours – violet, blue, green, yellow and pink – relate to each other in such a way that, if one assembles them as they would be in the colour circle, they describe the shape of a pentagon:

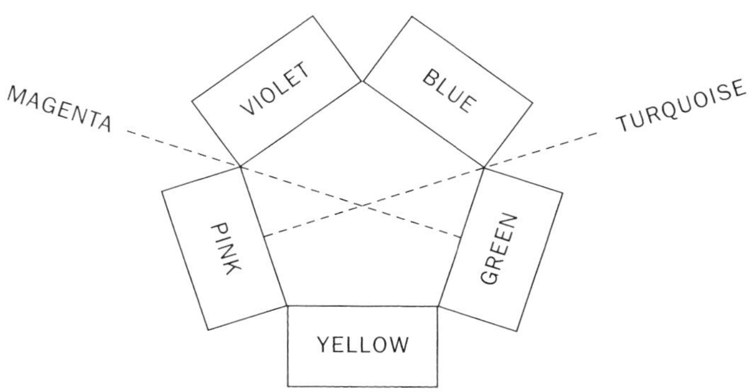

Each colour is in such a position that its complementary would be exactly between the two colours opposite, e.g. turquoise, being complementary to pink, is not actually painted, but if it were, it would lie between the blue and the green. Similarly, magenta, the complementary to the painted green, would lie between the actual violet and pink. This is the rationale behind my unstable situation because the missing complementaries are all evoked by the colours actually present, and this applies right around the whole group. At the same time, neighbouring colours are fusing visually: if the yellow is next to the pink a fugitive orange appears; and again, if that same yellow is bordered by the green or even by the blue, different yellow-greens appear. So I am dealing with both at once – the fusion of harmonies and the evocation of complementaries. This is the framework within which I articulate the colour event of the painting.

RK: *It seems to be a perfect example of the principles underlying all your colour work. If one were to strip the paintings bare of what they are, namely works of art, one would be left with these two phenomena, colour-fusion and the simultaneous contrast. I wonder if you constructed this astounding 'pentagon' before making the paintings?*

BR: No – simply because I couldn't. I think there is a naïve and widespread misunderstanding about theories of colour. Take the colour circle, or rather the function of the colour circle: it is a purely theoretical concept existing in the mind but not in our actual experience. Nobody can ever paint it out 'correctly' because the moment one tries to visualise what has been proved by optical experiment you get involved with pigment – and all the scientific purity is lost. I could teach the so-called principles of my work to anyone in, say, half an hour, but I doubt if it would be of much use. Because once you get involved with colour reality you are immediately faced with an immense range of variables which govern your vision. These cannot be isolated intellectually without distorting the facts of sight. I discovered the colour structure of the Song *of* Orpheus paintings simply by trying to get a specific colour sensation.

RK: *In what way?*

BR: Well, I realised that I needed more colours than just three if I wanted to do without a white or grey ground. So I had to open up and re-relate my group of colours. It was rather like Divisionism in reverse: instead of dividing up the sensation of colour I had to find my 'building blocks', the particular hues and shades that could best generate an envelope of coloured light. For example, I knew that I would need the presence of a red, but as it had to work with all the other colours it had to be implied rather than stated; that is to say, I looked for something that would *behave*

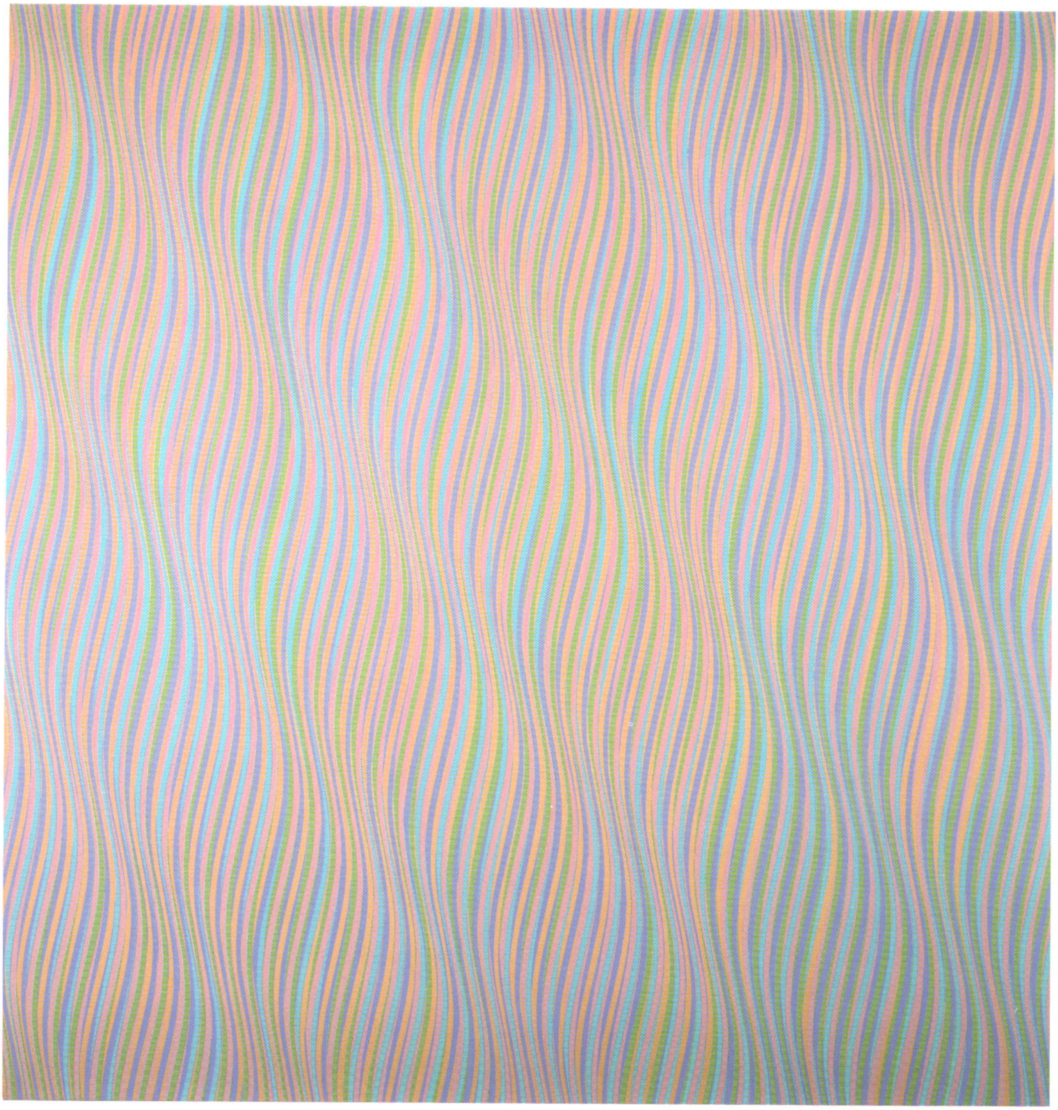

Andante 1 1980

as red. So eventually I paired violet and pink which between them, in the context of the other colours, generate different reds. In the same way of course the particular pitches of the blue, the green and the yellow had to be found. It's a question of working entirely through relationships, you see. Only afterwards I realised that the colours could be placed in that 'pentagon' I showed you. I could never have constructed it in advance because I would not have known what to look for.

RK: *I wonder what you are looking for now. The studies in your studio suggest that you are shifting ground yet again.*

BR: Yes, I have to. I think that there are now too many colours and that this hinders a true colour character. In fact, I have only become fully aware of the problem of colour-bias through doing these new paintings and by looking at the paintings of Turner and Monet again. All painting which focuses on the perception of colour seems to have a problem with iridescence.

RK: *You mean the kind of 'rainbow look' which occasionally surfaces in Turner and Monet? It can make the paintings look 'unnatural', as though the colour has got out of control.*

BR: 'Unnatural' is rather a loose term. What one means perhaps by 'natural' colour is what has been achieved by Matisse. His paintings always show an awareness of colour totality. But each colour maintains its own characteristics – being sustained, and not submerged by others.

RK: *Is that your intention, too, now?*

BR: In my own way, yes. I am getting into an area of such delicacy and refinement that I feel it cannot be right. I adjust and adjust and the whole thing is poised so precisely that I fear it is too vulnerable, too rare an endeavour to be healthy. I need something more robust, something stronger. If what I now understand is really true, it should take bolder treatment. I would like to make the duality of colour more clear. Its identity has to be preserved but at the same time it has to stand, I think, a certain degree of modification through interacting with others.

RK: *It seems to be inexhaustible, ploughing that field, and very fascinating. But when you are working at your north-light table, trying to get the colours right, often, I know, struggling with one colour for days – aren't you worried sometimes that people might think your activity superficial or even irrelevant?*

BR: Well, the whole venture of being a Modern artist could be called irrelevant and superficial. But leaving aside that aspect of your question: if one wants to do something at all, which is fundamental to being an artist, one soon realises that as a Modern artist you have to find something to do it with. It can be anything provided it takes you out of yourself and helps you to act freely. Earlier I chose form, and later colour, which I believe to be more precise because it is closer to our experience of the real world. Unstable and incalculable, it is also rich and comforting. For a painter it is an ideal vehicle because it can be both a revelation and merely the surface of things.

RK: *One of your favourite authors, Marcel Proust, would certainly agree with you. In his essay* On Reading *he says about painters in general, and Monet in particular: 'This surface with which they charm and disappoint us, and beyond which we would like to go, is the very essence of that in a sense depthless thing – a mirage arrested on a canvas – which is a vision. And the mist which our eager eyes would like to pierce is the last word in the painter's art. The supreme effort of the writer as of the artist only succeeds in raising partially for us the veil of ugliness and insignificance that leaves us incurious before the universe.'*[3]

1 "Perception Is the Medium" (1965), reprinted in *The Eye's Mind*, 1999, pp.66–68.
2 The term 'plasticity', which has become central to Riley's thinking since the mid-1980s, is further explained in *According to Sensation* (1990), pp. 91–101, and in *Chromatic and Plastic Interaction* (1996), pp. 147–167 [in this volume]
3 Marcel Proust, "Days of Reading (1)", in *Against Sainte-Beuve and other essays*, Harmondsworth 1988, p. 211.

Completed in April 1978 for *Art in Australia*, but not published. This is the only text dealing extensively with the colour structure of the 'curve paintings' of 1974–78 which were included in Riley's 1978–80 retrospective exhibition. First published in *The Eye's Mind: Bridget Riley*, 1999, pp. 89–104.

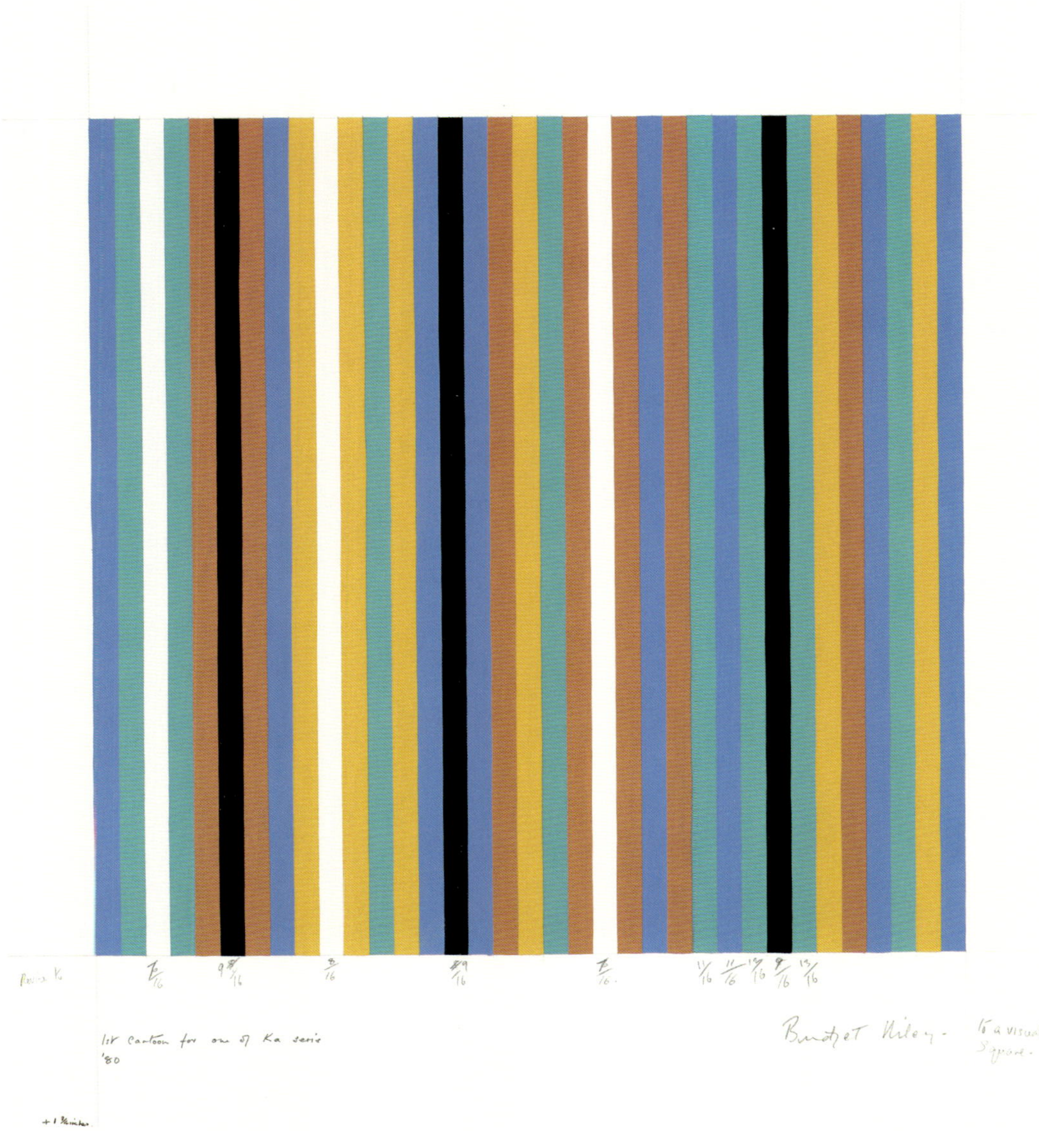

1st Cartoon for one of *Ka* Series 1980

Bridget Riley's Pictorial Thinking
1984

The place Bridget Riley has now been holding for twenty-five years in contemporary art still has the reputation of being a kind of enchanted castle. Although her paintings undoubtedly celebrate the riches of what one can see, they seem to defy penetration. At one moment a pure radiating promise, her work can suddenly appear inaccessible if one tries to probe more closely. This experience can be so startling that some people never attempted to look again. But the disturbance is not the fault of the artist. The unexpected 'brush-off' is largely self-generated by the spectator. Nobody gains access to the feast of these paintings without having first abandoned the attempt to pin down the event occurring. Once the habit to arrest the thing seen has been discarded the violent reaction subsides and the initial disturbance yields to the pleasure of attending, with open eyes, the emergence and disappearance of pictorial relationships that continuously redefine themselves. Riley's paintings do not rebuff looking as such, but only that kind of penetrating attention that treats the work simply as an object of examination. Without dispensing with the intellectual preconceptions of sight, she insists that looking is primarily, before any objectifying intention, a way of participating in the universal movement of the visible world. That is to say, rather more part of a 'happening' than a means of investigation. The particular challenge of her paintings therefore goes beyond the visual phenomena that anyone can observe in them. Bridget Riley aspires to a state of perceptiveness that she herself has called 'a positive attitude to change'.

All major pictorial decisions, such as the employment of variable elements or the exclusion of overtly symmetrical relationships, are rooted in this attitude; and her rejection of any dogmatic or systematic approach springs from it. Nevertheless Riley's procedure is by no means wayward, the result never ambiguous or fragmentary. Quite the reverse. Steadiness – not stubbornness – is her *forte*, the unity and singularity of a painting her aim. The acceptance of change becomes truly 'positive' only when the primacy of movement is no longer opposed to stability, but is allowed to establish its own momentum, its specific measure and structure. When Bridget Riley gained recognition in 1961 with her well-known black-and-white paintings, she was surprised to discover that this important point – the particular structure of the pictorial event – was barely noticed. Far from illustrating the textbooks of perceptual psychology she had found the first formula for her artistic intent: movement as a sudden, cyclic switch between stable states of order and momentary phases of upheaval and collapse. Even at that time she knew that this dramatic scenario was too dependent upon the dissolution of something firm and rigid to be more than a beginning, however spectacular. She therefore tried from these early days to make use of the greater flexibility of colour. But the experiments made between 1963 and 1965 never left the studio because the mere 'coloration' of the complex structures of the black-and-white work did not produce a satisfactory result. Colour remained inert, decorative – a simple illumination of form. Instead of pursuing this abortive direction further, Riley side-stepped her immediate interest. Practising a positive attitude to change also implies to be able to wait. Working for almost two years (1966–68) exclusively in coloured greys she acquired an insight that was crucial to all her subsequent work: developing colour energies required a reduction of formal complexities.

The final breakthrough happened in 1968 with the discovery that elongated forms such as stripes and curves, placed vertically or diagonally against the horizon of perception, were capable of setting off fleeting but clearly visible haloes and zones of immaterial colour. However minute

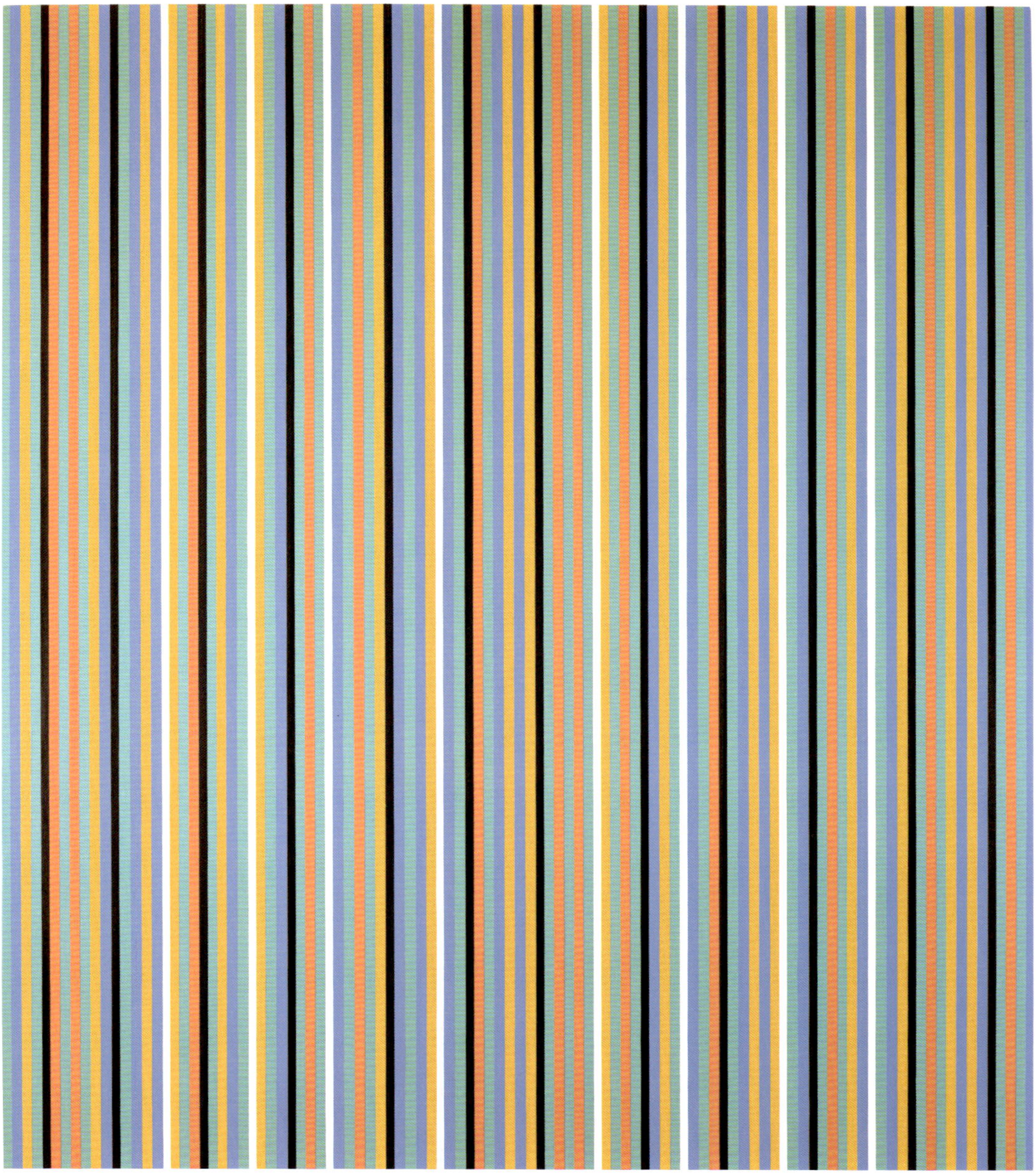

Après Midi 1981 (detail, overleaf)

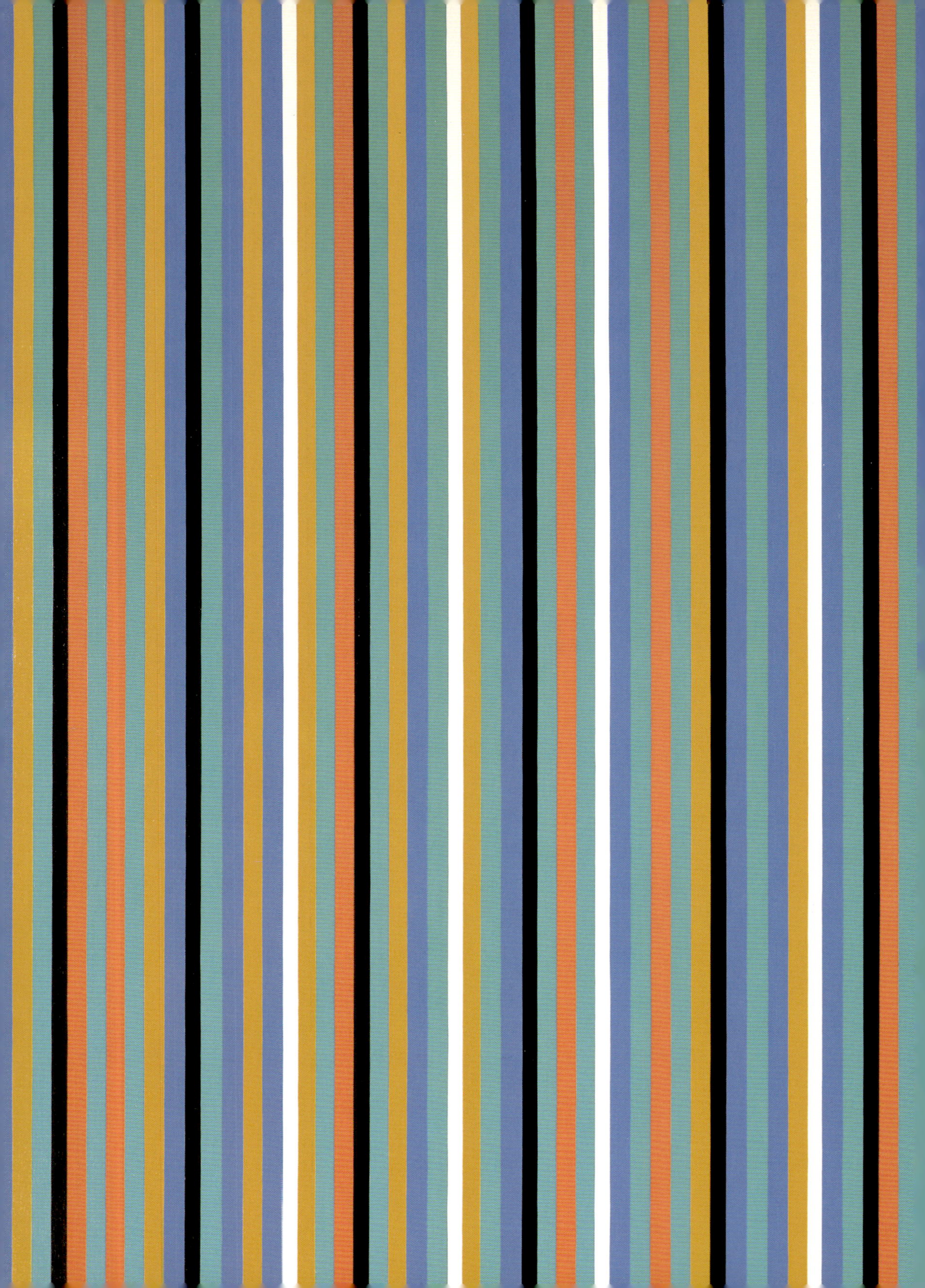

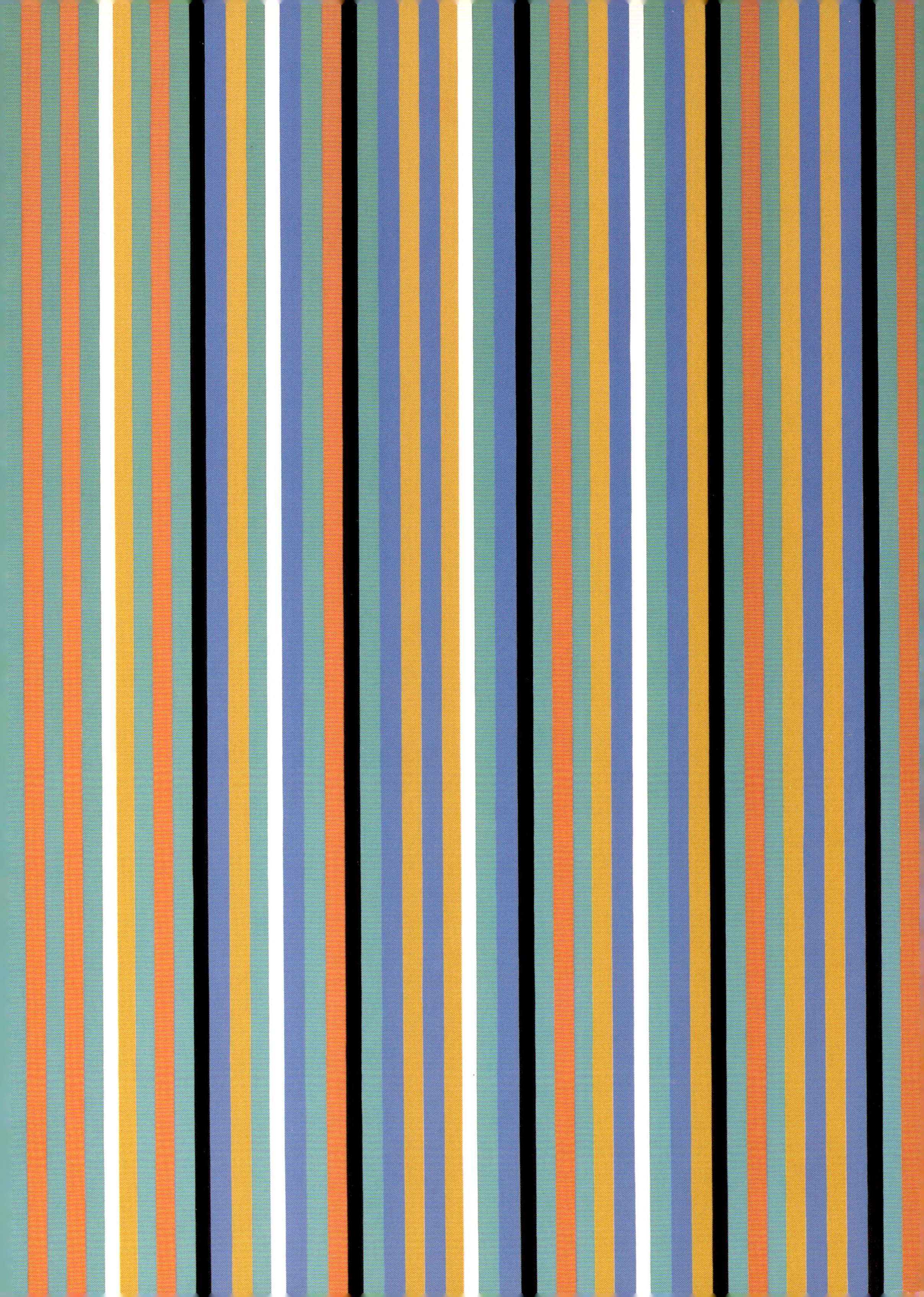

and ephemeral this phenomenon may seem, it is the key to the magic transformation which since has been at the centre of Riley's work: two, three, four or five colours, alternating with each other, give rise to an event of such vivacity and chromatic abundance that the objective facts of the painting literally recede behind this effect. For the disembodied glow of colour 'along the edges' is no delusive will-o'-the-wisp but a clear indication of colour's surreptitious insurrection against the confines of form. It follows a certain pattern of behaviour that can roughly be described by four simple laws:

- First of all, there is the phenomenon of *colour-spread*: each chromatic colour which borders on a neutral, white or grey area infiltrates the immediate border zone; and this spreading is all the more pronounced the smaller the tonal difference between the two areas is (yellow, being a light colour, is more prone to spread into white than blue).
- Secondly, colours which are neighbouring one another in the spectrum tend to *fuse*: yellow attached to red shifts towards orange, turquoise next to blue towards blue-green – and this fusion is helped, once again, by a common or approximately equal level of tone between the hues.
- Generally the approximation of the different lightnesses and darknesses within the natural range of hues towards a common middle-tone seems to be an essential prerequisite for the free intercourse of colours amongst each other. The elimination of the tonal difference not only allows for additive mixtures in the eye of the beholder but also facilitates the effects of *colour contrast*. As a rule, Riley tries to avoid the direct complementary opposition, as for instance red against turquoise (i.e. bluish green), because the open simultaneous contrast would only enhance the colour polarity and thus consolidate the formal demarcation. She prefers to join turquoise with brick red (i.e. yellowish red), establishing a kind of 'near-opposition' that will be destabilised by the hidden simultaneous contrast: the yellowish red will be pushed towards a full red while the turquoise takes on a stronger bluish tinge.
- A very special instance of this self-regulation of colour vision, which has been first observed by Delacroix, is the *induction* of the so-called 'third colour' that completes the colour totality in any daylight situation. In a landscape for example, which is dominated by the colours of sunlight, vegetation and the sky, our eye will inadvertently register

> a certain red frequency as well (Monet's 'lilac'): as a necessary completion of the basically triadic structure of the colour phenomenon. This explains the surprisingly strong red-violet sensation prompted by the blue-and-yellow formations in Riley's recent stripe paintings.

But these chromatic effects, although employed by the artist, are by no means the motive of her work, let alone its content: they cannot even be observed in the same purity that the analysis purports when they occur within the collective sensation of a painting. The criteria of Bridget Riley's pictorial practice are of a different order. On one hand she explores in numerous studies the relationships of a chosen group of colours, trying to find the particular steps, sequences and rhythms that may release the inherent energies. Mere 'local' colour, lack of space and perceptual 'streakiness' are the main reasons for rejection at this point. On the other hand she simultaneously aims at harnessing the emerging visual forces. The released energies have to be couched in such a way that they don't dissolve, congeal or break loose in a tumultuous manner. Exploring and assessing the intrinsic scale of the situation – what range the prompted activity may command or require – is therefore a decisive step in Riley's working process. Until the mid-1970s the regular repetition of white intervals, frequently alternating with dark grey bands that accentuated the rhythm, played an important role in this. As 'resonance areas' they accommodated the discharge of the colour energies and allowed the firm structures to 'breathe'. However, since the painting *Pæan* (1973) this sort of organisation slowly lost its dominating role because Riley's concept of pictorial unity was shifting. Instead of aspiring for a virtually homogeneous whole she tried to put a stronger emphasis on particular groupings. While previously the various activities of colour were summarised by a kind of golden or silvery light, in the work of the late seventies – and in the curve paintings of the period 1976–78 in particular – the correspondences between distinct blocks of colour emerged as a unifying factor. Saturated clusters respond to pearling *glissandi*, granular passages are contrasted with diffuse ones. And Matisse, no longer Monet, seems to be the point of reference – the new keyword being 'the plasticity of the medium'.

Since 1981 Riley's paintings show clearly what she means by this term. On a visit to Egypt in the winter of 1979/80 she discovered the art of the tomb painters who managed to recreate the splendour of daylight in subterranean darkness, and as a result she felt encouraged to shift her own 'palette' towards relatively pure and brilliant hues. In addition she

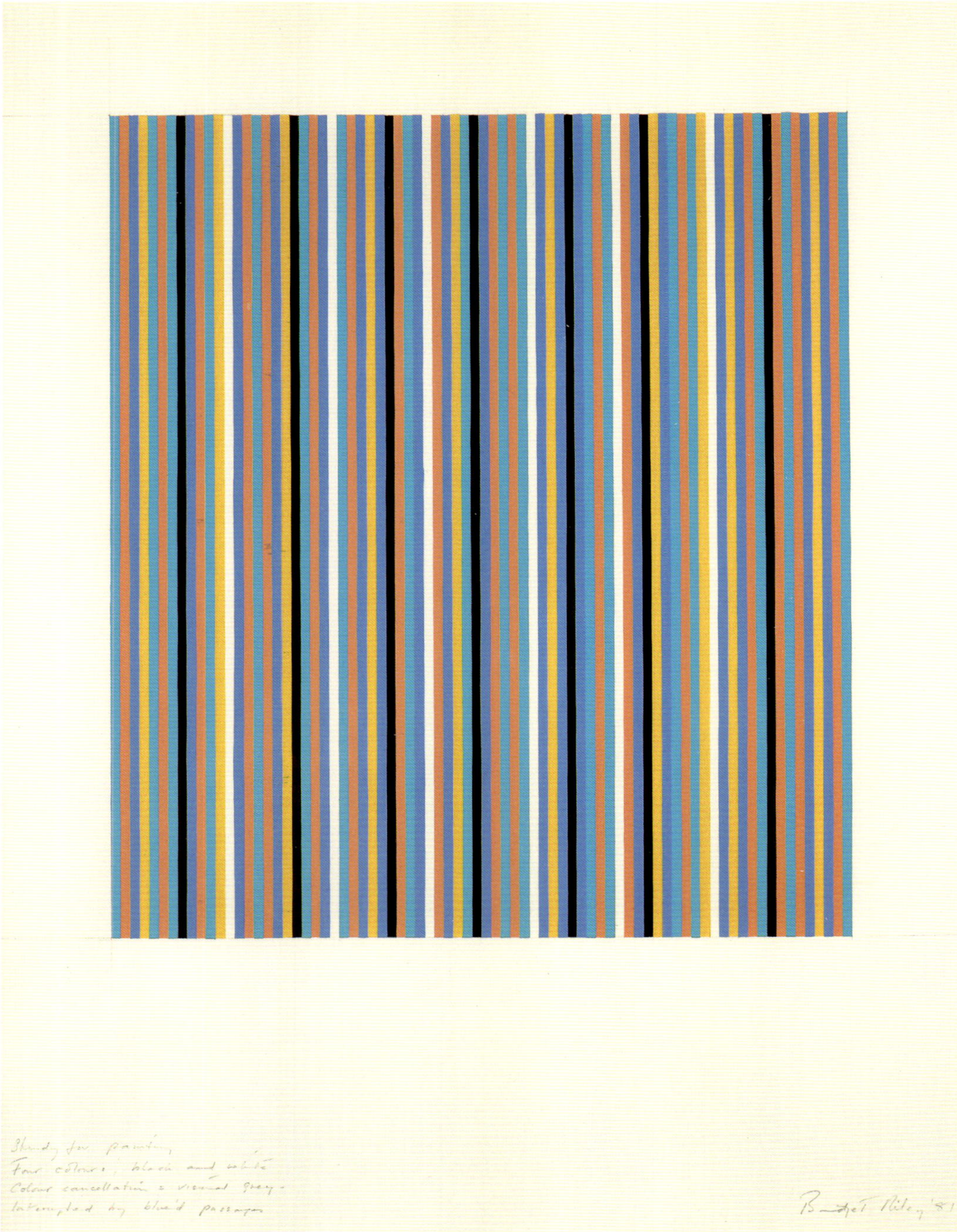

Study for painting, Four colours, black and white Colour cancellation = visual grey. Interrupted by blue'd passages 1981

changed from acrylic to oil colour because of the higher saturation of the medium. A luminous turquoise sets the mid-tone level, to which the other colours – brick red, yellow ochre, blue and apple green (yellowish green) – now relate; and recently the introduction of pale lilac has taken over the role of the white intervals. But it is not simply the higher intensity and contrast of this group of colours that is responsible for the plastic impact of these paintings; nor can the increased structural density be solely ascribed to the widening of the stripe element. The new depth and volume are rooted in a different compositional approach. The appearance of the paintings no longer springs from the structural positioning of colours on the surface of the canvas, but rather the other way round: sensation now precedes articulation. Instead of letting the powers of perception become visible, Riley has begun to organise the sensations provided by her perceptual use of colour. Where she needs the sensation of shadow, she may put a brick red next to apple green; a warm golden look could require the same green being enclosed both sides by the same red; a flaming light she mixes by joining red with yellow ochre, a dull, milky one by combining this yellow and lilac; and in her range of 'perceptual greys' she is pairing near-opposites in a method of modulation: a soft silky grey for instance may be obtained by juxtaposing Blue-Yellow-Blue / Lilac-Green-Lilac / Turquoise-Red-Turquoise. This *painting with composite colour perceptions* is nevertheless no licence for 'painterly' liberties. Bridget Riley has relinquished the firm structural basis of her black-and-white paintings for a new, radically unstable *motif*. As she starts with highly changeable elements she has to find the picture plane within the spatial shifts of colour: going *with* and going *against* the advancing and receding momentum of sensations that are inseparably linked to the presence of colour – and yet at the same time not chromatic at all. The 'plasticity of the medium' is her working title for building the unfathomable depth of experience pulsating in colours. 'With my last paintings', Riley says, 'I have the feeling as though the place I have been building for many years has become inhabited.'

Introduction to the catalogue accompanying the exhibition *Bridget Riley. Ölbilder und Gouachen* at Galerie Reckermann, Cologne 1984. This is the first time this text has been published in English.

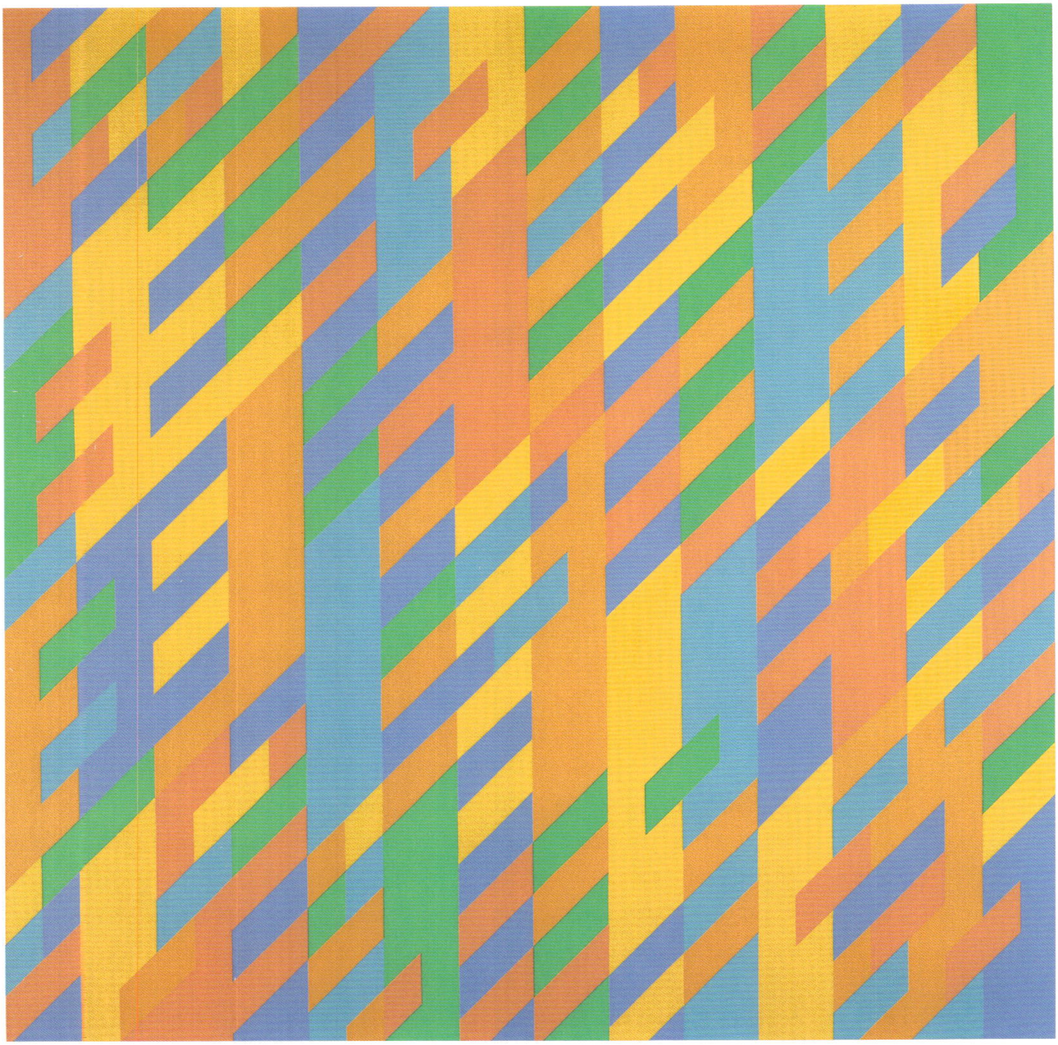

Bloom 1987

According to Sensation

Conversation

1990

ROBERT KUDIELKA: *When I visited your studio in 1985 I saw some of the last stripe paintings you made. Subsequently you introduced narrow regular diagonals and then increased the scale of all units, orchestrating large areas of colour. Throughout that period you retained a strictly limited palette. In several respects your recent paintings display marked differences. What prompted you to make these changes?*

BRIDGET RILEY: In the mid-1980s I felt that if I continued in the direction my work was taking it would inevitably lead to over-refinement. Those selected limitations, disciplines and attitudes which had previously provided grit and grist to my mill might now, unless I discarded them, get in the way of any real development. As one can see in Matisse, to preserve a freshness in working it is important to go back sometimes to first principles.[1]

RK: *And yet these new canvases do not seem to be pared down further – quite the reverse in fact.*

BR: No. Nevertheless they have been preceded by dispensing with a few notions such as the exclusivity of an absolute, extreme stance, rigorous control, even *the new*. In making them I am trying to use a way of working which as an Abstract painter I might have considered obsolete earlier. It seems to me that Abstraction, in the bare eighty odd years since it began, may be only at a similar stage in its development to that of the Italian Primitives.

RK: *But what about the contribution of an artist such as* Mondrian? *Surely you would not regard him as* primitive?

BR: No, not at all, he's just the opposite. Mondrian is a kind of Giotto in Abstraction in that he took abstract art beyond any naïve state of icon making, giving it plastic values and relationships which can only be compared in their potential to those which Giotto introduced into figurative painting.

RK: *In what way do you relate to* Mondrian? *I can see that there could be a connection to his late paintings, particularly to* Broadway Boogie-Woogie.

BR: I've always loved that painting. In the 1960s I even tried to make a full-scale copy of it. But that little exercise taught me that one cannot get into and take off straightaway from a great work of art, especially a late one. Better to go back to earlier, less formed stages. Mondrian's roots lie in Synthetic Cubism, out of this came the entire body of his work. If one looks, for instance, at Picasso's *Portrait of a Young Girl* (1914) one sees that he has eliminated the distinction between the figure and its surroundings and redefined this relationship through the collage technique as an open flowing rhythm. Mondrian turned this particular spatial quality, determined as it is by pure relationships, into the basis of a plastic art which 'destroys', as he puts it, any concrete assertion of the elements with which it is constructed.[2]

RK: *But the 'destruction and annihilation' of which* Mondrian *speaks is not the same as the perceptual dissolution in your work.*

BR: No, certainly not. He wants to bring about a kind of dynamic opposition in which all factors – line, form, colour etc. – lose their separate existence and simultaneously retain their different character. Whereas I used to try and push the elements to such a point that they hovered on the brink of sheer sensation...

RK: *And now?*

BR: It's different – in fact almost the opposite. Right up to, and in some ways including, the stripe paintings I used to build up to sensation, accumulating tension until it released a perceptual experience that flooded the whole as it were. Now I try to take sensation as the guiding line and

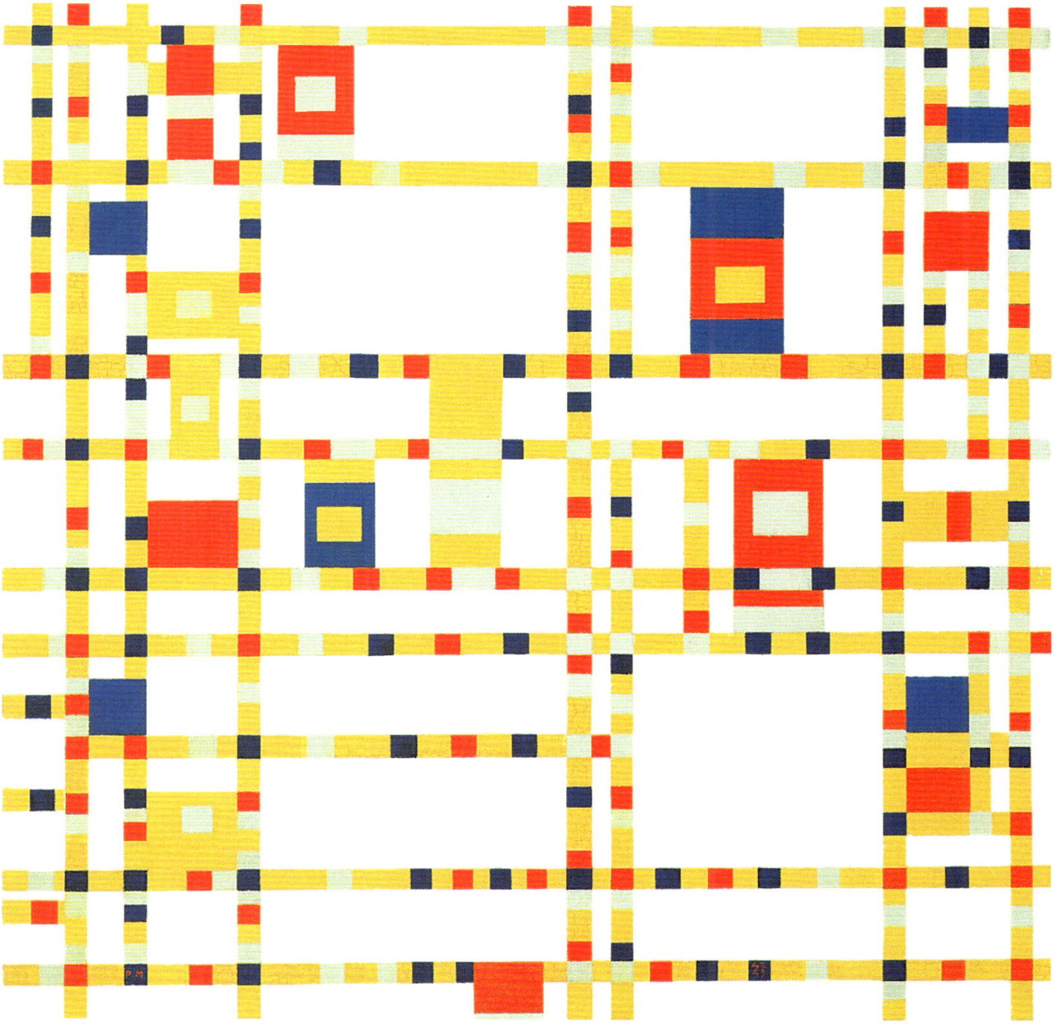

Piet Mondrian
Broadway Boogie Woogie 1942–43
Oil on canvas 127 × 127 cm

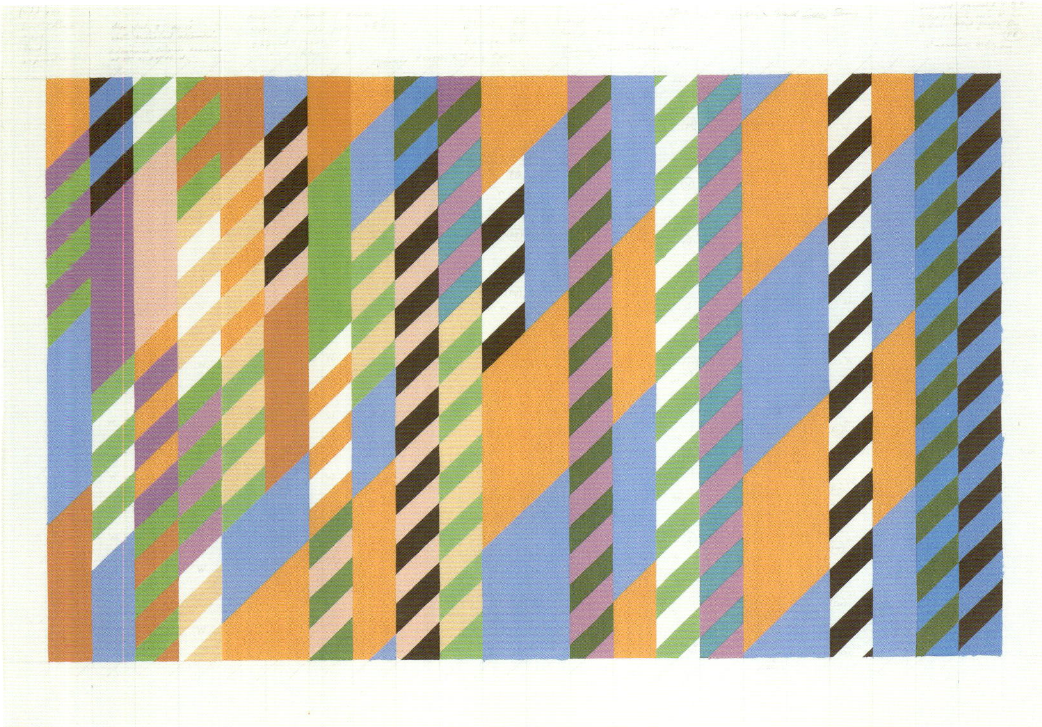

Rough study. July 2nd 1991

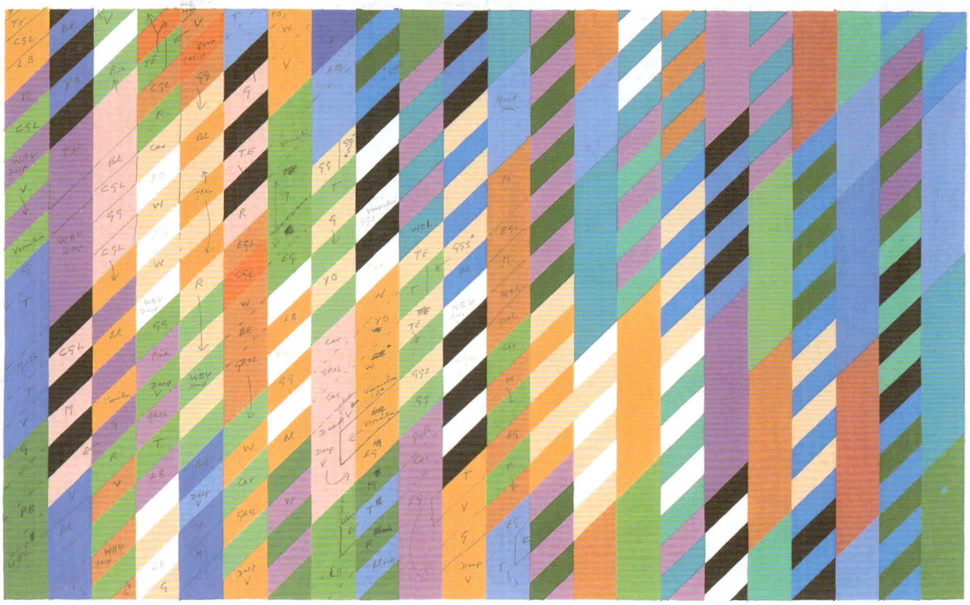

Rough study. July 4th 1991

build, with the relationships it demands, a plastic fabric which has no other *raison d'être* except to accommodate the sensation it solicits.

RK: *The result is a remarkable change on two counts, in the type of sensation produced as well as in the fabric that carries it. Pure visual effects and chromatic interaction in particular are much less prominent; and the even colour structure that came after the compact imagery of the black-and-white work now seems to have been overtaken by an entirely different attitude to the whole process of pictorial organisation.*

BR: Well, I wanted more. A way of working which allowed me to get to grips with plastic issues, to get closer to the real problems of painting. I threw out notions of what the result should be. I crossed the vertical register with a strong diagonal, upsetting the balance of the canvas. That gave me time. I could work against those directional forces, counteracting them through colour and rhythm.

RK: *What then is your objective if not compositional harmony?*

BR: If one is trying to give sensation a leading role one is dealing with something elusive, essentially unstable, and highly responsive. When it is going well everything you do, even the smallest change made, will affect the entire field. In order to get somewhere one has to have two things in mind: to keep the spatial flow of the painting open and, at the same time, to hold it in place through continually checking it. I suppose this could sound like a paradox, but only if one thinks in logical terms. In painting, it seems to me, *contrast* is the basic relationship. Even that which appears to be harmony is actually a harmony of contrasts, be they spatial, directional, formal, chromatic, tonal, etc.

RK: *Obviously colour is still very much on your mind, although the new paintings seem to be less concerned with 'colour for colour's sake'.*

BR: Yes. I no longer treat colour in a purely perceptual way. Sensation of colour is a different thing, it takes in attendant qualities, so to speak, such as glitter or sombreness, buoyancy or weight, dull glow or full brilliance, impalpability or density, softness or hardness – in short a surprising variety of sensual relationships.

RK: *What about this curiously unpredictable space? It seems to me as if the colour activity which you played out in the past chromatically has now been turned into an abstract spatial movement.*

BR: I think of space as another plastic agent grounded in colour organisation. As you know, colours can adopt different planes, similar ones or approximately the same, according to the context in which they are placed. So a certain green, for instance, may be pushed forward by one group of relationships and nearby the same green, with different

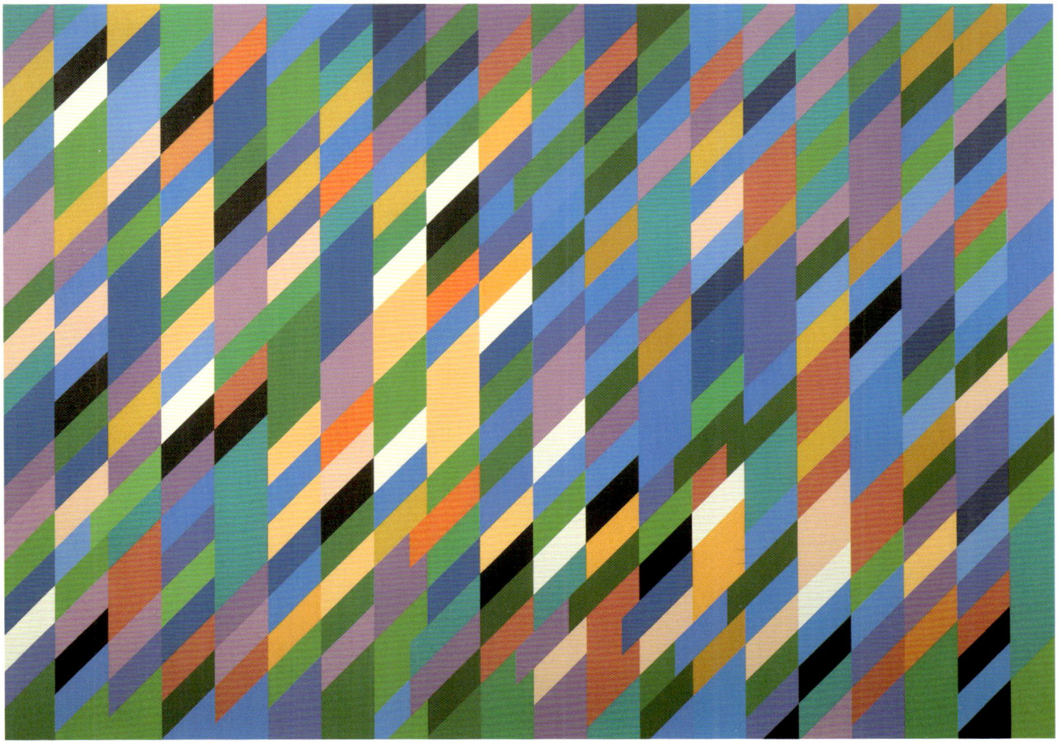

Close By 1992 (detail, overleaf)

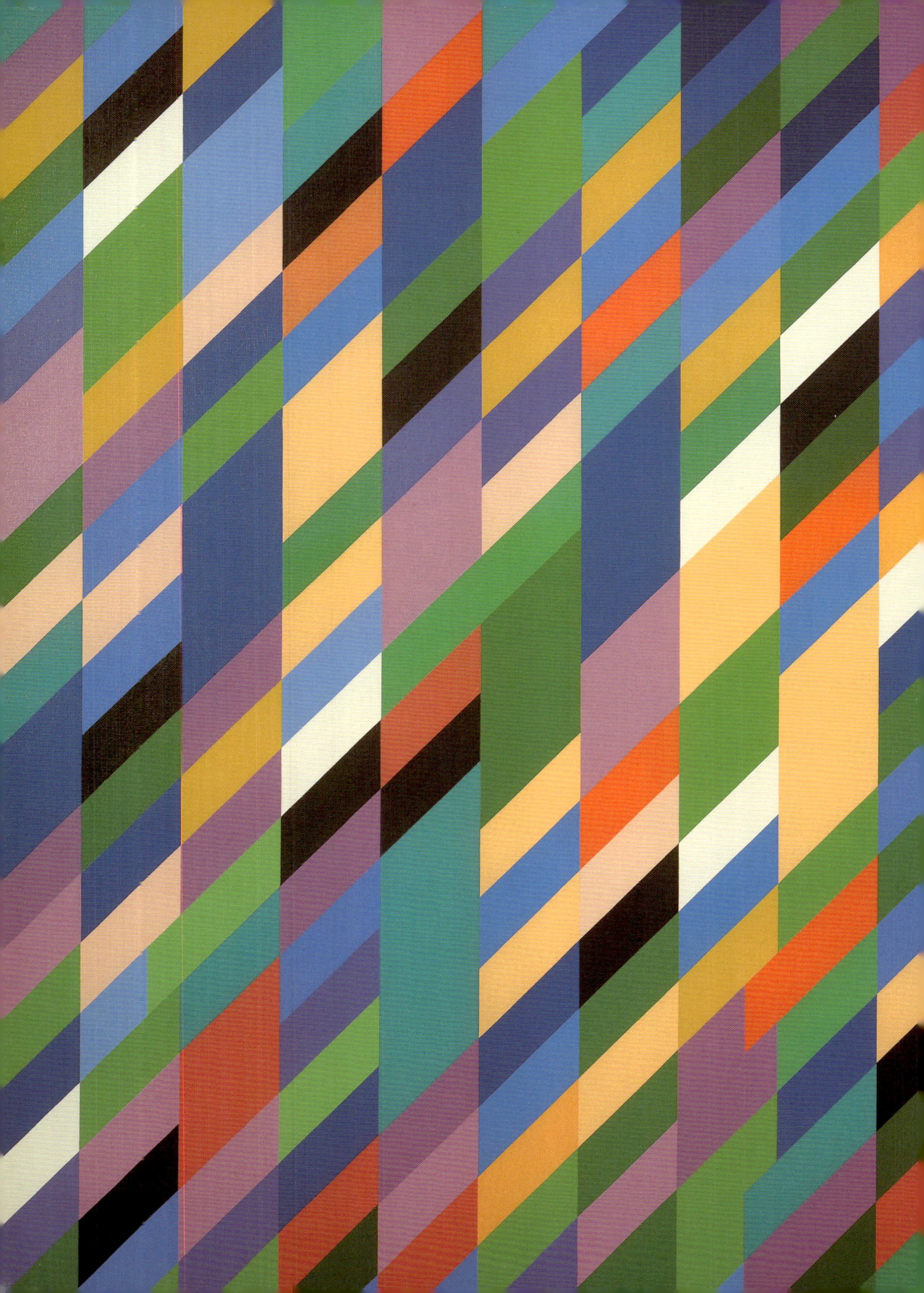

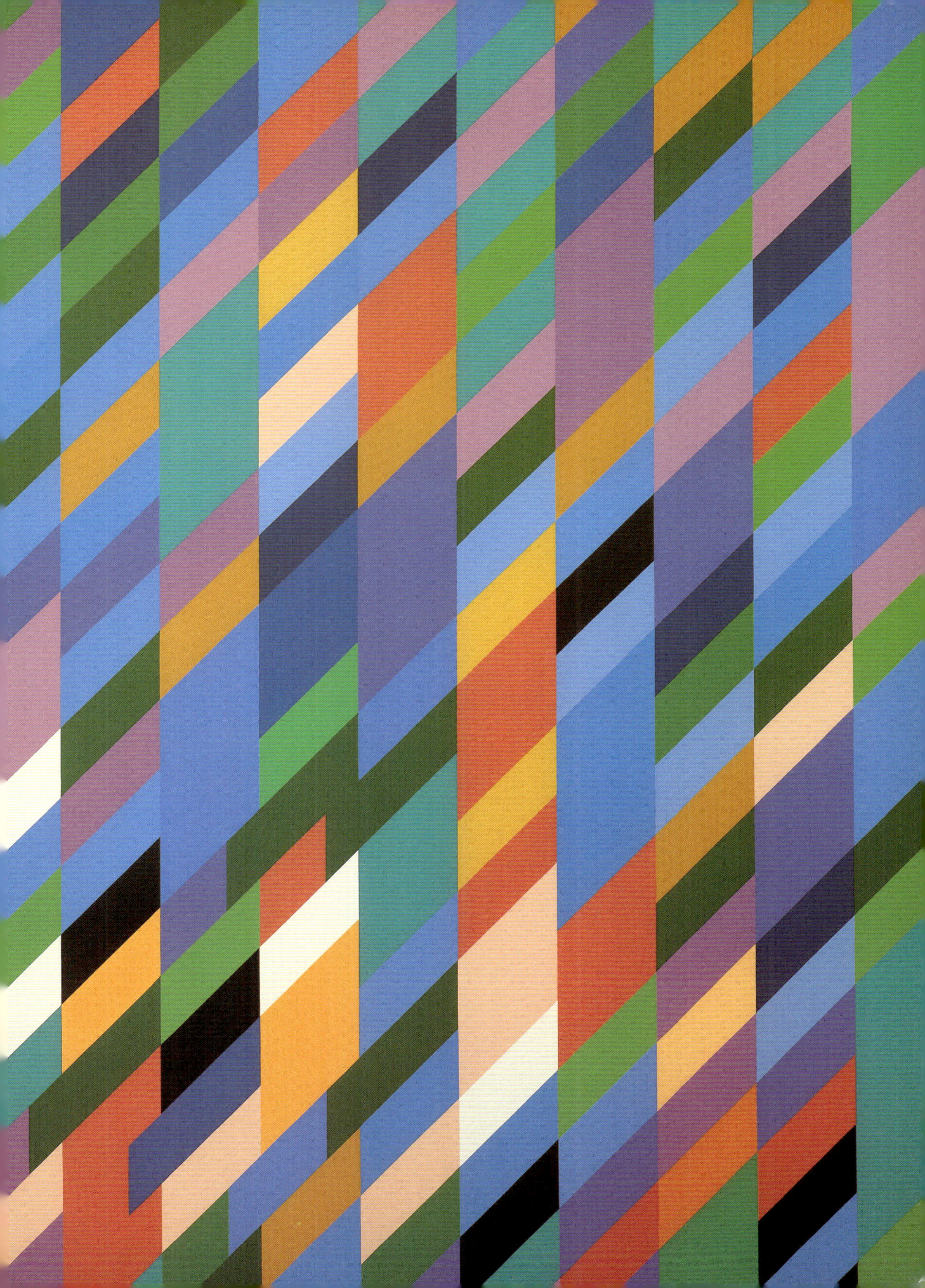

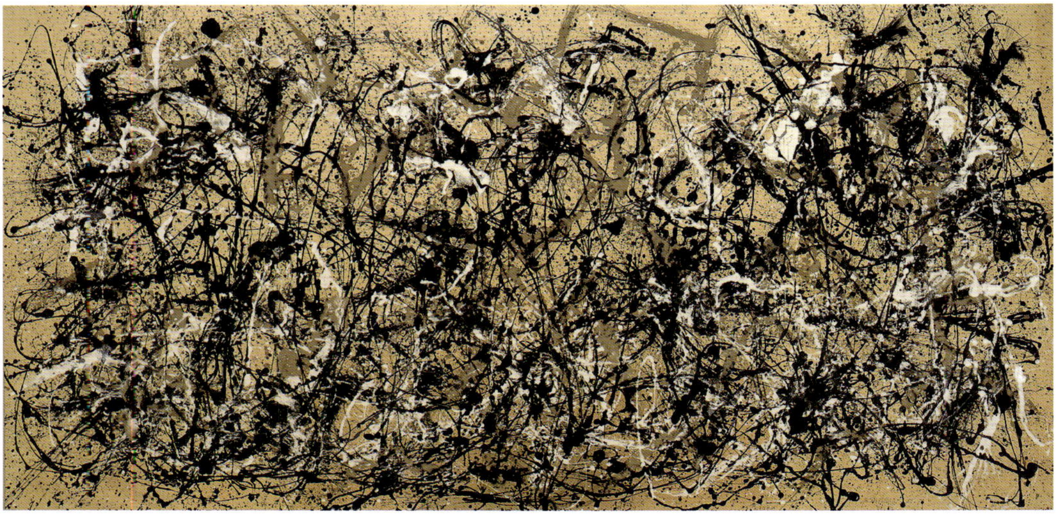

Jackson Pollock **Autumn Rhythm** 1950

affiliations, may counteract that step by drawing back. Meanwhile adjacent colours may be taking up spatial positions which emphasise, modify, or even reverse the planes of those greens. In this way a gentle kind of emerging and receding syncopation arises that can pick up pace, sometimes developing into a rhythm.

RK: *But the dynamism is not just cumulative, is it? In looking at your new work one is made aware of a rhythm alternating between the recognition of a specific area and the sudden realisation of the field as a whole. There are always firm and clear constellations which can be spotted and discerned spatially – one plane of colour distinct from another. But in those moments when the eye periodically switches to a simultaneous view of the totality of the canvas this assessment collapses, giving way to a completely different reading. The undeniable depth of the paintings doesn't seem to operate on a figure-ground relationship – not even in the sense of ambiguity.*

BR: No, it has to be an *abstract* space. That is to say, if sensation alone is the yardstick, then the painting has to be a place that allows for the relatively independent workings of sensation. Although in the objective world sensations are always prompted by something or other, they are not necessarily bound to whatever may trigger them off. They have a life of their own, as every painter knows when he is working: they change, but not in any logical way; sometimes one may not even notice them, only to find them turning up again with unexpected force; but, above all, they are *coherent* – without being in any way continuous. Disruption, friction, sudden ease and deceptively smooth passages all play an important part in the web of sensation.

RK: *It is, then, this working experience that has led you to discard the criteria of the unified image?*

BR: Yes. It's simply not enough to operate from the closed world of a specialised ideal. If a painting is to be a work, a work that aspires to the condition of art, it is obliged to express the tenor of existence. There is no escaping the changing pulse of our experience. To assert, for instance, a holistic image or the even distribution of incidents as a viable expression amounts to counterfeit, mere 'fabrication'. Art has to be expressive of the urgency and failure, love and inadequacy that drive human endeavour.

RK: *Expression – that's the term, I think. Despite your reference to Mondrian I have the feeling that your new work is somehow closer to that of Jackson Pollock.*

BR: I see little significant difference between the two. *Autumn Rhythm* meant as much to me as *Broadway Boogie-Woogie*.[3] After all, sensation is not a question of style.

1 A recurrent theme in Matisse's writings which is summed up in his "Letter to Henry Clifford" (1948) in a metaphor often referred to by Riley: 'Indeed, if gardens were not dug over at the proper time, they would soon be good for nothing. Do we not first have to clear and then to cultivate the soil in season? – The preparatory work of initiation, of renewing, is what I call "cultivating the soil".' In *Matisse on Art*, ed. Jack D. Flam, London 1973, p. 121.

2 For Mondrian's understanding of 'destruction' see J. J. Sweeney's posthumously published "Interview with Mondrian" (1943), in H. Holtzmann and M. S. James (eds), *The New Art – The New Life: The Collected Writings of Piet Mondrian*, London 1986, pp. 356–357. Riley has emphasised the importance of this aspect of Mondrians work in both her writings on the artist, "Mondrian: the 'universal' and the 'particular'" (1995) and "Mondrian Perceived" (1997), reprinted in *The Eye's Mind*, pp.194–197 and 183–191 resp.

3 The conjunction between Mondrian and Pollock is a staple point of reference in Riley's thinking. See also *Bridget Riley 1992*, p. 140 [in this volume]

Published in the catalogue accompanying Riley's exhibition at the Sidney Janis Gallery, New York, in March 1990. The title was chosen in response to a question raised by a painting by Jasper Johns, *According to What* (1964). Riley saw this painting in 1965 and always regarded the query in the title as the crucial issue for the modern artist. She wanted to emphasise with her answer a recent shift of her orientation. In 1992 it was used for the Hayward venue of the 1982–1992 retrospective exhibition which showed her move from a perceptually orientated way of working to the primacy of 'sensation'. Reprinted in *The Eye's Mind: Bridget Riley*, pp. 114–120.

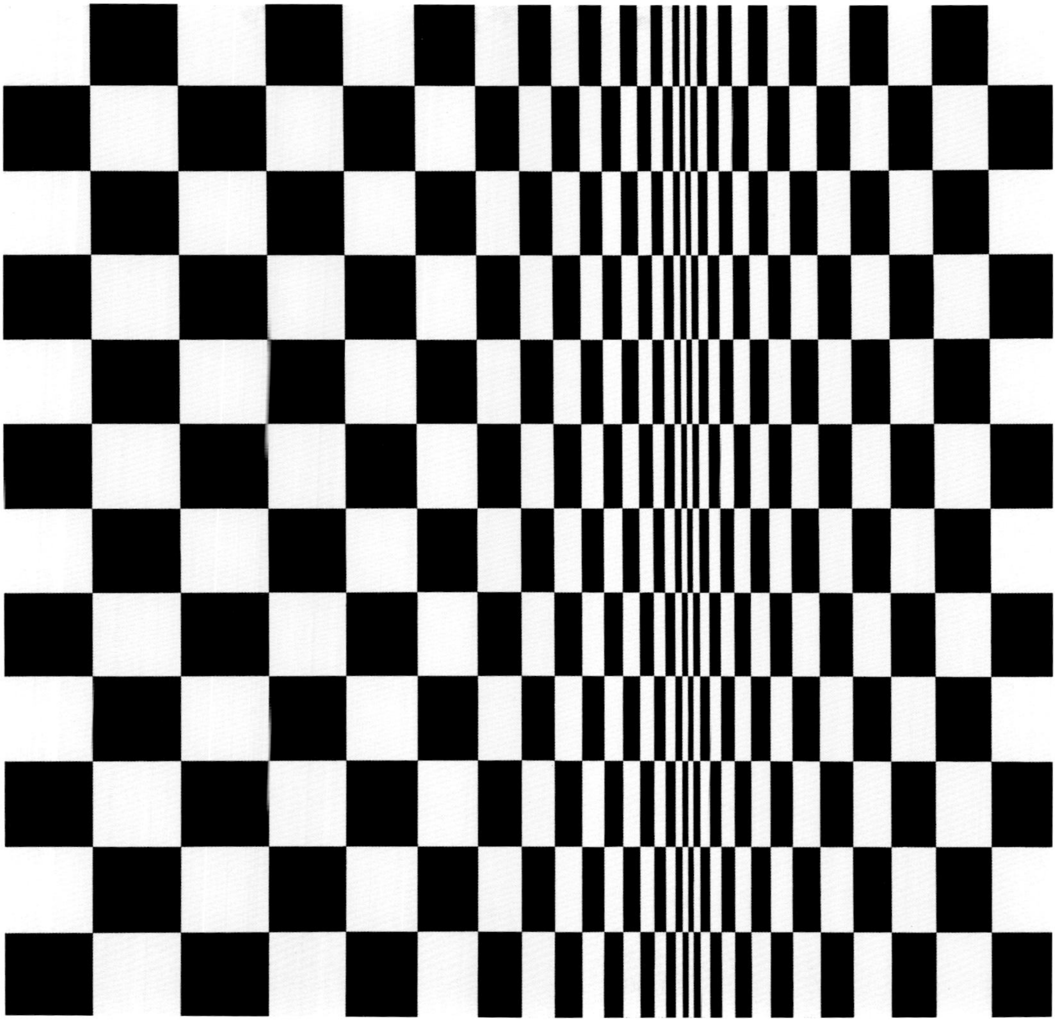

Movement in Squares 1961

Paintings 1982–1992

1992

The development of Riley's painting during the 1980s is marked by two decisive turning points. It began with a fundamental change in her use of colour, prompted by a visit to Egypt in the winter of 1979–80. This led to a major alteration in the spatial character of the paintings which, in the spring of 1986, precipitated a change in formal organisation: diagonals were introduced to counter the previously dominant vertical stripes and, within a few months, a new pictorial theme emerged.

However, Riley's work has never evolved in such an apparently straightforward, single-minded fashion. The seemingly continuous progress of her painting from black and white to grey, from coloured greys to pure hues, and finally from few colours to many is a misleading mirage. In the 1980s when Riley began to lecture on her work for the first time, she took great care to point out the cyclic character of her progress, the recurrence and continual transformation of certain themes, devices and approaches. At the same time she tried to assure her audience that they did not need to know about these considerations to enjoy her paintings. But knowing about the inner metabolism of the work does add considerably to that enjoyment. It aids a fuller understanding of the area which Riley's work occupies now – before it moves on to close further unforeseeable circles.

The intellectual pleasure in tracing these imaginative turns and returns should not, however, obscure the fact that the driving force of the work is not rooted in any preconception of art or some such similar ambition. Everything in Bridget Riley's work springs from and is returned to the sensation of *looking*. Her descriptions of Old Master paintings in the catalogue of her exhibition *The Artist's Eye* (National Gallery, London 1989) provide evidence of the highly sophisticated practice of looking which informs her most recent work. But this interest did not originate in museums. 'Long before I ever saw a major painting, felt the need to share an experience, knew the excitement of invention or painted my first watercolour, I had been fortunate enough to discover what "looking" can be.'[1] This revelation occurred in the artist's childhood in Cornwall during the Second World War. The biographical details are simple. In Riley's childhood paradise there was no electricity, water had to be fetched from a brook, and her mother tried to divert herself from worries about her absent husband by taking long walks on the cliffs with her two daughters. In none of this is there any clue as to what kind of 'looking' it was which made Riley into an artist, and she herself did not explain it until the 1980s when she found a new relationship with nature through her pursuit of colour. So enigmatic is the inner circle in which her art evolves that Riley first found a way of talking about the shaping of her visual life in Cornwall when she made paintings like *Cherry Autumn* (1983) and *Coxcomb* (1984), which quite obviously reflect the intense coloured light of the South of France. Because of this surprising connection between the recent work and her remote beginning a passage from the "Pleasures of Sight" (1984) is worth quoting here:

> 'Swimming through the oval, saucer-like reflections, dipping and flashing on the sea-surface, one traced the colours back to the origins of those reflections. Some came directly from the sky and different coloured clouds, some from the golden greens of vegetation growing on the cliffs, some from the red-orange of the sea-weed on the blues and violets of adjacent rocks, and, all between, the actual hues of the water, according to its various depths and over what it was passing. The entire elusive, unstable, flicking complex subject to the changing

qualities of light itself. On a fine day, for instance, all was bespattered with the glitter of bright sunlight and its tiny pinpoints of virtually black shadow – it was as though one was swimming through a diamond.'[2]

Such flights into the crystal element of vision do not lend themselves to landscape painting. But equally one does not necessarily turn into an abstract painter by virtue of sheer visual excitement. Other influences were at work too, especially during the crucial period 1959–60. Many of these have long since been absorbed or lost their validity, but three primary sources of her art can still be identified:

1 *Klee's "The Thinking Eye".* Although her painting differs in almost every respect from Klee's, Riley shares with him a firm belief in the importance of a continuing dialogue with nature and an understanding of work in natural, organic terms: the process of 'genesis' being superior to any formal result.[3] But what Klee chiefly revealed to her more than thirty years ago is the distinction between the theoretical concept of abstraction and abstraction in painting. Klee's definition has become entirely her own: 'To be an abstract painter does not mean to abstract from naturally occurring opportunities for comparison, but ... to distil pure plastic relations.'[4] Riley's pictorial structures are based on the primacy of such pure relationships over any given formal vocabulary. Although for descriptive purposes it is scarcely possible to avoid referring to 'stripe' or 'rhomboid' paintings, such classifications are absolutely meaningless by themselves. In Riley's view there is no such thing as 'geometric art': 'If one judges works of art only according to what they "look like", one should not be surprised if one eventually gets an art which merely looks like art.'

2 *Seurat's "méthode".* Clearly it didn't need Seurat to awaken Riley's interest in perception. What she owes to him is rather the insight into the difference between a scientific or technical method and a creative one. When, in 1959, she copied a painting by Seurat and then practised his method on her own, she soon discovered (as Matisse and others had done before her) that the methodical restriction to five basic 'portions' of colour in any given daylight situation did not at all guarantee, let alone determine the pictorial result. The opposite was the case: painting became highly demanding. In 1987 she conducted a colour workshop at the Salzburg Summer Academy in which she repeated

her own 'Seurat experience'. After the students had apprehensively begun to acquire the fundamentals of Seurat's method by copying a reproduction of a painting, they were amazed by the freedom of choice to which they were exposed when they tried to apply this method independently. 'Seurat gives you everything you need for making a painting', Riley explained, 'and then he tells you that you have to invent your own!' His method forces one to make up one's mind – literally – point by point. For Riley, this resoluteness enforced by self-imposed limitations has become the quintessence of creative work: to have no other course except through making decisions. She calls her own way 'working from a basis', proceeding *from* and working *with* freely chosen regulations and conditions – as opposed to aiming *towards* a particular objective.[5] The so-called 'Egyptian palette' of 1980 was such a 'basis' that immediately necessitated a revision of the formal structure. Conversely, the introduction of the diagonal units opened up a new avenue of working with colour.

3 *Stravinsky's* "*Poetics of Music*". If there was ever any doubt, the colour paintings of the 1970s finally made it clear that Riley's 'mathematics' are musical and rhythmical in inception rather than diagrammatic or methodological. She does not think in terms of numbers and equations but 'sees' relationships, proportions and correspondences. However, it is not only this musical streak in her visual intelligence which attracts her to the ideas Igor Stravinsky expounded in his lectures, *The Poetics of Music* at Harvard University in 1939–40. Riley's own artistic credo can be found in the lecture "On Musical Composition" in the plea for limitation which rejects the Romantic notion of creative freedom: 'My freedom thus consists in my moving about within the narrow frame that I have assigned myself for each one of my undertakings. I shall go even further: my freedom will be so much the greater and more meaningful the more narrowly I limit my field of action and the more I surround myself with obstacles. Whatever diminishes constraint diminishes strength. The more constraints one imposes, the more one frees one's self of the chains that shackle the spirit.'[6]

This is making a case for a classical (by no means classicist) modern art which does not strive for self-expression, messages or symbols but the meaning of which is the result of fulfilling and even 'over-fulfilling' its limitations (like the music of Haydn and Mozart, for example). Riley

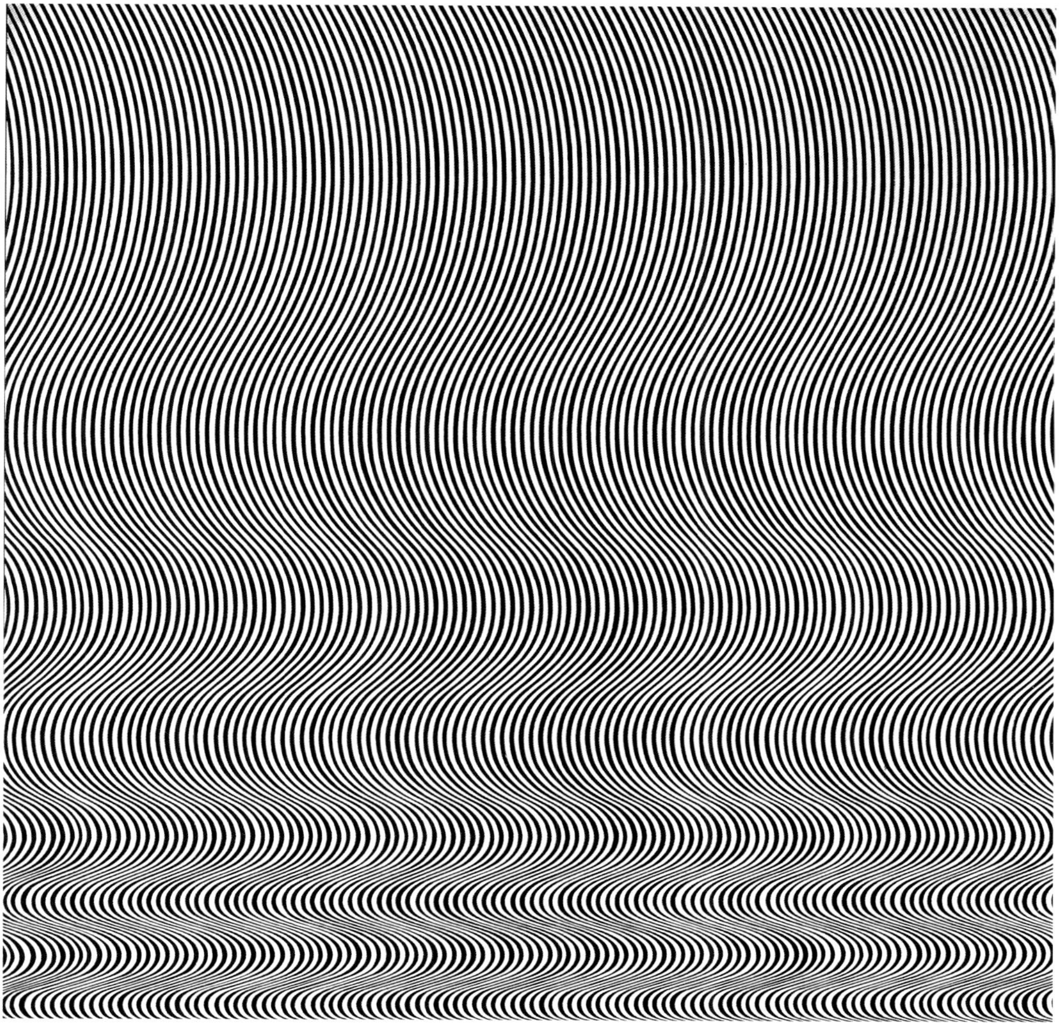

Fall 1963

herself also uses a poetic example: 'If the modern artist is no longer subject to external restrictions, then this simply means that he has the freedom to set himself limitations, to invent, so to speak, his own "sonnet" form.' Her development combines two almost opposing tendencies – towards maximum richness of the medium on the one hand and the readiness to break new ground on the other. Each reflects, in its own way, an awareness of the critical limit. The formal re-orientation which occurred in 1986 was partially a result of the recognition that paintings like *Saraband* and *Burnished Sky* (both 1985) had become so rich and complex in colour that a lapse into mere refinement was unavoidable unless a new 'obstacle' in Stravinsky's sense was found.

'Nothing important really gets lost' – this firm conviction concerning the sacrifices in the studio is evident in the thirty years of Riley's development. In the work of the 1980s two early features of her art surface which had already appeared in *Movement in Squares* (1961), a key painting of the black-and-white period. Firstly the bold intervention in the equilibrium of the field by a dramatic dislocation that in turn creates the need to regain stability. In *Movement in Squares* it is the evenness of the square format (characteristic of much of her early work) that is disrupted by an off-centre stress in the image. In the recent paintings a similar strategy brings about an equivalence of the diagonal axes: by articulating only one direction – the rising thrust – the whole composition has to be weighed against this powerful accent. And even in the preceding stripe paintings this anti-symmetrical bias is present though in a more subdued form. The open formation of the coloured bands is in fact distinctly 'two-sided' in the sense that there is always a contrast between left and right, between what Riley calls – in an oblique musical analogy – an 'entrance figure' and a corresponding 'return'. *Movement in Squares* also helps one to understand a fundamental principle of Riley's pictorial world: in the realm of perception, in contrast to logical conception, any clear and unambiguous statement requires the inclusion of its opposite; for instance, without the constant height of the squares the change in width – the movement in squares – would not be perceived as movement. This constant counterpoint can clearly be seen in the work of the 1980s, although there – as in most of the early paintings – it is the vertical register that provides the constant against which the dynamism of colour and space is pitched. Other aspects of *Movement in Squares* are specific to the 'Riley sensation' in its earliest form. The progression of the black and white areas is rhythmically organised in such a way that the suggested 'reading' of the sequence in the compressed zone, where the white elements begin to

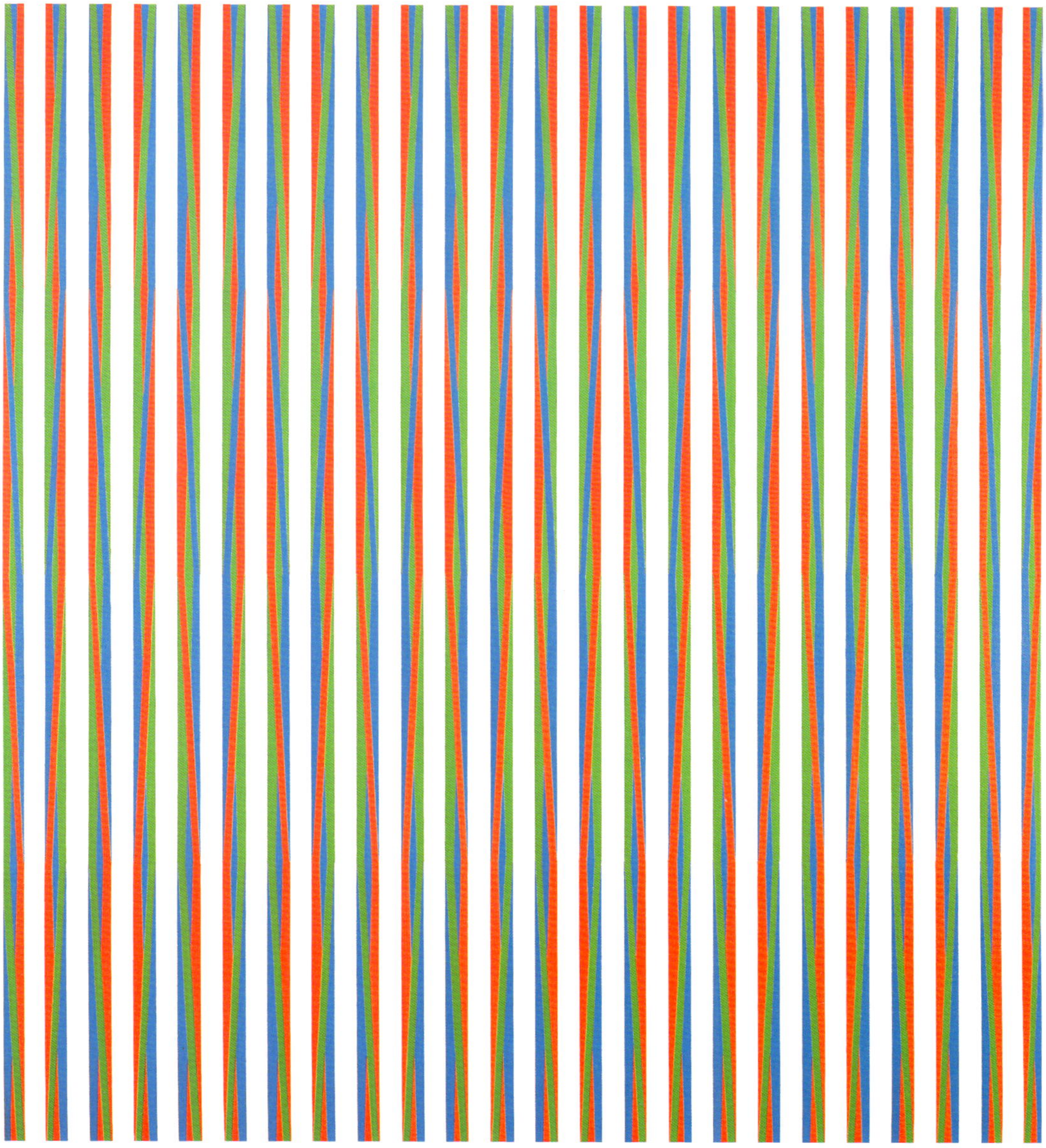

Zing 1 1971

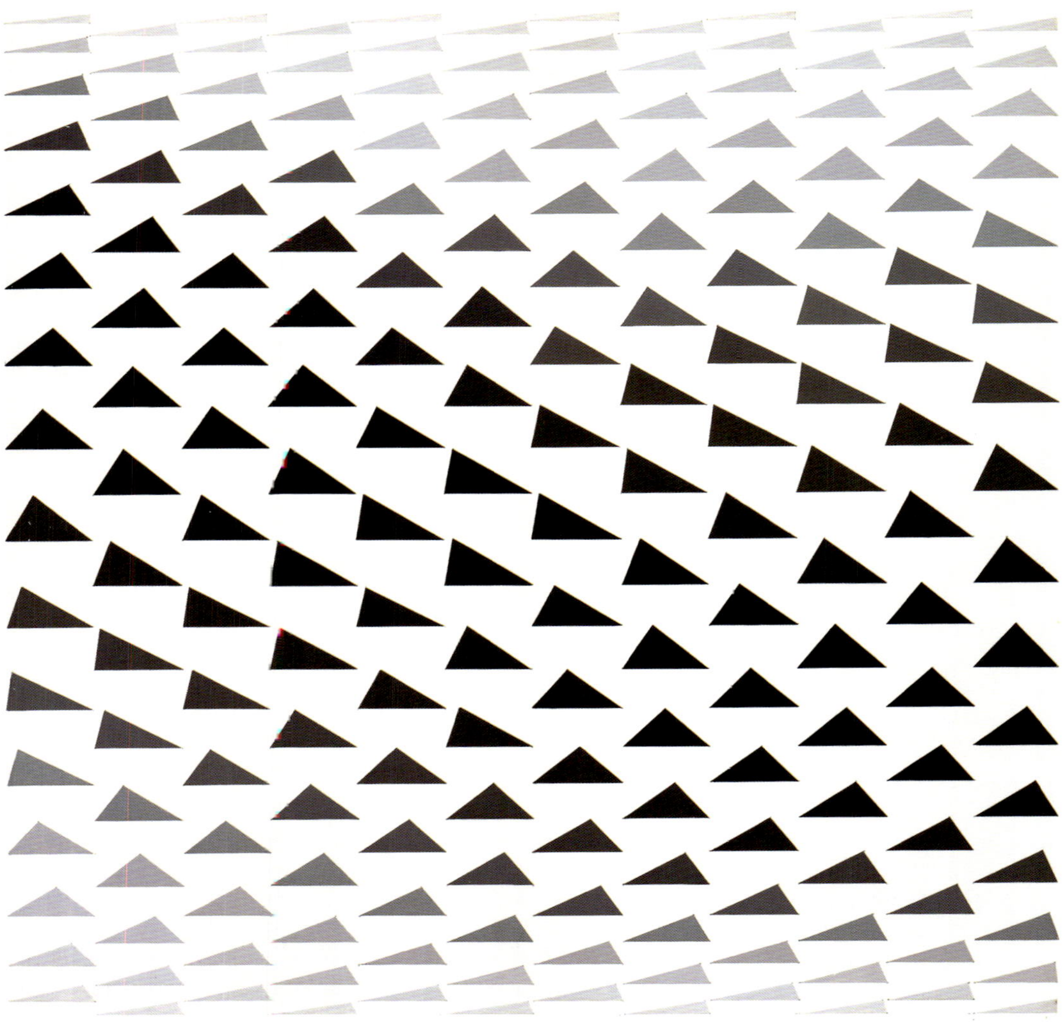

Turn 1964

appear bigger than their black pendants, is momentarily disrupted, before the visual control is regained. In 1960, Riley herself described this cycle in the following way: 'The basis of my paintings is this: that in each of them a particular situation is stated. Certain elements within that situation remain constant. Others precipitate the destruction of themselves by themselves. Recurrently, as a result of the cyclic movement of repose, disturbance and repose, the original situation is re-stated.'[7]

However, modifications of this periodic rhythm may also be found in later works despite the various transformations Riley's first 'sonnet form' has undergone. One has to resist the temptation to match similarities in appearance in order to find out what is specific to the work since 1980. For instance, an early zig-zag painting such as *Descending* (1965–66) seems amazingly close to the recent diagonal compositions. But it only 'looks like' that. The difference is in fact profound and it concerns the pictorial organisation. At a very early stage, around 1963–64, a structural prototype emerged in Riley's work that withstood many changes and even the introduction of colour. After a spectacular climax with *Blaze* I (1962), the tight and explosive structure of the paintings began to yield to a more open organisation. The painting that heralds this shift in Riley's work is *Fall* (1963). Instead of deriving from a descriptive progression of forms, the sensation of movement here springs directly from the cumulative repetition of a single curving line. In reproduction the theme of the painting is difficult to see. It is the horizontal interplay between the curves to the right and left of the vertical that in the compressed area shuttles across the repetitive register, without breaking loose. (Indeed, this disintegration does not occur, nor does the *moiré* effect interfere, when the actual size of the painting – 141 × 141 cm – allows a proper scale for the event.) Once this principle of a counter-movement to the actual formal structure has been grasped the connection with the early abstract colour work is easier to see. Eight years after *Fall* Riley made *Zing* I (1971), a colour painting which is strikingly similar in organisation, although the pictorial means are now completely different. Bands of coloured stripes which are continually 'twisting' around each other are accumulated through repetition and produce horizontal zones of variously tinted light which traverse the vertical formations. The relevant link between the two paintings is not, as it might seem, the so-called iterative structure. Identical repetition as a compositional principle is the direct consequence of a more basic requirement. The type of visual tension that would drive form and colour to the edge of dissolution could only be generated by evenly charging the entire picture plane. An elementary 'basis', a kind of bedrock of Riley's

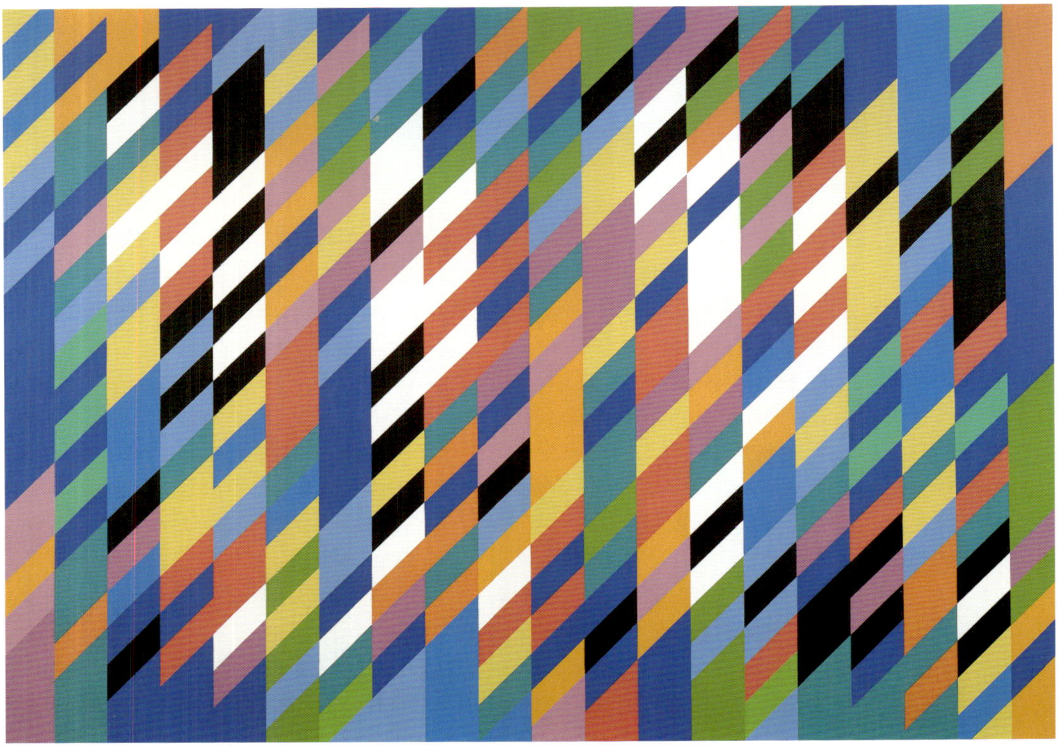

Gaillard 1989

work since 1964, demanded that the unity of the painting be organised as a homogeneous whole.

And this is the hub of the matter. During the 1970s Riley had increasingly become aware of this 'restriction to the whole' and searched for a way of overcoming it without losing the dynamism which she regards as indispensable to her work. In 1980 she found a workable solution. Her paintings have since left the structural concern of totality a long way behind. The relative autonomy of the parts – be they formal, spatial or colouristic distinctions – is the fundamental characteristic common to both the stripe and rhomboid paintings. The extent of the change in pictorial unity becomes apparent if one compares a painting such as *Gaillard* (1989) with a work of the early period, *Turn* (1964). Both are attuned to an exhilarating note, a sense of twisting and turning in every direction; and in each of them this sensation is carried by small individual units which are arranged in vertical bands and display a diagonal dynamic. But the difference in the way the paintings are built could scarcely be greater. *Turn* has been developed entirely out of a conception of the total picture plane. The grey sequences turn progressively; the width of the triangles is constant while their depth changes according to a regular increase and decrease; the steady shift of their points always follows one of the steep diagonal divisions in the vertical compartments and the diagonal reverse occurs on a straight front which runs through the base of the triangles nearest to the right angle. In *Gaillard* by contrast the last vestiges of a control over the whole field, the vertical register and the one-sided diagonal bias, become the very elements against which the colour structure seems to be pitched. White loosely indicates a horizontal counter-balance, red and orange dominate the full stretch of the opposite diagonal, black and yellow circulate in open, unconnected loops, and a range of blues, supported by greens and violets, permeates the constantly shifting space. In the studio these dense, inextricably layered structures are built up piece by piece with coloured papers of different sizes (nicknamed 'zigs' in studio parlance because their directional counterparts – the 'zags' – are missing). Riley says she is 'trying to use a way of working which as an Abstract painter I might have considered obsolete earlier.'[8] Matisse, in using cut and coloured papers, liked to quote Chardin's motto: "I put it in and I take it out until it works."[9]

Clearly it is colour that is responsible for this transformation. In the early 1960s Riley had experimented with colour, but her formal means at that time did not allow colour to be turned into a pictorial energy comparable to that of the black and white contrast. 'To create a colour-form, not coloured forms'[10] was her initial ambition. Only when she began to work with coloured greys in 1965–67 did she begin to see a way towards her first pure colour paintings. Apart from the subtleties of visual rhythms and tempi, the *Drift* and *Deny* paintings develop the opposition of colour and tone inherent in the basic contrast between scales of warm and cool greys. Their theme is an inversion: when the contrast between light and dark is greatest the colour contrast disappears, and as the tonal contrast diminishes the colour contrast emerges. Thus the 'cool' oval forms in *Deny 2* (1967) at their lightest pitch glitter with an almost metallic sheen, like silvery leaves, while in those passages where they come close to the tonal level of the uninflected 'warm' ground, the contrast between greenish blue and red is activated and creates that coloured mist which can be recognised even in a black and white reproduction. Here, beneath a grey veil so to speak, is an important characteristic of colour behaviour: colour begins to interact if adjusted to a common tonal level. This practice remains a part of her work until roughly 1986 (and it explains among other things the relatively high tone of the blue in the 'Egyptian palette'). But before she could turn this rule of 'behaviour' into a means of pictorial 'conduct' – to quote Bryan Robertson's distinction[11] – a sacrifice had to be made which, in view of the luxuriance of the *Deny* paintings, seems rather harsh. In 1972 she described the crucial balance at stake: 'In my earlier work, when I was developing complex forms, the energies of the medium could only be fully released by simplifying colour to a black-and-white constant (with occasional grey sequences). Conversely colour energies need a virtually neutral vehicle if they are to develop uninhibitedly. The repeated stripe seems to meet these conditions.'[12] The change in 1980 re-affirmed this move in the context of the colour work itself: for the sake of the strong colours of the 'Egyptian palette', Riley had to abandon the structural intricacies of her curve paintings and revert to the plain stripe as a formal 'vehicle'.

Chant 2 (1967) is the archetype of Riley's initial, spare use of pure colour. Red and blue stripes in two different combinations – blue surrounding red, red surrounding blue – regularly alternate as they extend across the surface. The width of the bands rhythmically increases and decreases while the white intervals between them remain constant. When this ingeniously simple painting was shown at the Venice Biennale in 1968 it caused quite a stir because the composition seems to mysteriously open out in the centre to convey the sensation of an unplumbable depth radiating an intense, subtly coloured light. No colour theory lies behind this, simply the basic observation that colours bordering on white

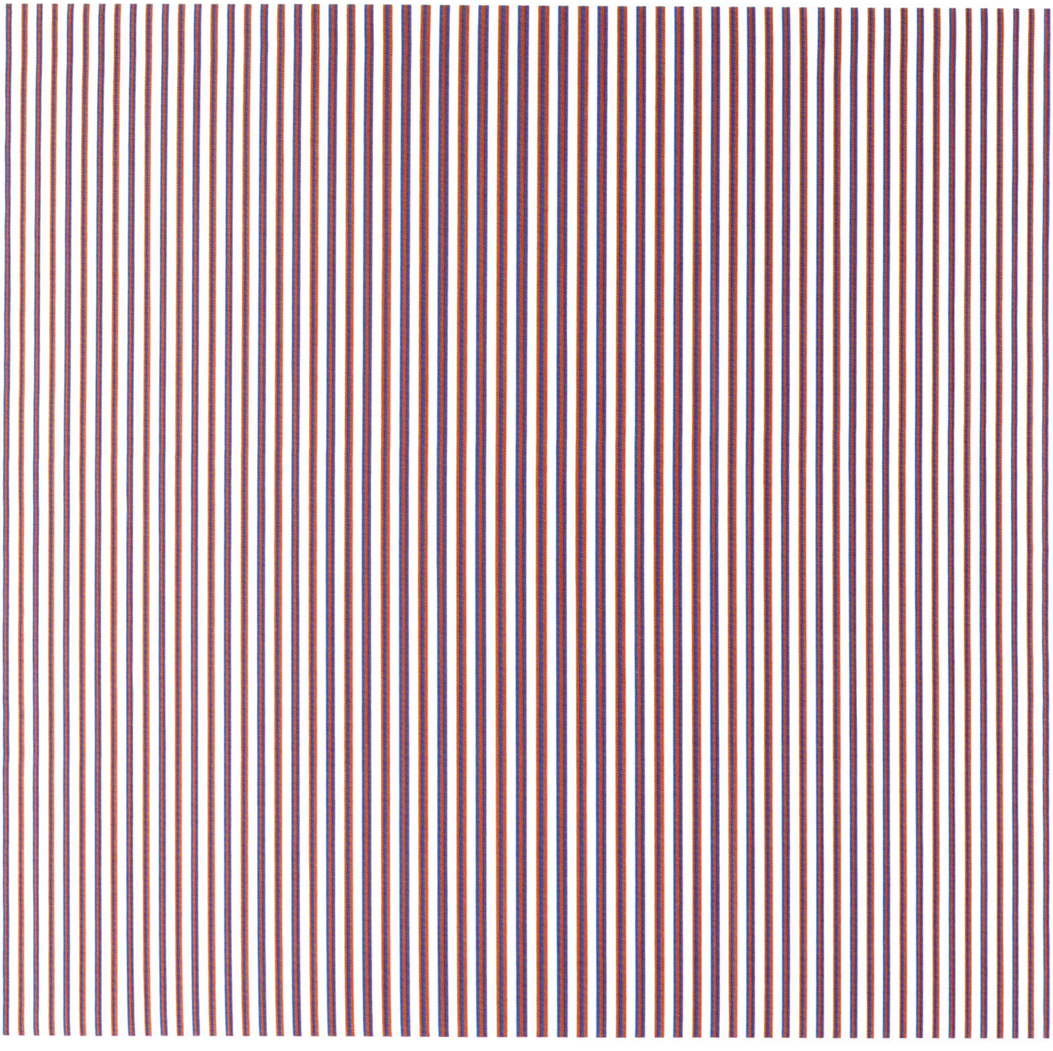

Chant 2 1967

Aurulum 1978

can do one of two things: either directly bleed and fuse or induce contrasting colours. The blue-red-blue combination gives off a blue shimmer, the red-blue-red band flickers with yellow-orange at its edges. When put to work with a precise sense of scale and rhythm, these two opposing tendencies of colour energy avail a surprising wealth of pictorial possibilities. Nevertheless, Riley soon realised that there were restrictions, too. This 'basis' apparently did not allow for more than three colours in each painting since its effectiveness depended on the interaction between colour and light. Similarly the white ground was indispensable to accommodate the free play of sensations, although, of course, it was also a formidable barrier. The vertical stripe seemed to have an almost unchallenged superiority over any other structural element. At the beginning of the 1970s, therefore, Riley worked hard on extending her formal means, and in doing so came up with some surprising inventions – such as the 'twisted' stripes in *Zing 1* which, by virtue of their long thin points, exaggerate the critical 'edge exposure' essential to the discharge of coloured light. In the monumental painting *Paean* (1974) she succeeded in achieving an open orchestration of composite colour blocks anticipating for a moment the developments of the 1980s. But she could not follow this up, partly for personal reasons, partly because she was not yet fully conscious of what stood in her way: it was not so much a formal as an organisational problem – the underlying concept of wholeness.

Instead of tackling this problem directly she re-introduced in 1974 the curve element into her work and continued to work in this vein until 1981. This was a period of gradual colour development, progressing step by step towards a fuller palette. The workmanlike approach Riley brings to her art gives her the nerve to complete a course which to outsiders may look like an *impasse*. Even when the end of the road is already in sight, she will arrive at it slowly as though she knew that only by doing so will she find the turning-point which starts her off on the next stage of her journey. The return to the delicate, linear curves which she had previously used in *Cataract* (1967) led to the discovery that she could introduce the twisting colour bands of *Zing 1* into these upright curvilinear fields and create free-floating clusters of colour. *Aurulum* (1977) for instance is from the period when the white ground was being progressively eliminated: at first by a pure grey, then by a coloured grey and finally by the addition of a pair of colours between the three main colours. All five colours used in this painting – blue, pink, yellow, violet and green – are relatively pale. And in the *Song of Orpheus* paintings of 1978 the colours almost seem to disappear – so perfect is the balance achieved towards the end of this engagement with coloured light. The consequent attempt to intensify the colour led only to making them seem darker and heavier. It is arguable that some of the most beautiful paintings Riley has made belong to this period. But in 1981 she closed this chapter of working towards the totality of light by making one last curve painting in which she reversed all the colour frequencies towards black. She called it *Withdraw*.

By then the visit to Egypt in winter 1979–80 had produced unexpected results. The term 'Egyptian palette' which Riley herself uses might suggest that she brought back these colours almost like a souvenir. But nothing from the outside world gets into her work in that manner. The decision to recreate the colour she had seen in the Tombs of the Workmen (that is, the artists) in Upper Egypt only occurred to her after the opening of her retrospective in Tokyo that followed the journey to Egypt. And in any case it would be very difficult to relate Riley's palette of brick-red, ochre-yellow, blue, turquoise and yellow green to the actual Egyptian colours since her intention was to recover the particular colour sensation from memory. The first series of small paintings employing the new colours has the title *Ka*, the Egyptian name for the 'double' of every living creature. If there is an explanation for this response then it may be found in a certain elective affinity of the creative spirit: Riley was struck by the degree of abstraction the Egyptian artists achieved in establishing those 'pure plastic relations' (Klee) which evoke the brilliance of daylight in the darkness of their tombs.

Apart from a necessary return to the use of the stripe element, the immediate consequence of this palette was a change in painting technique. For the sake of greater intensity and saturation of colour Riley turned from acrylic to oil paint in 1980. Slight shifts within the colour balance may be explained by the fact that each painting is developed, including full-size cartoons, in gouache on paper before being executed in oil. This allows for individual adjustments when the colours are finally mixed in the oil medium. But beyond such technical concerns, there was a shift towards sensation as the basis for change in the pictorial structure. The stages of Riley's development in the years 1980–85 may be described as follows: at first black bands articulate the colour orchestration (*Summer's Field*, *Luxor*, *Serenissima*, *Rose Rime* – all 1982), then this structural support is dispensed with (*Greensleeves*, *Cherry Autumn* – both 1983); finally via an intermediary step of substituting lilac for white (*Coxcomb*, 1984), the limits of the palette are overturned by a burst of colour (*Saraband*, *Burnished Sky* – both 1985).

The new form of pictorial organisation can be discerned right from

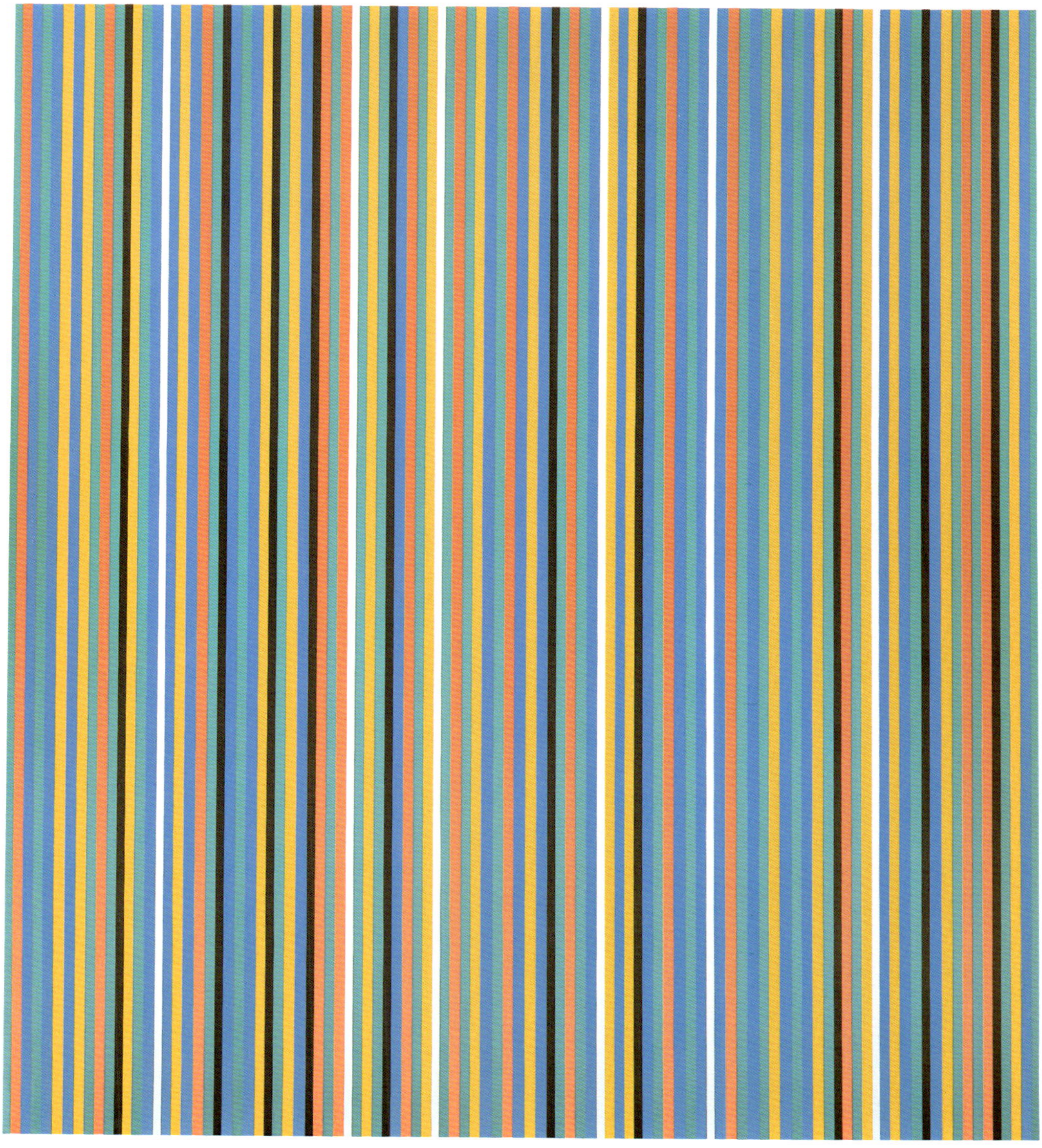

Luxor 1982

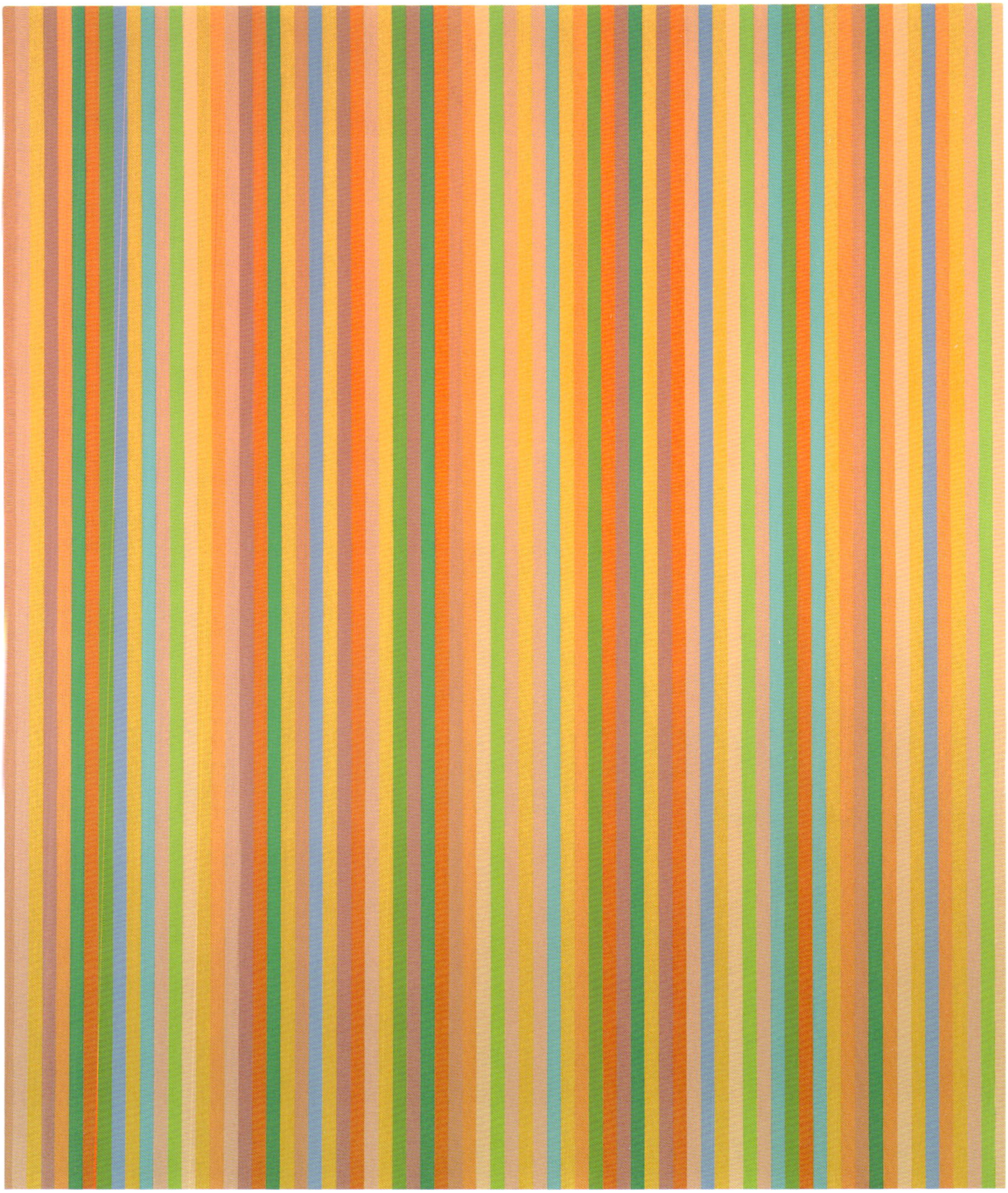

Saraband 1985

the beginning. The black bands no longer establish a regular measure like a musical beat or metre, but act as genuine rhythmical accents which both drive and check, contain and break the colour development. Similarly the white intervals have lost the primary role they once played in accommodating the chromatic activity. Now they serve, depending on their position in the painting, a double function: either as plain pauses, 'breathing spaces' between the blocks of colour, or as sudden clearances which set free the high, flaming accents of bordering colours. But more importantly, a similar contradictory orientation seems to govern the use of colour itself, as the first group of paintings shows. Where the colour development moves predominantly in oppositions (turquoise-red, blue-yellow) – as in *Serenissima* and *Rose Rime* – a vivid pearly grey suffuses the entire colour field; but as soon as a few strong harmonies are struck – like the turquoise-blue chords in *Summer's Field* and *Luxor* – alternating banks of composite colours suddenly spring up. In the first group this disruptive energy is firmly controlled by the tight tension of the black bands. However, once this armature was removed the self-generating dynamism of colour appeared. In *Greensleeves* this is counteracted by recreating the stabilising function of black with a colour, green, but this approach was not pursued further because it led to a simple harmonising of the colour intensity. Instead she followed the direction indicated by *Cherry Autumn*: to build this uneven, jerky, irregularly fluctuating space out of its own tensions and antagonisms. *Cherry Autumn* (1983) is a key painting in Riley's development because it shows her making the connection that three years later resulted in another major re-orientation. Her initial interest in the chromatic and luminescent aspect of colour's energy (the Neo-Impressionist heritage) was slowly superseded by the realisation that colour's prime potential, at least in *painting*, was somehow *spatial*. Or, as she herself prefers to say: 'plastic' – since it is not a space which colours create around themselves, settling within it, but a highly contested and unstable property which they make up and even fight out, so to speak, between themselves. In 1984 and 1985 she used her time in Vaucluse mainly for experimenting with new formal structures because by then she already was convinced that this plasticity could not be properly developed nor sufficiently organised by means of vertical stripes.

In retrospect one can see that the stripe paintings of 1980–85 hold a unique position in Riley's work in the sense that they mark the apex of her transition from the earlier, chromatic use of colour to the spatial and 'plastic' emphasis of the most recent paintings. Indeed, at moments she came very close to realising a dream of every colourist – to make the spectator oblivious of form. After incorporating in paintings like *Coxcomb* that 'perceptual lilac' which her five colour palette had long been reflecting back to her, she went one step further and in *Saraband* and *Burnished Sky* (both 1985) attempted to compensate for the absence of a horizontal axis by broadening the colour range, particularly in the red area. Her analysis of Renoir's colour in the spring of 1985 – during the great retrospective at the Hayward Gallery – obviously bore fruit. And yet, the opulence of these paintings also reveals that, once again, a creative period was drawing to a close. The title *Burnished Sky* alludes to the blackish grey which impinges on one's eyes in places of high atmospheric purity and intensity of light – like the desert, for instance.

The change, when it finally occurred, was drastic. In the spring of 1986 Riley produced the first studies which include the kind of short diagonal 'hatching' that can be found in *Gentle Edge*. Another painting of the same group is called *Broken Gaze* – the perfect mirror of her first colour vision had been broken. These transitional works are few in number since Riley soon saw the ghost of the old structural totality returning. She reacted against this violently by increasing and roughening the scale of the diagonal fields and by dislocating rhomboid fragments of various sizes within the vertical register. 'That gave me time', she explains, 'I could work against these directional forces, counteracting them through colour and rhythm.'[13] This approach – which in principle has governed all the rhomboid paintings – represents the closing of the most recent cycle in Riley's studio practice. The procedure of dislocating a chosen form and relocating it in a new structural context had been applied once before, in a group of circular images related to *Blaze I* (1962), although at that time dislocation was a method as well as the pictorial theme itself.[14] In 1986, however, this device became a means of finding a new form of expression altogether. It can be seen emerging in the works of 1987 (*Ease*, *Into Place* and *Stream of Change*). As the development went on, the principle of displacement took quite a different character, as can be seen in the form and colour relationships of *New Day* (1988). Whereas in *Blaze I* it came close to distortion, dislocation is now employed in a way analogous to the musical technique of transposition, with the difference that, in transposing and developing her 'themes', Riley has to create new pictorial 'harmonies' in each painting.

The work since 1986 has progressed in a way which makes it clear that this change of direction was not just formal or conceptual. It is as though the imaginary edifice which Riley has been building for more than twenty-five years has begun to be 'inhabited' and developed from within.

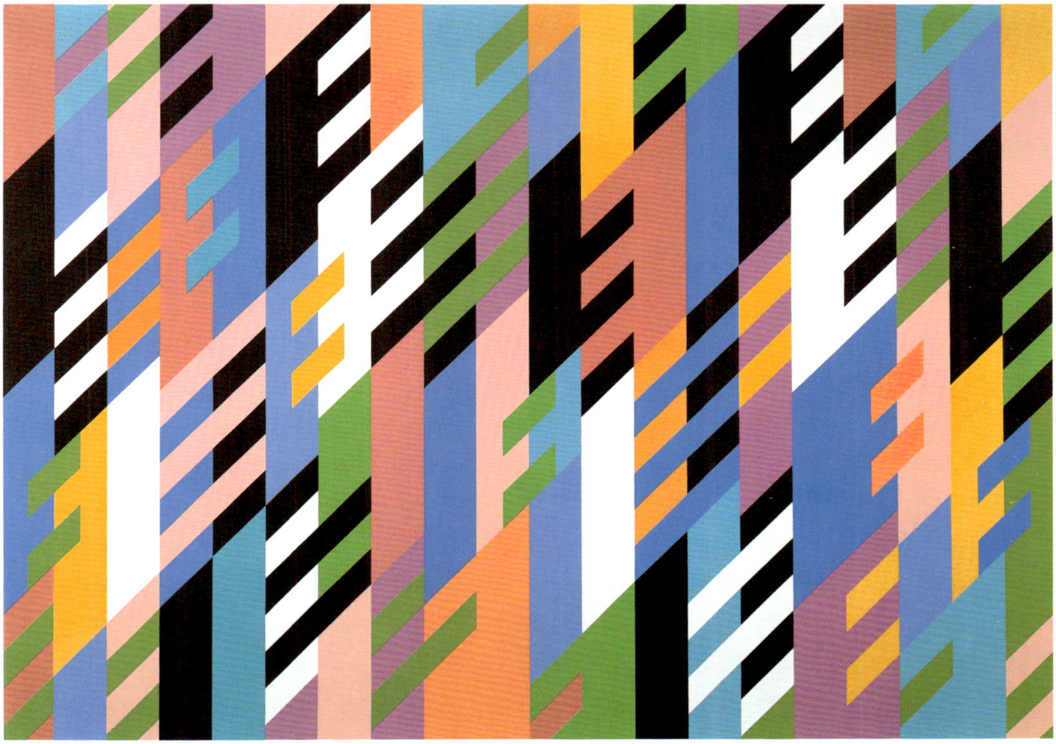

Justinian 1988

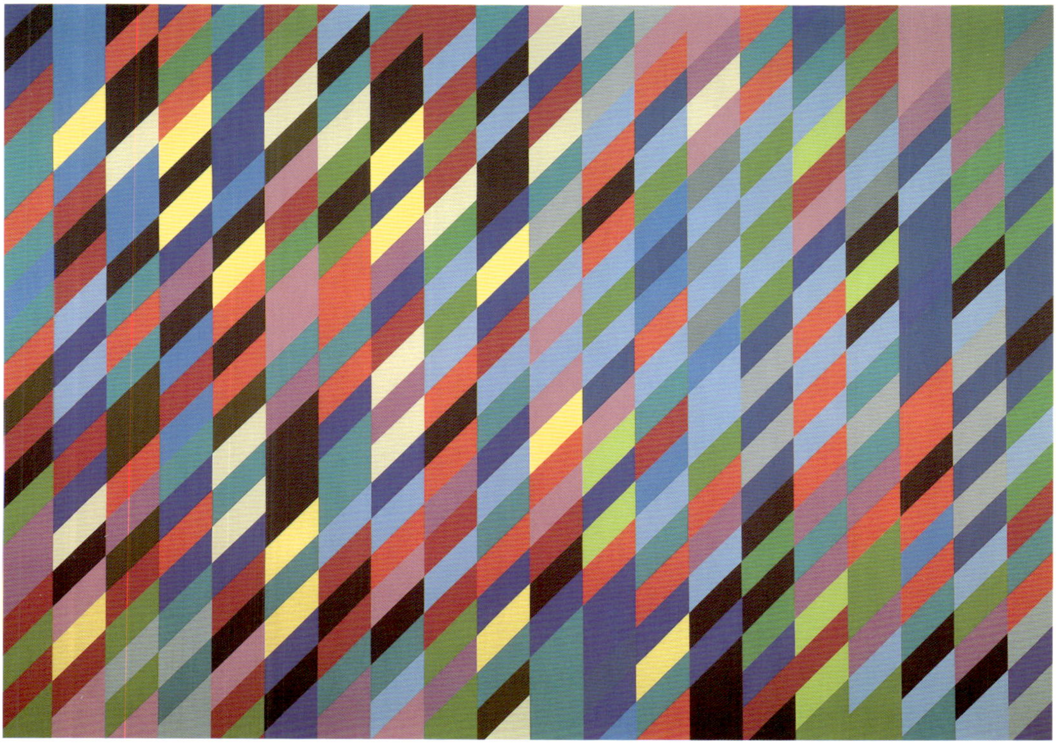

Cool Place 1990

Unlike any previous period, the present phase of her painting seems to be driven less by the need to intensify than by a longing to deepen the work, according to the familiar cycle of feeling: 'repose, disturbance, repose'. The rhythmic pace of *Into Place* and *Stream of Change* is answered by the almost hieratic, ceremonial presence of the paintings of 1988 (*Justinian*, *New Day*) in which black for the first time figures as a colour: both as a deep hue and as a 'plastic' weight indispensable to the wide horizontal format. In 1989, however, the pendulum swings back, the solid blocks of colour are dissolved again, she even abandons, as can been seen in the transition from *Debut* to *Gaillard*, the fencing of the main dramatic event by a flat, firm area round the edges of the canvas. And with the temporary exclusion of black in paintings like *Certain Day* (1989) the colour frequency is stepped up to a point where it becomes almost weightless and effervescent. But, in 1990, *Cool Place* and *November* introduce compositional factors which stabilise the work. There is strong emphasis on the 'other side' of the painting: a still area – mostly off-centre to the right – which counters the more active entry passage on the left-hand side, sometimes acting as the 'eye of the storm' (*Set Fair*, 1990). All paintings since have an increased density of colour provided by earth colours and broken hues (magenta-grey, 'stone', 'apricot', and many others). In the most recent paintings, *Cromarty* (1991) and *High Sky 2* (1992), Riley makes use of an irrational proportion of one third to two thirds, a so-called *álogon* in musical terms, in the diagonal element which at certain points disrupts the vertical register.

The new sumptuousness of colour (between fifteen and twenty colours in each painting) has been achieved at the price of virtually extinguishing what seemed for a long time the hallmark of Riley's art: the overt chromatic actions and interactions, the iridescent lights and unexpected fusions of colour have all disappeared. By penetrating the peculiar space of colour, part of that colour's magical outward appearance is lost. Instead, a firmly interlocking and at the same time dramatically shifting fabric of sensations has emerged, a visible paradox which the artist refers to as 'plastic'. The term plastic originally does not relate to any three-dimensional or intrinsically sculptural quality as Mondrian, who also used the term, knew. It was coined in late Antiquity to describe a particular formative force in nature. However, the originator of the modern European use of the term plastic is the English 17th century philosopher Ralph Cudworth. In his book "The True Intellectual System of the Universe" (1678) he argues that there is an 'Inward Principle' to the universe which makes all its natural parts, physical beings as well as human sensations, act 'regularly' and 'artificially' though 'without any deliberation or studied consideration'. And then he gives the following definition of how this 'plastick nature' operates:

> *"And therefore though it be One, yet notwithstanding it consists of Different and Contrary things. For the being Hostility in its Parts, it is nevertheless Friendly and Agreeable in the Whole; after the same manner as in a Dramatick Poem, Clashings and Contentions are reconciled into one Harmony. And therefore the Seminary and Plastick Nature of the World may fitly be resembled to the Harmony of Disagreeing things."*[15]

'That sounds like Cézanne', Riley remarked when she had read this passage. Possibly. It is certainly the way in which she has made colour work in her recent paintings: as a unity in and amongst contrasting colours. The biggest circle which Riley closed in the 1980s is the imaginative one. She set out to rediscover the legacy of the great French colourists of the 19th century; and the form of colour painting she eventually accomplished 'may fitly be resembled' to a conception of plasticity that is of best English extraction.

1 "The Pleasures of Sight" (1984), reprinted in *The Eye's Mind* (1999), p. 30, and in the Tate Gallery retrospective catalogue *Bridget Riley* (2003), p. 213.
2 Ibid.
3 Maurice de Sausmarez's book *Basic Design: The Dynamics of Visual Form*, London 1964, includes reproductions of student work made under Riley's supervision during her last period of teaching (at Croydon School of Art, 1962 – 64). Two of the drawings show 'a measured analysis of a shell to arrive at the fundamental geometry and rhythm' while the third is a proportional study on the relationships between the stem and the leaves of a tree. All on p. 67.
4 Paul Klee, "Abstract?", in Jürg Spiller (ed.), *Paul Klee. The Thinking Eye*, translated by Ralph Manheim, vol 1, Lund Humphries 1961, p. 72.
5 'I am sometimes asked "What is your objective?" and this I cannot truthfully answer. I work "from" something rather than "towards" something.' Personal statement in Maurice de Sausmarez, *Bridget Riley*, London 1970, p. 91. Reprinted in *The Eye's Mind* (1999), p. 79.
6 Igor Stravinsky, *The Poetics of Music*, Cambridge Mass.: Harvard University Press 1942, p. 65.
7 "Perception Is the Medium" (1965), reprinted in The Eye's Mind (1999), pp. 66–68, and in the catalogue of the Tate Gallery retrospective exhibition *Bridget Riley* (2003), p. 207.
8 *According to Sensation* 1990, p. 92 [in this volume]
9 The French original is even more understated: "J'en remets, jusqu'à ce que ça fasse bien". Quoted after D. Fourcade (ed.), *Henri Matisse, Écrits et propos sur l'art*, Paris 1972, p. 163.
10 *Conversation* 1972, p. 22 [in this volume]

11 Bryan Robertson, "Introduction" to *Bridget Riley. Paintings and Drawings 1951–1971*, London 1971, p.8.
12 *Conversation* 1972, p. 20 [in this volume]
13 *According to Sensation* 1990, p. 97 [in this volume]
14 On the early theme of 'dislocation' cf. Maurice de Sausmarez, *Bridget Riley*, London 1970, pp. 45–31. See also *Building Sensations* 1999, p. 173 [in this volume]
15 Ralph Cudworth, *The True Intellectual System of the Universe*, facsimile reprint of the London 1678 edition, Stuttgart 1964, p. 152. This source has been brought to my attention by Dieter Rahn who has researched the history of the term 'plastic' in his book *Die Plastik und die Dinge*, Freiburg: Rombach, 1993, p. 12 f.

Commentary on the paintings selected for the exhibition *Bridget Riley: Paintings 1982–1992*, Nürnberg: Verlag für Moderne Kunst in cooperation with South Bank Centre London, 1992, pp. 30–48. An English version of the German catalogue (originally conceived for the shows in Nürnberg and Bottrop) was printed for the two subsequent British venues: Hayward Gallery, London and Ikon Gallery, Birmingham.

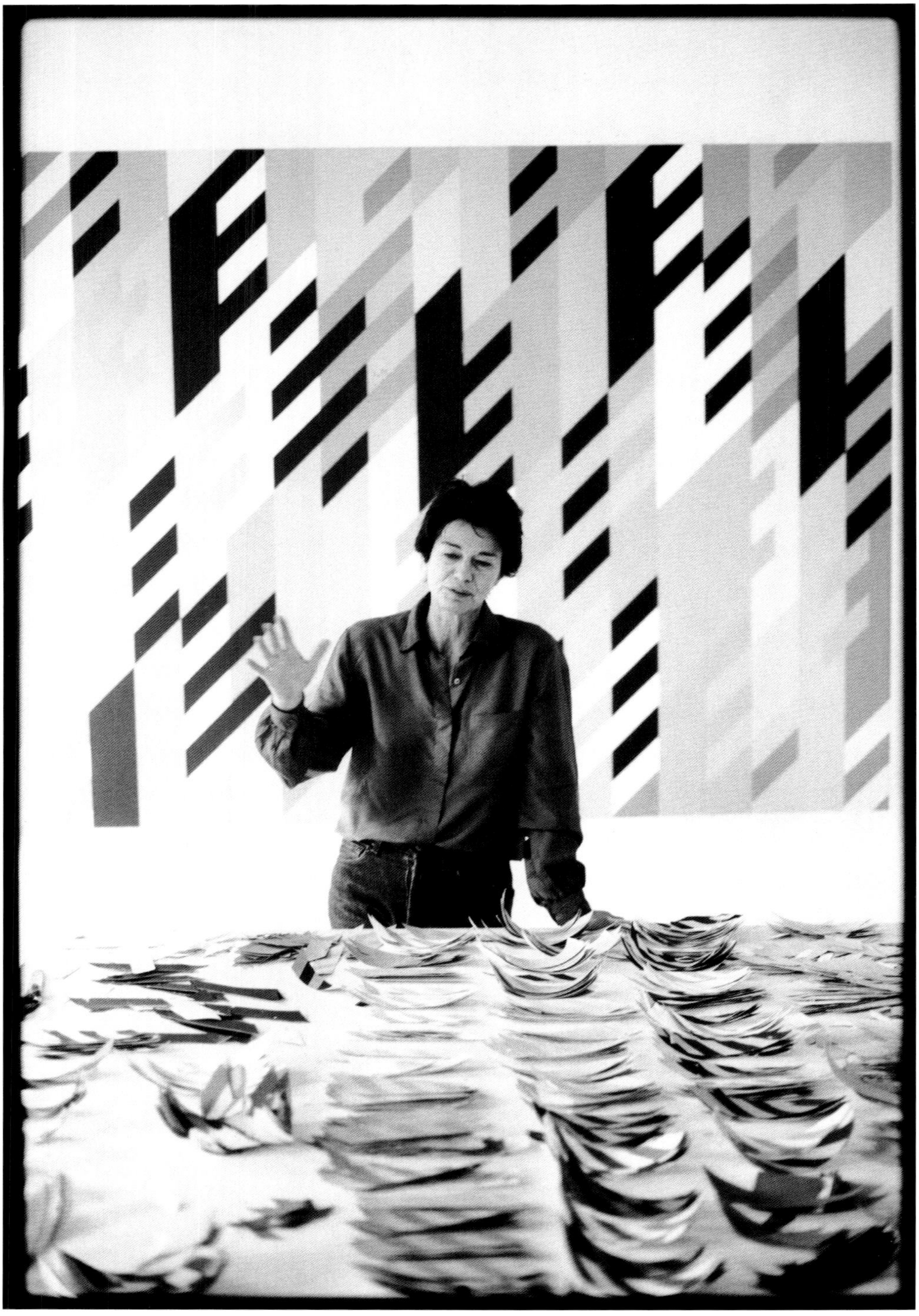

Bridget Riley

1992

In March 1972 Bridget Riley and I visited Munich together. The trip was exciting right from the moment it began in Zurich where the car broke down in the middle of traffic. Bridget, to my surprise and irritation, seemed to enjoy the disruption. She believes, I think, that it is in the nature of machines to break down from time to time and that their ultimate fate is to break down utterly and forever.

Soon after our eventual arrival in Munich by train we banished the unfortunate way the trip had begun from our minds. In the Alte Pinakothek there are more than enough things which – quite unlike the motor car – become increasingly powerful the more you get to know them. On that visit Bridget especially enjoyed looking at Altdorfer's *Battle of Alexander*; admiring the undulating rhythm of the massed lances, and of course she was thrilled by the unique collection of Rubens. But the indelible impression which that visit to Munich left on both our minds had little to do with looking at works of art. In fact the high point of the

(opposite)
Bridget Riley in front of *Justinian* 1988

trip was an early spring day of a kind which only seems possible in the foothills of the Alps, a day of utmost clarity when light evenly floods space, endowing everything with equal presence and filling the air with an extraordinary, almost tangible brightness. And at that time of the year when the new leaves cannot compete with such brilliance the effect seems more hallucinatory still.

From the museum we had wandered over to the Hofgarten where we found a table already laid with a white cloth beneath some trees whose branches were still bare. A few other people had also been tempted outside by the glorious promise of summer. It was about midday. A waitress brought us glasses of wine which sparkled yellow and green. The light grew brighter and stronger every minute. I do not exactly remember what we were talking about (most likely paintings) when Bridget stopped and exclaimed: 'Look at it! Just *look* at it!' I have noticed on similar occasions that this urgent demand can also be accompanied by a direct injunction: 'No, don't look *at* it, just glance!' On that day in Munich there was indeed nothing to look *at* in the proper sense of the word, no particular incident or object to be observed. It was rather as though we were sitting in the middle of an all-enveloping event. Although it would have been possible not to notice the full extent of what was happening, it was certainly, I think, well within the capacity of human sight to discern and analyse particular effects. But no one was obliged to attend the show. The other people went on eating and enjoying themselves without taking much notice of the light and colour dancing all around them. They might perhaps have blinked rather more often than usual.

Strangely enough, such amiable indifference was entirely in keeping with the performance of which they were unwittingly a part. Nature is indifferent to her audience. Bridget Riley believes that true appearance is best revealed through the casual glance – and then only momentarily. Although there were good reasons for ascribing everything to the power of the sun, light itself did not appear as the main actor in the drama. The bright, almost palpable shine which filled the air disintegrated into countless fragments, colours, reflections and shadows which in turn seemed to destroy the solidity and weight of objects. A dense, irreducible element, the matrix of appearance imposed itself upon the eye with its own unique sensations. The light blue of the spring sky which faded away in the distance to infinity was caught up between the black branches of the trees seen against the light and became there a shade darker. Meanwhile, on the gravelled surfaces of the garden, the blue reflection of the sky was sharpened with the sparkle of local hues and animated by shafts of sunlight. Patches of luminous colour, entire islands so to speak, and small jewel-like nuggets covered the ground, alternating with deep cast shadows. Simultaneously, reflections of light, the disembodied relatives of this dappled patterning, danced across glasses, tables, clothes and faces until they were absorbed by either light or darkness. Sometimes these reflections changed colour as they went, and sometimes not: from bright red to blue, even from white to white, from light yellow to a middle tone the actual colour of which was no longer identifiable. This vein-like system of layered shades and colours with their thin, subtly varying tones seemed like some elastic, pliable structure, which gently swayed as it spread over everything, even the figures which actually were moving beneath the trees. It made one think of a closely worked veil which moved within itself, or even of some permeable medium which crystallised momentarily, only to become fluid again. Once the measure of attention had been exhausted, Bridget Riley leaned back and said: 'And some people complain that my paintings are too dazzling to look at – that they are positively unnatural!'

This episode reveals two things: that a relationship exists between Bridget Riley's art and nature – and something of the unique character of that relationship. The fact that she maintains and cultivates such a relationship at all and, as an abstract artist, sustains her art with it is in itself highly unusual for someone of her generation. Most painters, whether abstract or figurative, in the second half of this century have tended to think of nature as something over and done with in the evolution of modern art: at most a point of departure but certainly no longer the lifeline of their art. For this reason Riley was little understood when, starting with her earliest paintings in black and white, she persistently referred to the affinities between her work and nature. If people explained this reference at all, it was in terms of 'optical laws' which, it was thought, could be seen at work in the paintings. Thus a proper understanding of Riley's art was delayed for many years. The fact is that, for Riley, 'literal abstraction' – the process of abstracting from experience – is the essence of everything abstraction in art is *not* about. The paintings of the late 1980s counter this misconception more effectively than any argument. The impression provided by these densely structured compositions, with their disseminated light and incalculable depths, their varying rhythms and incidents may initially he daunting. However, we know this space instinctively: diffuse but bright, shallow and yet unfathomable, a world which shifts without moving place and which, in spite of the diversity of its constituent parts, has nevertheless an inner logic of its own. This is the world of sensations, though seen in a way radically opposed to introspection: unfolding, branching out, enveloping – as though experienced from the 'interior of a tree'. This image, which is Riley's own, does not allude to those bare, transparent ghosts in the Munich Hofgarten but to a handsome edifice in full and heavy leaf – like the magnificent oak which stands outside her studio in the South of France.

In this respect the long-postponed question of Riley's specific links with nature becomes more important. How and in what respect does this kind of painting relate to nature if it does not abstract from it in any conventional way? For it is clear that these diagonally organised pictorial structures do not remotely relate to the form of any real tree (as Mondrian's studies of trees do, for example), nor do they bear any resemblance to any other kind of natural object. It is equally obvious, however, that such a particular world of forms and colours which affect the senses so directly and resoundingly cannot simply be fabricated on the drawing board with the aid of a few calculations or random strategies. It is a genuine invention which has been forged in response to a need and both this need and the means to meet it result from the organic progress of the work itself.

Bridget Riley's painting has been developing now for more than thirty years. At irregular intervals she seems to encounter and pick up again certain issues and problems which she has tackled and seemingly settled at an earlier stage of her development and then, by re-engaging with them, she simultaneously transforms and clarifies some of her basic preoccupations. The relationship to nature is a prime example of this. Although she has never been in doubt about it as a point of departure, she did not know for a long time where it was leading her. Only in the transitional phase of the 1970s when she began to see what she calls the 'Medusa's Head of colour' did she realise that the solitary path she was taking actually led through a well cultivated, if at the time generally ignored, field. The gulf between nature and abstraction had already been discovered and explored by the great colourists of the nineteenth century. The major retrospective exhibitions of the late 1970s and especially two in New York – *Cézanne: The Late Work* (Museum of Modern Art, 1977–78) and *Monet's Years at Giverny: Beyond Impressionism* (Metropolitan Museum of Art, 1978) – helped her to understand this.

One of the principal achievements of the French painters of the period usually referred to as Classical Modernism was to uncover the fundamental problem of abstraction in painting while working from nature, *sur le motif*. It is a problem which had remained concealed for most of the history of art: how does one deal with the difference between the way we normally 'see' things and their actual visual appearance? For most of our daily preoccupations it seems to be of little significance that there is no 'real' local colour in nature (as Delacroix realised) or that 'near' or 'far' in perception do not correlate with their objective positions in space. But to the painter *sur le motif* every single colour or plane appears as part of a continuum of relationships from which it cannot be isolated without distortion, and the totality of this experience is only perceivable as something dependent upon its relative parts. That meant that the visible unity of nature could only be rendered indirectly by means of an analogous structure of colour and space within the painting. In their different ways Monet's '*enveloppe*' and Cézanne's '*harmonie générale*' met this challenge.

Riley was aware of such 'equivalent' approaches to nature. In 1959–60, on the threshold of her independent work, she had studied Seurat's *méthode* very closely and made a number of paintings in the Neo-Impressionist manner. But it was not before she had developed her own fully abstract language and began to work with colour, that she finally discovered the basic reason for such sophisticated methods: that the true face of nature was visibly veiled. Her re-involvement with Classical Modernism in the late 1970s alerted her to the fact that these painters had to refrain from direct representation because, objectively speaking, the problem that colour presents cannot be resolved in those terms. All colours vary according to their context and this 'relatedness' is in no other way accessible than through the particular changes it effects.

This discovery had a decisive influence on her own use of colour in the 1980s. Even more important however was the impact this insight made upon her understanding of abstraction. There was a second route to abstract art which had somehow not been followed up by its originators at the beginning of the century. If nature visibly eluded depiction, as the great 19th century painters had seen, then the idea of aiming 'beyond' representation – towards some sort of 'absolute' – was also wide of the mark, an all too theoretical concept, however much it may have contributed to the formal liberation of art. Could it not be that the turning away from representation was simply an unavoidable move, necessitated by perception, in order to prepare for and build up a new relationship with nature? Riley was enormously encouraged by this insight. Cézanne's tight modulations and Monet's fugitive lilacs have rarely found a better advocate: 'They *saw* it', she insists. In 1975 she had a studio built in the South of France. Ever since the early 1980s she has worked there for several weeks in the year – *pour me nourrir*, as she says, quoting Matisse.[1]

It would be a mistake, however, to conclude that Riley in the 1980s has become an 'Abstract Impressionist'. Whatever such a term might mean in an art history book (and it comes to mind with astonishing ease, probably just as easily as the phrase 'optical effects' did once upon a time), for Riley rendering an impression without an actual subject would be as absurd as trying to extend the soaring of the lark by removing the resistance of air and gravity. Confronting nature directly is the misguided way, so to speak, by which the Impressionists discovered the creative paradox that it is only through withdrawing from depiction that the artist can come close to those aspects of nature which provided an initial impulse. Without such critical concepts recording one's sensations in front of the motif leads to nothing but a chance agglomeration of disparate impressions.

Riley's attachment to the great *plein air* colourists strengthened her resolve not to rely on any kind of external reality. If Monet and Cézanne had to retreat to the edge of abstraction *sur le motif*, why should it not be possible to do the reverse, to develop a relationship with nature from working within abstraction itself? Riley's newly built studio in the South of France deliberately has no window overlooking the splendid panorama of the plateau of Vaucluse. And in leaving the house and walking on the hillside in the hour before dusk when the colours are released from the domination of the sun, she is not 'hunting for visual sensations', not searching for 'material' for her paintings. It is rather like someone returning home after a perfectly normal day at work. Yet it is not quite so normal. When she had completed the full-size cartoon for *Dark Light* last winter she remarked: 'Isn't it curious that nature immediately looks so much better once I've got a painting together?' That is roughly how the balance between the making of abstract art and nature should be seen.

This is, of course, an intimate view of the artist's practice. The outsider who looks at the paintings for the first time seems to be confronted by a completely different experience. The paintings appear seamless, built up inch by inch from exact geometric forms. And this unremittingly tight structure nowhere allows the spectator to adopt a particular viewpoint or the illusion that he is looking out at something. It seems entirely calculated to provide a totally unpredictable experience: the movements of the eye as it discovers relationships within the painting, their accompanying dislocations and the irretrievable moment when the formal structure of the painting disintegrates. In the late oils and watercolours of Cézanne there is a similar kind of drama which takes hold of and pervades the entire picture plane. But precisely this comparison with Cézanne makes the specific character of Riley's painting – her own *petite sensation* – more clear. While Cézanne makes visible a dramatic sensation experienced in front of the motif, Riley builds up a dramatic momentum within the painting to make the spectator 'see' in a way that is initially disturbing but perhaps ultimately not so dissimilar. Since 1962 when David Sylvester, reviewing her first individual exhibition, identified and commended this 'disturbing element'[2] in her work, little in principle of the 'Riley sensation' has really changed. It may have seemed as though the vehemence of the paintings was becoming less marked as a result of the introduction of colour during the first period of coloured 'stripe' compositions (1967–1973) and even amiably dissolving in the 'curve' paintings which followed it (1974–1980). But the energetic charge returned in force with the second group of coloured 'stripe' paintings of 1980–1985, and since 1987 the intensity and resonance have increased in the diagonal compositions. What has changed, however, and this tremendously so, is the sheer volume of the visual event. The sharp, instantaneous presence of the black-and-white paintings has steadily been expanded and eventually given way to rich and complex occurrences which are highly differentiated in themselves. As a result, the imaginative place in time which the 'Riley sensation' both demands and avails has become, as she herself puts it, more 'inhabitable' for the spectator – as well as for the artist herself.

Today it is difficult to imagine the hysteria which was once provoked by the 'disturbing element' in Riley's paintings, although significantly there were no casualty reports when it first put in an appearance. Bridget Riley's work is an interesting case in the history of the reception of modern art. Those who saw Riley's earliest exhibitions, and especially the critics of the time, clearly looked at the paintings long enough to notice that the visual disturbance which accompanied the beginning of the experience did not persist until the end. It was only later that it became fashionable to rave about the aggressiveness of the 'patterns' and (from the point of view of art politics) opportune to complain that one's eyes were hurting when the controversy caused by the exhibition *The Responsive Eye* in 1965 at the Museum of Modern Art, New York, was at its greatest. That was the dazzling moment in Riley's career (which in some eyes has left a deep black after-image ever since) when all of New York, and not just the art world, was at her feet. The hypocrisy culminated in an accusation that was epitomised in the polemical headline of an article by Thomas B. Hess, the editor of *Art News*: "You can hang it in the hall" – No one could stand pictures like these in a living room![3] Time and Riley's international following, especially those who have collected her work, have revealed the error of this all too partisan outrage. It is precisely when you live with the paintings or get to know them intimately over a period of time that you come to wonder how it could have happened that, in all honesty, you once felt a little provoked yourself. For, after the first dazzling impact, a very special form of adjustment takes place. It is almost the opposite of becoming accustomed to the paintings. It is enough to leaf through a glossy magazine to get an idea of how permissive we have become in tolerating violations of our colour vision. But becoming inured to experience in this way is entirely different to the process by which the eye is gradually trained to appreciate the surprise and stimulation which occur only *after* the first unsettling experience in front of Riley's paintings. In 1963 Anton Ehrenzweig came up with a striking analogy in the foreword to the catalogue of her second exhibition: 'We have to submit to the attack in the way in which we have to learn to enjoy a cold shower. There comes a voluptuous moment when the senses and the whole skin tingle with a sharpened awareness of the body and the world around.'[4]

Riley changes our way of looking. And she does this successfully *with the aid* of our sense of sight because what she asks us to do is by no means unnatural. The demands of her art are neither at war with our common perceptions of nature nor do they violate the physical characteristics of our perceptual faculties. Even the most vibrant of her black-and-white paintings will not make the spectator feel more dizzy than the view of sunlight filtering down through the leafy crown of a tree or the sight of the gentle swaying of a field in the summer wind. And in any case none of them is remotely as dazzling as the silvery flash and flicker of an ash tree in an approaching storm or the glitter of light dancing across the tousled surface of sea in the evening sun. There have also been objections that the paintings trick the eye with 'optical illusions' or that they are incompatible with a leisurely view from an armchair. Riley's own testimony 'I have never studied "optics"', in her rejoinder to the American polemics "Perception Is the Medium" (1965)[5], did not immediately clear her from the suspicion that she had recourse to text books on optics. But the progress of science certainly has done. It is an amusing side-light on the hazards of scholarly objectivity to go through the long list of publications by perceptual psychologists and physiologists who began to exploit Riley's paintings as 'examples' and 'proofs' of their own insights and arguments – without, however, realising that the evidence provided by reproductions and details is dubious (to say nothing of the nonchalant attitude to reproducing paintings upside down or the wrong way round). Photographs and reproductions are always misleading (or, at best, simply *aides-mémoire*) because the 'Riley sensation' can only occur fully when each work is seen on its proper scale. It is in the *exactness* of each painting – and that includes everything, not just the format – that this *petite sensation* becomes a totality and acquires the kind of force which defies inquisition. Both Sylvester and Ehrenzweig recognised independently that the precipitous effect of Riley's pictorial world is not at all optically mechanical but rather equates with a well-known shift in dramatic performance. 'The disturbing element is not only imaginative in conception', Sylvester observed, 'but has the sort of rightness in its placing a good actor has in his timing – it seems at once unexpected and inevitable.'[6] The protagonist of this visual drama is of course not a person but our own point of view. Ehrenzweig found a suitable metaphor for this imaginative conception: 'We sometimes speak of "devouring" something with our eyes. In these paintings the reverse thing happens, the eye is attacked and "devoured" by the paintings.'[7] Far from being subject to aggression the spectator precipitates any loss of visual control *himself* by trying to dominate the process of looking, to arrest and contain what is seen. In short, the momentary disturbance is the result of the attempt to put oneself 'in the picture', so to speak.

These observations on the drama of Riley's painting are striking. But in scope and content they are restricted to the early black-and-white works. The iconoclastic effect provoked by the 'Riley sensation' only occurred in its most direct and fierce form in the paintings made between 1961 and 1963, and assumed its ultimate, definitive expression in *Blaze* (1962). After that the explosive tension relaxes until it all but subsides during the transitional phase of 1965–1967 when coloured greys replace the contrast of black and white, and then the introduction of pure colour in 1967 instigated a major shift in direction. Although there is a lyrical tone in the work of the 1970s, it does not follow that colour in itself is responsible for this quieter mood, as the most recent paintings show. Rather the drama of confrontation has been superseded by quite the opposite strategy of drawing the spectator into the work. 'They should stealthily engage and disarm you', Riley has said of her paintings.[8] Colour seems to have enabled her to proceed from the disruptive shock of making us 'see' to the full experience of what looking her way feels like. In this sense the work has become more 'inhabitable' because colour leads the spectator towards the magical domain which he can enter if he is prepared to look *with* the visual current instead of struggling against it. The paintings strike a high festive note, but the formal movements suggested to our eyes – those arcs, loops, shifts and jumps, sudden stops and slow turns, crossings and returns – are thoroughly familiar. We know them as part of our peripheral vision, from that oblique view 'out of the corner of one's eye'. They are the most natural patterns of seeing which we use and practise daily if we are aware of our surroundings.

Riley's opposition to the widely held view that any visual experience outside our focus of attention is contrary to the human spirit has continued since the 1960s. She has never made any secret of her convictions: 'Our bearings still suffer from the concept or suppositions of Renaissance theory, which is "man as the measure of all things". But man is only a part of a bigger whole and this whole is neither centripetal nor centrifugal. It is much more open and egalitarian.'[9] This is to be understood neither literally as the rejection of single viewpoint perspective nor too generally as an ideological justification of abstraction. Her statement about the position of man relative to the larger whole is based on the only evidence she really trusts – her work in the studio. In other words, the spectator's sudden loss of focus in front of the paintings is not the outcome of a cunning aesthetic strategy but the direct reflection of the artist's creative engagement in her work.

Riley's relationship with nature, the very lifeline of her work, cannot be determined by any stable point of reference such as a principle or subject, or by obliquely accommodating it in the context of a *motif*. She has described this very special relationship with great lucidity in "The Pleasures of Sight" (1984). The essay starts with a long and lyrical account of incidents which formed her 'visual life' and ends with a sober and razor-sharp piece of analysis: 'But whatever the occasion might be, the pleasures of sight have one characteristic in common – they take you by surprise. They are sudden, swift and unexpected. If one tries to prolong them, recapture them or bring them about wilfully their purity and freshness is lost. They are essentially enigmatic and elusive. One can stare at a landscape for example, which a moment ago seemed vibrant and find it inert and dull – so one cannot say that this lively quality of sight is simply "out there in nature", or easily available to be commanded as wished. Nor is it a state of mind which, once acquired, can bend the most stubborn and unrewarding aspect of external reality to its own purposes. It is neither the one nor the other but a perfect balance between the two, between the inner and the outer. This balance is a sort of convergence which releases a particular alchemy, momentarily turning the commonplace into the ravishing.'[10]

Such is the paradox of Riley's relationship with nature. The point of connection is at once very familiar and equally remote. The 'lively quality of sight' cannot be grasped either objectively or subjectively because it consists of an unforced convergence of perception and emotional experience, of an incalculable 'Sympathy of the Universe' (Shaftesbury). It is for this reason that the momentary 'alchemy', the metamorphosis of the plain and insignificant into something magical, will not allow itself to be artificially manufactured or artistically staged. One cannot gain access to these sensations (or at least not in such a way that they take on an equivalent liveliness of their own) by projecting a spontaneous feeling for nature, however deeply felt it might be, onto natural sites and objects. The recovery of this precious elixir, those 'pleasures of sight' which are familiar to all people, seems barred, and there is probably only one way, however uncertain, to circumvent this barrier – and that is through the kind of abrupt reversal which Riley has negotiated.

This is the ingenious circle. The answer to the second part of the question – in what respect these paintings relate to nature – in fact clears the field for the primary, essentially artistic problem: how does Riley's art connect with such an elusive stimulus? The resolution has now been on the table for a long time. Bridget Riley first achieved an independent voice after a grave personal and artistic crisis during the winter of 1960–61 which resulted in repeated attempts to paint one ultimate, absolutely black picture. It was out of the failure of those attempts that the black-and-white paintings emerged which within four years catapulted her to the problematic heights of stardom in the visual arts. This break of continuity and the departure from what for the first half of the twentieth century has been the customary route to abstraction – the evolutionary one taken by Kandinsky, Malevich and Mondrian – was at first either not noticed or quickly obscured by art historical analogies between 'Optical Art' and 'Neo-impressionism' based on the similarity of the perceptual approach. The break was nevertheless real and is fundamental to the abstract work. The obvious lack of recognition may partly be due to the fact that Riley herself kept this literally dark area of her development undisclosed for a long time, both for personal reasons and also because of real insecurity. But during the 1970s, a period she describes as 'a time of taking in', she finally caught up with that point on her elliptical progress. In 1975 and 1976 she made many visits to her parents' home in Cornwall where her mother had fallen seriously ill, and there, renewing contact with the scenes of her childhood, she began to read Proust, casually at first, but then with a growing sense of engagement. The recognition was so important to her that she began to compile a personal index of the *Remembrance of Things Past* on the long train journeys to the country. The novel illuminates a seemingly enigmatic paradox that is summed up in the final pages in a single sentence given to the fictional painter Elstir: 'You can make a new version of what you love only by first renouncing it.'[11] This jewel from what Beckett calls 'Proust's treasury of nutshell phrases'[12] is a variation on the central theme of the book – that reality which every direct description will invariably fail to represent can only be recreated indirectly through the agency of involuntary memories. Proust's basic insight into the creative cycle of loss and recovery affected Riley deeply. It made her more confident in her chosen path of rigorous abstraction by striking an echo in quite different, apparently unrelated corners of her world – in Cézanne's lesson of the 'sacrifice' and in her distant but passionate feeling for the paintings of Jackson Pollock.

If there is a single, essential clue to Riley's sudden turn to abstraction it is, in spite of all stylistic differences, the work of Jackson Pollock. It is even possible to imagine that it was from his example of attaining extreme states that the idea came to her of making one ultimate statement in a painting. For the young artist, the impact of the great Pollock exhibition at the Whitechapel Art Gallery in the winter of 1958 was 'shattering'. It awoke her to the dangerous but electrifying truth that any creative attempt to enter into a more vital and rewarding relationship with reality might require a complete renunciation of appearances and artistic devices. Pollock had crashed right through the barrier, no matter how high the price had been. 'I am nature' – Pollock's defiantly rebellious remark[13] – strikes an echo in a rough and inconvenient tendency of Riley's own involvement with nature. This brusque, abrasive quality contributes to the irrepressible brio of the early work by adding an almost flippant note, dismissive of all the elderly whispers of the art world. And this unruliness can be retraced in the harmonic frictions disrupting the majestic rustle of the latest paintings which, in organisation and rhythmical density, seem curiously related to Abstract Expressionism. But it is only a distant echo. The note of tragedy has obviously been excluded. No matter how tempting the thought, Riley's painting is no more 'Abstract Expressionism with constructive means' than 'Abstract Impressionism'. Right from the beginning the 'pleasures of sight' stood between her and Pollock's 'organic intensity'.[14] And there is also – let us happily admit it, although she makes little of it herself – a touch of female intuition which tells her that nature will always remain impregnable, no matter how radical and self-destructive the attempt to identify with it. But most importantly, at the end of the 1970s a mountain appeared on Riley's horizon: the artist (not the painter, the *artist*) Cézanne, that wild, uncouth temperament who provided such overwhelming proof of Proust's insight into the workings of the creative spirit. In his memoirs *Ce qu'il m'a dit* Gasquet recorded one of Cézanne's curiously casual jolted trains of thought: 'One has to sacrifice what one feels – you understand, it is enough that one feels. One never loses this, one's feeling. Not that I condemn it.'[15] It was an amazing insight conveyed in a wonderfully halting fashion. Whatever one sacrifices, a passionate desire for expression or the love of nature, and even for what one makes the sacrifice, whether for apples or landscapes or for curves and stripes, is basically unimportant. The decisive thing is that one makes a sacrifice because by doing so one loses nothing – other than the preoccupation with oneself. 'You can't simply go for being an artist as such', Riley said in an interview in 1988, 'the example of Cézanne makes it plain that you must be workmanlike in what you do.'[16]

Once the magic word – 'workmanlike' – has been spoken, the bewildering paradoxes of Riley's work unravel and produce a fully rounded meaning. It is not just that nature external to the artist cannot be reached directly. There is yet another aspect of abstraction, a practical view from the inside, which appears totally strange if considered in any theoretical way. Because of their professional sympathy for Cézanne's ethos of objectivity, art historians often find it difficult to see that his submission to the *motif* was by no means an ascetic restraint but, on the contrary, enabled him to properly articulate the monumental scale of his feelings. Visitors to Riley's 'work place' in London – four floors of studios and a living space under the roof – are often surprised by the strangely purposeful atmosphere, a mixture of urgency and gentleness, concentration and ease, in which she collaborates with her assistants. The surprise is justified. This calm and steady application contains Bridget Riley's impenetrable – because entirely open – secret. She makes her art like a workman who performs a particular essentially limited task to the best of his abilities. She knows that it is not at all necessary to tear yourself apart. It is enough to move out of the way, to avoid the interference of self-consciousness with the mainspring of human nature, which she quite unaffectedly calls 'spirit', by diverting the focus of attention to self-imposed limitations. In 1989 she defined this cunning, downright practical conception of 'art' with reference to Cézanne and the Western tradition: 'Painters have always needed a sort of veil upon which they can focus their direct

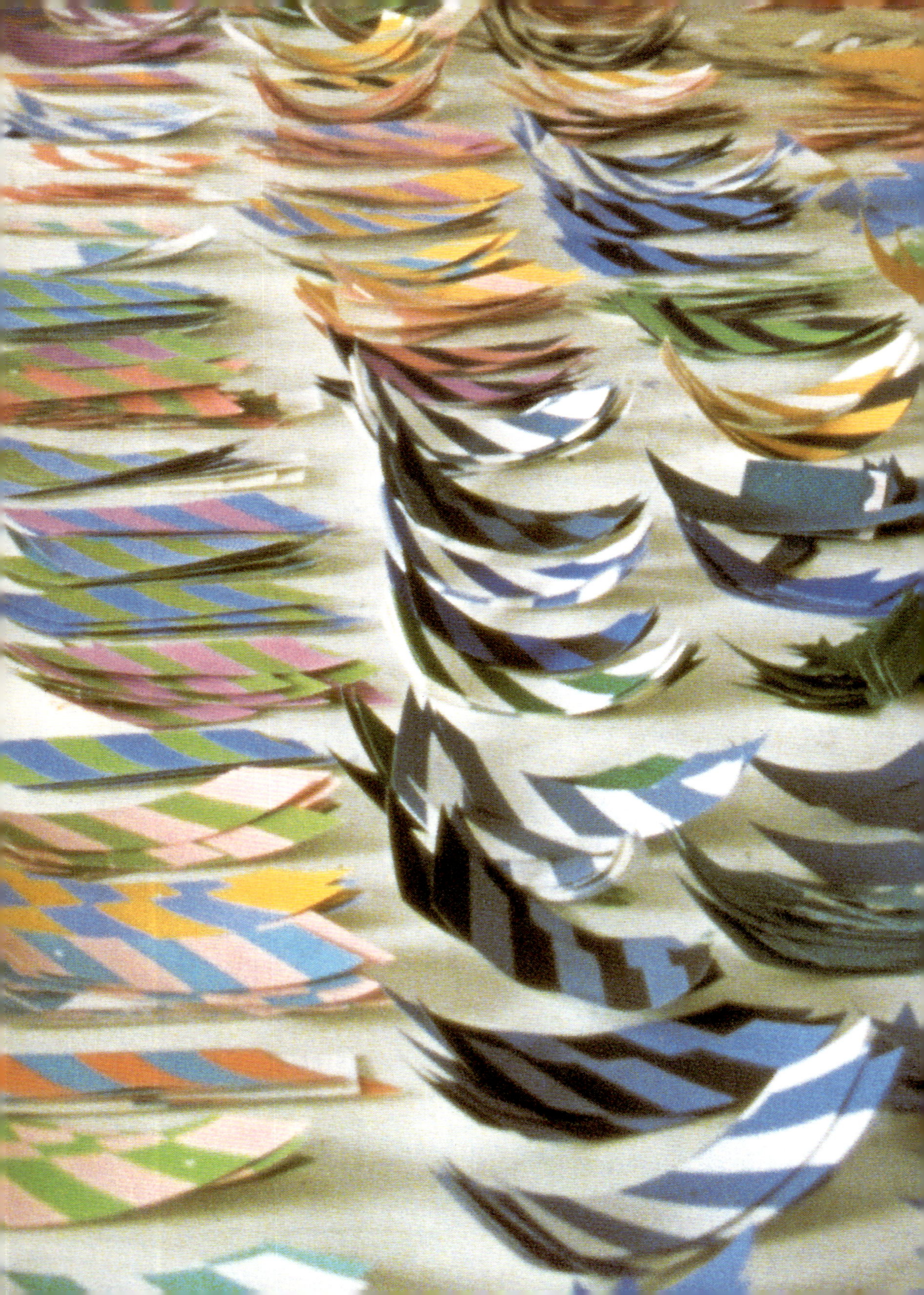

attention. It's as though the more fully the consciousness is absorbed, the greater the freedom of the spirit behind. In the tradition an important aspect of this veil was given by mythology and the Bible. If these spiritual perspectives are no longer available, the alternative is not plain realism. At the most, the painter may be led through the pursuit of his art, like Cézanne was, to 'realise' the veil of reality us such.'[17]

The image of the veil is obviously not coincidental. It is the nearest metaphor to what she herself is painting. Everything in Riley's art, other than the experience it creates, is part of a seamlessly woven veil. She sees and treats her mathematical forms with a lack of reverence that is incompatible with Constructivist orthodoxy. The geometric elements are just familiar and malleable enough to be used in the transformation of the 'commonplace' into the 'ravishing'. The paint quality itself, the physical surface of the paintings, is anonymous and bland because the 'lively quality of sight' is plainly not hand-made. But apart from a professional respect for the craftsmanship of her assistants she does not attach special status to the immaculate execution of her paintings. If there were another, better and more practical way of making a painting (if, say, Pollock's 'dripping' was more open to organisation, to revision and adjustment) then she would probably have no inhibitions in painting that way. For Riley's pictorial methods are only vehicles – 'agents' as she says – in a process of transformation. They serve firstly to banish from the picture plane all the findings, observations and suggestions gathered by chance, as well as any direct intrusion of taste. And if such paraphernalia nevertheless insinuate themselves into the painting, then the chosen means are sufficiently 'at arm's length' to bring them to light immediately and allow their removal. This is not for the sake of some obscure 'purity' or pretended 'absoluteness' of vision. With good reason Bridget Riley devotes much of her time outside the studio to cultivating her visual life: in 'nourishment' from nature, in the dialogue with older art and on the many journeys she has undertaken. She finds it difficult to deny herself the delights of genuine pictorial representation, but this denial is essential in order to allow for the lengthy, intimate and unaccountable process of trial and error by means of which the fabric of the painting begins to assume a character of its own. At times during its making the structure will have looked shockingly convoluted and chaotic, almost inaccessible, and at other moments it may have appeared to have fallen apart completely, sunk into inertia. But then quite suddenly, and in a way which always takes Riley herself by surprise, the web of relationships prompts just the reaction which restores to her the 'lively quality of sight', her *petite*

(opposite)
Bridget Riley's work table

sensation which had seemed unattainable by more direct means. This recovered sensation is not quite like anything previously known. The world of sensations seen as from the 'interior of a tree' is not a combined reflection of the inner human world and the outer natural world but an amalgam of perception and sensation refined through and obtained by the process of abstraction.

On the occasion of Riley's first European retrospective in 1970–71 Bryan Robertson described this characteristic property very pertinently when he spoke in the introduction to the catalogue of the 'unsentimental economy' of the artist's feelings.[18] Indeed, there is no oversensitivity, not a smidgin of grandiloquence and not a trace of raw and unprocessed experience in Riley's art. The balance is perfect. Just ten years later it was this 'sentimental education' which John Russell, in an allusion to Flaubert's novel, celebrated as the revelation of her retrospective in 1978–80.[19]

Having restricted her use of colour to three, at the most five hues until virtually the end of the 1970s she has now arrived at a palette of approximately one hundred carefully selected colour values; about thirty blues and greens and around twenty shades in the red and yellow areas. From these she selects a carefully weighed and restricted 'colour bracket' for each painting, not unlike a musician who chooses a particular key. However, the 'unsentimental economy' has been retained even within abundance, as though nature itself had a hand in it.

After Bridget Riley had given a lecture at the Berlin University of the Arts in December 1990, a female student came forward at the end of the discussion and said, in a slightly awkward way, that the colours of the new paintings seemed to her somewhat excessive, overwhelming – like stained glass windows in a Gothic church. 'You couldn't have said anything more beautiful', Riley replied, 'it was worth coming here for that alone!' It is fair to assume that Bridget Riley was imaginatively reborn in the 1980s. An avowed member of the 'workmen's' guild she has quietly ascended to the caste of warriors whose coat-of-arms is the last entry in Delacroix's journal: 'The first merit of a painting is to be a feast for the eye.'[20]

1 In the case of Matisse this 'nourishment' meant working from the model and modelling in clay. See Clara T. MacChesney, "A Talk with Matisse" (1912), in Jack D. Flam (ed.), *Matisse on Art*. London 1973, p. 50–53.

2 David Sylvester, "Bridget Riley", *The New Statesman*, 25 May 1962.

3 Thomas B. Hess: "You can hang it in the hall", *Art News*, Vol. 64, No. 2, April 1965, p. 41 ff. The last sentence of this polemic, which is as vacuous as it has been influential in putting down the exhibition *The Responsive Eye*, runs: "And if it causes a headache, you

can hang it in the Pentagon". (p. 50).

4 Anton Ehrenzweig, foreword to the exhibition catalogue *Bridget Riley*, Gallery One, London 1963.

5 Bridget Riley, "Perception Is the Medium", *Art News*, Vol. 64, No. 6, October 1965, p 32 ff. Reprinted in *The Eye's Mind* (1999), pp. 66–68, and in the catalogue of the Tate Gallery retrospective exhibition *Bridget Riley*, ed. Paul Moorhouse, London 2003, p. 207.

6 See note 2.

7 See note 4.

8 "The Pleasures of Sight" (1984), in *The Eye's Mind* (1999), p. 34.

9 Bryan Robertson, "Introduction" to *Bridget Riley. Paintings and Drawings 1951–1971*, catalogue of the Hayward Gallery retrospective exhibition, London: The Arts Council of Great Britain, 1971, p. 14.

10 *The Eye's Mind* (1999), p. 32.

11 Marcel Proust: *Remembrance of' Things Past*, transl. C.K. Scott Moncrieff, vol. 12, London 1931, p. 467. The original French reads: 'on ne peut refaire ce qu' on aime qu' en le renonçant.'

12 Samuel Beckett, *Proust*, London 1931, p. 17.

13 Pollock's reply to Hans Hofmann when the latter saw Pollock's painting for the first time and remarked: 'You do not work from nature'. Quoted after Bruce Glaser, "Jackson Pollock: An interview with Lee Krasner" (1967), reprinted in Pepe Karmel (ed.), *Jackson Pollock: Interviews, Articles, and Reviews*, New York: Museum of Modern Art, 1999, p. 28.

14 On this basic concept of Pollock see the author's essay "Abstraktion als Antithese. Vom Sinn der Entgegensetzung in der Malerei Piet Mondrians and Jackson Pollocks", in H. Poos (ed.), *Kunst als Antithese*, Berlin 1990, pp. 211–240.

15 Quoted after P. M. Doran, *Conversations avec Cézanne*, Paris 1978, p. 152.

16 "Personal Interview" (1988), reprinted in *The Eye's Mind* (1999), p. 25.

17 "The Colour Connection" (1989), reprinted in *The Eye's Mind* (1999), p 173.

18 Bryan Robertson, "Introduction" to *Bridget Riley. Paintings and Drawings 1951–1971*, London 1971, p. 18 (cf. note 10).

19 John Russell. "The Cogency of Bridget Riley", *The New York Times*, 28 January 1979.

20 Eugène Delacroix, *Journal 1822–1863*, Paris: Librairie Plon, 1982, p. 808.

Introductory essay to the catalogue of the exhibition *Bridget Riley: Paintings 1982–1992*, Nürnberg-London, 1992, pp. 3–28.

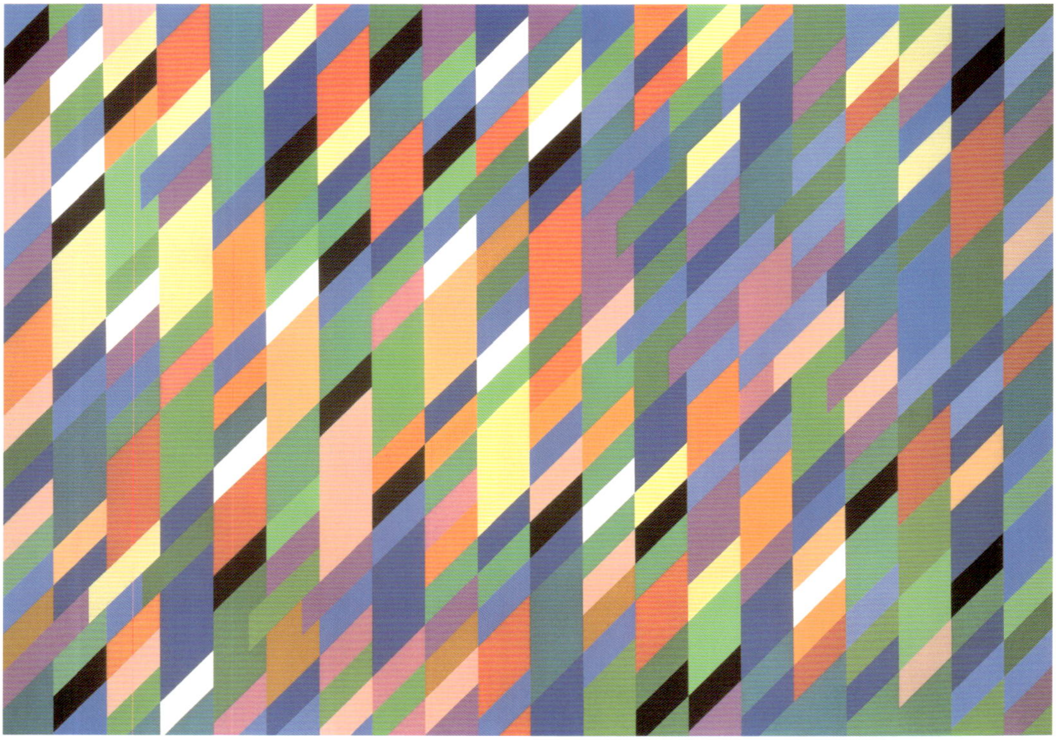

High Sky 2 1992

Chromatic and Plastic Interaction

On the functioning of pictorial colour in the work of Bridget Riley

1996

In the years 1871–73 Hermann von Helmholtz toured several cities in Germany giving a series of lectures titled "Optical Observations on Painting". Although this was at precisely the same time as the germination of Impressionism he makes no mention of this contemporary development in painting. Since his habilitation on "The Theory of Composite Colours" (1852) the physiology of the senses had been a central area in his research and the act of looking a favourite subject. But the scientist Helmholtz had too firm a humanist grounding not to begin by admitting the limits of his competence: 'Compared with those who have long been familiar and well acquainted with the wonderful region of art I must appear like a wandering traveller who has entered through steep and stony border mountains, although in doing so I have reached some points which offered good views.'[1] This turns out to be a charming understatement. With regard to the relationship of light and colour in perception Helmholtz makes it unmistakably clear that, whatever the tradition may have thought of it, for the modern physiologist the concept of imitation of nature in art is simply a theoretical surreptition. In a strictly empirical sense no colour sensation can be represented adequately. Throughout all the four parts of his series of lectures runs the thesis that the painter does not perform a 'transcription of an object' but the 'translation of an impression into another scale of sensations which belong to a different order of stimulation in the perceiving eye and through which the organ speaks a different language in its responses to the outside world.'[2]

Despite its old-fashioned scientific phraseology this statement still defines the persistent problem of pictorial colour in a pertinent and appropriate manner: no transcription of an object but the translation of an impression into a different scale of sensations. The insight of the scientist shows how liberating a view from the 'border mountains' sometimes can be for the specialists in the plains, particularly when scientific prowess is paired with a broad understanding of the subject. The battle for modern art in Germany might have been spared a great deal of tub-thumping and nonsense had the interested public, including art historians, taken notice of Helmholtz's argument because he described, quite unintentionally, the radically new plastic problem which the French painters of Classical Modernism had encountered. Instead of simply making sketches and studies from nature which could then be developed into compositions in the studio according to the established patterns of landscape painting, the artists *en plein air* tried to be faithful to an unprecedented experience. Nature empirically perceived is not a preformed image which only required depiction but a spectacle of light and colour which eludes imitation. Perhaps Helmholtz's formula 'no transcription – translation into a different scale of sensation' is still the best resolution of the paradox that in some of Monet's most successful paintings such as, for instance, the series focusing on the Japanese Bridge (1899–1900), nature seems to be present with an almost hallucinatory immediacy, though probably no single colour value would stand the test of empirical verification.

This astonishing historical coincidence is by no means diminished by the fact that Helmholtz's own concept of art as propounded in "Optical Observations on Painting" is rather less original.[3] The scientist and lover of art, who made some illuminating observations on Veronese's colourism, remained firmly within the boundaries of the classicist academic tradition thinking that the necessity of 'translation' offers the artist the chance of 'refinement of the sensory impression'.[4] In a similar way Roger de Piles, the advocate of the Rubenists in the 17th century dispute over which took primacy, colour or drawing, had argued the distinction between the natural colour phenomenon ('couleur') and pictorial colour ('coloris'). He recognised, like Helmholtz, that pictorial colour is obviously much less brilliant than colour in nature and consequently asked for a 'science de coloris' from the painter to compensate for this discrepancy. The painter should off-set the loss of 'éclat' and 'vigueur', which he ascribed to the flatness and the observational distance of the picture in general, by a 'savante exaggération', a skillful distortion or lie for the sake of truth.[5] But be it either refinement or compensation, the tendency is in principle the same. Both the modern scientist and the critical scholar of painting can imagine the translation only as a transport of one and the same thing, i.e. the colourfulness of colour – with at best the possibility of improvement. The true metamorphosis, that in the transition from one scale of sensations to another the character of sensation itself might change, remains outside their scope.

Such a transformation is indeed difficult to envisage and would have to be regarded as fairly improbable if it had not in fact been achieved. How else could colour appear in a painting if not as colourful? But at the high point of the colourism of French 19th century painting a painter challenged the seeming evidence of this logic. Quite apart from scientific insights and objections any enquiry into pictorial colour has to take into account such surprises and challenges of a principal nature because a subject lies at the heart of its pursuit which is not only a scientific matter to define and explain. This is an essential difference from other art historical topics such as, for instance, the iconographical or semiological change of the colour blue from Fra Angelico to Yves Klein. Where pictorial colour is at stake painting is not only an object but also an 'organ' – to quote Schelling's famous phrase – of recognition: not only a witness but also a partner in the investigation of a subject matter which is more changeable than the scientific approach presumes and at the same time more objective than the art of interpretation would like it to be. The characteristics of pictorial colour do not change continuously or permanently, but when they do change, when by translating perceptual colour into the picture plane the sensation of colour itself is changed, as in the paintings of Cézanne, then a new field of exploration is opened up for both the art of painting and scientific enquiry.

Cézanne and the Depth of Colour Space

The problem as such is familiar: in Cézanne's painting the chromatic quality of colour is secondary to its spatial function in the picture plane. However, it is essential to see that this is achieved not just by adding a new compositional factor, but rather that the particular space of the paintings seems to spring from a hitherto unknown absoluteness of colour perception. The painter Cézanne seems to *see* more empirically, as it were, than the physiologist Helmholtz would have thought possible for our sense of sight. On the 23 October 1904 he wrote to Bernard: 'I am absolutely certain that an optical impression (une sensation optique) is formed in our visual organ which causes us to order the planes represented by colour sensations (les plans representés par des sensations colorantes) *according to light*, half-tone and quarter-tone.' That is to say, initially we see only coloured planes in different positions and distances to each other which we *then* start to distinguish and to order as steps of lightness and darkness, as Cézanne emphasises by underlining 'par la lumière'. But we do not do this on the basis of perception, not as painters as he shrewdly remarks: 'La lumière n'existe, donc pas pour le peintre.'[6] For a painter (as a picture maker, not as an explorer of nature) light does not exist apart from colour like some sort of achromatic source, or as an independent reflection on a coloured surface, but is always a colour among colours. In other words, the difference between colour and light in the practice of painting is in itself simply a difference of colour.

This absolute truth to perception from the outset leads to consequences which do not comply with the well-known cliché of the difference between Cézanne and the Impressionists as a comparison between a painting of Monet's Japanese Bridge, *Le Bassin aux Nymphéas* (1899, The Art Museum, Princeton University), with a similar motif by Cézanne, *Le Pont* (1888–90, Pushkin Museum, Moscow), shows. Cézanne's painting is clearly more 'superficial' in the sense that he bases his pictorial organisation solely on the 'planes represented by colour sensations', whereas Monet by underpinning his radiant colour explosions with a firm tonal structure relates less directly to perception. A black-and-white reproduction of his work proves that this is not only due to the often assumed 'photographic eye' of the arch-impressionist, because the extremes of light and dark are reduced in favour of a mid-tone pitch conducive to the effect of colour, and the transitions are developed continuously, without abrupt cuts or breaks. In short, the magical natural glitter of colour brilliance in Monet's painting takes place in a pictorial space which is *not* formed by pure colour sensations alone – but more traditionally, by the compositional support of a light-dark continuum.

With Cézanne this is quite different. Here no continuous tonal underpinning carries the colour organisation. The particular planes of colour seem to work out their common space amongst each other as a perceptual quality which is different to but not separate from colour; and most importantly, this perception of space comes into being through the exercise of sight itself instead of conditioning and accommodating our vision in advance like a formal projection. Contrasts of different sorts – such as chromatic shades, tonal intervals, varying quantities, changing tempos and opposing directions – engage our eyes in a rhythm which seems to be anything but a steady flow. The distinctions of here and there shift abruptly depending on where one focuses, and yet return periodically. Thus for instance the sharply broken passage in the middle under the bridge seems to jump momentarily far beyond the neighbouring planes – only to sink back the next moment, when the eye moves towards the trees on the left, into the area of reflections of the bridge construction. As one continues looking this changing perception of near and far discloses a space the dimensions of which far exceed the tunnel-like projection of Monet's view under the Japanese Bridge, although Cézanne's space does not rely upon a construct of depth and, if one looks at the individual planes as such, appears rather disrupted and shallow. Maurice Merleau-Ponty has said of this space: 'The depth of the painting (as well as the painted height and width) presents itself from one-does-not-know-where [on ne sait d'ou], springing up from the pictorial support.'[7]

Nevertheless Monet's painting appears to be more colourful – but only because we recognise our usual colour impression in it, though in a heightened, celebrational form. As a rule we do not experience colour in the first instance of sensation as Cézanne treats it. In spite of our habitual modern sensualism we are always looking for objects in space long before we note their colour or even become interested in it. These are the simple metaphysics of everyday life which one may find either fascinating or problematic. Be this as it may, as active people in the world we are to an astonishing degree colour-blind because there seems to be no need to pay attention to colour as such in order to orientate ourselves. We behave rather like the spectator at a black-and-white movie who does not miss colour, seeing it implicitly as it were; or like the art historian who seems to be oblivious to the fact that he might have overlooked something when he mentions the colour of a painting only in passing. It is precisely this peripheral presence of colour in our daily experience which Monet re-creates in the scale of pictorial colour, with all its specific characteristics: surprising, fugitive, precious, and benign. He establishes an equivalent for the experience of physical space by supporting his colours with a coherent modelling of light and dark tones. Hence the impression of a magical hyper-reality – whereas Cézanne's colourism confronts us with the enigma of a radical change, a transformation of experience. In his painting the objects on whose surface we normally see colour figure merely as positions or places of colour, and the space in which everything exists is constituted by the correlation of these places.

It would be silly to try and explain this change in the mode of perception by a physiological hypothesis or even to justify it as a wilful expressive distortion of the 'normal' way of seeing.[8] All the real challenges in art are not disposed of by explanations. They are either slowly settled by increasing familiarity or they are corroborated in their viability by repetition and development. Significantly both applies to Cézanne's unusual organisation of the 'sensations colorantes'. The astonishing popularity of the great Cézanne exhibitions of the past two decades has impressively shown to what extent human perception is flexible and malleable – and this in the interest of a more satisfactory conception and recognition of what has been *seen*, because the majority of people visiting these exhibitions will not have gone for the sake of art alone. But what is even more important, through their assimilation of Cézanne's approach, artists in this century have confirmed the significance of this change in our concept of space.

One cannot speak of a direct and determining influence of Cézanne in this regard because each time cognizance of the level of his endeavour has to be regained before any correspondence can take place. The sporadic and discontinuous development of this issue is therefore integral to it. Thus the spatial character of the colour planes played an important role for both Matisse and Picasso at the beginning of the 1920s when they tried to consolidate their earlier achievements. Whereas after the Second World War the aesthetic positivism of American art with its liberating simplifications 'flatness', 'space', 'what you see is what you see' seemed to have rendered obsolete the old distinctions between the surface of the canvas and the picture-plane, between colour as phenomenon and as pictorial element. But in the arts the jettisoning of ballast is often only the start of a new assessment of true weights. In the past two decades painters such as Frank Stella and Bridget Riley who in the 1960s belonged to the most radical exponents of a break with the dead conventions of European painting have increasingly realised the necessity of reconsidering the category of pictorial space if painting is not to deprive itself of one of its most particular characteristics. Whereas Stella – of all

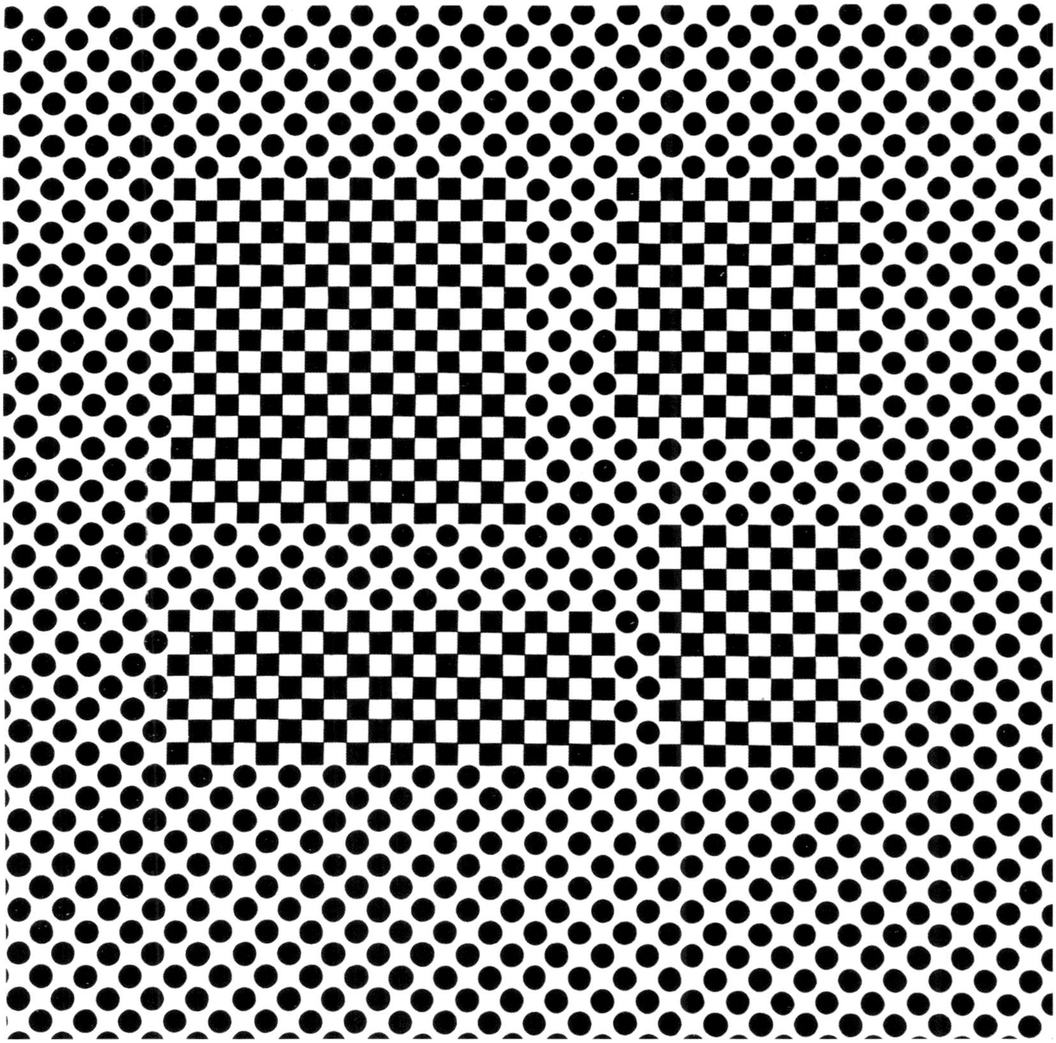

Hidden Squares 1961

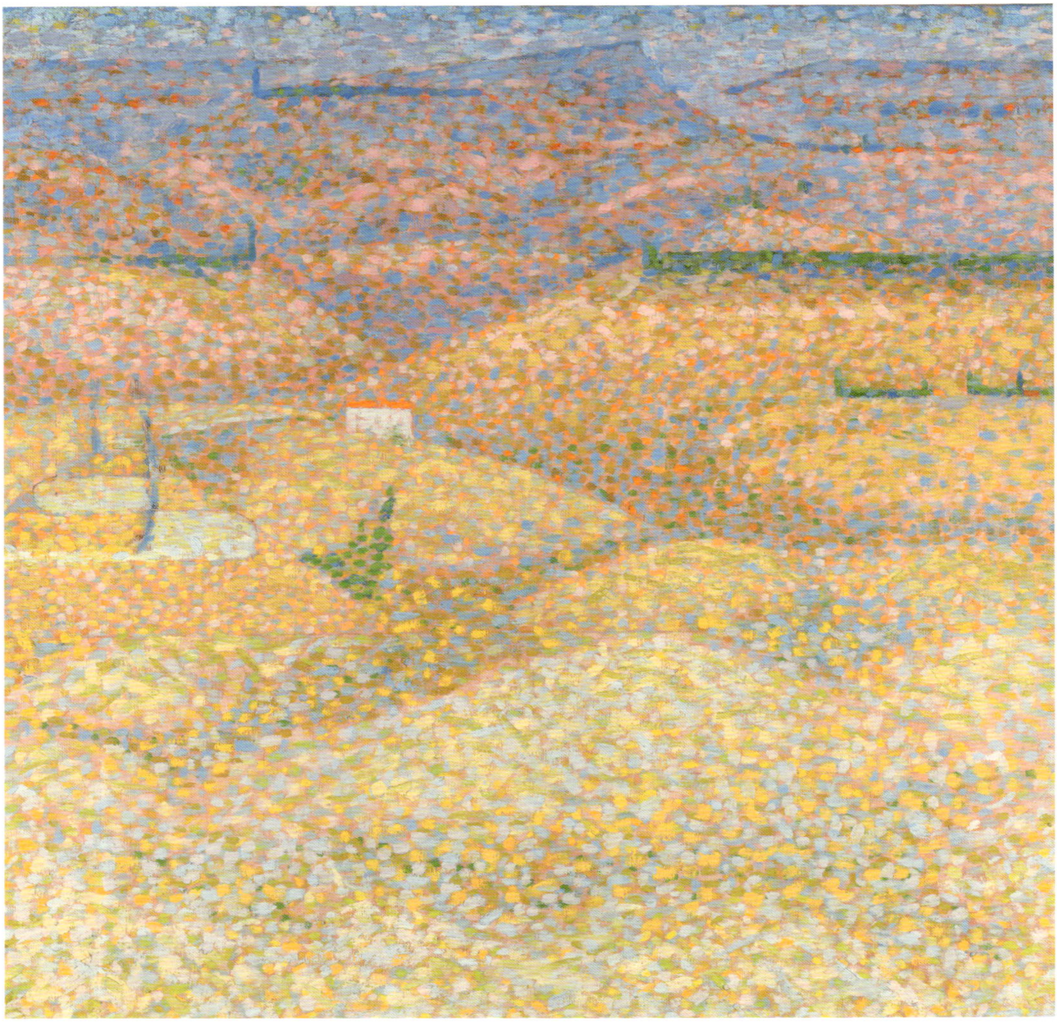

Pink Landscape 1960

American painters – discovered for himself the dramatic spatial performances of Caravaggio and Rubens,[9] the English painter Bridget Riley has accomplished in her development the transition from a primarily chromatic organisation to a plastic spatial concept of pictorial colour.

Bridget Riley: From 'Chromo-luminarisme' to 'Plasticity'

Riley's starting point at the end of the 1950s was the Neo-Impressionism of George Seurat. In retrospect her last big figurative painting, *Pink Landscape* (1960), reveals the extent to which the unmistakable dynamism of her abstract paintings already informs this early phase. Riley diverges from the orthodox method of 'chromo-luminarisme' (Signac) by not confining the divisionist analysis and the pointillist application of colour simply to the adequate representation of colour's appearance in light. Instead, the motif of hovering midday heat in the hills around Siena shortly before the outbreak of a thunderstorm, seems to have offered a pretext to chromatically evoke the moment of dissolution of the pictorial subject into a turbulent event threatening the synthesis of perception. The dominant contrast of orange and pale blue is intensified rather than harmonised by the derivatives of pink and yellow-green; and the additive totality of the colour impression has been replaced by an explosive disintegration of the pictorial structure.

The rigorous black-and-white works of the 1960s with which Bridget Riley became a leading exponent of the emerging Op art movement have only temporarily and superficially concealed this origin of her art. The reversal of the optical synthesis aiming at a release of the constituent contrast energies also governs her treatment of the abstract forms of geometry as *Hidden Squares* (1961), a typical painting of the early years, makes plain. Again the structure is poised at the critical point where the dissolution and genesis of form equal each other, although now this is no longer achieved via the depiction of a natural phenomenon but as an immediate manifestation of a 'state of mind' (Riley) which affects the spectator directly. Thereby the black-and-white contrast does not merely act as a description of forms. As in the tonal studies of Seurat the achromatic black and white is used as a kind of quintessence of the contrast energy in colour. Thus the beginning of the explicit colour work in 1967 does not amount to a principal re-orientation but only extends and modifies the prevailing dramatic conception. While the organisation of the black-and-white works culminated in the cyclic recurrence of strictly controlled upheavals of perception, with the introduction of colour contrast these moments of sudden disturbance receded in favour of the diffusion of disembodied coloured light.

In the years 1967–79 Bridget Riley concentrated exclusively on the generation and articulation of coloured light under the particular conditions of pictorial colour. As opposed to the 'chromo-luminarisme' of the Neo-Impressionists the works of this period do not relate to any pre-existing reality whatsoever, neither to natural observation nor to abstract optical laws. Each painting formulates a connection of visual events or happenings which will take place in this particular way solely among the selected elements, according to their specific scale, and within the unique constellation of the structural framework.[10] Only the way of procedure can be somehow generalised: at first two, then three and eventually five colours are juxtaposed on a white ground in such a way that two alternative forms of 'behaviour' can happen: either the colours optically mix, from a faint colour spread to a full fusion, or they polarise one another leading in one instance to an increased intensity, in the other to a neutralisation of hue. However this general description does not take into account the crucial plastic problem with which Riley has been battling for a long time. She realised that colour contrasts could not be activated by the same complex formal structures as the black-and-white oppositions. 'Colour energies need a virtually neutral vehicle if they are to develop uninhibitedly', she summarised in 1972. 'The repeated stripe seems to meet these conditions.'[11]

This formal restriction seems to have stimulated rather than inhibited the constructive inventiveness of the artist as can be seen in the ingenious structure of *Zing 1* (1972). It consists of the even repetition of vertical bands each of which contains three stripes in red, green and blue which mutually cross each other in a manner not unlike the twisting of ribbons. If one reads this device from top to bottom first green diagonally crosses the other two colours, then red passes over blue and green, followed by blue through green and red, and finally green again, closing the sequence. This four-times crossing (called in Riley's studio parlance 'colour-twist') effectively de-stabilises the colour identities because the supporting stripes as they taper into acute points can no longer protect the particular colour they carry against the influence of neighbouring hues. Within the colour bands as well as along the edges of the white intervals between them the local colours of the painting shift into their opposite extremities: blue into blue-violet and blue-green, green into turquoise and yellow-green, red into orange and carmine. Moreover, through the paired mirroring of the twisting bands horizontal zones of vividly changing colour-light expand across the canvas flooding the vertical structure of the painting with a luminous totality of colour.

The possibility of releasing this disembodied light depends on a condition which became comprehensible to its full extent only when Bridget Riley had moved away from it. Despite all advances and shifts in her pictorial structure the conception of the space in which the colour activity takes place remained remarkably constant from the first sparse stripe combinations right up to the full colour clusters of the curve paintings at the end of the 1970s. No matter whether we see the discharge of colour against a pervasive white ground or alternating with successive grey sequences, whether the perceptual tints appear to dissolve into a diffused shine or – very rarely – to glow against a dark field: in all cases the area of this interaction is a homogeneous achromatic continuum turned towards the spectator without a sense of 'depth' as it were. This evenness and unity of space may be an obvious prerequisite of a painting primarily focused on the relationship between colour and light, as the precedent of Monet shows. But for an abstract approach which does not confront the vagaries of colour in nature such a reduction is rather a restriction of the range of pictorial possibilities than a real advantage.

Interestingly Riley's own criticism did not tackle directly, as one might have expected, the 'even distribution of incidents' as she herself calls the pictorial convention that emerged in the wake of *all-over painting*. The re-orientation of her work in 1980 was prompted by a dissatisfaction with the limitations of the colour presence in her paintings that had been mounting for quite a while. The two feats of her art – the dispersal of local colour in ethereal *arpeggios* and *glissandi* to which the onomatopoetic title Zing alludes, and the dissolution of the single colour identities in a luminous totality – had gradually, as she came to master them, revealed certain insufficiencies which she tried to improve upon. The changing from acrylic to oil paint helped to increase the brilliance and saturation of colour, and in dispensing with the uniform field organisation in favour of specific groups and blocks she aimed at emphasising the 'colour character' as she calls it. However, despite the urgency of her efforts the decisive push came from outside. During a visit to Egypt in the winter of 1979/80 Bridget Riley discovered the palette of the ancient Egyptian painters that had remained constant for more than 2000 years. Although initially she felt no more than an unexpected excitement at this discovery, a few weeks later in London she began to re-create these colours from memory: a brick red, an ochre yellow, one blue, two greens (yellow and blue green), as well as black and white.

The response to such a remote stimulus does not seem quite so strange when one recalls that the task given to the Egyptian painters, to preserve the radiant riches of life in the eternal night of the tombs, literally fulfils the directive which Cézanne gave to Emile Bernard: 'The light thus does not exist for the painter.' Riley's 'Egyptian palette' is, broadly speaking, as authentic as a free appropriation can be, including the significant divergence that the blue is raised in tone to a similar pitch as the red and the two greens in order to facilitate chromatic interaction. There was initially no intention to change the concept of releasing the light energies inherent in colour. The new stripe formations differed from the preceding ones only in their replacing of the luminous overall sensation by a free rhythmic grouping of bands which exhibited distinct and contrasting colour characters. Two opposing activities can be observed: where colours are grouped in their natural order (red-yellow, blue-green) strong harmonies appear which can, when they enclose one another (e. g. yellow-red-yellow), develop into accents of such brilliance that they seem to 'flame', as it were. Conversely a kind of optical *sfumato* of transparent grey begins to cloud the colours when oppositions (red/green, blue/yellow) and contrasts of intensity (blue/red) prevail and are extended to full chords.

It is important to see that this change in the structure did not affect the continuous space of the paintings while the colour groupings were still controlled by a rhythmic beat of black strokes and white intervals. The blendings, echoes, and discrepancies were firmly kept within a taut lateral flatness which seemed only to open up towards the spectator, impenetrable in its frontality. But when Bridget Riley eliminated the black bands the sensation changed. *Cherry Autumn* (1983, Birmingham City Art Gallery) is a key painting in this regard. Although all the means of the new colour organisation – cumulative highlights and neutralising contrasts, block-like fusions and broken passages – can be found in this painting it is not the shallow expanse of colour which determines its appearance but a dynamism from an unexpected depth. Instead of simply corresponding amongst each other in one and the same plane, the juxtapositions, pairings and groupings of colour seem to spring up from 'one-does-not-know-where', adopting different positions in space. Or, in another way of reading the painting, the planes appear at changing distances in perception. The first puzzle, whether the blue-green bands are in front of or behind the ridge-like formations of yellow-green-yellow, and where in relation to this the red/green constellations figure, soon disappears as one realises that this fluctuating space is in itself

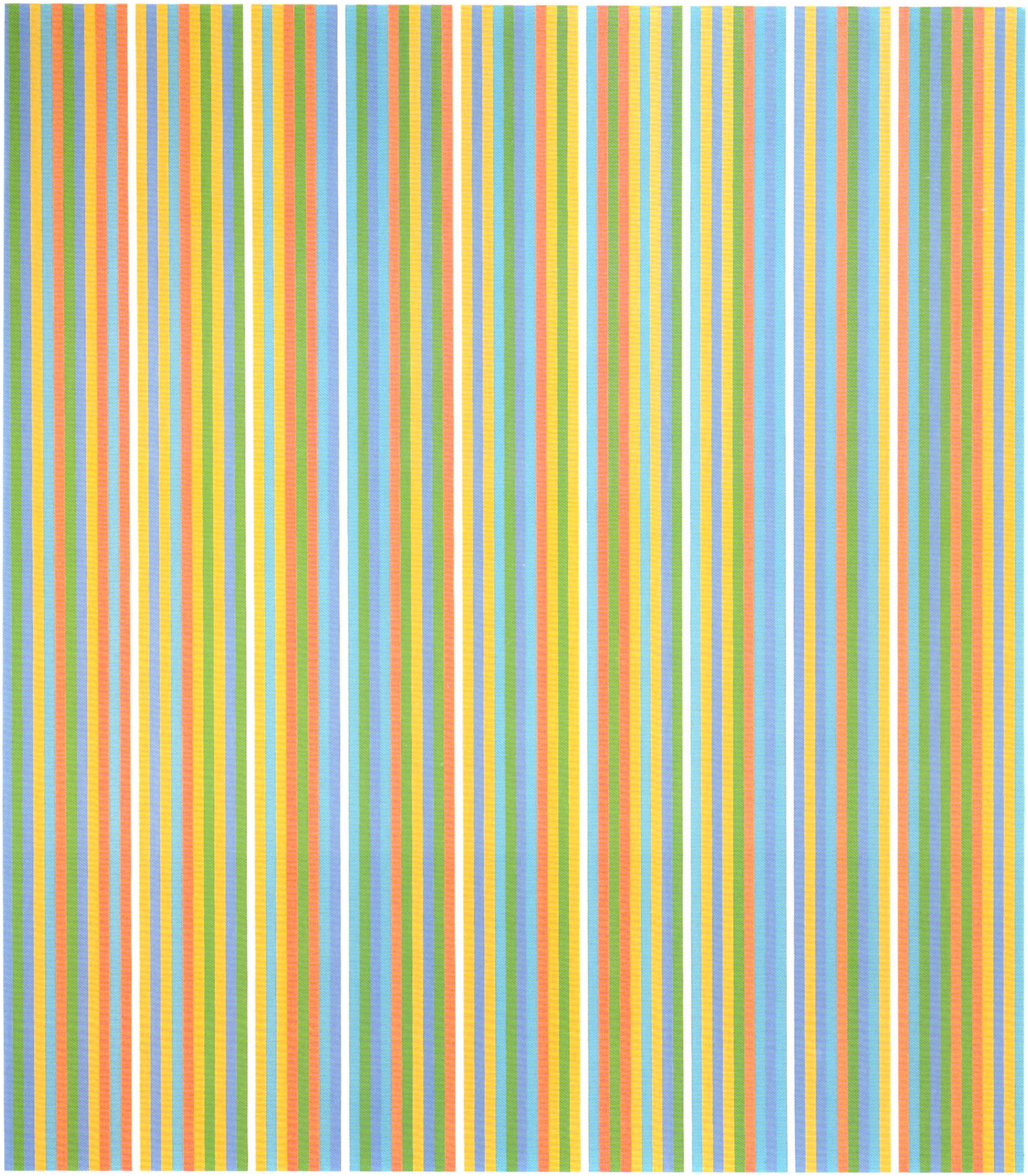

Cherry Autumn 1983

clearly and firmly built. The greatest plastic depth of the painting opens up towards the centre while towards the sides the *repoussoir* effect of colour diminishes.

This discovery was fundamental. Starting from primarily chromatic interests rooted in colour divisionism Riley had rediscovered on the basis of autonomous pictorial colour the problem of the 'planes represented by colour sensations'. Although at the beginning she still believed that both forms of colour activity – the chromatic and the spatial – could be reconciled she soon realised that the luminous interaction of colours across the surface and the shifting tensions of the 'plasticity of the medium', as she describes the spatial potential of colour, in fact obstructed one another. In 1986 she therefore discarded the formal restrictions which she had adopted for the sake of chromatic interaction and went for the development of colour's spatial qualities. Asked in 1990 about this sacrifice of the colour magic which for more than a decade was connected with her art, she answered: 'Well, I wanted *more*. A way of working which allowed me to get to grips with plastic issues, to get closer to the real problems of painting. I threw out notions of what the result should be. I crossed the vertical register with a strong diagonal, upsetting the balance of the canvas. That gave me time. I could work against those directional forces, counteracting them through colour and rhythm.'[12]

The particular steps of this major change were shown in the exhibition *Bridget Riley: Paintings 1982–1992* which in 1992–93 toured several venues in Germany and Great Britain.[13] *High Sky 2* (1992, Neues Museum, Nürnberg) can be seen as a culmination and a conclusion of this critical phase. The previous stripe formation has been transformed into a vertical register of wide bands that is crossed in its full extension by a grid of parallel diagonals which follow exclusively the rising direction from bottom left to top right. Far from simply serving as a scaffold for colour this structure puts forward the dynamic imbalance against which all the configurations and rhythms of colour are pitched. For this Riley employs a greatly extended scale of colour which along with the basic contrasts includes a broad range of tones and shades and is specifically selected for each painting. In *High Sky 2* the palette consists of 20 distinct hues apart from black and white: six variants of green and three of red form the basic colour contrast, and this main axis is supported and modified by four blues, two violets, two shades of orange and a group of pale yellows and reds which Riley calls 'cream', 'pink' and 'apricot'.

The general disposition of the colours seems at first glance to emphasise in a broad and loose manner the absent counter-diagonal. Starting with big light blocks and driven, as it were, by a flock of black and white rhomboids a predominantly green formation travels from top left to bottom right, tightening and taking on tempo as the passage loses body and weight. But this literal counter-action – the volume of colour opposing the linear direction – is only the compositional framework within which the loops of perception, the real movement of the painting, take place. The turbulence of the rising and falling arcs is both enhanced and at the same time checked by a qualitative distinction of 'places' in the painting. For instance there is a noticeably darker patch in the upper right quarter, consisting of blue, green and violet. Through the extension and reduction of the rhomboid units by one third, this area is rhythmically accentuated so that it appears to turn anti-clockwise. It is due to such frictions and abrupt changes that the circulating momentum is sustained and the colour perception generates a distinctly fluid sense of space which continually shifts. Riley has precisely described this genesis of pictorial space from opposing local distinctions:

> "I think of space as another plastic agent grounded in colour organisation. As you know, colours can adopt different planes, similar ones or approximately the same, according to the context in which they are placed. So a certain green, for instance, may be pushed forward by one group of relationships and nearby the same green, with different affiliations, may counteract that step by drawing back. Meanwhile adjacent colours may be taking up spatial positions which emphasise, modify, or even reverse the planes of those greens. In this way a gentle kind of emerging and receding syncopation arises that can pick up pace, sometimes developing into a rhythm."[14]

The spatial range of *High Sky 2* is still, however, rather confined. The compositional emphasis on the counter-diagonal and the contrast relationships of colour provide a coherent tension in the picture plane which only allows for a limited play of depth. But the more recent paintings are explicitly engaged in that non-illusionistic depth particular to colour perception for which the artist has been searching since the mid-1980s: 'Pictorial space is deep in the sense that there is nothing behind, as it were, no ultimate base or distance to which it relates.'[15] In *Reflection 1* (1994) the composition strongly resembles a musical development of composite colour themes, 'colour compounds' (Riley), which, as our perceptual activity becomes involved, take up distinctly different positions above and below one another. Although the lightest tones

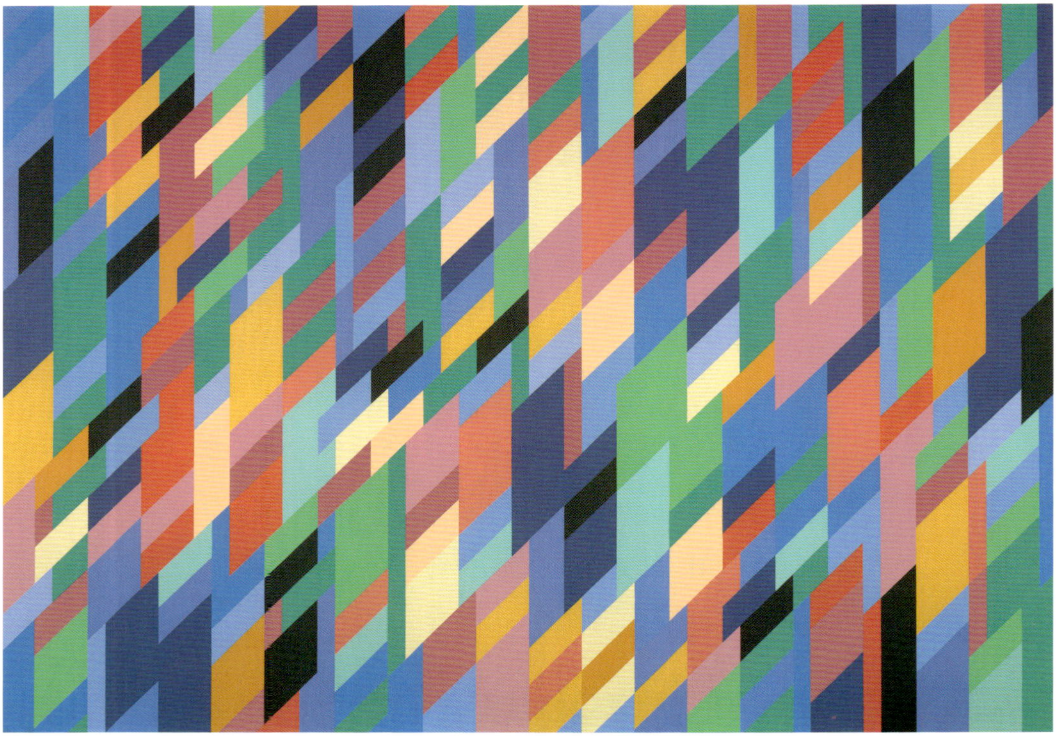

Reflection 1 1994

altogether seem to dance like twinkling reflections above all the other colour planes, the effect of depth is not based – at least not predominantly – on light-dark relationships. Those nearly black rhomboids for instance, stating the deepest tonal level, seem in some constellations to belong also to the highest or nearest spatial positions. The increased span of the colour space appears to spring from a more general change in the structure. The subdivision of the vertical register by an irregularly recurring proportion of one third permits more flexible transitions, and this new flexibility in the metre is supported by more differentiated and more subtle colour relationships. One of the major motifs, a 'compound' of blue, black and red, is modulated by derivatives of blue-red and violet towards a kind of blue tenor in such away that even strong green notes are included despite their latent contrast. Only the spurious yellow, orange and bronze shades form a direct though unobtrusive opposition, a flanking sub-motif which is related to the main theme simply through the similar tonal level of 'cream' and 'apricot', i.e. pale ochre and rose-yellow. It seems as though Bridget Riley has begun to modify and complement the primacy of contrast, which she had brought from her earlier light-orientated paintings into the new plastic space of colour, in favour of a new pictorial order which encompasses both harmonies and contrasts.

Colour as the Element of Sight

Building with the plastic interactions of colour has a certain dramatic function in Riley's painting. But her particular practice nevertheless allows a more general reflection on the concept of European colourism. The function of colour in painting does not seem to be confined to colourful appearance as such. When Bridget Riley herself was asked 1989 to select an exhibition from the collection of the National Gallery in London she presented under the title "The Colour Connection" to the surprise of many people, also a painting by El Greco and two works by Poussin.[16] And in her lecture "Colour for the Painter" at the Darwin College, Cambridge, she argued that Titian had not found his way to colour painting through a chromatic interest alone. The first stage of his development up to the *Assunta* (1518, Chiesa dei Frari, Venice), she claims, is distinguished by the invention of a particular form of 'drawing with colour'.[17]

One can indeed understand the origin of explicit colour painting at the beginning of the 16th century as the answer to a problem which had been thrown up by the projective perspectival construction of pictorial space: the positions of the objects in a mathematically construed space do not necessarily coincide in our visual perception with the planes of their colour. The unstable spatial relationships of colours amongst each other required a different, more flexible form of organisation than the fixation of points, directions and proportions in a static monocular system. In this respect Titian's conception of pictorial colour as a 'simile of creation', described so brilliantly by Theodor Hetzer still retains its singular importance.[18] But the structure of a 'potential totality' (Hetzer), in which the unity of colour is created and re-created anew for each painting through the transition and the mutual transformation of the single hues, no longer seems to be the exemplary solution par excellence. Besides this radically de-stabilising, insubstantial way of treating colour, other forms such as for instance the musical-architectural edifices of Veronese and Poussin can claim their own place as genuine articulations of colour space. This extension of the traditional concept of colourism seems to be all the more necessary as some of the most advanced artistic contributions to the problem of pictorial colour in the 20th century have been built upon the factor of mobility in our sight. This may be briefly indicated here by a reference to two paintings which despite all stylistic differences show a surprisingly similar organisation of colour: Picasso's still-life *Mandolin and Guitar* (1924, Guggenheim Museum, New York) and *Odalisque with a Tambourine* (1926, Museum of Modern Art, New York) by Matisse.

Picasso's painting is a genuine modern equivalent to the grand *nature morte* of the tradition. Although clearly built according to the Cubist principle that the contours of the figurative forms do not coincide with the areas of the colour planes, the composition forgoes the original sparseness of the concept. The effort of interrelating figure and space in the flatness of the picture plane has given way to a sovereign display of perceptual depth. Black, white, red, brown and ochre yellow – the traditional interior colours – form discontinuous planes which, in different sizes and modified in themselves, cut through the full expanse of the painting. Only loosely attached to their particular figurative incident they seem to compete directly with an intrusion of blue in different shades and tones. Depending on whether one concentrates on the autonomous function or the figurative significance of colour in the painting, these planes change their positions and prompt quite different ways of reading. For instance, the composite sky blue in the open doorway to the balcony seems to penetrate right through to the immediate foreground where it is imaginatively mirrored directly below the table of the still-life, suggesting a pervading air of light, sea and freshness. But at the very moment our glance is diverted to the similarly blue shadow tracks to the left and right of the door, this atmospheric invasion suddenly withdraws into an indistinct prospect disclosing the greatest perceptual distance. All the other planes behave in a comparably ambivalent though less contrary manner. Picasso shows plastic interaction in an almost pure state, as a *staccato* of contrast effects in which the particular hues mainly serve the suggestion of feeling.

The *Odalisque with a Tambourine* on the other hand immediately reveals the approach of the colourist. The strong chromatic accents – the turquoise of the decorative cloth on the left, the red floor, the blue in the window and the green and yellow chair in which the nude is posed – are all equated in a similar mid-tone to support the pure colour relationships. But the painting also betrays the lesson which Matisse learnt during the winters spent in Nice since 1917/18: to establish a spatial and plastic depth it seemed necessary to introduce tonal values. According to a simple logic of contrast, the area of colour as such is 'put into light' by massive black accents – most notably on the extreme left, in the closed shutter and in the shadowed part of the chair. Within the area of autonomous colour-light the respective hues are virtually never darkened but only further 'lightened' in different degrees. In this respect the nude occupies a central position because in her body alone all tonal levels – from the deepest black of the facial mask to the highest lights of yellow ochre – are coherently present. The other planes of tone act as remote echoes and expedients of this figure, extensions in a space of almost physical elasticity. The most daring connections, such as the passage of the light mauve from the curtain at the window via the blouse of the odalisque to the reflection on her lower leg, show an inconspicuous credibility as part of this gliding structure. It is perhaps this which defines colour painting at its most exclusive: that we are not only solicited to see *in* colour – but are simultaneously made aware of the fact that we are looking *at* colours as well.

The conventional studio motifs of Matisse and Picasso are as different from the abstract events of Bridget Riley as they are removed from Cézanne's *réalisation* of the colour sensations before nature. But despite this essential incomparability of their art, all these artists in their work convey with their different means a somehow similar artistic contradiction. Normally nobody conceives visual reality as it is presented in these works. Nevertheless these 'translations' into a different scale of sensation, that is into the unique plastic domain of pictorial colour, are not simply artificial abstractions. By diverting the spectator's attention from his usual attitude of noting colours as attached to objects and making him see within the particular structures of pictorial colour, painting seems to have the power to momentarily re-create that essential agility and vividness of looking which all fixed pictures miss – and which the cinematic ones will never re-capture. Only colour in the picture plane seems to be capable of stealthily equating with the natural drama of sight.

1 Hermann von Helmholtz *Vorträge und Reden*, Braunschweig, 1896, p. 95.
2 Op. cit., p. 110.
3 Helmholtz's thesis almost certainly came to the attention of the Neo-Impressionists. Joan Ungersma Halperin has pointed out in her brilliant study *Félix Fénéon. Aesthete and Anarchist in Fin-de-Siècle Paris* (New Haven-London: Yale University Press, 1988) that by 1878 a French translation of the lectures, *L'Optique et la Peinture*, already existed to which Fénéon obviously relates in his monograph on Signac (1890), although without explicit reference (op. cit., p. 126 and note 16, p. 385 f.)
4 *Vorträge und Reden*, p. 134.
5 Roger de Piles, *Cours de peinture par principes* (1708). Ed. by Jacques Thuillier. Paris: Gallimard, 1989, p. 150 f.
6 P. M. Doran, *Conversations avec Cézanne*, Paris: Macula, 1978, p. 44.
7 Maurice Merleau-Ponty, *L'Œil et l'Esprit*, Paris: Gallimard, 1964, p. 68 f.
8 The discovery by neurobiology that the perceptions of form, colour, movement and space are based on a differentiation and separation of functions in our brain only helps to understand better why these particular factors of sight are to a certain degree variable in their coordination. For the problem of "segregation" and "integration" in our perception of form, colour and movement see Semir Zeki, "The Visual Image in Mind and Brain", in *Scientific American*, special issue "Mind and Brain", September 1992, pp. 43–50. – On the separation between the perception of objects and of space in particular cf. Fraser A. W. Wilson a. o., "Dissociation of Object and Spatial Processing Domains in Primate Prefrontal Cortex", *Science*, 25 June 1993, vol. 260, pp. 1955–1958.
9 Frank Stella, *Working Space*, Cambridge, Mass. – London: Harvard University Press, 1986.
10 In a recorded conversation with the artist, "Perception and the Use of Colour", E. H. Gombrich emphasised the objective legitimacy of this 'dialogue with the medium' for the exploration of the colour phenomenon. In *Bridget Riley, Dialogues on Art. With Neil MacGregor, E. H. Gombrich, Michael Craig-Martin, Andrew Graham-Dixon and Bryan Robertson*. London: Zwemmer, 1995, pp. 39–43 [second edition 2003, pp. 39–45]
11 *Conversation* 1972, p. 20 [in this volume]
12 *According to Sensation* 1990, p. 97 [in this volume]
13 Cf. the catalogue text to this exhibition *Paintings 1982–1992*, pp. 122–126 [in this volume]
14 *According to Sensation* 1990, p. 97 [in this volume]
15 "Bridget Riley in conversation with Alex Farquharson" (1995), reprinted in *The Eye's Mind* (1999), p. 132.

16 *The Artist's Eye: Bridget Riley*, exh. cat. of the National Gallery, London, 1989. The other painters included in this exhibition were Titian, Veronese, Rubens and Cézanne. The catalogue introduction "The Colour Connection" has been reprinted in *The Eye's Mind* (1999), pp. 142–173.
17 "Colour for the Painter" (1993), in *Colour: Art & Science*, ed. by Trevor Lamb and Janine Bourriau. Cambridge University Press, 1995, pp. 31–64.
18 *Tizian. Geschichte seiner Farbe* (1936). Reprinted in *Schriften Theodor Hetzers*, ed. by Gertrude Berthold, vol. 7, Stuttgart: Urachhaus, 1992, pp. 39–304.

The German version of this essay is based on a paper given during a symposium on colour at the Bauhaus-Universität in Weimar and was first published in *Who's afraid of… Zum Stand der Farbforschung*, ed. Anne Hoormann and Karl Schawelka, Weimar 1998, pp. 133–156. The present English translation was included in the exhibition catalogue *Bridget Riley. Ausgewählte Gemälde – Selected Paintings 1961–1999*, Kunstverein Düsseldorf in association with Hatje Cantz Publishers, 1999, pp. 41–60.

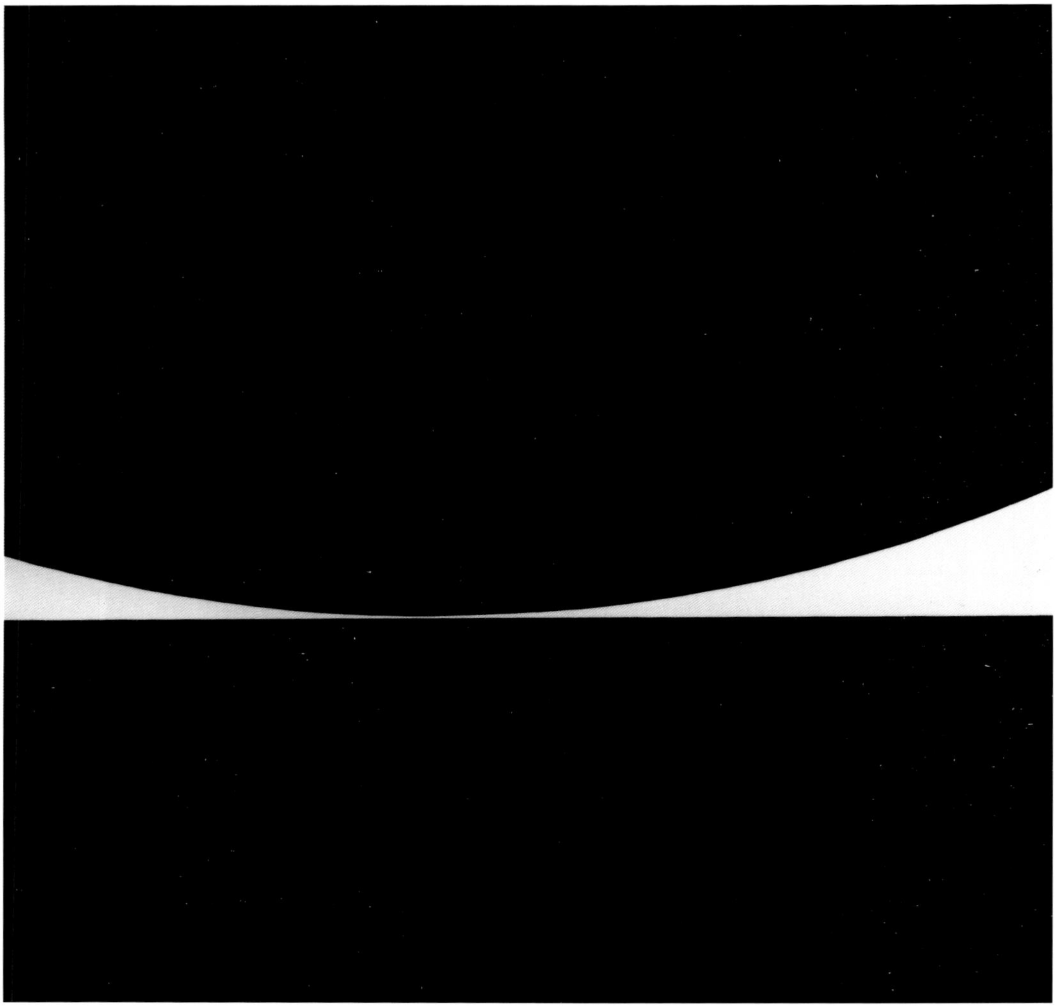

Kiss 1961

Building Sensations

The early work of Bridget Riley

1999

> *We find certain things about seeing puzzling, because we do not find the whole business of seeing puzzling enough.*
> Ludwig Wittgenstein[1]

During the winter of 1998/99, Abbot Hall Art Gallery in Kendal mounted a small retrospective of Bridget Riley's work. In the first room many of her celebrated black-and-white paintings of the early 1960s, such as *Movement in Squares*, *Blaze 4* and *Pause*, were brought together. It was interesting to see the curiosity and circumspection with which the public approached these works. People spent a considerable length of time looking and comparing, reading the catalogue and pointing things out to each other, returning to certain paintings and changing their place of viewing. Young people seemed impressed and some of the elderly visitors went up close, lifting their spectacles to see more clearly what they were looking at. No one in this gathering behaved as though they were in any

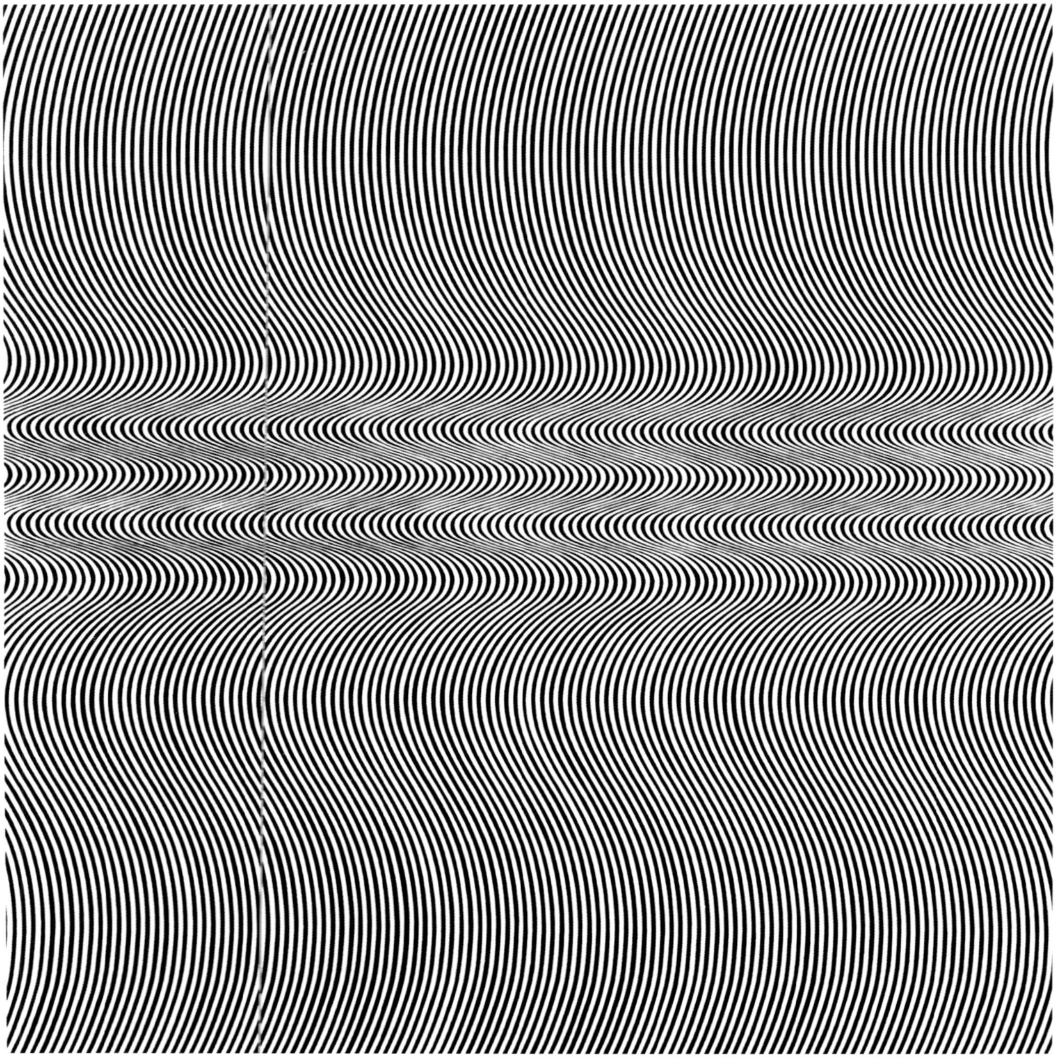

Current 1964

way threatened or in imminent danger.

Some thirty years ago the general attitude to Riley's work was quite different. Even those who were open-minded and prepared to encounter a new experience could not help being affected by the fashionable view of what they were going to see. In 1965, at the height of the excitement surrounding the *Responsive Eye* exhibition at the Museum of Modern Art in New York, which launched Riley's reputation, the contemporary art world seems to have been engaged – partly innocently, partly deliberately – in generating a peculiar sort of myth. Riley's work became the centre of a critical tale of violence and aggression inflicted on the spectator by so-called Optical art, and this view persisted right through the 1970s. Even supporters called her paintings dazzling or blinding, relating the experience to states of hallucination and 'feeling high'; the majority, however, denounced them as mindless, nauseating and detrimental not only to the standards of art, but almost physically harmful. Erich Sokol, the cartoonist, put his finger on this hysteria when he drew a woman desperately trying to save her husband from being sucked into the centre of Riley's painting Fission.

It could be said that the composure of today's spectators merely demonstrates that the novelty of the work has worn off. But this would mean that the effect was never merely physical, and makes it even more interesting that people who now see the paintings for the first time seem to be quite at ease with them. It is also beside the point to claim that the artist herself has paved the way to a more balanced response by refraining in later paintings from the violence of her early pieces. Although the element of instability in Riley's work has undergone several transformations since she moved from her black-and-white paintings to her present preoccupation with colour, the tension between structural firmness and shifting perceptions, so particular to her, has remained remarkably constant. Both these rationalisations are inadequate because they overlook the beginning of Riley's public career. Following her first solo exhibition at Gallery One in London in 1962 she rapidly gained a certain measure of international recognition without which she would never have been invited to participate in the *Responsive Eye* exhibition; and during these three years there was no review complaining of 'eye-bashing', although the disturbing factor built into her work was observed right from the beginning. In his review of the show at Gallery One, David Sylvester clearly saw this quality and recognised its balance within the work:

'The disturbing element is not only imaginative in conception but has the sort of rightness in its placing that a good actor has in his timing – it seems at once unexpected and inevitable. This proposing and disposing of order seems no mere game with optical effects, it seems to symbolise, dramatically, an interplay between feelings of composure and anxiety.'[2]

In drama and the other arts, the sensation of unstable situations and identities shifting between disruption and restitution is well-established and accepted as a viable 'imaginative' equivalent to life. So why was this recognition denied in painting? With hindsight it is clear that the exhibition *The Responsive Eye* coincided with the start of the controversy between Minimalism and Modernism in American art.[3] Visual complexity did not suit either camp. Riley's paintings were aesthetically too energetic and demanding to fulfil the need for 'disinterested contemplation' which Clement Greenberg had put forward as the historical role of Abstraction in his essay 'The Case for Abstract Art' (1959).[4] Conversely, the intricacy of her structures must have looked to the partisans of 'holism' and 'non-composition' like the epitome of that 'fussines' (Frank Stella) and 'juggling' (Donald Judd) which they associated with European art.[5] It was the current taste for blandness and vacancy – post-painterly or conceptual – which could not help but feel challenged and confused by Riley's work.

Thirty years later the situation has certainly changed, although it has not necessarily led to a more appropriate understanding. Ironically Bridget Riley now figures, for many of her new admirers, as the 'last Modernist' in painting as though her work had never been condemned as a deviation from the Road to High Art. It is time to lay aside these various clichés and try to see Riley's work in its own terms. The exaggerated attention paid to its 'effect' has obscured its true character for far too long. There is an astonishing lack of plain observation in the reviews and appreciations of the past twenty years. Talking about the 'blinding' quality of the work has become a licence not to bother with it any further and prevented a long overdue rediscovery. None of Riley's paintings have been created to bring about an optical effect as such; they are built, with a unique inventiveness and ingenuity, to house that particular sensibility for disruption and instability which is all her own.

An Equilibrium at Risk

There was no such thing as Op art when Bridget Riley first showed her paintings. The opening sentence of Sylvester's review states: 'Bridget

Riley is a hard-edge abstractionist.' The big, flat, sharply delineated areas of *Kiss* (1961), fully justify this classification. Of course, the elusive optical flash at the point where the curvilinear shape almost touches the straight form beneath seems to herald further developments. But this harbinger can easily divert attention from a more important aspect. Being based on a square format the unequal division of forms and masses in *Kiss* lays out the ground plan of Riley's earliest pictorial order.

Traditionally painters have tended to avoid working within equal dimensions because it does not give a bias from which to start. But for this very reason Riley seems to have chosen the square as the basic format for most of her paintings right up to 1967. It provided a static equilibrium which could be upset by asymmetrical divisions. In *Kiss* the total field is divided twice, horizontally as well as vertically, each time in a ratio of approximately two to one. The edge of the straight form delineates the horizontal division whereas the near touching point of the large curved shape above indicates the hidden vertical.

The recurrence of such bisections in later paintings shows that there is no mathematical system behind it. Although some of the measurements may come close to the Golden Section, they are not established by that proportional device. Nevertheless there is a certain range within which these divisions are positioned whether they are horizontal or vertical. Either the proportions are clearly irregular as in *Kiss* and *Cataract 3*, in *Movement in Squares* and *Pause*; or these divisions are just off centre, narrowly avoiding symmetry, as in *Serif*, *Crest* and *Current*. Furthermore, there is another option which refines the use of this destabilising factor. Instead of being apparent the asymmetrical disposition can be hidden, as in *Black to White Discs*, *Breathe*, *Arrest 2* or *Cantus Firmus*. Such latency heightens the sensation of a given equilibrium at risk.

As Riley developed her means an important extension to this structural device emerged that is still effective in her recent work. In circular compositions such as *Uneasy Centre* and the *Blaze* paintings the axial asymmetry has been turned into a displacement of the centre. But as the few remaining preparatory drawings for these works show, this displacement can take on a wider role. In the *Study for Broken Circle* (1963), for instance, the coherent form of the circle is dismembered and reassembled in a new way. This treatment can also be found in *Fission*, where two different formal progressions, one long and one short, are displaced cross-wise so that a tension arises which gives the painting its name. From about 1963 onwards dislocation becomes a basic building practice in Riley's work, independent of formal changes and even of the move into

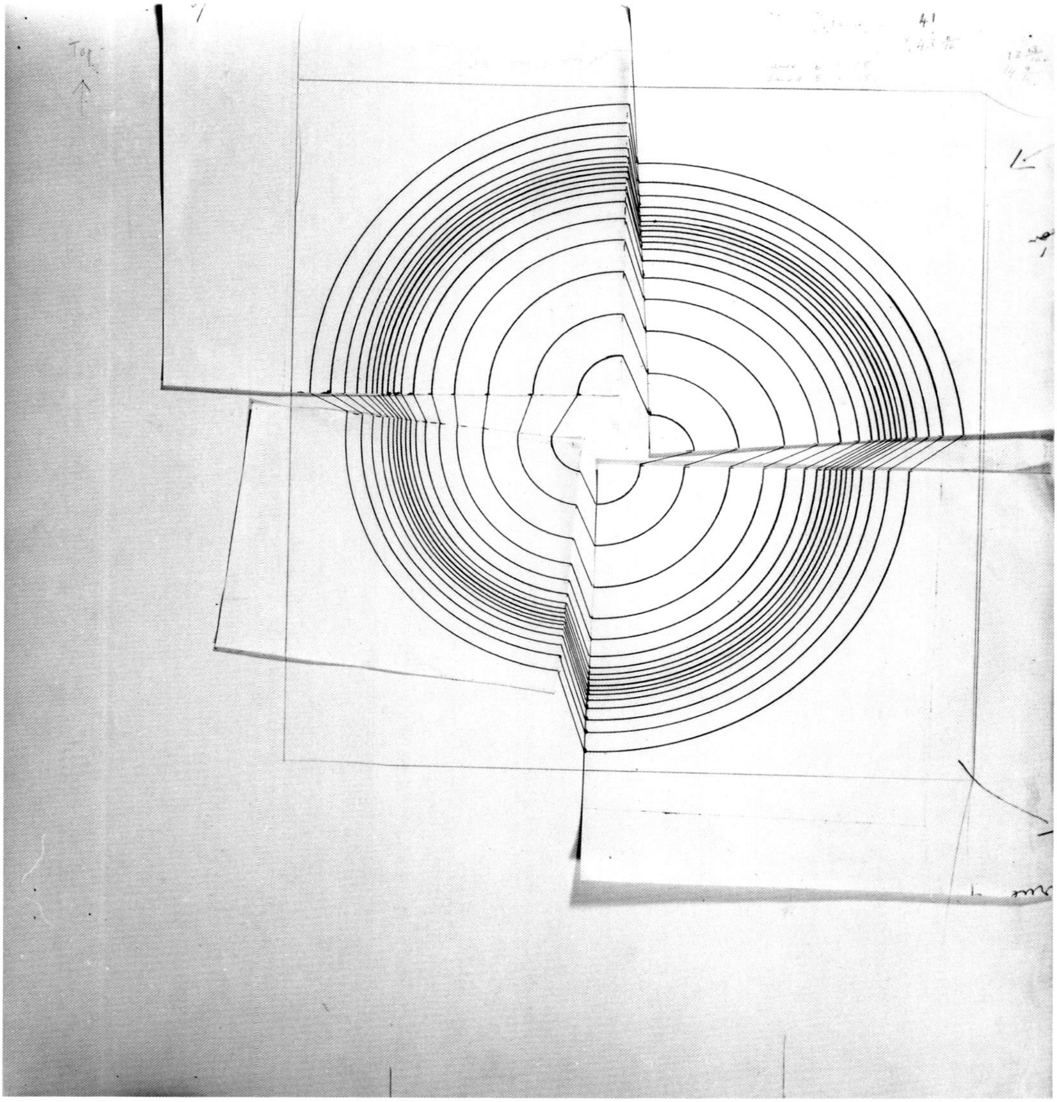

Study for Broken Circle 1963

colour. For instance, in *Where* the tonal movements are dislocated in such a way as to form a regular tripartite structure which recurs in different forms in later paintings. Eventually this principle of breaking up a given unity and reassembling it encompasses both ends, as it were, of the building process. In the paintings which Riley began in 1986 the continuity of the vertical bands is broken up by a diagonal, and this upheaval is counteracted and rebalanced by the dislocation of the rhomboid colour forms it produces.

This later development emphasises that destabilisation and disruption in Riley's work is never an end in itself but a crucial step in transforming a static equilibrium into a dynamic one. A stable position is turned into a balance between stability and instability. It is obvious, however, that on the basis of *Kiss* alone it would not have been possible to push ahead with considerations of such extreme abstraction. *Kiss* shows only the ground plan of Riley's pictorial world, the means and methods to construct it still had to be found.

Progressions – Formal and Tonal

There were only a few early paintings done in a similarly intuitive manner, among them *Horizontal Vibration* (1961) and *Serif* (1964). Both are characterised by areas of compression and expansion achieved through the varying widths and intervals of the black and white bands, and it is clear that *Serif* is a kind of reprise prompted by the curve painting *Crest*. In 1961 Riley had already begun to look for a structure that would allow her to articulate and develop her interests more satisfactorily. The discovery took her by surprise. While working on a sequence of black and white squares she suddenly found that by steadily diminishing their widths she could generate a movement, and in one long working session, as she remembers, she completed *Movement in Squares* (1961), the only painting done in such bravura manner.

The progressive structure of this painting could look like an abstract version of a Futurist depiction of movement, and Riley's earlier interests in Futurism – particularly in Giacomo Balla – seems to confirm this connection. But there is an essential difference. *Movement in Squares*, and all subsequent paintings using progressive sequences of form and tone, does not represent movement in its successive phases, but enacts it autonomously in the picture plane. That is to say, we perceive these sequences as movement, rather than reading them as chains of incident, because they are pitched against a constant. With *Movement in Squares*,

Riley discovered for herself the plastic principle that in order to define an experience she had to bring in its opposite. The squares 'move' because, while their widths decrease, their heights remain the same.

However, this progressive reading precipitates yet another kind of movement, a sudden dissolution which periodically engulfs the entire pictorial field. It is as though the accumulation of tension in the compressed zone leads to a momentary flash or disturbance. But this disruption is never final, it is held in check by the overall structure. Stability is regained, only to be challenged again, in what seems to be a cyclic process. In 1965 Riley herself described this momentum:

> 'The basis of my paintings is this: in each of them a particular situation is stated. Certain elements within that situation remain constant, others precipitate the destruction of themselves by themselves. Recurrently, as a result of the cyclic movement of repose, disturbance and repose, the original situation is re-stated.'[6]

This perceptual phasing, which E. H. Gombrich related to the periodical momentum of Western music,[7] reappears in many variations and guises throughout her work. But it is particular to the early black-and-white paintings that one can read the score, so to speak, before the performance starts. The spectator can survey the structure, distinguish and perceive the progressive sequences, and yet is still drawn into the cadence with which the cycle begins again.

In *Fission* (1963) the character of the performance is changed according to the different structural potential of the chosen element. The progression of a circle to an oval is read in reverse as an expansion towards the full form, and because the units do not touch, as the squares did, the whole field behaves differently. The distress caused by the rupture of the vertical axis is 'healed' by long looping arcs which curve diagonally across the canvas. Because of this greater flexibility the sequence of circles to ovals proved to be one of the most fertile themes in Riley's repertoire. As *Where* and *Pause* (both 1964) show, the formal progression can be combined with tonal sequences from light to dark, to create more subtle and complex sensations.

Tonal progression was first introduced as a theme on its own in *Black to White Disks* (1962), Riley's largest canvas to date. The painting accommodates a centrally placed diamond of evenly spaced identical discs which advance and recede according to a successive modulation of tone. Although the fullest sequence from the palest grey on the left to the black

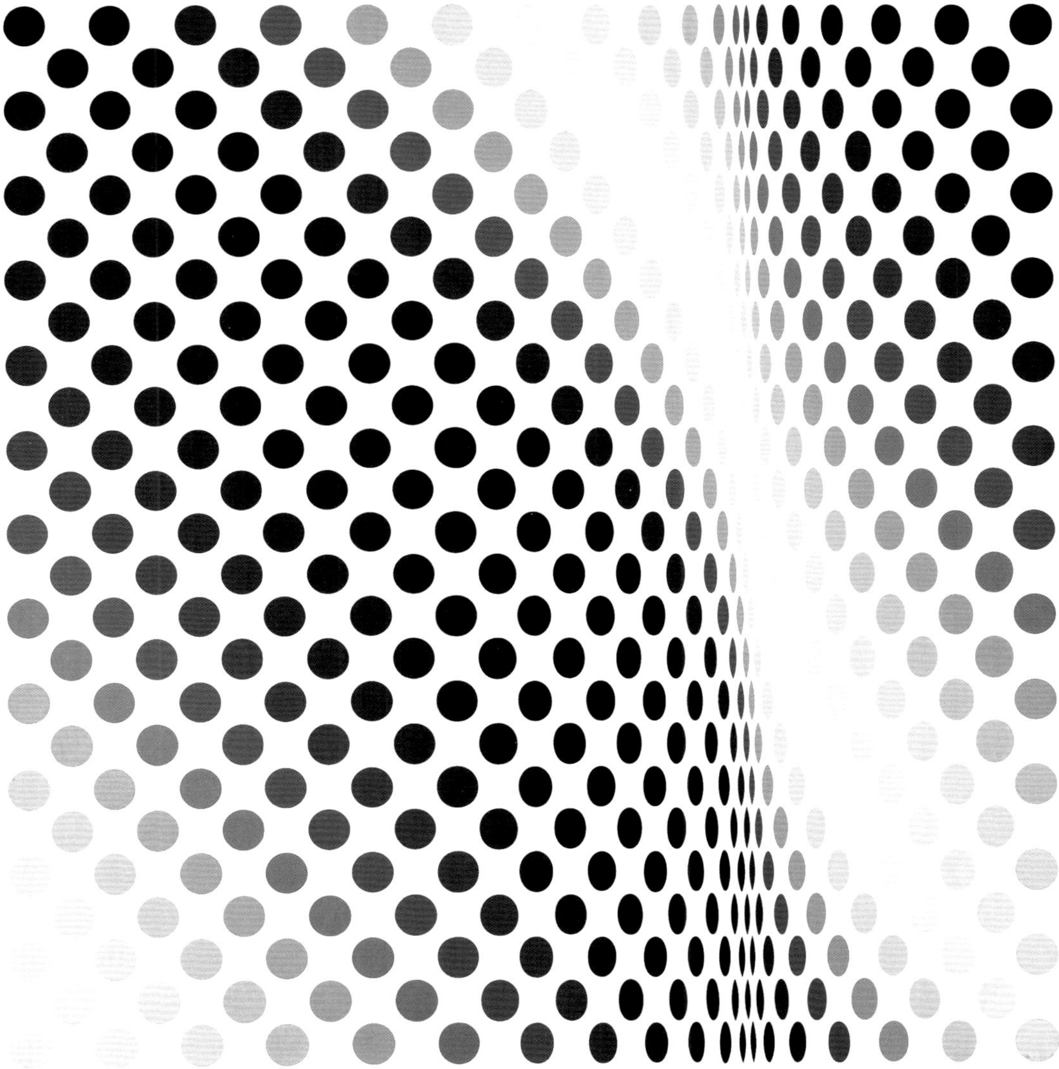

Pause 1964

is longer and slower than its reverse on the right, the suggestion of symmetry is so strong that the eye tends to cling to the vertical centre of the diamond until one discovers that the true tonal centre of the image, the line of absolutely black discs, is just a little to the right. Such veiled, subliminal moves play an important part in the fabric of Riley's paintings right through to the present day. But in her early studio practice this tonal structure also lent itself to a kind of cross-breeding with formal progressions, resulting in a method of differentiating visual time.

Where and *Pause* are both about the modification of a basic formal movement through the different visual tempi provided by tonal sequences. In *Where*, two different gradations to and from a central grey – one quick, the other slow – are imposed on a regular structure of increasing and decreasing forms, with the result that the shifting paces completely change the character of the space. The underlying compression becomes almost explosive, and only the dislocation of the tonal sequences relieves the tension. *Pause* is a much more mysterious painting. Here the shift of tempi veils the structure altogether. As often in Riley's work a clue is given at the top and the bottom of the painting, because even in contriving the most elusive and enigmatic sensations she remains a builder, erecting a painting rather than inscribing it on a flat surface. Along both edges one can see that the two tonal movements from black to the palest grey – one in thirteen and the other in seven stages – do not converge with the formal structure which clearly echoes that of *Movement in Squares*. By turning these sequences inside out as they travel down and across the painting, the absolute black circle in the top left corner becomes the slimmest oval in the compressed area at the bottom. In reverse, the palest grey circle at the bottom right moves up through the compression turning into an oval just off centre at the top. And yet, however rigorously these concerted movements may be fashioned, they eventually combine to form a light and serene divertimento.

With such complex organisations the stable starting point of the original scenario was slowly eroded giving way to an instant sensation of flux and motion. This development is most apparent in a group of paintings employing a device which in Riley's studio parlance is called 'point movement'. Their archetype is *Shift* (1963). The scale study reveals how the triangles are brought about. A regular vertical and horizontal register provides a constant proportion of width and height while the moving points of the triangles are established by a crossing diagonal. It may be noted that this is already a step from the progressive phrasing of single units towards the organisation of a total field. But in the actual painting

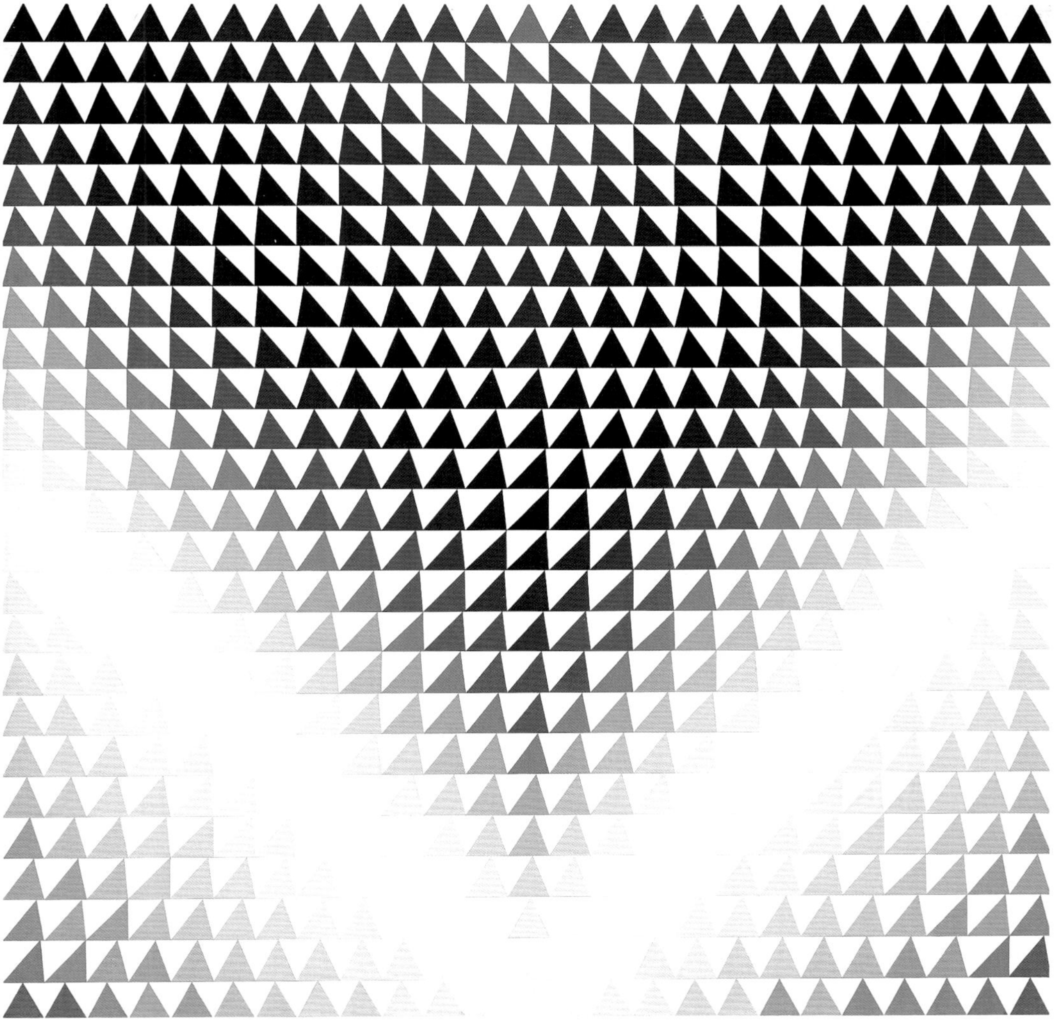

Burn 1964

the literal scenario of the 'cyclic movement of repose, disturbance and repose' can still be recognised. The points of the black triangles in the vertical compartments move progressively in one direction, then turn, and finally re-turn back into the original direction. The key-units for this organisation are the rectangular triangles. They can be seen along the top and the bottom of the painting, and they mark the turning-points within the structure. While the first change of movement drops steadily through the addition of one triangle each time, the return back into the original direction is increased by a ratio of two units. As a result the centre passage opens out like the segment of a fan until it spans almost half the height of the painting. Conversely the long return movement is gradually reduced to a succinct clause in the bottom right corner, one right-angle against another.

The two subsequent paintings however, *Shiver* and *Burn* (both 1964), can no longer be seen in this way. It takes close analysis to discover that the highly energetic field of shifting directions in *Shiver* is controlled through firm structural divisions also marked by rectangular triangles. The total structure is divided by a pair of V-shapes which together form a hidden chevron. In the enclosed area at the top, all the diagonals of the point movement 'lean forward' and straighten up towards the middle, before swinging back to their original position. The central chevron area is made up of repeated parallel movements, all the same length and all 'tilting backwards'. The return in the lower part repeats the upper movement, but in reverse sequence, the diagonals 'tip downwards' from an almost upright position and straighten up again. But this description of the formal means of the painting conveys little of its sensation. *Shiver* is the pure visual equivalent for certain states of being. They may be identified with the actual title of the painting, but Riley remembers that at the time she was also thinking of the beaded skirts and rapid little movements of the Shimmy – a dance popular in the Twenties.

It is the advantage of such rigorous formalism that it can structurally encompass a variety of meanings. Paradoxically this requires that the artist lays aside any direct interest in content, as Riley has shown in her recent writing on Bruce Nauman's formalism.[8] She was surprised that an artist of such different persuasion should in some of his best pieces employ literally the same formal procedures as she herself has done: repetition, reversal, dislocation, asynchronism, and accumulation of density. The only criterion for the successful articulation of an experience seems to be the unadulterated response to the specific plastic conditions in hand. In *Burn* she has given a fine example of this secret of formalist expression. By turning the structure of *Shiver* on its head she upset the equilibrium, and in trying to counteract the dislocation of weight she introduced the two tonal movements diffusing the gravitational pull downwards. But in adding this further complexity it became apparent that the scale had to be changed to a coarser grain to withstand the intense dissolution of the field. The result is not only a different sensation, an expressive paradox like 'cold heat', but a painting that exposes a critical contradiction that has emerged in Riley's pictorial world.

Images and Fields

As early as 1963, Norbert Lynton noted a divergence between two distinctly different groups of paintings in Riley's work: 'image paintings' and 'field paintings'.[9] The first group contains all the images using dislocated circles, like *Uneasy Centre* for example, and is epitomised in the *Blaze* paintings. They are among the most explosive structures that Riley invented, because they carry the principle of dislocation directly into the 'quintessential and most dramatic space of all', as Bryan Robertson remarked: 'the distance between the spectator and the canvas.'[10] Far from being merely a geometric form amongst others, the circle is seen as the mirror image of our focus in looking; and by dislocating this relationship Riley touches the core of our vision.

This is undoubtedly an iconoclastic act and it is not by chance that Anton Ehrenzweig, the great theoretician of iconoclasm in twentieth-century art, wrote one of the best analyses of Riley's early work.[11] But it should also be seen that there is a steady, consistent move after 1963 to open up the all too immediate confrontation between the eye and its mirror. Although the surprising smallness of many of Riley's early works is due to the fact that they can only function and display their potential when they are encompassed by our view, the development of the work in general, and in particular the theme of point movement, shows that Riley began to undermine this confinement. The concern with images gave way to a more open field organisation which she attributed at the time to the example of American painting: 'open space, shallow space, a multifocal space as in Pollock.'[12]

By 1965 the conflict of orientation seems to have been resolved. The zig-zag theme which had been instrumental in the powerful impact of the *Blaze* paintings was finally concluded in *Descending* (1965), a classic field painting. In an even vertical register every other division is a curve which progressively traverses the painting in a slow, dropping movement;

and the dislocation in the zig-zag fabric brought about by this irregular gradient is no longer tense and spasmodic, but a sharp and angular ripple across an open field.

It is interesting to see that this shift had already begun in 1963 with a theme that by-passed the main preoccupation with structural progressions. In *Fall*, *Current* and *Crest*, Riley articulated the sensation of a whole field simply by re-iterating and amassing a particular curve. The only other structural devices are the irregular proportions governing the areas of contraction and expansion. Even more than the complex edifices of *Pause* or *Shiver* these repetitive structures, despite their graphic firmness, generate an immediate sensation of flux. Particularly in *Current* (1964) one can see the new structural problem posed by this 'virtual movement', as Riley calls it. Although there could be no 'return', as in the original scenario, because there is no stable starting point, the visual frequency unleashed had nevertheless to be contained. Only before the actual painting can one properly appreciate the master stroke: the horizontal zones of parallel arcs in the areas of compression do not break loose but are firmly held within the tension of the curvilinear field. The change of scale in reproductions usually falsifies this sensation by producing a moiré-effect instead.

The increasing involvement with this immediacy of perception brought about new forms of field organisation which were essential in preparing the ground for the move into colour. In *White Discs 2* (1964) Riley created a powerfully elusive sensation by deleting parts of the regular structure spanning the field. Once the 'white discs' have started to emerge under one's eyes it is not difficult to intimate the complete field of black discs. In a similar way, although with entirely different means, *Breathe* (1966) calls directly on sensation. This phalanx of elongated triangles is clearly built with an off-centre organisation consisting of a short and speedy movement on the left and a long, slow one to the right. But the grand, voluminous pulse, the 'breath' of the painting, is nevertheless puzzling, and it is with a mixture of surprise and delight that one realises that it is through an ingenious distraction of our attention that this sensation is achieved. The pace of the progressions is dilated by moving in steps of two instead of one by one.

The connection between *Breathe* and the formal organisation of the *Orient* paintings is so obvious that with hindsight one might think that the transition to colour could have been more direct than it actually was. But for Riley using colour was not simply a problem of finding an adequate form, it required a profound revision of her pictorial approach which had so far mainly been based on the principle of contrast and

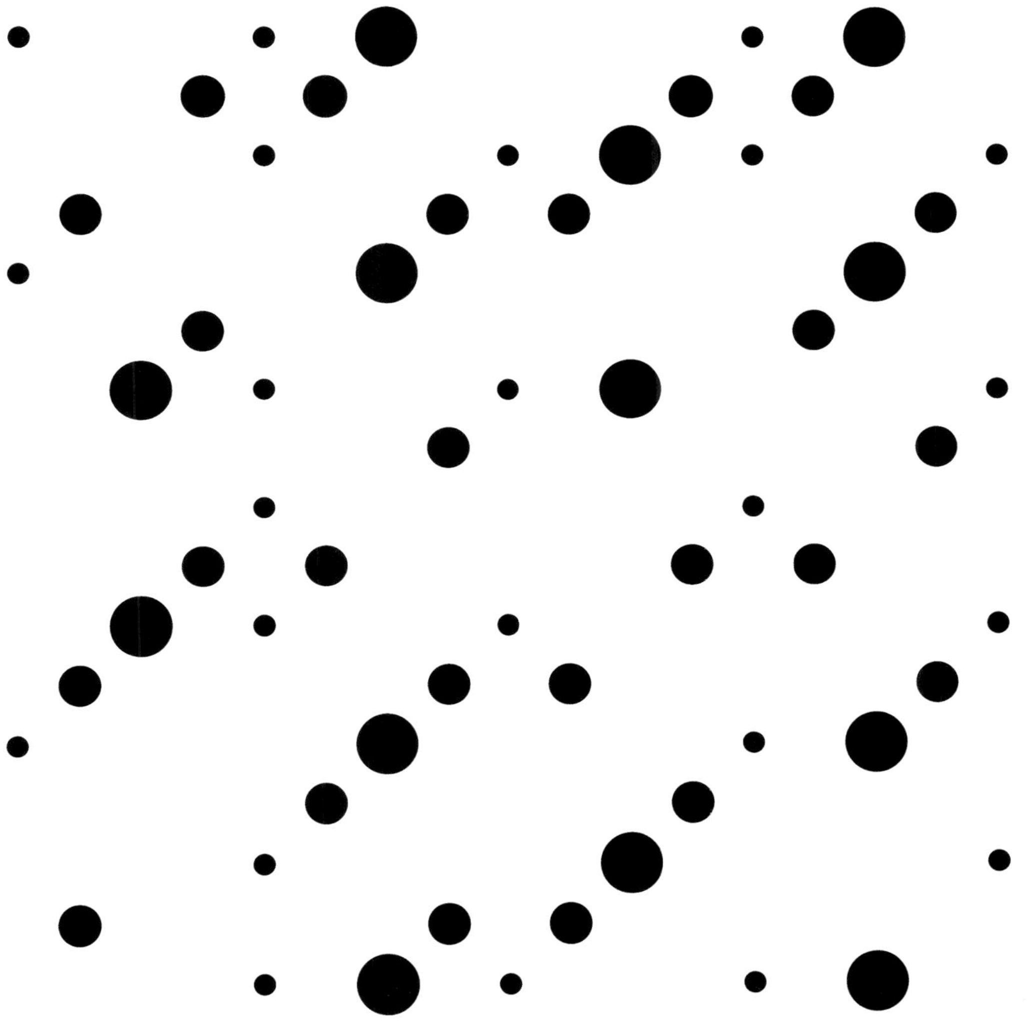

White Discs 2 1964

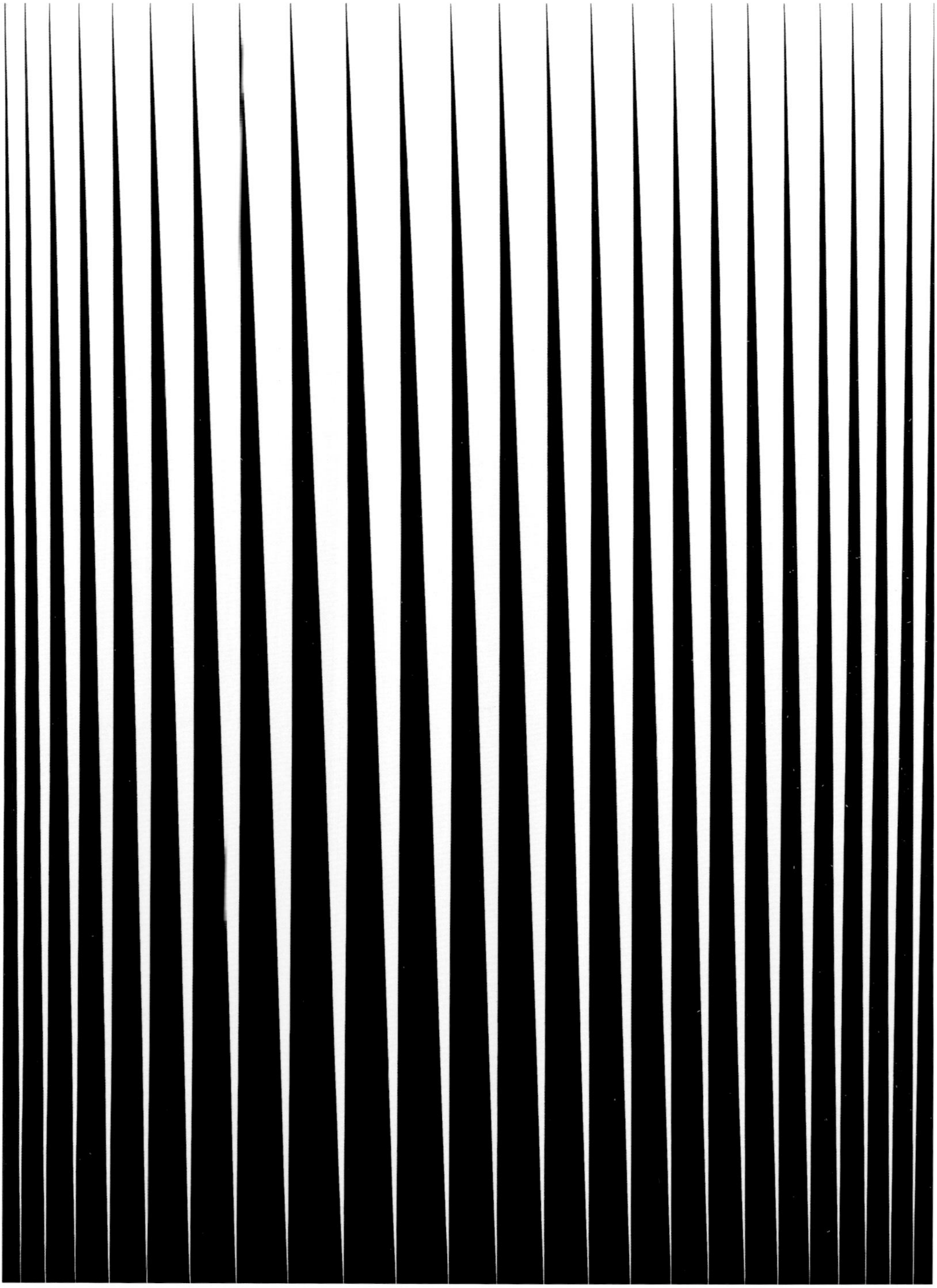

opposition. With the introduction of grey this reckoning had already begun to change, and another clue seems to have been provided by structures in which the physical presence of form and contrast have been considerably eroded. *Static 1*(1966) is all about virtual movement and perceptual energy. The actual structure of minute ovals turning in different directions and at different speeds is barely discernible in this even, highly-charged, field. It was this achievement of having turned the picture plane into a field of pure disembodied energy that, together with the infinite range of delicate shades available in grey, allowed Riley to make the transition from her black-and-white work to pure colour painting.

The Transition to Colour

In his monograph on Bridget Riley (1970), Maurice de Sausmarez reproduced a study of 1965 which shows that Riley had tried to apply colour within the structure of her earlier black-white-paintings. But she soon realised that a bigger step was required, a kind of denial of previous practises and attitudes, as she later explained in referring to the *Deny* paintings: 'I didn't choose the title *Deny* by chance. The whole group of paintings grew out of, and away from, the absolute opposition of black and white. I wanted something which operated on more levels, was capable of more development, had a more grey'd quality, like the indeterminate nature of reality.'[13]

The complexity of *Deny 2* (1967) can be seen as operating on several different levels of 'denial'. Obviously the structural movement of the ovals works against the regular grid which supports them. The basic theme is the slow spin of a slender upright oval – vertical to horizontal, and back to vertical again. At the edges of the canvas one can see the two different forms of progression: along the top and the bottom the return sequence simply reverts, whereas down the sides one long complete turn-over takes place. The regular half-way position of the horizontal ovals draws one's attention to the internal organisation of the movement. The total field is divided into four equal compartments in which the units are moved around in such a way that the uppermost sequence is reversed in the lowest, and vice versa. But what is more, these four quarter field movements are related to one another in a complementary way. In the top half of the painting the horizontal oval in the middle moves successively down and out towards the edges of the canvas, while in the lower part the movement rises from the vertical ovals in the corners to meet in the centre. This results in a sensation simultaneously centrifugal and

(opposite)
Breathe 1966

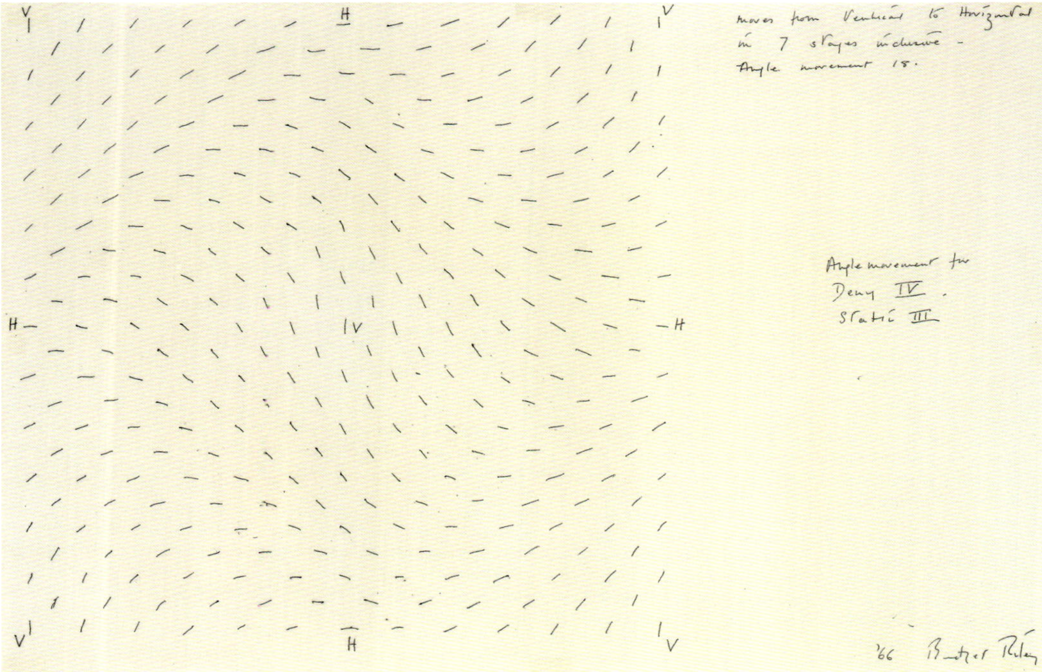

Angle movement for *Deny 4* and *Static 3* 1966

centripetal. All formal agents seem to be dispersed and drawn together at the same time.

In sheer formal terms this structure is not unlike that of *Static 1*, but in *Deny 2* Riley has 'denied' the simple black and white contrast by introducing an opposition between a warm reddish grey for the ground and a cool bluish grey for the ovals within a common tonal harmony. Furthermore, the bluish grey of the units is organised in three different tonal gradations which in turn 'deny' the structural developments. If one once more uses the edges of the canvas as a guide one can see that there is a slow progression from light grey to middle grey, a fast one from light to dark grey, and again a slow one from dark to middle grey. They combine to form a diffused dark area at the bottom, clearly reminiscent of the V-shaped dissolution in *Burn*.

As with the complex point movements, however, the description of the operative means falls short of the actual appearance of the painting itself. The sombre elegance of *Deny 2* springs from an unexpected visual opposition between colour and tone. Where the tone of the ground and the ovals are equal the colour contrast between red and blue emerges. In reverse, where the light-dark opposition is at its maximum, the colour differentiation, in a supreme, perceptual form of 'denial', is virtually suppressed. So at one extreme there is an almost metallic glitter, reminiscent of shining leaves turning in the wind, and at the other, our sense of depth and distance is lost in a soft, shadowy mist.

With the *Deny* paintings one has the feeling that, if only one could lift a veil, one would stand in the light of *Chant* and *Late Morning*. But again, there was no such direct continuation. *Deny 2* was an end rather than a beginning, the culmination of a development that includes *Turn* as well as *Shiver*, *Burn* and *Static 1*. The real advance was prepared for by a group of paintings on which Riley worked concurrently. She had in fact introduced warm and cold greys for the first time in 1965 when she began to extend the curve theme of *Crest* and *Current*. By enlarging the body of the curve the visual speed was slowed down and the alternation of warm and cold greys provided a subliminal tension. However, the main aspect of this group of paintings – called *Arrest* – was a complex interlocking between the formal structure and sequences of coloured greys. In *Arrest 2* (1965) a steep diagonal fall of curves on the left corresponds to a larger and shallower rise on the right, both movements being slightly bowed. The progression of warm and cold greys obliterates this off-centre organisation in two ways. Firstly, a fast sequence from dark to light grey transgresses beyond the formal division, and then, most importantly, a second, slower tonal movement starts in the actual centre of the square format with a sharp contrast between the palest grey and the deepest saturated black. *Arrest 2* is a magnificent display of the dynamic stillness that can be effected through the interrelationship of opposing thrusts and weights.

However, as a first step beyond mere tonal modulation the *Arrest* paintings did not lead much further. Rather, in working with coloured greys on a large scale Riley seems to have familiarised herself sufficiently with the still remote problem of colour to realise two things: that intricate formal structures would inhibit the presence of colour, and that the greatest forte of the curve was not the weight it could carry but its long supple edge. The solution did not come at once. But when it was achieved in *Cataract 3* (1967) it looked both inevitable and quite unexpected.

The formal structure of the painting is quite simple – an even diagonal displacement of one and the same curve. The whole stage belongs to what happens to colour, *with* colour and *through* it. Sharing the same curve, two coloured greys – one red, one turquoise – travel in close proximity the full span from a tonally equal, chromatically neutral grey to the full untempered colour contrast. But as soon as they draw nearer to the area of open brilliance something extraordinary takes place, the colour seeming to break loose from its formal vehicle. This may be due partly to the familiar displacement of the area, partly to the high frequency of the curvilinear field and partly to the granular friction which Riley has unobtrusively built into the gradation. The sequence, instead of proceeding smoothly, advances by always moving on, in a kind of 'roll over' rhythm, from one stage before the last (that is to say 123 / 234 / 345 etc). But whatever the cause may be, the result is visibly there: a cool, fresh, rosy aura envelopes the heart of the contrast, shimmering and sending off sparkles, like dancing reflections, into the greyer areas of the painting. With *Cataract 3* the transformation of the original cyclic scenario, 'repose, disturbance, and repose', was almost complete. Colour could obviously be put into action in an analogous way, as a sensation embracing the tension between an actual hue and its dissolution in coloured light.

There was only one more step to be taken, the relinquishing of the grey envelope. In *Chant 2* (1967) this is accomplished. The colours are reduced to a pair of red and blue, the strongest chromatic contrast, and the forms are simplified into stripes, the most neutral structural vehicle possible. But from these stark means a painting of great presence and authority is extracted. Red and blue in two different combinations, red surrounding blue, blue surrounding red, alternate as they spread across the canvas. The width of the bands increases towards the centre while the white intervals remain constant. Depending on the spectator's distance, the painting offers two different but interrelated experiences. Up close one can see the radiation of colour energy along the edges of the bands: the blue-red-blue combination gives off a dark blue violet shine, whereas the red-blue-red band appears as a lighter red violet and flickers with a luminous yellow orange. As one steps back these elusive details give way to a powerful collective sensation. In the centre, where the broader bands are amassed, an unplumbable depth opens up, radiating an almost colourless light.

Chant 2 was shown at the Venice Biennale in 1968 together with *Late Morning* (1967–68), the other great painting that confirmed Riley's breakthrough to pure colour. A wide horizontal canvas of well over three metres, it is based on a continuum of regular periodic units which carry a cumulative momentum. The pace is set by the brilliant red chord consisting of two red stripes facing one another over a white interval. This steady pulse is accentuated on one side by an adjacent blue stripe which, through minutely graduated, acts as an asymmetrical constant beat. On the other side an overt progressive movement from blue to green provides a rhythmic flow in response to this driving thrust. It is organised according to the artist's 'roll over' principle, drawing out a mere

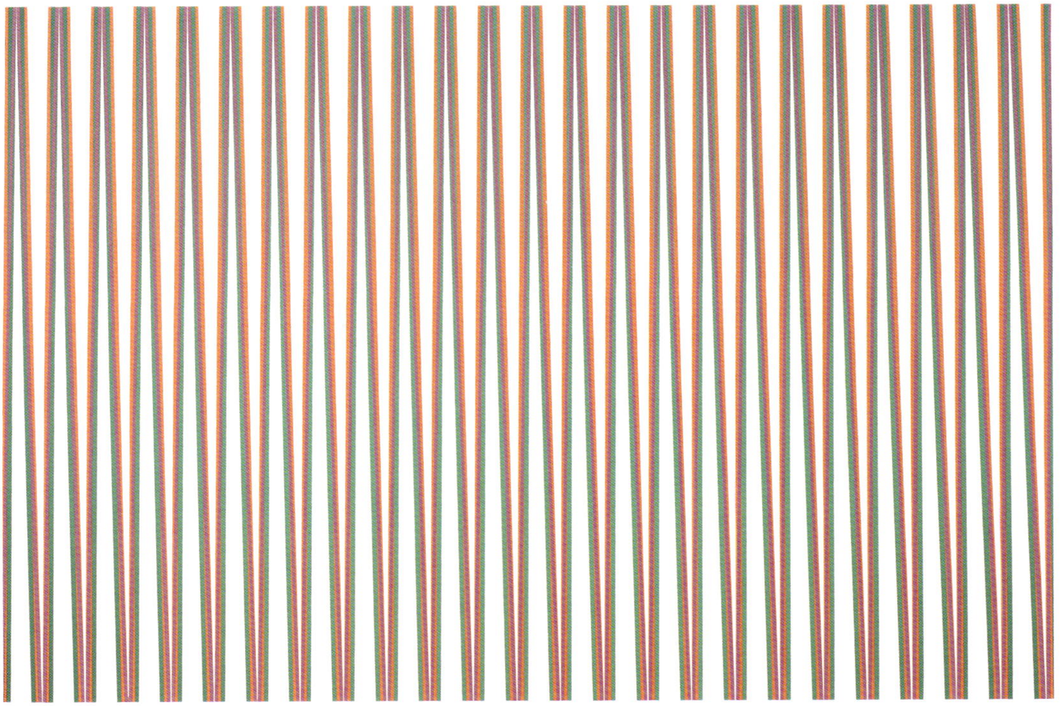

Orient 4 1970 (detail, overleaf)

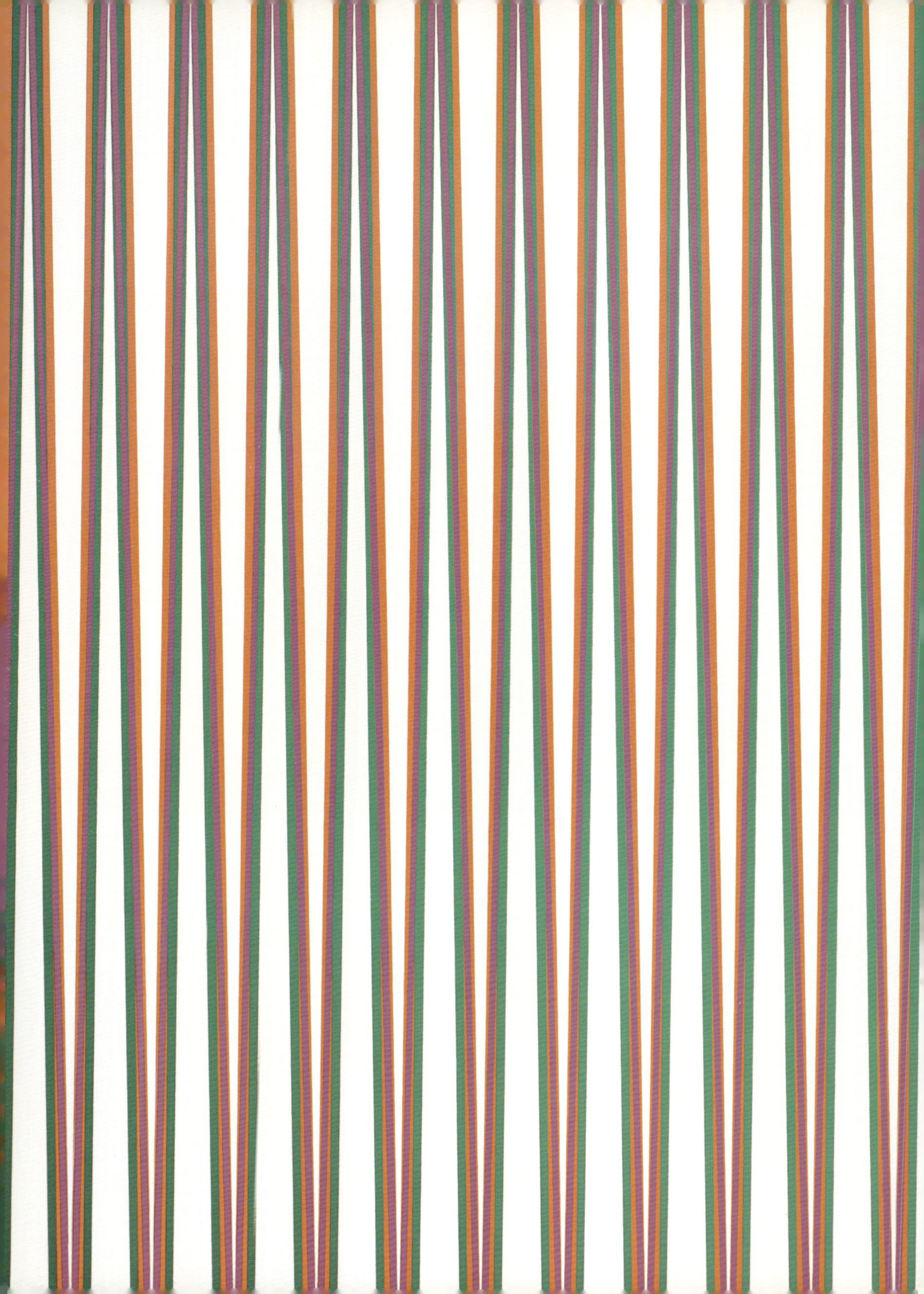

ten stages to a span of thirty positions. But this movement is not continuous. The whole passage is subdivided into three phases and rearranged in a dislocated manner. Instead of beginning with blue or green the first part on the left starts from a central position of turquoise. This appears like a premature echo anticipating the second part which advances from blue to turquoise and continues through into the third part where it culminates in yellow green. With this sequence being mirrored on the right side, the total organisation describes a circular movement encompassing the instantaneous sensation of a volume of pale yellow light emerging in the centre. In a talk at the Tate Gallery in September 1994 Bridget Riley said that she chose the title *Late Morning* because the sensation reminded her of that hour in the Midi just before noon 'when the heat is about to reach its zenith and the air is alive with the dry sound of cicadas.'

Extending the Range

The breakthrough to colour resulted in a burst of activities which can roughly be divided into three developments. First of all Riley started to explore the new terrain she had found through *Chant* and *Late Morning* (*Rise 1*, *Byzantium*, *Orient 4*). Then, having discovered certain limitations she made various attempts at strengthening the intensity of colour and giving more body to the fugitive sensations (*Zing 1*, *Cantus Firmus*), and finally she re-introduced the curve element to give her newly acquired experience with colour a more sympathetic form (*Entice*, *Aurulum*, *Song of Orpheus 5*, *Andante*).

The first group shows the extent to which colour changed her pictorial practice. Formal complexity was sacrificed for the unassertive character of stripes and bands, and for some time *Chant 2* remained the last square format because the extension and opening up of the scope of vision seemed as essential to the release of colour activities as the confinement had been to her explosive black-and-white images. The big horizontal format entered Riley's repertoire. In retrospect she wrote: 'In the same way that I had to sacrifice distinctive forms in order to release the energy of colour-light, it was necessary to increase the scale of the event in order to prevent focused looking.'[14]

The paintings *Rise 1*, *Byzantium* and *Orient 4*, are each based on a palette of three colours only, without any gradation. After *Late Morning* Riley gave up this kind of colour progression, developing colour's perceptual interaction instead. The relationship of the three chosen colours is therefore crucial. *Rise 1* is made up of orange, violet and green, *Orient 4* operates on the triad of magenta, turquoise and ochre. These are, as David Thompson saw, 'colours which are already biased towards other colours,[15] that is to say composite colours which destabilise each other to form new perceptual identities. However, on close comparison one realises that these colour groups are selected according to a familiar principle because two of them always seem to work more actively together, thus forming a contrast to the third one. The orange and violet in *Rise 1*, for instance, when juxtaposed provide a cool carmine red to which the green then acts as a contrast. Likewise, the blue sensation produced by the green and violet pair is counteracted by the orange. In short, the principle of unequal balance reappears in Riley's colour calculations.

But the paintings are not demonstrations of colour theory. The apparent 'phenomena' of Riley's colour paintings are, in fact, sensations which can only happen under precise conditions, within the specific scale, pitch and frequency established by the plastic structure of the particular painting. So it is indispensable to the upward movement which gave *Rise 1* its name that the horizontal structure of the bands is organised, for the first time since *Horizontal Vibration*, in a purely perceptual way. Only in this context can the most powerful colour accent – the carmine of the orange backed up by the violet, exert its visual pull. *Byzantium* (1969), on the other hand, is not only made up of a different group of colours, red, yellow-green and blue, but the even diagonal organisation of two alternating bands, red enclosing either yellow-green or blue, sets up a tension that creates a completely different sort of colour interaction. The extreme displacement of the vertical axis unleashes a vigorous counter-thrust to redress this imbalance. The whole field reverberates with disembodied energies striking a grand, ceremonial colour chord: purple, gold and white.

The powerful tension of *Byzantium* alerts one to a fundamental paradox in the new colour paintings which explains why Riley increasingly preferred the vertical emphasis for her structures. The perceptual activity of colour seems to be at its most intense when it is seen as a horizontal spread against the vertical forms that carry it. But in order to give some pull to this horizontal diffusion she introduced the steep angle of elongated triangles in a group of paintings all titled *Orient*. The result is a tense 'zone-ing' of the field which in *Orient 4* is further differentiated by a new structural element. It may be remembered from *Shift*, *Pause* or *Deny 2* that, when Riley was involved with progressive movements, cross-over passages played an important part in her plastic vocabulary. In the colour work this concept seems to have been transformed into a literal 'cross over' device, a band of two colour stripes crossed by a third. *Orient 4* shows the enormous potential of this device. The basic pair of turquoise and ochre is crossed by magenta in a regular stroke. Thanks to the tapering points of this magenta stripe, thinning out at the top and bottom of the canvas, the colour relationships within each band are destabilised, giving rise to an astonishing range of colour sensations. The magenta itself travels from a violet inflection at the top to a pinkish orange at the bottom, the turquoise turns towards blue in the middle before settling in a greenish shade, and most dramatically, the ochre shifts from a yellow variant through a warmer rosy tint to a burnt orange appearance. These may be very faint incidents in themselves, but amplified through repetition they gather considerable force. The firmly spanned structure of *Orient 4* opens up into an orange and reddish zone across the top and a blue and greenish one at the bottom.

Extension and amplification were initially important means to accommodate and harvest the profusion of dispersed coloured light. But with time and experience Riley became increasingly concerned with stabilising and substantiating this elusive experience. *Zing 1* shows one direction in which she proceeded. By multiplying and increasing the cross-over device she acquired a new structural element called, in her own studio parlance, 'colour twist' – although the literal association of twisting ribbons is misleading. It is in fact a form of movement which allows all three colour stripes in a band to mutually cross one another in turn. In *Zing 1* there are four diagonal crossings in each band. At the top, green crosses over red and blue, then red crosses blue and green, followed by blue crossing green and red, and finally at the bottom, the sequence returns to its starting position with green again crossing red and blue. This sets off a multitude of minute colour inflections, in effect a virtual colour totality, which in the tight repetitive structure of *Zing 1* is firmly held together in glittering horizontal zones, recalling the compressed intensity of the curves in *Current*.

Although this was only one direction which Riley pursued, *Zing 1* shows very clearly the limits of the attempt to enhance the presence of colour energy as such. Mere intensification would not lend more body and volume to sensations which by their very nature are fugitive and immaterial. So it must have seemed an alternative to tackle the problem from another angle. Between 1970 and 1973 Riley made a whole group of paintings in which she tried to give more weight and density to the play of colour by re-introducing black and grey sequences. *Cantus Firmus*

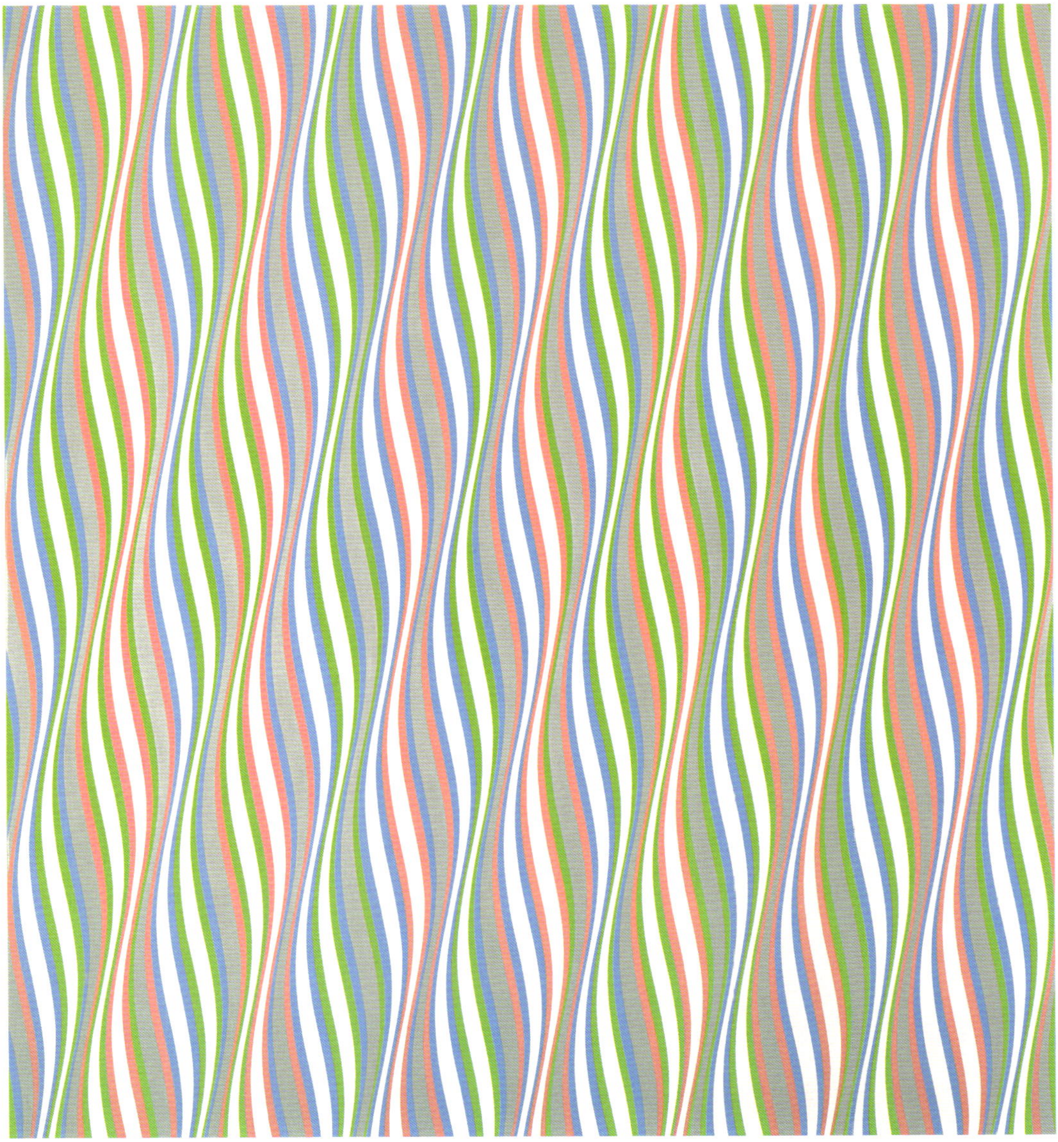

Entice 2 1974

(1972–73) is the most successful of these canvases because, despite its reduced colour presence, it is a masterpiece of pictorial building. The impression of a powerful spatial movement is so strong that it takes some time to realise that almost all the component parts of this painting are identical and constant. *Cantus Firmus* is built on a regular alternation of black, white and grey bands which are surrounded by bands of three colours mirroring one another: olive, magenta and blue facing blue, magenta and olive etc. Both the periodic repetition of this colour constellation and the width and sequence of the black and grey bands are constant. Only one factor, the grey, moves from a mid-tone pitch at both sides of the painting in two different progressions – slow on the left and quicker on the right – towards a dark grey, virtually indistinguishable from the black bands close to it. This off-centre organisation is buried in a manner comparable to *Black to White Disks*. But the sensation is completely different. However reduced the colour activity may be, the fusion with the greys destroys the notion of a regular metre as well as the perception of any continuity in tone. The width of the bands and their planes in space seem to glide and fluctuate, disclosing a dense and yet curiously permeable space.

Re-introducing and transforming earlier themes and devices is obviously one of the ways in which Riley proceeds. Sometimes this produces an odd unruly painting but it can also open up unexpected territory. At first glance *Entice 2* (1974) seems simply to combine the curve element with greys, rather in the manner of *Cantus Firmus*. A vertical curve is diagonally displaced so that a continuous field of narrowing and widening forms emerges, every third interval carrying a constant grey of the same tonal pitch as the colours which flank it. There also seems to be a repetition of the blues, greens and reds which mirror each other across the white intervals. But this order is deceptive because the continuity is undermined by rhythmic syncopations attracting and evading our attention. Identical colour pairs are interspersed with contrasting pairings, and the apparent overall organisation harbours a number of hidden accents and shifts, the most notable of which is the emphasis towards warm greens and reds on the right side.

In spite of the power and novelty of this image, Riley did not carry it further. As with the earlier choice of stripes she never goes for 'imagery' as such, but rather for pictorial function and the sensation conveyed. In this way a structural observation in *Entice 2* seems to have indicated a change of direction. The narrowing of the curves in the pinched parts virtually severs the curvilinear field, and these acute passages seem to have suggested a new role for colour twists used in paintings such as *Zing 1*. In turning three colours around a curvilinear axis Riley saw the possibility of accumulating groups of disembodied colour across the surface, quite independently of the previous confinement to horizontal zones. This became the dominant approach in her work for the next few years.

Aurulum (1977) is already a highly developed painting. One clue to the building up of complexity in Riley's work is her ability to take small and steady steps. First, she let the colours down with grey to facilitate their interactions; then, lightening and clearing them again, she explored the two different structural possibilities inherent in turning colours around a curve: tight twists and open expanding loops. And eventually, with paintings like *Aurulum*, the white intervals gave way to pale tinted greys which act as a conduit for the spread of colours.

The whole field of *Aurulum* is organised in two ways, firstly, by changing the number of curves carrying the same sequence of colours, and secondly, by reversing this sequence within the continuous formal structure. Each colour movement involves seven cross-over stages. At the top left corner, for instance, it begins with blue, rose and yellow-ochre crossing in turn, continues with a full repeat of this sequence and finishes with blue again at the bottom. Varying the number of curves carrying the same progressions and steadily shifting their positions along the diagonal drop of the field creates vivid clusters and chords of luminous colour. These golden, pink and yellow sprays are supported by a hidden inversion of the initial colour sequence to yellow-ochre, rose and blue. Through this a slight inflection is added to the loose *glissandi*, lending a kind of iridescent bloom to the painting.

It seems almost impossible to go beyond such subtleties. But having trained her vision in this high-keyed colour fluctuation Riley went one decisive step further. In the *Song of Orpheus* paintings she split up the grey intervals which so far had served as receptacles for the colour activity into two more hues. This meant that the whole balance of colours 'already biased towards other colours' had to be readjusted to a shifting constellation of five colours: violet, blue, green, yellow and pink. In *Song of Orpheus 5* (1978) this palette is separated into two different colour twists. A theme of three colours, pink, blue and green, is interlaced with another consisting of two, yellow and violet. Their intricate structural relationships truly defy penetration. But far from being confused the result in sensation is a clear contrast between rippling green and yellow clusters and hazy rose passages working against one another.

By the time Riley painted the *Song of Orpheus* paintings she had achieved her primary objective, to find a footing in colour, though with an unexpected consequence. In 1992 she said in conversation with Michael Craig-Martin:

> 'I saw that the basis of colour is its instability. Instead of searching for a firm foundation, I realised that I had one in *the very opposite*. That was solid ground again, so to speak, and by accepting this paradox I could begin to work with the fleeting, the elusive, with those things which disappear when you actually apply your attention hard and fast.'[16]

So successful was this achievement that, if one views the *Song of Orpheus* paintings with an open unfocused gaze they come precariously close to dissolving into coloured light. But this of course provoked Riley's building temperament. However subtle and refined her paintings may become from time to time, the cultivation of sensitivity is not her aim.

In the curve paintings after 1978 this tendency towards evanescence is counteracted by deepening colour and modifying the overall organisation. One of the very last curve paintings, *Andante* (1980–81), shows how far this could be carried. Green, turquoise, violet, magenta and dull orange-ochre are the constituent colours which are organised in a new plastic way. Instead of regular or periodically recurring rhythmic patterns, broader structural considerations are brought into play. Vivid accents of green, in conjunction with turquoise and violet, flash across a bed of warm colours which draws upon interactions between magenta, dull orange-ochre and, once again, violet. This free disposition of the curving colour twists includes a shift in the colour emphasis. Whereas in the larger part of the painting reddish interactions prevail, the balance is reversed in the lower right side in favour of a cool blue-green giving weight to the sharp breaks and interjections of these colours elsewhere.

In 1981 when Bridget Riley completed *Andante*, she had already begun to extend and transform this free perceptual organisation. The broad simple colour band reappeared, carrying a palette of unprecedented strong and bright hues. After ten years of intense involvement with chromatic interaction Riley had shifted the basis of her work once again; and this not for the last time in the past two decades. Such changes are neither capricious nor deliberately engineered in pursuit of novelty. She herself scorns any value attached to change as such, because to her sensibility movement is an essential condition of preserving the vitality of life. In this sense the rich and continuous development of her work, now spanning more than forty years, is a rare and precious achievement in itself.

1 Ludwig Wittgenstein, *Philosophical Investigations*, translated by G. E. M. Anscombe. Oxford, 1989, p. 212e.
2 David Sylvester, 'Bridget Riley', *The New Statesman*, 25 May 1962.
3 Although from today's point of view Minimal art is subsumed into 'Modernism', this was not so at the time. The supporters of Clement Greenberg's view of the evolution of Modern art were opposed to the claims of the Minimalists, as one can see from Michael Fried's essay "Art and Objecthood", 1967. One of the critical points was the notion of 'presence', whether the picture plane was an area in its own aesthetic right or simply a physical fact among the other objects existing in the world. The whole debate is well documented in *Minimal Art: A Critical Anthology*, ed. Gregory Battcock, London: Studio Vista, 1969.
4 Clement Greenberg, *The Collected Essays and Criticism*, ed. John O'Brian, 4 vols., University of Chicago Press 1986–93, vol. IV, p. 80.
5 'Questions to Stella and Judd', interview by Bruce Glaser, 1964, ed. Lucy R. Lippard, 1966. In *Minimal Art*, op. cit., p. 150.
6 "Perception Is the Medium" (1965), reprinted in *The Eye's Mind* (1999), p. 66.
7 Bridget Riley, *Dialogues on Art. With Neil MacGregor, E. H. Gombrich, Michael Craig-Martin. Andrew Graham-Dixon, Bryan Robertson*, ed. R. Kudielka. London: Thames & Hudson,[2]2003, 1995, p. 43.
8 Bridget Riley, "Nauman's Formalism" (1999), in *The Eye's Mind* (1999), pp. 212–16.
9 Norbert Lynton, "London Letter", *Art International*, vol. VII, no. 8, October 1963, p. 84.
10 Bryan Robertson, "Introduction" to *Bridget Riley. Paintings and Drawings 1951–1971*, catalogue of the Hayward Gallery retrospective exhibition, London 1971, p. 7.
11 Anton Ehrenzweig, "The Pictorial Space of Bridget Riley", *Art International*, vol. IX, no. 1, February 1965, p. 20–24.
12 "In Conversation with Maurice de Sausmarez" (1967), reprinted in *The Eye's Mind* (1999), p. 62.
13 *Into Colour* 1978, p. 68f [in this volume]
14 Op. cit., p. 70 [in this volume]
15 David Thompson, "Bridget Riley", *Studio International*, vol. 182, no. 935, July–August 1971, p. 21.
16 Bridget Riley, *Dialogues on Art*, (2003), p. 60.

First published in *Bridget Riley: Paintings from the 1960s and 70s*, texts by Lisa G. Corrin, Robert Kudielka, Frances Spalding, London: Serpentine Gallery, 1999, pp. 23–33.

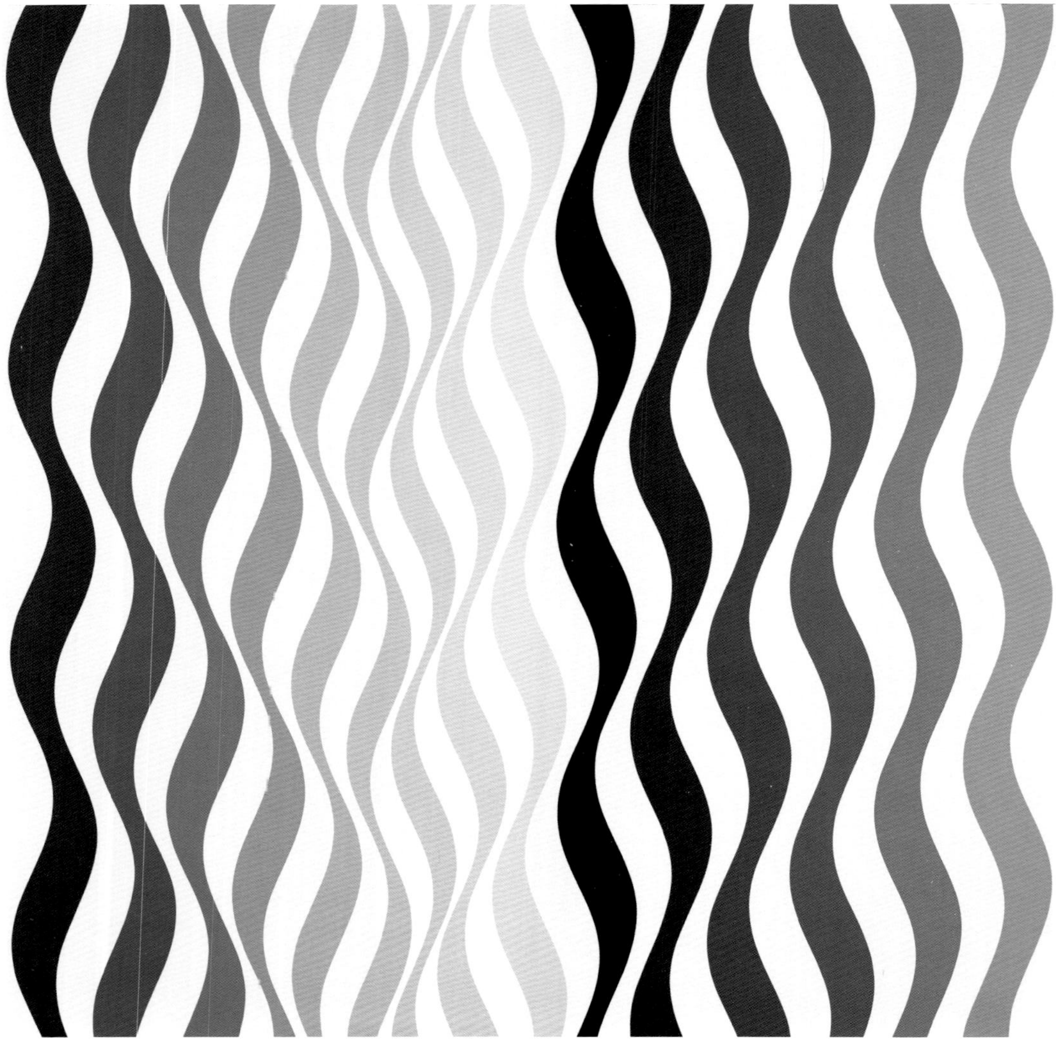

Arrest 2 1965

Supposed to be Abstract

Conversation

2001

ROBERT KUDIELKA: *Your recent success in New York, 35 years after the Responsive Eye exhibition, is remarkable in that you haven't been celebrated as a figure from the past, but as a contemporary. Reviewing your show at the DIA Center for the Arts, Peter Schjeldahl wrote that looking at a collection of your paintings from 1961 to 1984 is like 'opening a time capsule and finding today's newspaper.'*[1] *Why do you think this is so, this feeling of looking at work that is new and not at all 'dated'?*

BRIDGET RILEY: Maybe it is because I have always tried to avoid making tasteful decisions. Of course it is inevitable that there are fashions and styles at any given time but I don't think that these form a sound basis. Or may be it is because my view of past art is critical and appreciative rather than historical. No matter how much you love and respect the past, you simply have, as an artist, to stand on your own feet.

RK: *But this independence from the various academies of Modernism has had its price. With the renewed interest in your work some of the old clichés have also* *reared their heads: the idea of a psychedelic background to your images and the notion of a computerised approach to painting in particular.*

BR: Aren't they two extraordinary opposites? The computer and psychedelia? During my opening at DIA two young girls appeared: 'We are painters', they said, 'abstract painters – were you on drugs?' 'No', I replied. 'Thought not!', they said and, with an air of triumph, they vanished.

RK: *The association with the computer is more difficult to untangle, I think. It has long gone outside the confines of the art world. There was an American introduction to a well-known textbook on database design and applications several years ago which featured your 1961 painting* Movement in Squares *on the cover – without crediting this image to you, implying that it could have been devised by a clever computer programmer.*

BR: Some people first made this connection in the late 1960s and I used to dismiss it without further thought, partly because it was irreconcilable with my working methods in the studio, and partly because I knew nothing whatsoever about computers. I can see now that it is the 'binary' look of my black-and-white work, which appealed to those who were familiar with computer logic. Nevertheless the connection is superficial and misleading, as one can see by the continual use and even the increasing popularity of my early paintings for illustrations in computer textbooks.

RK: *You mean that even skilled computer wizards, with highly sophisticated design programs, cannot produce equally striking and convincing images on their own?*

BR: Exactly so. The computer may be excellent at manipulating a given set of data or information, it may even, once it has been instructed, generate variations on my paintings ad infinitum. But it cannot initiate those very particular kinds of dramatic structures which I wanted in my black-and-white paintings in the 1960s. A computer simply does not understand what I called to myself the 'sense of inevitability'; and its mind would go blank when faced with the task of constructing a visual order which produces and accommodates disorder without yielding to it – as I did in *Movement in Squares*.

RK: *This may be why computer analysts are inclined to read your black-and-white work the wrong way round. Both the database design publishers and a recent German book titled* Computer und Kunst *by Erwin Steller reproduce* Movement in Squares *upside down – with the short passage on the left and the long one on the right. And indeed if one regards the painting only numerically there is no difference – in terms of the increase and decrease of its elements – without taking into account the third factor: the perceptual dissolution which relates the two unequal black-and-white movements.*

BR: You can't experience those black-and-white paintings if you only

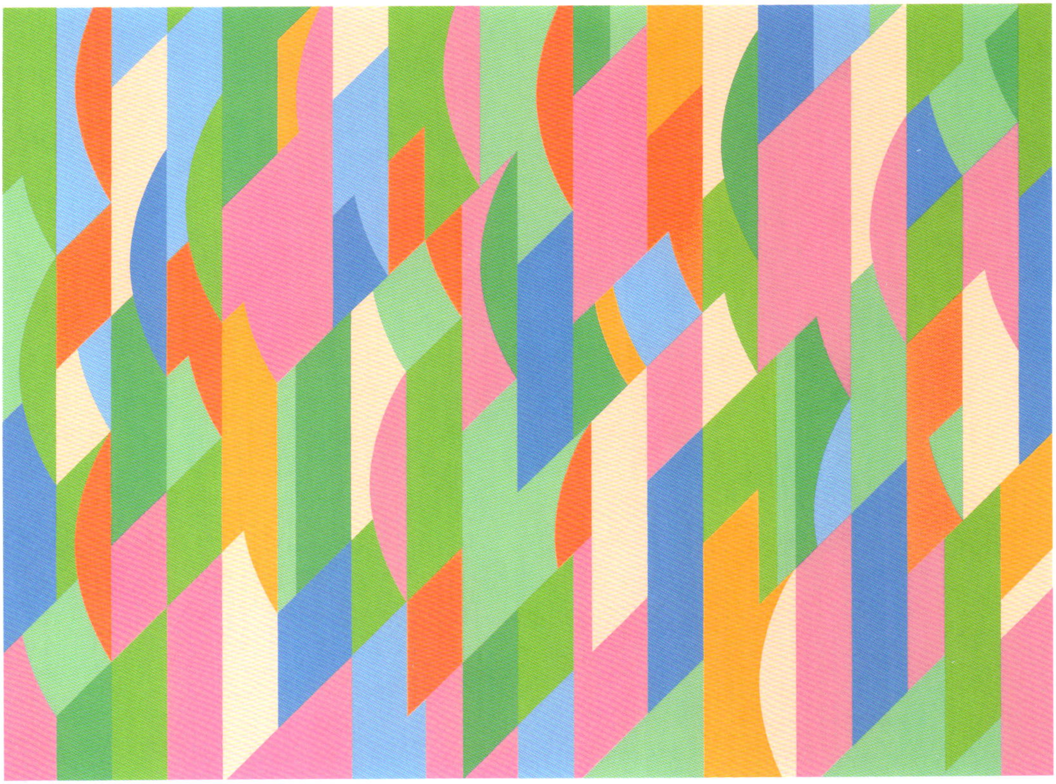

Lagoon 1 1997

count and measure their elements instead of *seeing what they do.* Everything in the painting – contrast, weight, unit, scale and speed – functions in such a precise way that together they precipitate a state in which each seems to momentarily lose its particular role and characteristics, before recovering this particularity again. At the beginning it was essentially a cycle of repose, disturbance, and repose.

RK: *This cycle, of which you have frequently spoken,*[2] *is a three-fold structure rather than a binary one and seems to be essentially a cultural configuration.* E. H. *Gombrich pointed out, in his conversation with you, that this structural concept of your work is, at least in Western music, the basis of all music: 'the possibility of a resolution of a discordant sound in a cadence.'*[3]

BR: I believe this happens in Shakespeare's sonnets too. In the one which opens 'Shall I compare thee to a summer's day?' he proceeds, beautiful line by beautiful line, to dismantle the comparison until he reaches the nadir, beauty obliterated 'by chance, or nature's changing course, untrimmed'. There, with tremendous verve, Shakespeare reverses direction, the sonnet climbs again. Beauty is recovered and its immortality ensured, in the only form he can support – as a work of art.

RK: *But this three-fold structure only applies to your paintings of the early 1960s, doesn't it? Then the scenario changed.*

BR: Well, it may be that this had something to do with my feeling that the black-and-white structures were almost too complete. At first I could not find a place in them for colour, or a way in which I could introduce it. What I needed were some more fluid, intermediary modes, which would allow me to break through the straight alternation. So I introduced greys, first neutral and then coloured, and through this I found a way to handle pure colour. Colour turns out to be the perfect vehicle for me because it is made up of harmonies as well as contrasts, and though unstable and fugitive, it also comes through as a powerful presence in its own right.

RK: *It is interesting to see that after 1968, when you introduced pure hues, your work with colour was dominated by two main tendencies for nearly 30 years. In the first place the formal complexity was radically reduced to accommodate the activity of colour; and through this the range and richness of colour grew until it reached a point where it could dictate the formal requirements. It seems to me that the introduction of a dynamic diagonal in 1986 was rather more an attempt to organise the increased colour differentiation, which had gradually emerged, than a return to formal complexity. Some of your paintings – such as* High Sky 2 *(1992) – could include anything up to twenty-five distinctly different colours. But since 1998 this has changed drastically: the palette is now limited to four or five colours – and the forms appear big and surprisingly simple.*

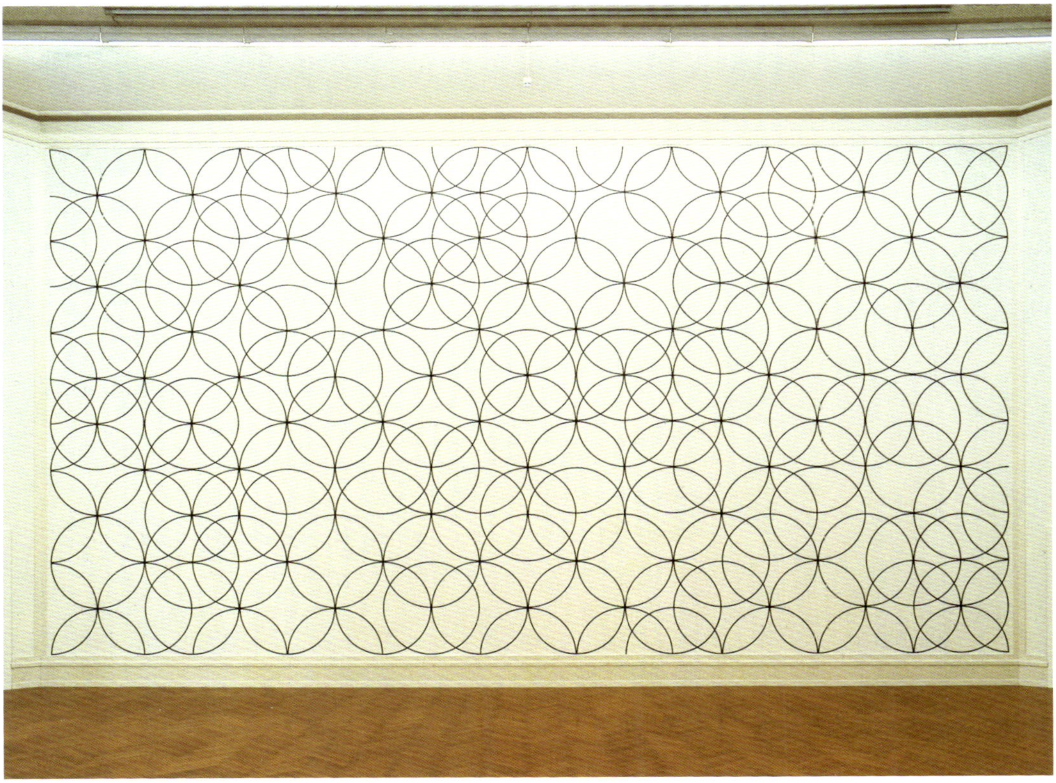

Composition with Circles 1 1998

BR: The change is not really so surprising, I think. It began back in the mid-1990s when I tried to give fuller reign to the curves and arcs which had been filtering through the colour organisation of my diagonal paintings. For a long time I tried simply to introduce parts of circles, based on the slice-like segment at which one arrives if one divides a circle vertically into six equal parts.

RK: *I remember studies and a few paintings, such as* Lagoon 1 (1997), *in which this curvilinear element appeared among the rhomboid forms. But initially the curves were bent to the left only, in opposition to the prevailing diagonal thrust, and the scale of the units and the range of colours employed were not much changed. Only in 1998, after two years of extensive probing and many trials and errors, did you arrive at the perpendicular swing, the paring down of your palette and the explosion of scale. What finally prompted this rapid resolution of what was obviously an intricate problem?*

BR: Well, many factors suddenly came together. There was the wall drawing for the Kunsthalle Bern (1998) in which I used circles on a big scale, though simply as linear elements. There I realised that the new spatial structure, which was beginning to emerge, would need a rethinking and simplification of colour relationships.

RK: *Just as years ago the use of pure colours had forced you to simplify your formal means?*

BR: Yes. Perhaps the most surprising thing was that the curve did not allow me to add a new form to those I was already using. It took over and emphasised the feeling of gravity through its curvilinear swing. The colours and their proportions took on different weights and consequently the balance between them became more fluid.

RK: *From the outside this looks like a shift in orientation within familiar territory. If the preceding rhomboid paintings with their structural density were reminiscent of Cézanne's small constructive planes, the new work shows a certain affinity to Matisse's late paper cut-outs – except for the underlying rhythm.*

BR: I suppose the fact that I had been working with cut-out pieces of paper for a long time...

RK: *Almost twenty years is certainly a long time!*

BR: Well, true – once I began to use curved shapes with those big flat areas of colour, the association probably became inevitable. But as you said, the structure in my work differs very much from Matisse in that it is supported by a rhythmic underpinning, some layers of which are apparent, while others remain latent.

RK: *The interplay between overtness and latency seems to be a recurrent factor in your work. In earlier paintings such as* Black to White Discs (1962) *or* Cantus

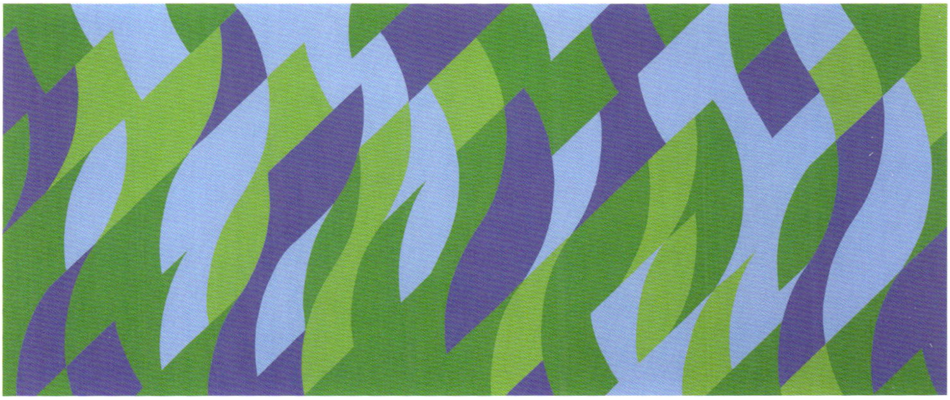

Parade 2 2002

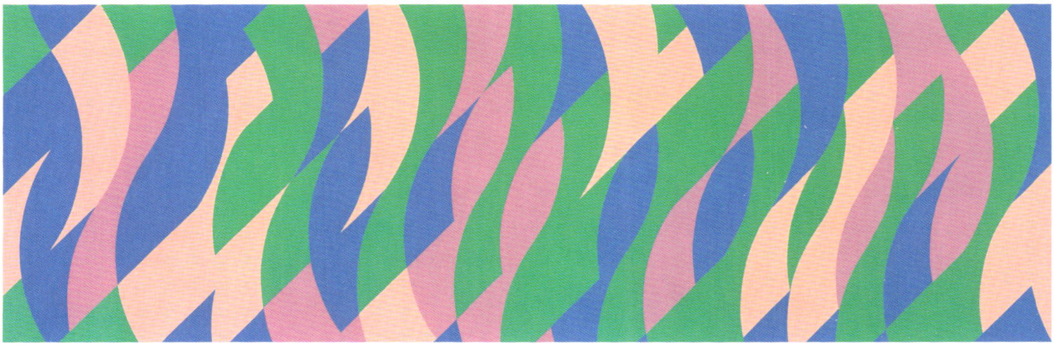

Evoë 3 2003

Firmus (1972–73) *it was often a basic formal device that was hidden by and within the appearance of the work, whereas now layers of different rhythms seem to support, obscure, and even oppose each other.*

BR: You played me a fascinating piece of music by György Ligeti recently...

RK: *You mean the six* "Études pour Piano" *he wrote in 1985, all of which work with the rhythmic phenomenon of 'simultaneous layers of different tempi' (Ligeti)?*[4] *The piece I played you, the so-called* Warsaw Étude, *is based on sixteen fast pulses per measure. There are however passages in which the right hand of the pianist accentuates every fifth pulse and the left every third – thus creating the sensation of superimposed melodic layers. The resulting perceptual complexity reminds me very much of the paintings you have been making since 1998.*

BR: Perhaps the only significant difference might be that in my work the rhythmic layers are not the same but are varied in their structural character as well. Paul Klee, who was a good musician himself, realised that in one respect painting had a considerable advantage over music: it could make the simultaneity of different rhythmic patterns clearly perceivable.

RK: *In looking at your new work one can still detect a basic vertical structure underlying the whole. Although seldom shown in the drawing itself, it nevertheless controls and stabilises the dynamism of the curves. 'My curves are not mad', Matisse said, 'I have derived constant benefit from the use of the plumb line.'*[5]

BR: He's right, of course, he must have learnt this early on from academic figure drawing. The vertical is an essential structural element in organising curvilinear weights and balances. The sheer physical necessity of breaking up the big canvases of *Evoë* and *Parade 1* (both 1999–2000) into panels of two and four gave me an opportunity to emphasise that latent vertical structure.

RK: *Now, a powerful diagonal is played against this stabilising register, very much as it was in the preceding group of paintings. But in the new work it has a different dynamic effect. The sharp parallel cuts, all accentuating the diagonal rising from bottom left to top right, seem to literally drive the rhythm of the paintings.*

BR: The drive is really brought about by the third element, the curve, which defines and shapes the rhythm. When played through a series of arabesques the curve is wonderfully fluid, supple and strong. It can twist and bend, flow and sway, sometimes with the diagonal, sometimes against, so that the tempo is either accelerated or held back, delayed.

RK: *Just by itself the formal description is very revealing. The swing of the curve and the increased rhythmic complexity have added a feeling of body and weight to your colour work. The abstract, essentially musical organisation has become infused by a new sense of almost physical elation. When I look at paintings like*

Evoë and Parade 1, I can't help thinking of primeval dancing or the ancient iconography of the Bacchanal.

BR: To tell you the truth, when I had finished *Evoë* and was thinking about it's title, I toyed with the idea of calling it "Bacchanal without Nymphs", and another painting, still untitled, "Bacchanal without Satyrs". But then I remembered just in time that I am after all supposed to be an abstract artist.

1 Peter Schjeldahl, "British Flash: Having Fun with Bridget Riley and Damien Hirst", *The New Yorker*, 6 November 2000, p. 104
2 Cf. "Perception Is the Medium" (1965), reprinted in *The Eye's Mind* (1999), pp. 66–68.
3 Bridget Riley, *Dialogues on Art*, ed. R. Kudielka, London: Thames & Hudson, 2003, p. 43.
4 György Ligeti, *Études pour Piano, Premier Livre*. Erika Haase, Piano and Harpsichord. *col legno* Musikproduktion, AU-031 815 CD.
5 *Matisse on Art*, ed. Jack D. Flam, London: Phaidon Press, 1973, p. 112.

First published in *Parkett*, no. 61, May 2001, pp. 22–26.

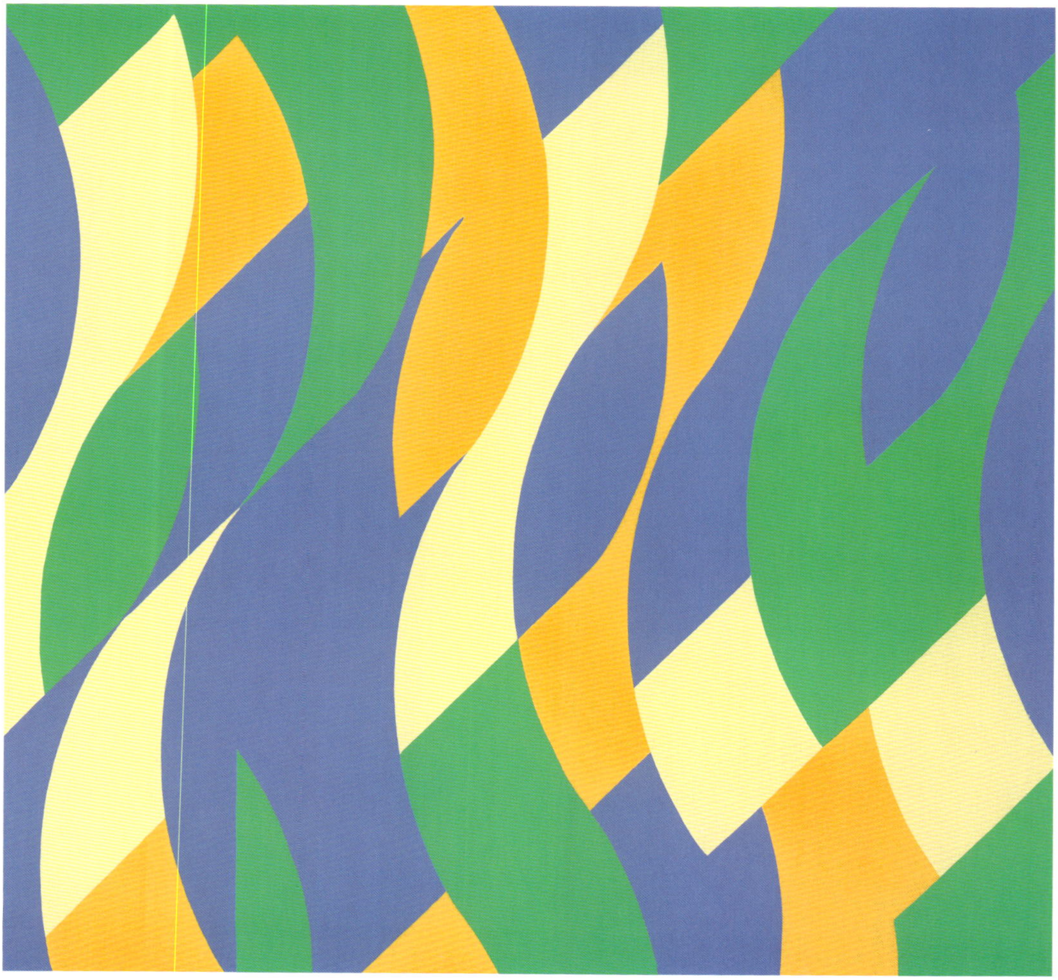

Rêve 1999

Abstract Figuration

On Bridget Riley's recent curve paintings

2003

> *The court ladies wore the so-called jûni-hitoé meaning 'twelve-layer' garment. It consisted of an outer robe of gorgeous brocade and embroidery and twelve or even more silk undergarments of different colours and shades which were arranged in such a way that each robe was slightly smaller and shorter than the one below it, so that a beautiful colour stratification might be visible at the neck and the outer edges of the sleeves.*[1]

In June 2000 when Bridget Riley showed her new curvilinear paintings for the first time, at Waddington Galleries in London, she was surprised to find that they seemed to be immediately accepted. At the opening of the exhibition the late Bryan Robertson, who had followed her career since the early 1960s and organised her first retrospective at the Hayward Gallery, in 1971, said to her: 'This is the easiest work you have ever done.' Indeed the appearance of the paintings seems to be much less demanding than that of the preceding rhomboid images, or of any earlier group.

The number of colours in *Rêve* (1999), *Parade 2* (1999–2000) and *Evoe 3* (2003) is limited to four and the structure is characterised by broad, curved shapes moving at an even pace across the canvas. Only after a while does one become aware that this ease is not the result of a simplification or mere enlargement of the formal elements, but a triumph of Riley's structural ingenuity. The works' apparent boldness and simplicity completely conceal the fact that they embody distinctly different layers of *ordering*. In fact, these paintings could be said to be the outcome of the most complex conjunction of pictorial factors Riley has ever attempted.

It would be futile to deconstruct these layers in an attempt to lay bare the essence of the work. No reality lies 'behind' or 'underneath' these paintings. The final compound is the body of experience, as has been said of the famous robes of the Heian Period: 'The garment *was* the person; it was the direct symbol of his or her personality.'[2] However, the different strata of composition in Riley's recent work are not merely superimposed to form a cumulative image. They are interlaced in such a way that each new level of ordering opposes the preceding one. This interplay between assertion and dissolution, composition and de-composition, generates the inner dynamism of these paintings and encourages an analytical approach as a preliminary to a more rewarding way of looking.

Combining opposing layers of construction has been a device fundamental to Riley's paintings, ever since she introduced tonal progressions into her black-and-white work. In *Pause* (1964), for instance, the transformation of circles into ovals carries the superimposition of light to dark grey sequences diverging both in tempo and in structural registration. As a result the two movements hold each other in suspension, they form – a pause. This approach culminates in *Deny 2* (1967) in which a regular grid is 'denied' by the revolving movements of the oval elements, upon which in turn tonal progressions of different paces are imposed, and the whole structural complex is set in a cool, bluish grey that contrasts with the warm grey of the ground. Obviously such an intricate fabric could not be extended, but by breaking down her formal vocabulary into thin stripes of colour, as in *Late Morning* (1967–8) for example, Riley began to build up a similar counterbalance with the perceptual interaction of colours. The stripe paintings of the late 1960s and early 1970s, as well as a considerable number of the subsequent curve paintings, are based on the opposition between the vertical organisation of the actual surface hues and the horizontal spread of luminous, disembodied colours. Instead of simply extending limitations, or overthrowing compositional devices, Riley confronts different forms of ordering aimed at a tension between stability and instability. It is her way of establishing the vital contradiction that she admires in Mondrian's 'dynamic equilibrium',[3] and in Klee's concept of 'unstable balance'.[4]

The particular development evinced by the paintings created since 1997 lies in the range covered by such contradictory structures. There is still that vertical register that underlies most of Riley's abstract work. However much her themes may vary, the top to bottom relationship underpins the general layout and formal extension. But the new curvilinear movements also incorporate the biggest destabilisation of this vertical bias. In 1986 Riley crossed the vertical register with a field of parallel diagonals rising from bottom left to top right. For the next ten years she worked with this dynamic opposition until she began to connect the regular vertical pulse with the diagonal subdivisions through circular segments. The reintroduction of a curved element in 1997 eventually resulted in the recent group of paintings.

At first glance the vertical foundation of the movements is hard to discern in the paintings. In fact *Rêve* is one of the few paintings in which an actual vertical can be found in the bottom left of the work. But if one traces this line imaginatively upwards, one realises that the perpendicular swing of the first fully reversed curve is twisted around the same invisible vertical. Moreover, once alerted to the presence of such a metre, the spectator begins to sense the regular pulsation and, consequently, visual perception itself becomes more acute. For instance in *Réve*, and indeed in all subsequent paintings, one notices a recurring free-floating element, which looks like a lancet. Scattered across the canvas in numbers, these shapes loosely resemble a fall of petals. But how is it, then, that these tilted elements seem so firmly integrated into the structure? Closer inspection provides the clue. The two formative curves are slightly trimmed along the top left and bottom right, and if a connecting line were to be drawn between these two trims it would reveal the vertical register that forms the spine of the new work.

If the vertical grid is a fairly subliminal device, the parallel diagonals severing the pictorial field play a more prominent role in the formation of the paintings. On one hand they seem to drive the movement, giving rise to a number of distinctive shapes. There are the big, blade-like cuts and giant commas that seem to simply press forward. But there are also the more ambiguous shapes that ride the crest of the movement. In *Rêve* one finds the slender, waisted shapes created by two diagonally displaced undulating curves and the tilted squares with two curved sides that punctuate and accelerate the flow. These latter two forms have become indispensable to Riley in drawing out a rhythm horizontally, because the diagonal fissions not only act as driving agents, but also provide an essential opposition against which the power of the curves can rise and gather momentum.

Although this opposition is a new function of the diagonal structure, it could be said to fulfil part of Riley's original intention in introducing this one-sided thrust in the late 1980s. 'I wanted *more*', she has said in explanation of her move, 'a way of working which allowed me to get to grips with plastic issues, to get closer to the real problems of painting'.[5] The key word here is 'plastic'. By upsetting the balance of the vertical band structure she created a tension that demanded drastic compositional operations such as the displacement and re-allocation of whole units in the pictorial fabric in order to counter this imbalance. As a result, the strong block-like formations of *New Day* (1988) appeared and, by establishing an open interplay of weights, stabilised the underlying dynamism and the disturbance of the field. In 1989, when a group of these early rhomboid paintings was shown at the Galerie Schlegl in Zürich, Franz Meyer, the celebrated ex-director of the Kunstmuseum in Basel, said to the artist: 'If one might associate the space of your earlier colour paintings with landscape, then one could say that you are now beginning to work with a kind of figure space.' His diagnosis of Riley's shift of interest was remarkably perceptive. That summer the National Gallery, London, presented Riley's *The Artist's Eye* exhibition for which she had selected seven great colour paintings from the collection, all characterised by dense, figurative compositions and animated by a diagonal dynamism.[6]

Reading the catalogue interview accompanying this exhibition, it becomes clear that some of Riley's descriptions of the selected paintings foreshadow aspects of her own subsequent work. The motif of the 'entry figure' leading into the painting from the left-hand side, for example, that she observed in Rubens' *Peace and War* (1629–30) clearly has an abstract equivalent in her recent paintings.[7] In the same way her term 'collective figuration', coined for Titian's *Bacchus and Ariadne* (1521–3) and Poussin's *Triumph of Pan* (1636), could be applied to her new compositional approach.[8] Nevertheless her aim of an increased plasticity could not be achieved solely through the means employed in *New Day*. The almost hieratic firmness of this work's pictorial formation conflicted with Riley's other reason for introducing the diagonal emphasis: 'I wanted to be able to go around a painting, to take your eye upwards, downwards and diagonally across in all sorts of ways and rhythms that I could not manage

(opposite)
Final study for Curvilinear Grid 1998

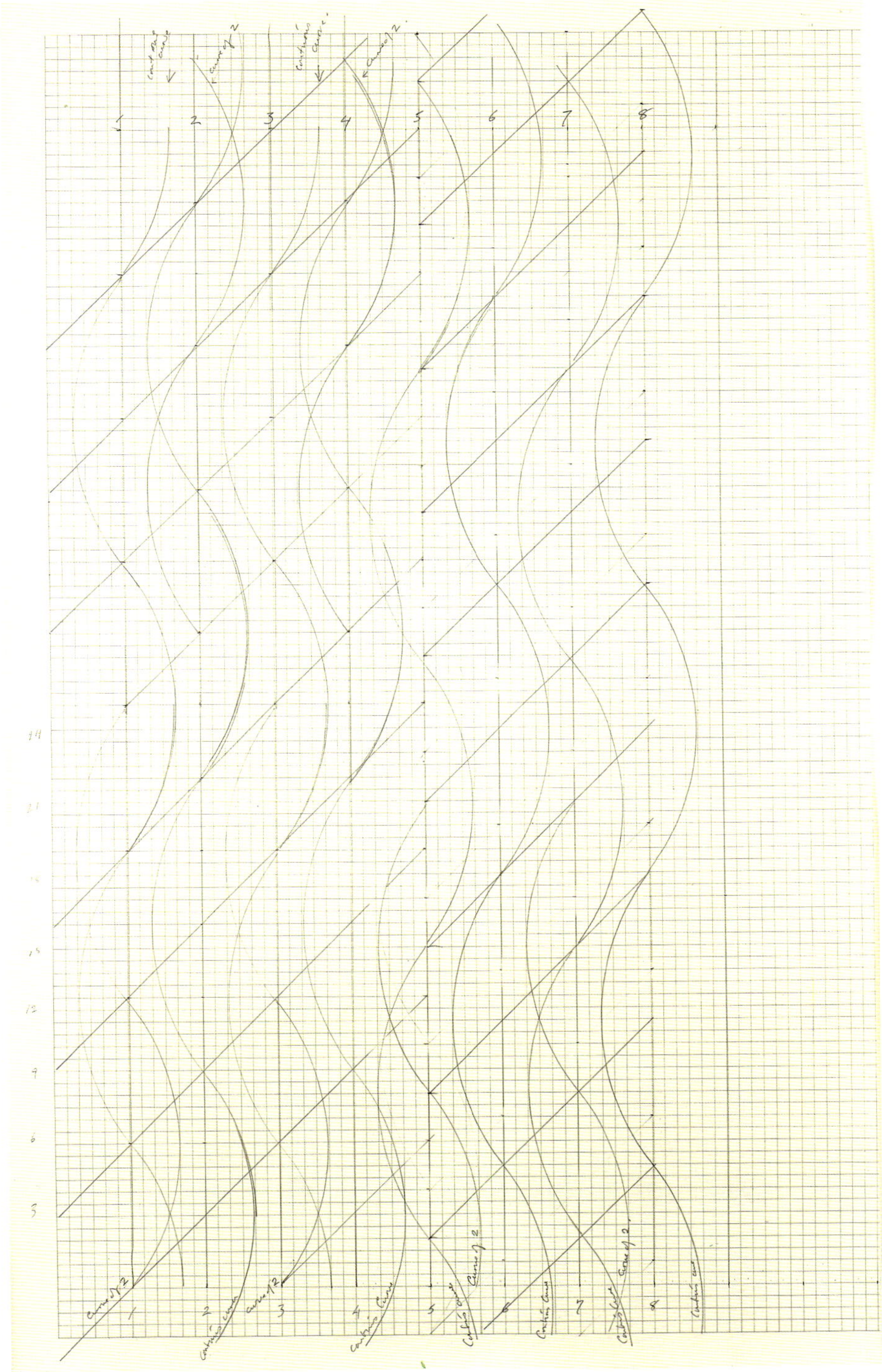
1
2
3
4
5
6
7
8

with just the vertical bands.'[9] What was needed was a more fluid and flexible space than the one provided by the block-like constellations. Consequently the paintings of the early 1990s seem to move in virtually the very opposite direction to a constructive consolidation. The big compounds of rhomboids are broken up, giving way to glittering passages of smaller shapes that act almost like brushmarks, and the number of colours increases accordingly until each painting may resonate with up to twenty or more specific hues.

With hindsight one can see that this renewed dissolution of the pictorial fabric prepared Riley for an unprecedented mode of circular composition. In practically all of her later rhomboid paintings the colour movement is introduced by a strong accent in the top left corner and descends with and against the formal diagonal until it reaches a point – usually just off centre right – from which it is reversed. In the area on the right-hand side of *High Sky 2* (1992) this circular return is clearly visible, and its revolving tendency is enhanced by a new structural device: the amplification, and occasional reduction, of the blue, violet and green rhomboids by one third of their width.

The employment of a tripartite proportion in addition to the straightforward repetition and multiplication of the basic rhomboid unit was of seminal importance. It allowed for a 2:3 ratio in the rhythmic structure, which was a device frequently employed by composers of vocal music in the Middle Ages, as a means of both enhancing and deflating dynamic tension. This shift of metre can also be found in Baroque dance music of the seventeenth century, for instance in the *Courante*, and again in the nineteenth century, when it was favoured particularly by Chopin, Brahms and Liszt.[10] In *Reflection 1* (1994) one can see how Riley developed this device in her later rhomboid paintings. The extended 1/3 and 2/3s divisions intermittently suspend the regular vertical register creating a temporary rhythmic dislocation. The resulting disturbance acts in two ways: slowing down or accelerating the tempo, before the regular pulse resolves these frictions again.

Apart from adding to the rhythmic complexity of the rhomboid paintings, the tripartite proportion eventually offered a way of reintroducing a curve element. Having worked for quite a while with virtually circular movements, in the mid-1990s Riley began to search for the structural means that would allow her to include actual curvilinear shapes in her compositions. *Lagoon 1* (1997) shows an early step in this direction. In the centre of the painting a blue rhomboid form encompassing six basic units is joined by a curved fragment, a green crescent of an equal length.

But the apex of this curve extends to only two thirds of the regular width of the rhomboid. Riley had found that a fuller curvature could not be contained by the underlying vertical and diagonal frameworks. Moreover, the reduced curve initially did not allow for a swing in both directions. All curvilinear elements in *Lagoon 1* are directed towards the left side, pressing against the diagonal thrust.

It was nearly two years before a satisfactory solution emerged. This lengthy interval was due not only to the extensive preparatory work on *Composition with Circles 1* (1998), a temporary wall painting measuring 5 × 9 metres commissioned by the Kunsthalle Bern, but also to the rigorous decisions required to fully integrate the new curve element. First of all Riley had to reduce the number of colours – *Lagoon 1* still comprises eight hues – in order to cope with the structural complexities. She had always known that complex colour relationships and dense formal structures do not sit well together,[11] and just as she had reduced her formal vocabulary to the repetition of stripes in 1968, she now had to restrict her range of colours to accommodate the added formal complexity. All paintings made after *Rêve* are based on a palette of four or at the most five colours. At the same time it seemed to be necessary to increase the scale of the imagery, and consequently the size of the canvases, to allow for the kind of spatial resonance demanded by a curve that could swing both ways. However musical the rhythmic structuring of the new paintings may be, the decisive change brought about by the curvilinear element was the introduction of a virtually physical sensation of weight into Riley's pictorial world.

For a long time the most puzzling aspect of this development was the balance of the colour relationships. Although Riley had intuitively arrived at a working colour bracket with the four colours of *Rêve* – blue, green, yellow and yellow ochre – she did not immediately understand its implications. Having worked for almost ten years with a broad orchestration of harmonies and contrasts it took her a while to find the new rationale intrinsic to the plastic problems which her work now presented her with. Certainly colour opposition was of primary importance because 'opposing' is a basic proposition of her pictorial logic. But what about the third position, the mediating and modifying factor that had become essential even since she introduced grey into the black and white work? In her early colour paintings such as *Orient 4* (1970), for instance, the three colours – cerise, turquoise and olive – encompass an opposition of red and green, and, through an emphasis on the blue tendency present in both cerise and turquoise, destabilise the contrast. The new work however

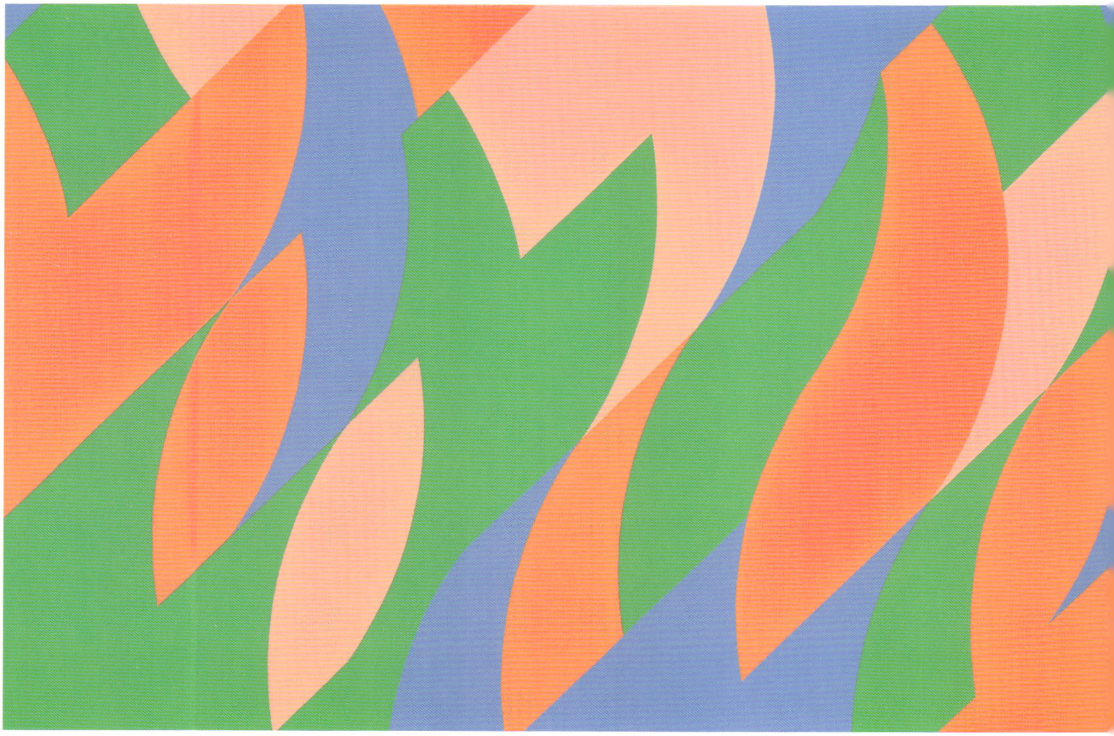

Paired Colours 2001

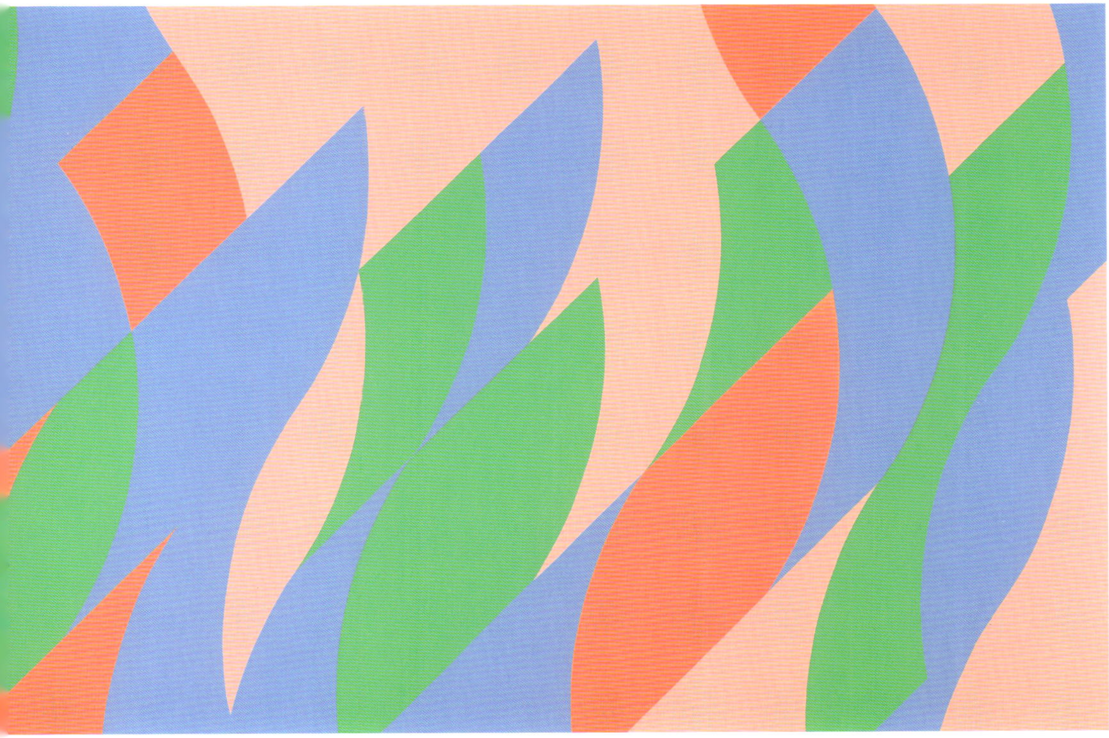

was no longer so concerned with overt colour interaction. In reviewing the group of paintings executed between 1999 and 2001, it is fascinating to follow the step-by-step establishment of an approach that is inherent in *Rêve*: two neighbouring colours (blue and green) form, with two opposite relations (yellow and yellow-ochre), a paired contrast mediated by an implied harmony (green and yellow-ochre).[12]

Very often in Riley's work blue and green, in a carefully attuned balance, form a kind of tenor against which a lighter pair of colours is pitched – magenta and pink in *Evoë 3*, or orange and pink in *Paired Colours* (2001). Occasionally two greens, one fully saturated and the other yellowish, are opposed by an unexpected contrast of blue-violet and pale blue in *Parade 2*, or of apricot and pink in the painting named after these colours *Apricot and Pink* (2001). This paired relationship, rhythmically disposed throughout the paintings, chromatically complements the formal structure, or rather the structural topography. For there are, strictly speaking, *no forms and intervals* in these new paintings. Each shape is an area delineated by the interplay of the diagonal and curvilinear orders and defined in its characteristics by colour. This is not unlike Mondrian's replacement of form by rectilinear compartments of weight and colour, except that Riley's complex layering of vertical, diagonal and curvilinear divisions enabled her to extract shapes that are surprisingly particular, although they do not attain an individual status. There is room for invention, but the range is nevertheless limited, constituting Riley's abstract cast of a 'collective figuration'.

The particular character of this working basis becomes clearer when one compares it with certain qualities Riley admires in earlier paintings. In 1997 she wrote a short piece describing the composition of Matisse's *Dance 2* (1909–10). In pointing out the different characteristics of the painting's five central figures she drew particular attention to their collective nature and to the equal status of figure and interval. 'The group, subject to the overall organisation of colour and rhythm and entranced by the act of dancing, lose their separate identities and become one pictorial form, one organic unit. And yet, figure by figure, interval by interval, how brilliantly Matisse shows the change of pace, mood and character. Each state, fast or slow, tense or relaxed, demonic or gentle is only an aspect of dance as a whole. One feels that they are interchangeable, that any one dancer could the next moment assume the role and gesture of another.'[13] This fluid, protean quality can be found in Riley's new abstract figurations, too, with one important difference. The five red figures in Matisse's painting are set against a background of blue and green, and although this background is flattened it is still a distinctly separate spatial plane from that of the figures. In Riley's curvilinear paintings, however, the spatial planes have become interchangeable to the degree that the figure-ground ambiguity is completed dissolved.

The elimination of this ambiguity marks an essential difference between Riley's new work and the Hard-Edge colour-field painting of the 1960s, which relied heavily on the figure-ground relationship. Thanks to the complex compositional stratification of her recent paintings there is no longer a stable ground plane carrying the painting, nor do isolated forms exist against some kind of background. Instead, the colour shapes shift, contrast and alternate in space according to a structural rhythm that is specific to each particular painting. In *Rêve*, for instance, the firmness of the composition almost conceals the surprising opposition between the two sides of the painting. Only after a while does one discern a virtually hallucinatory reversal: the very same blue that advances on the left side of the painting recedes on the right – and in its wake all the related colour planes reassemble in an unexpected way. In contrast to *Rêve*, *Evoë 3* is an overtly turbulent painting in which the spatial planes are continually shifting. The seemingly steady tenor of blue and green is kicked off dynamically, backwards and forwards, through the contrasting pink and magenta in each new constellation.

Such vivid changes in spatial positioning are of course facilitated by the absence of figurative recognition in abstract painting. But making use of spatial mobility has a telling history in representational work as well. Riley herself regards the two horsemen in the Panathenaic procession depicted in the West Frieze of the Parthenon as an informative example of plastic understanding both for sculpture and for painting. There again a collective figuration is created by rendering the limbs of the horsemen, and the heads and the legs of the horses, as 'interchangeable' angular shapes, in order to articulate an animated forward movement. However, this rhythmic device also permits an evocation of depth within the strict confines of relief technique. The second horseman, riding alongside and to the rear of the first, is perceived by the viewer as being in front, although both horsemen actually exist on the same physical plane in the relief. It is the sensation of movement, as opposed to the mere superimposition of images, which opens up a totally convincing plastic space.

There are other aspects of the Parthenon relief that demonstrate to what great extent the principles of building a visual rhythm remain objective despite historical distances and cultural differences. For instance, the bodies of the two horses are joined in a rising diagonal

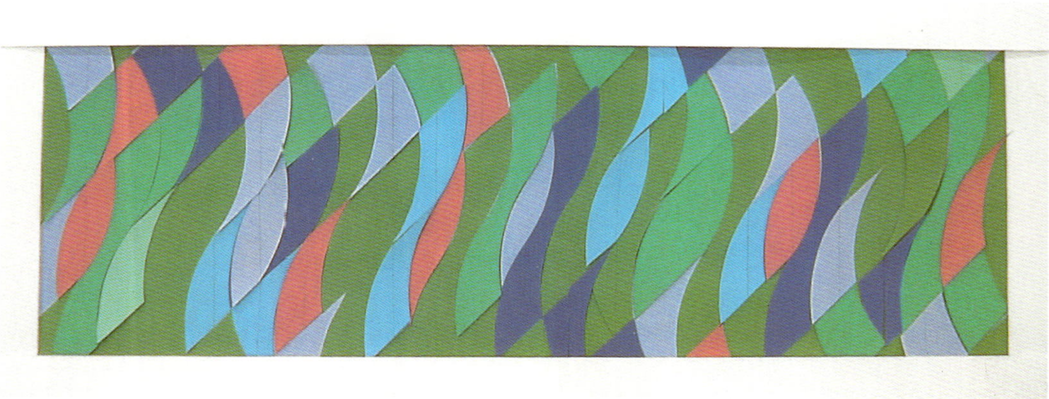

1

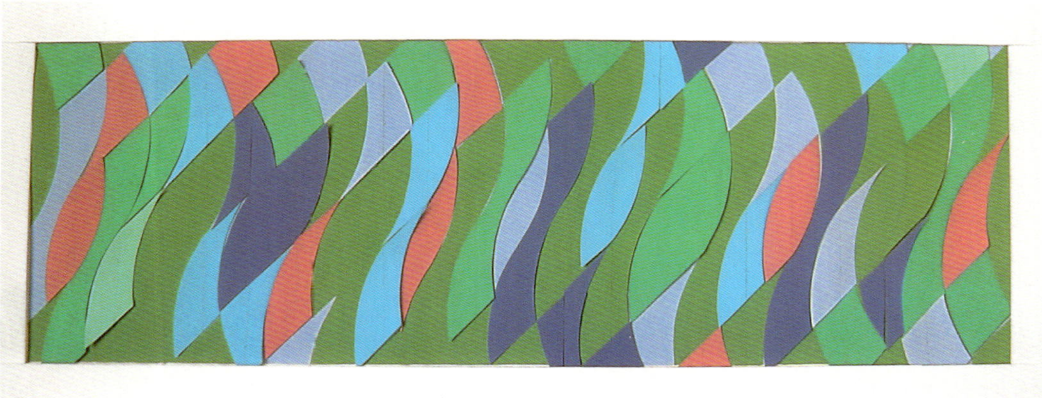

2

Collage studies for painting (in four stages) 2005

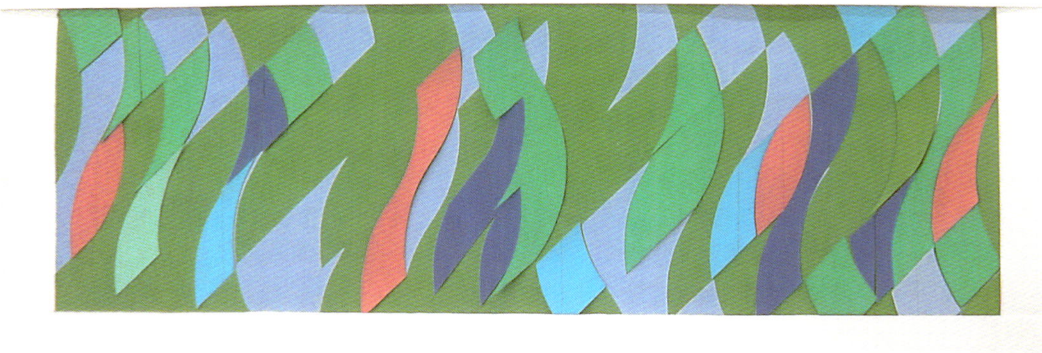

3

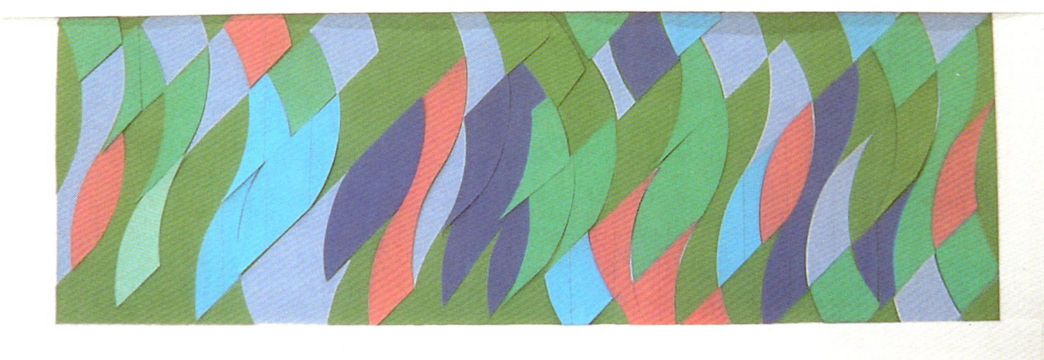

4

supporting the forward thrust, while a steep falling diagonal formed by the undulating shapes of the back of the first horse and the front of the second asserts the weight and power carried by this movement. One can even find a clear indication of the vertical balance, the plastic check as it were, in the virtual plumb lines connecting the head of the first rider with the hoof of the left back leg of his horse, and the hand of the second rider with the same point in his horse. But perhaps the most stunning device is the turning back of the first rider towards his companion. It is a clear, truly classic example of the perceptual fact that in order to make a directional movement visually plausible in the plastic arts, it is necessary to include or to suggest the opposite direction.

Riley has repeatedly emphasised the importance of this principle to her own work and has remarked on its presence in other works from the past.[14] In conversation with Neil MacGregor she analysed Mantegna's *Introduction of the Cult of Cybele at Rome* (1505–6) in these terms: 'The subject is the carrying of a statue into Rome. I was amazed to see that Mantegna holds together the narrow horizontal format of his frieze in one long, all embracing rhythm. The verve with which the first figure steps in, is stopped, cut short by the straight line of the statue, as though by an enormous comma; then this movement, introduced by the first figure, is picked up by the next two, turned round in the supplicating figure and continues in reverse until the very last figure where it changes back to echo the first.'[15] This description seems to anticipate the developments in her recent work. But, again, there is a decisive difference. Mantegna structures his frieze by extending the 'turning both ways' motif, so beautifully employed in the Parthenon relief, through groups and pairs of figures. The curve in Riley's paintings, however, seems to enable her to fuse these opposite directions into an almost simultaneous sensation. Instead of a steady epic flow, a dynamic concurrence of opposing movements is established, and the slender waisted shape made up of two diagonally displaced curves in the centre of *Rêve* is its emblem.

Riley did not dwell overly on this poised resolution. On the whole she has tended to avoid finite constellations, preferring an open and contradictory rhythm. Progressions, reversals and the interplay between successive reading and instantaneous sensation have been staple devices in her work since *Movement in Squares* (1961). So it is not surprising that with her new, layered method of composing she attempted the squaring of the circle, so to speak: a rhythmic movement based on the simultaneity of a progressive sequence and its reversal. This prompted an unexpected and initially rather awkward consequence because in order to carry the weight and draw out the dynamism of the new curvilinear structures she had to drastically increase the scale of her work. *Evoë 3* measures 193.3 × 581.4 cm, *Parade 2* measures 226.7 × 527.4 cm. To manage these enormous formats she split each painting into two canvases.

The simultaneity of the movements is, of course, not literal. Both works engender the sensation of concurrent, opposing developments by starting with a rhythmic cadence on the left side. In *Evoë 3* the large pink comma acts as an entry figure, pushing forward a dense muscular movement that seems to relax towards the centre. There it is momentarily delayed by two magenta lancets, accompanied by a pair of green, waisted shapes. These waisted shapes are then repeated, taking on weight, and, under the pressure of a pink hammer-like shape, initiate a second, more delicate sequence which is received by two big shapes, a magenta form resembling a bell clapper and a pink buffer, which swing the whole sequence back. If the initial movement had a falling momentum, the reversal rises upwards. It is carried by the step-wise ascension of the green shapes and helped by the apostrophes, which support the upward drift like little sails until this surging current meets the resistance of the passage initiated by the entry figure.

The same circular structure, which is perceived as a series of simultaneous events, can be found in *Parade 2*. But this painting is experienced in a remarkably different way, the character of the composition being almost opposite to that of *Evoë 3*. In the upper left of the canvas, at the point of entry, two related shapes in violet and yellow-green start the movement swiftly. It continues along a steep diagonal towards the centre where the impetus seems to vanish. But in that open green passage a curiously inert, violet shape, defined by two curves – one plain, the other undulating – picks up the momentum, setting the pace for a steady horizontal flow towards an area dominated by a pale blue configuration. This large sliced and interlaced shape echoes the cloud-like spread of the same pale colour on the left side and acts as a rebound of the entire movement. As *Parade 2* is clearly a two-sided painting, the reversal happens in two stages: firstly a broad phalanx advances towards the centre, and secondly, an elegant rise returns to the beginning.

In describing these two paintings one is unavoidably reminded of human gestures and movements. Riley herself admitted this: 'When I had finished *Evoë* and was thinking about its title I toyed with the idea of calling it "Bacchanal without Nymphs" and another painting, still untitled, "Bacchanal without Satyrs". But then I remembered, just in time, that I am after all supposed to be an abstract artist.'[16] There is indeed a painting by Poussin called A *Bacchanalian Revel before a Herm of Pan* (c. 1633) in the collection of the National Gallery, London, which has a somewhat related lateral rhythm. It begins with the entry figure of a nymph, who is turning back to hold out a bunch of grapes to two children while the forward thrust of her body partakes in a revel with two male dancers. Engaged in a complicated figure of dance this group is linked by three legs lifted in a parallel upward swing. This rising movement is countered by the falling diagonal of a tree behind which continues down to a group of four figures tumbling in the opposite direction to the dancers. All are linked by their gestures: the two running women and the satyr through the downward thrust of their arms, and the third woman, in the satyr's embrace, through reaching in the opposite direction. This hopeless resistance is not enough to reverse the whole chain of events, and in terms of content, is clearly not meant to do so.

Despite the obvious divergences there are sufficient similarities to beg a crucial question. If Riley in her recent work is so clearly involved with the spirit of exultant collective figurations, why does she not turn directly to the human figure? One answer is simply historical. The individual human figure has never been a vehicle for the expression of such states of being. It was the Bacchic and Arcadian mythology that lent itself to the celebration of an ecstatic reconciliation with nature in the arts even after the cultural validity of these pagan visions had long expired. When Poussin painted his bacchanals for Cardinal Richelieu and other humanist clients, they were anachronisms, replete with obsolete forms of imagery; and this is even truer of Picasso's recreation of the same mythical themes in the twentieth century. But what other pictorial language could be appropriate for the portrayal of these feelings?

The second answer touches upon the *raison d'être* of abstraction in modern art. Although Abstract art has many different and often contradictory meanings, one of its great possibilities, as Riley sees it, is its ability to give form to certain spiritual states that cannot be expressed by straightforward realism. 'Figurative painting without the relevant context of religion or mythology won't do – it's no longer a language. I think that an artist today has to totally accept this lack, has to start from a "placelessness", virtually as a point of departure. I can see no real alternative to abstract painting if, in fact, the painter wants to address those particular issues.'[17] In this regard her understanding seems to be very close to that of Mark Rothko, who saw his paintings as dramas, with the shapes and colours in the role of performers: 'They have been created from the need for a group of actors who are able to move dramatically without

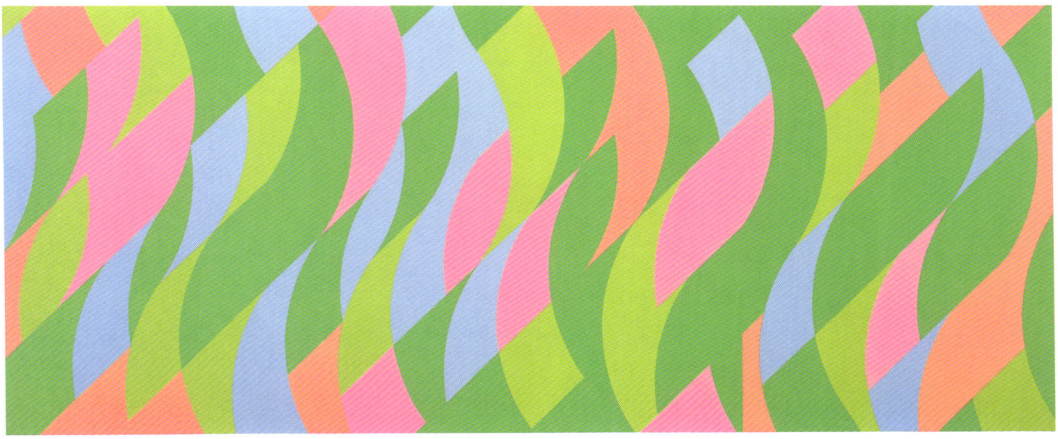

Two Reds 2000

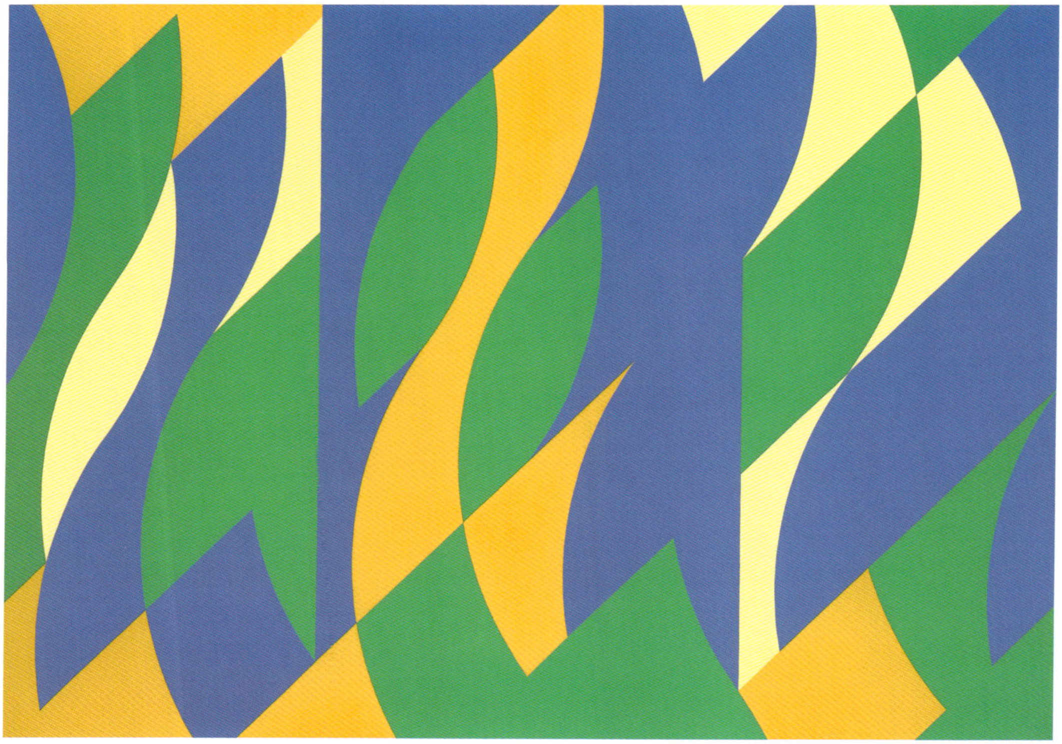

Painting with Two Verticals 2004

embarrassment and execute gestures without shame.'[18] Although Rothko's drama tends towards the tragic while Riley's seems to be coloured by almost the opposite spirit, the same could still be said of her abstract collective figurations. The complex rhythmic structure of her new curvilinear paintings allows her to express states of joy and elation without provoking the inference of self-reflection unavoidably connected with the human image.

The critical link between figurative art and this understanding of abstraction seems to be Matisse's work on the *Dance* decoration for Dr Alfred Barnes's Pennsylvania-based Foundation in the early 1930s.[19] The so-called *Paris Dance Mural* (1931–3) in particular marks an important step in his development of this theme. While the earlier *Dance* painting of 1909–10 retains a connection with the physical presence of the figures through the red colouring of their bodies and their mask-like faces, the recapitulation of the self-same cast of figures severs both these associations. The dancers of the *Paris Dance Mural* have no physiognomy and are a light, neutral grey that anticipates the final departure from any resemblance to flesh colour in the *Blue Nudes* of 1952. In accordance with this radical withdrawal from individual representation Matisse treats the human figure in an unprecedented way. Using the arcs of the three areas predetermined by the site of the commission, he fragments and dismembers the six dancing poses in order to re-assemble their parts in autonomous dynamic configurations. Each fragmented figure is 'cut in' from the edges and stretched to full tension within a sequence of rising and descending diagonals running through the three areas. The powerful dancer in the centre is even accompanied by formalised limbs, which are not fully accounted for by any of the figures in the neighbouring fields.

Looking at this rigorous figurative abstraction affords a clearer perspective on Riley's approach. Far from trespassing the confines of pure abstraction – whatever this may be – her recent work aspires to a similar collective sensation, though from primarily structural considerations. The shapes she extracts from the matrix of her layered orders can loosely be classified according to figurative attributes and associations. There are the waisted shapes of variable vivacity and volume; they are related to the cross-over spreading gestures, poses of maximum exultation, which are directly opposed to the softly curling, almost passive shapes; while the rhythmic beat is kept up by the big diagonal blades. These main characters are accompanied by a flurry of smaller, lighter accents: the lancets, commas, apostrophes and buoyant squares with two curved sides, which drive and punctuate the rhythm, riding the current or acting like little chinks of light. But being non-figurative derivatives, these elements can also adopt guises not necessarily related to the human figure. This becomes particularly clear in the most recent, scaled-down paintings Riley has made. The moment the almost physical sensation of weight recedes other areas of resonance open up, notably those of nature and of lively exchanges, such as conversations, competitions and conflicts, in general.

The colours in *Blues and Greens* (2001) are in themselves suggestive. But it is in fact the subtle balance of tones and hues that creates the sensation of deep and glittering vegetation. Three greens – a dark yellow-green, a turquoise and a lighter, slightly yellowish turquoise – are paired with two blues, a light and dark one, in such a way that the dark green and blue are of the same tone while the pale turquoise equals the light blue. However, this apparent harmony of tones and colours implies latent contrasts, which are released and intensified through the structural organisation of the painting. Despite the apparent tonal closeness there is a friction between the yellow-green and the blue, and provoked by the dominance of the greens the light blue takes on a reddish tinge and turns towards violet – an unexpected reminder of the perceptual activity that characterised much of Riley's colour work of the 1970s. The pervasive pulse of this low-key animation seems to be strong enough to turn our attention away from the connotations of dramatic action and to shift the associative character of these same shapes towards moving blades, leaves, bells, reflected lights, all rippling like new growth in a fresh breeze.

Subtle differentiation within a narrow bracket is, however, not the only direction in which Riley has extended her new range. *Two Reds* (2000) shows the opposite approach in terms of colour. Here the paired opposition consists of orange-red and magenta-red set against a dark and a light yellow-green, with pale blue of virtually the same tone as the mediating light green. The high colour contrast results in sudden shifts of pace and emphasis. But the rising turbulence is firmly checked by a clear distinction of plastic functions between the two sides of the painting. While on the left side the greens are carried into action by the other colours as it were, on the right they, by an ingenious shift of structure, themselves become the carriers of the movement. This dynamic two-sidedness within the coherence of one painting anchors and enhances the sensation of a rhythm advancing into two opposite directions simultaneously.

Given the fundamental difference that Riley's recent paintings do not unfold in one progressive direction of time only, looking at *Two Reds* is

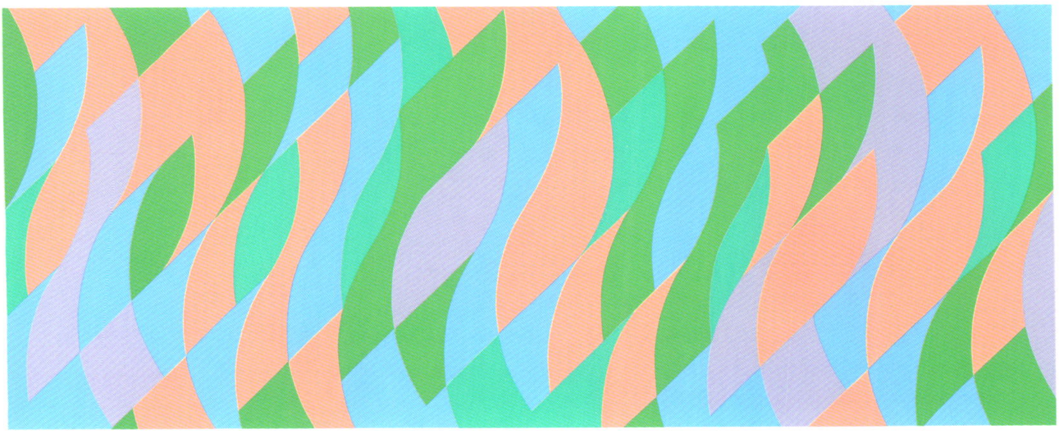

Enchant 2004

not unlike listening into an intense musical dialogue of the sort that Nikolaus Harnoncourt has observed in Bach's *Brandenburg Concertos*. In describing the final allegro of the *6th Concerto* he writes: 'Here, already with the first entry of the whole orchestra ... rhythm and metre are very firmly marked and at the same time called into question. Even though the movement begins with an up-beat involving a skip, it is already attached through syncopation to the third measure, so that one gets the impression that the violas begin the measure on the last eighth. The chords played by all other instruments decisively against this, but still on the beat, lead as in the first movement to a struggle for the "right" measure.'[20] It is a struggle that probably will never be resolved definitively in any work of art, let alone in life. On the contrary, to have kept this struggle alive, and to have deepened and strengthened it, as Riley has done over forty years of work, is an achievement to be celebrated.

1 Toshishiko Izutsu, "The Elimination of Color in Far Eastern Art and Philosophy", in Adolf Portmann and Rudolf Ritsema, *The Realms of Colour / Die Welt der Farben / Le Monde des Couleurs*, Leiden 1974, p. 434 (Eranos Yearbook, vol. 41).

2 Op. cit., p. 432.

3 See Riley's essay "Mondrian: the 'universal' and the 'particular'" (1992), reprinted in *The Eye's Mind. Bridget Riley, Collected Writings 1965–1999*, London 1999, p. 196.

4 This basic concept of Klee's teaching and its relationship to Mondrian is discussed in the author's contribution to *Paul Klee: The Nature of Creation*, London 2002, p. 82–83.

5 According to *Sensation* 1990, p. 97 [in this volume]

6 *The Artist's Eye: Bridget Riley*, exh. cat., National Gallery, London 1989. The conversation "The Colour Connection" included in this catalogue has been reprinted in a reduced form in *The Eye's Mind* (1999), pp. 142–173.

7 "The Colour Connection: In Conversation with Robert Kudielka" (1989), *The Eye's Mind* (1999), p. 161.

8 Op. cit., pp. 148, 166.

9 "Something to Look At: In Conversation with Alex Farquharson" (1995), reprinted in *The Eye's Mind* (1999), p. 131.

10 It is interesting to note that in the 1980s the composer György Ligeti experimented with a superimposition of rhythmic strata related to this ratio in his *Études pour Piano, Premier Livre*, written in 1985 (György Ligeti – Erika Haase, piano and harpsichord. col legno Musikproduktion, AU-031 815 CD). In the leaflet accompanying this disc the composer describes the structural principle of his pieces: 'The pianist plays coordinated, even pulsations in both hands. Superimposed onto these pulsations is a grid work of irregular accents which at times, however, progresses synchronously in both hands, thereby temporarily producing the impression of order. This impression slowly disintegrates as the accents in one hand begin to lag behind those in the other. In doing so the metric relationship is gradually blurred until we reach a point where we are unable to discern which hand leads and which lags behind. A state of order is in due course restored as the two successions of accents shift closer and closer to one another,

eventually falling simultaneously in the two hands, at which point the cycle begins anew.') Riley refers to one of these *Études* in *Supposed to be Abstract*, p. 208 [in this volume]

11 In 1972 she explained the transition from her complex black-and-white structures to her early colour paintings in the following way: 'Form and colour seem to be fundamentally incompatible – they destroy each other. In my earlier work, when I was developing complex forms, the energies of the medium could only be fully released by simplifying colour to a black-and-white constant (with occasional grey sequences). Conversely colour energies need a virtually neutral vehicle if they are to develop uninhibitedly. The repeated stripe seems to meet these conditions.' See *Conversation 1972*, p. 20 [in this volume]

12 This colour balance has a remote precedent in the palette of the tiled Safavid wall paintings of the seventeenth century. Called *haft-rangi*, 'Seven Colours' – technique, this palette consists of black and white, cobalt blue, turquoise and three warm hues, yellow, yellow green and ochre. In her colour-mixing studio Riley treasures a North African tile which is related to this Persian scheme.

13 The piece was commissioned by the *Daily Telegraph*, and published in an abbreviated version under the title "Pick of the Hermitage" in their weekend magazine, 27 October 1990, p. 55.

14 In "The Experience of Painting" (1988), for instance, she recalls another example of this contradictory logic of plastic representation: 'I discovered a well-known principle (it's always exciting when you find things for yourself): that you cannot have movement without its opposite – stasis. There is no change without a constant.' *The Eye's Mind* (1999), p. 123.

15 *Bridget Riley: Dialogues on Art*, ed. R. Kudielka, London 1995, p. 23. Neil MacGregor commented: 'That's a very musical way of analysing a painting.'

16 *Supposed to be Abstract* 2001, p. 209 [in this volume]

17 *Bridget Riley: Dialogues on Art*, 1995, p. 28. This concept of abstraction seems to be the reason why Riley, when speaking about her work, generally prefers to relate to the figurative art of the past. When in 1995 Alex Farquharson pointed out this tendency to her, she replied: 'I think abstract art should try to be as resourceful and as expressive as the great figurative art of the past [...] I would like to show that my abstract chromatic and formal means make as good and practical a basis to start from as figurative subject matter did in the past.' "Something to Look At"(1995), in *The Eye's Mind* (1999), p. 132.

18 Mark Rothko, "The Romantics were prompted ...", in *Possibilities* 1, Winter 1947–8, p. 84.

19 See Jack Flam, *Matisse: The Dance*, exh. cat., National Gallery of Art, Washington, 1993. This publication traces the evolution of the dance theme in Matisse's work from *Le bonheur de vivre* (1905–6) to the late paper cut-outs, focusing on the three major mural decorations of 1931–3: *Unfinished Dance Mural* (1931, Musée d'art moderne de la Ville de Paris), *Merion Dance Mural* (1932–3, The Barnes Foundation, Merion, Pen.) and *Paris Dance Mural* (1931–3, Musée d'art moderne de la Ville de Paris)

20 Nikolaus Harnoncourt, *The Musical Dialogue. Thoughts on Monteverdi, Bach and Mozart*, Portland, Oregon, 1997, p. 164. (The translation of this dense passage has been checked with the German original and slightly revised.)

First published in Paul Moorhouse (ed.), *Bridget Riley*, texts by the editor, Richard Shiff, Robert Kudielka and the artist, London: Tate Publishing, 2003, pp. 151–157.

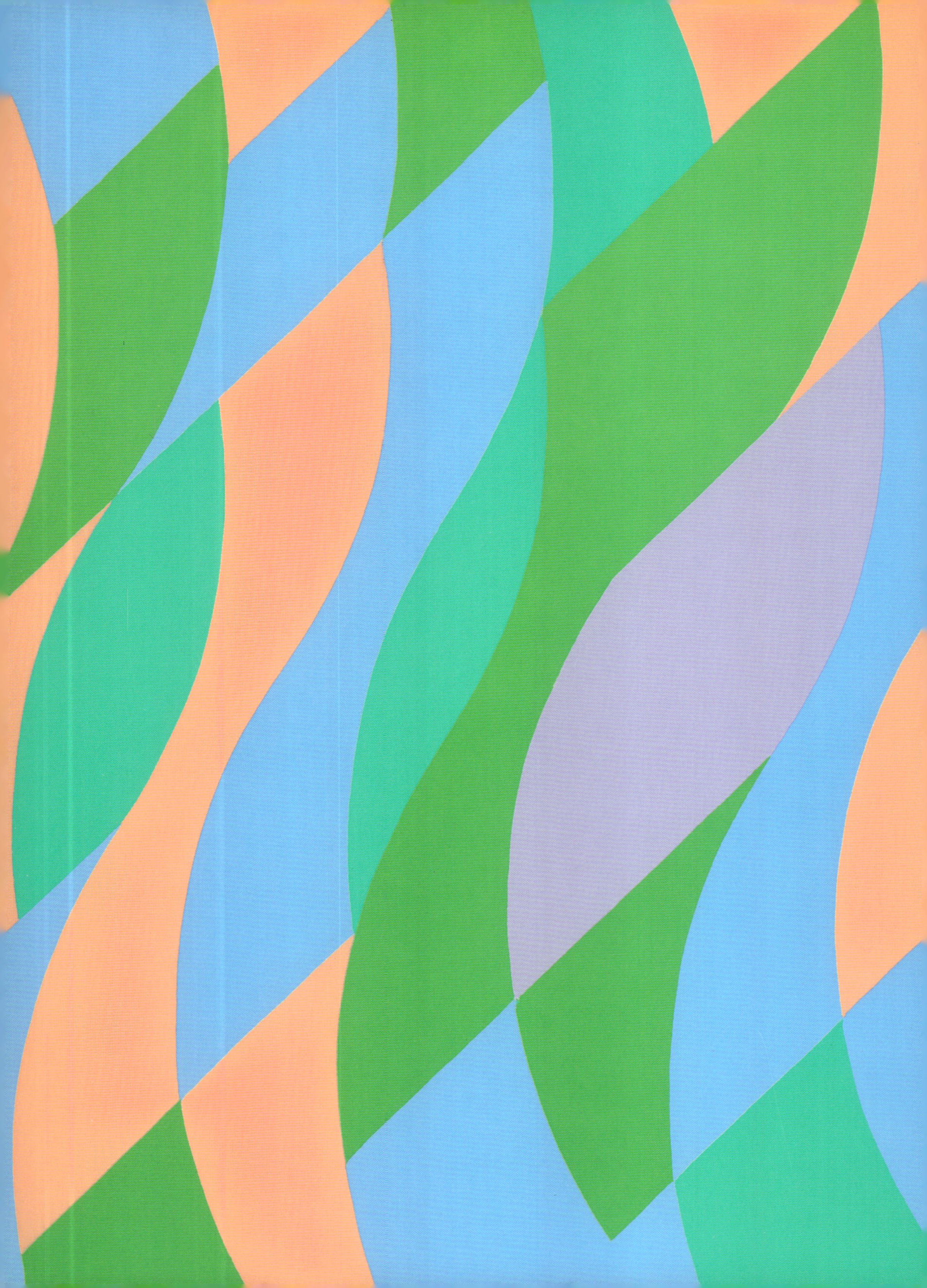

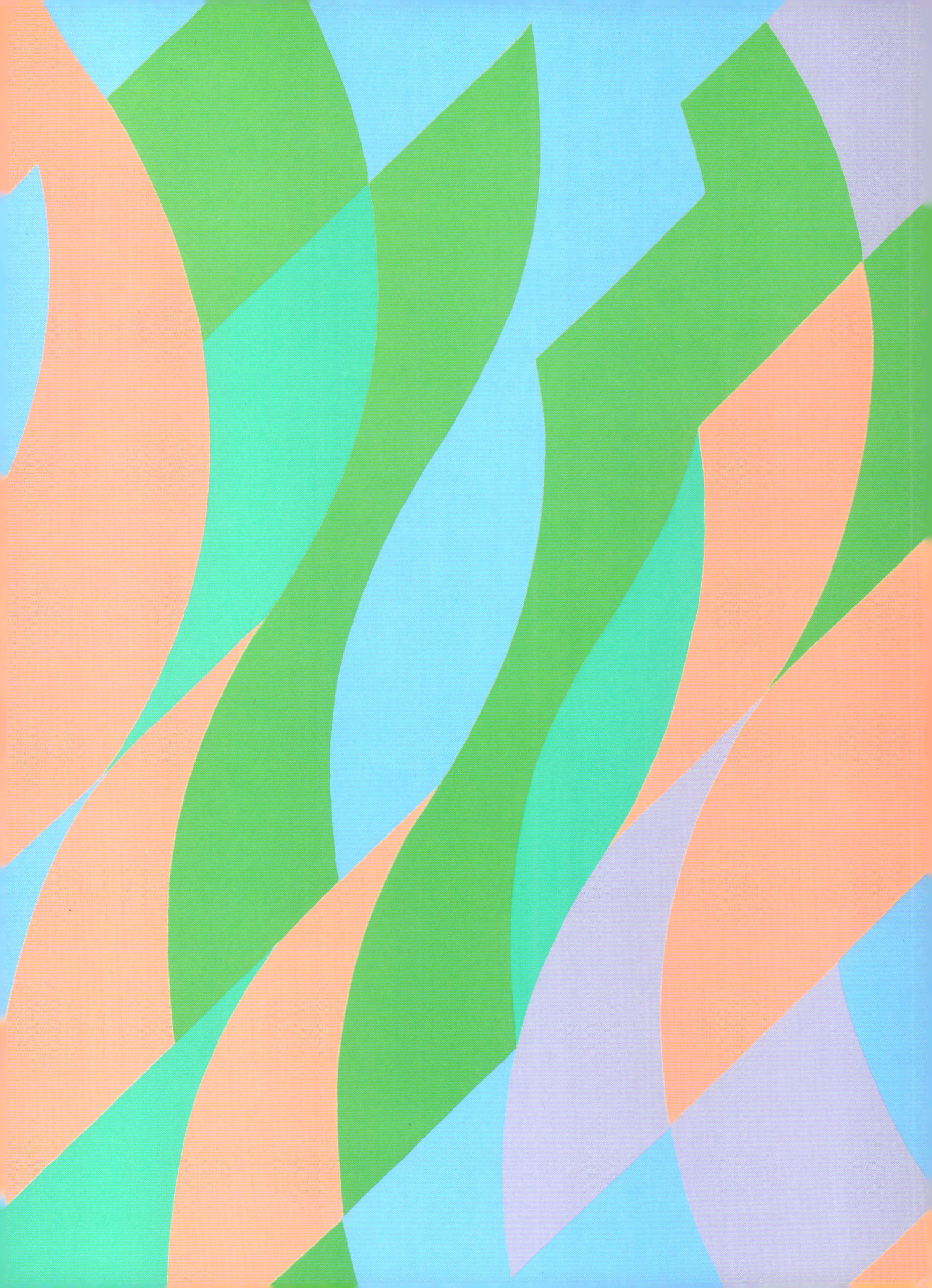

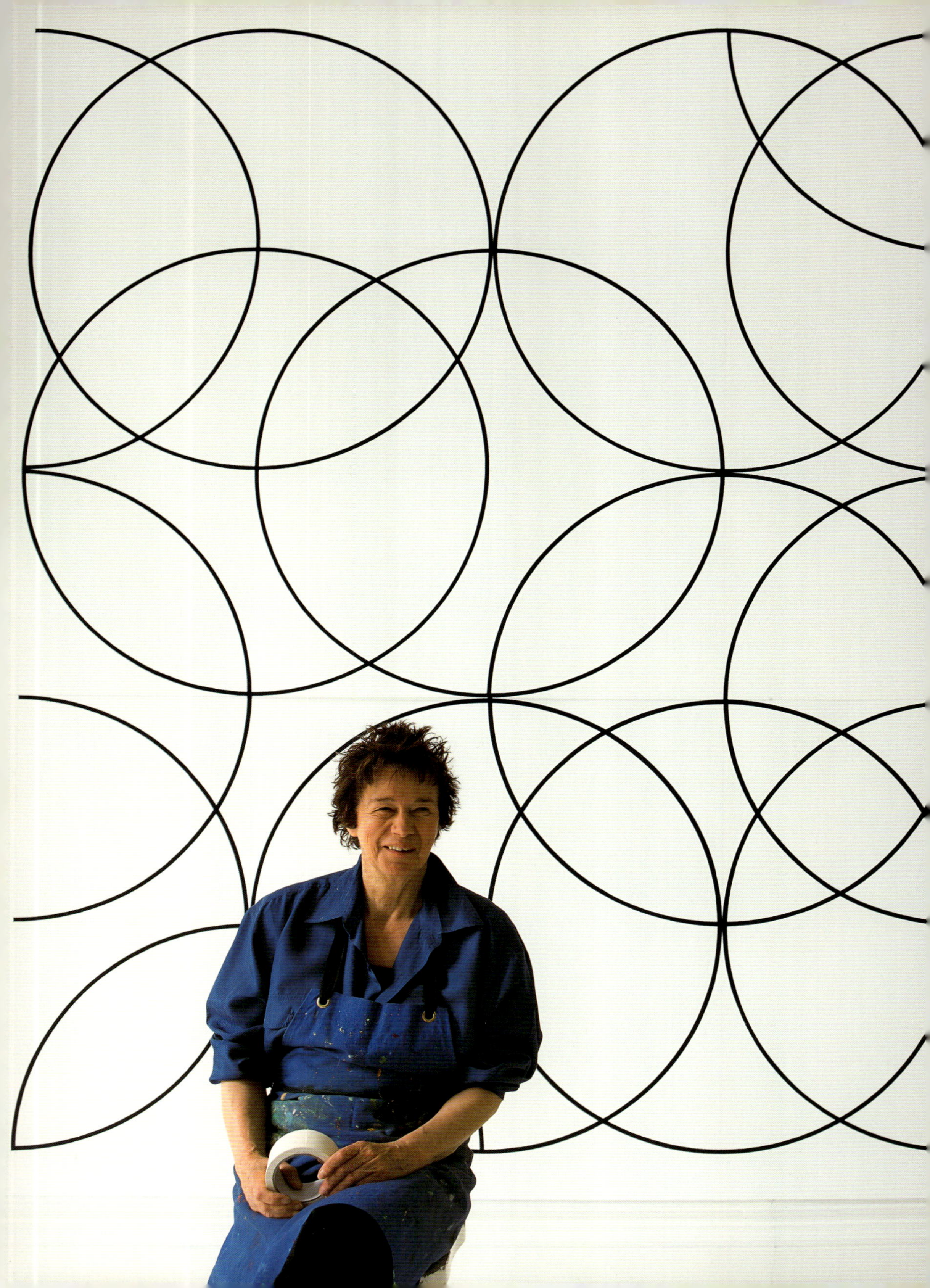

Biographical Notes

Compiled by Robert Kudielka

1931 Born in London.

1939–1945 Childhood in Cornwall. While her father is away in the armed forces during the War she lives with her mother, younger sister and aunt (a former student of Goldsmiths' College, London) in a cottage not far from the coast near Padstow. Irregular primary education by non-qualified or retired teachers who from time to time assemble children in the locality for lessons in subjects in which they have knowledge or interest. The beginning of Riley's interest in nature.

1946–1948 Education at Cheltenham Ladies' College. Thanks to an understanding headmistress she is allowed to organize her own curriculum, and chooses only art lessons in addition to obligatory subjects. Her teacher, Colin Hayes, later tutor at the Royal College of Art, London, introduces her to the history of painting and encourages her to attend the life class at the local art school. The Van Gogh exhibition at the Tate Gallery in 1947 is her first encounter with the work of a modern master.

(opposite)
Bridget Riley 2000

Enchant 2004
(detail, previous page)

1949–1952 Studies at Goldsmiths' College, London. For her entrance examination Riley submits, among other things, a copy of Van Eyck's *Man in a Turban*. She devotes herself mainly to the life-drawing class of Sam Rabin, who introduces her to the principles of pictorial abstraction: the autonomous construction of a body on a flat plane. She still remembers Rabin with respect, and later says: 'Life drawing was about the only thing I ever learned at art school.'

1952–1955 Studies at the Royal College of Art. A period of great frustration, partly because it is her first real experience of the art scene in London, partly because she slowly sees herself confronted with the unavoidable basic question of the modern painter: 'What should I paint, and how should I paint it?' Among her contemporaries are Frank Auerbach, Peter Blake, Robyn Denny, Richard Smith and Joe Tilson. She graduates with a BA degree.

1956–1958 Continuation of a long period of unhappiness. Nurses her father after a serious car accident and suffers a severe breakdown. Works in a glassware shop, teaches children and eventually joins the J. Walter Thompson Advertising Agency where her job is principally to draw the subjects which then formed the basis of the photographer's work. In the winter of 1958 she sees the Whitechapel Art Gallery's large Pollock exhibition, which makes a powerful impact.

1959 Stimulated by the exhibition *The Developing Process* at the Institute of Contemporary Arts, a joint project on the creative process devised by Harry Thubron and Victor Pasmore, she takes part in Thubron's summer school in Suffolk. There she meets Maurice de Sausmarez, who becomes her friend and mentor and who will write the first monograph on her work. The older painter and art scholar arouses her interest in Divisionism and Futurism and introduces her to primary documents of modern art (e.g. Klee, Stravinsky). In the late autumn she copies Georges Seurat's *Bridge at Courbevoie* from a reproduction.

1960 First year of her independent work. In the summer she and Maurice de Sausmarez tour Italy, admiring the architecture. At the Venice Biennale, she sees the large exhibition of Futurism. In the hills surrounding Siena she makes studies for *Pink Landscape* 1960, a key painting in her early development. In the autumn, she breaks with de Sausmarez and suffers a personal and artistic crisis. From repeated attempts to make one final, entirely black painting, originate her first black-and-white works, which to begin with are orientated towards contemporary Hard-Edge painting (e.g. Kiss 1961) but very quickly take on the unmistakable traits of her own pictorial identity.

1961 Beginning of the black-and-white paintings which, with ramifications, continue until 1966. It is a period of intense work. The painter Peter Sedgley remains her partner throughout the 1960s. In the summer they visit the plateau of Vaucluse in the south of France where Riley acquires a derelict farm which in the 1970s is transformed into her new studio. In London, on her way home one evening from J. Walter Thompson (where she works part-time until 1962 and remains by a happy mistake on the payroll until 1964), she shelters from a downpour in a doorway. It turns out to be the entrance of

Gallery One, whose director, Victor Musgrave, asks her in. She invites him to visit her studio to look at her work. In the following spring he hosts her first solo exhibition.

1965 Increasing recognition culminates in the inclusion of her work in the exhibition *The Responsive Eye* at The Museum of Modern Art, New York, in January. Richard Feigen simultaneously opens a solo show of her work which is sold out before the opening night. Josef Albers calls her his 'daughter' and Ad Reinhardt acts as her escort, to protect her from 'wolves'. She has become a 'star', to whom even Dalí pays tribute. But her success is double-edged. Fashion shop windows are full of 'Op' imitations of her work. With the help of Barnett Newman's lawyer she tries to take legal action against this commercial plagiarism, only to discover that in the USA there is no copyright protection for artists. Leading New York artists, realising the dangerous implications of this, start their own independent initiative. As a result in 1967 the first US copyright legislation is passed. Returning to London three weeks after the opening of *The Responsive Eye*, Riley has only one thought: 'It will take at least twenty years before anyone looks at my paintings seriously again.'

1965–1967 Period of transition in which she introduces into her painting sequences of coloured greys, as opposed to the neutral greys she had used earlier. The exceptional subtlety of these pictures and their titles (*Arrest*, *Drift*, *Deny*) carry the method of reversal further by compounding it. In the summer of 1967 she visits Greece. In the same year, with *Chant 1* 1967 and *Late Morning* 1967–8, she makes her breakthrough to pure colour. Along with the sculptor Phillip King she is chosen to represent Great Britain at the forthcoming Venice Biennale. That winter she meets Robert Kudielka for the first time.

1968–1969 Wins the International Prize for painting at the 34th Venice Biennale. She is the first British contemporary painter and the first woman ever to achieve this distinction. It is also the last prize awarded by the Biennale in its old form. The prize-giving ceremony cannot take place due to student protests. Along with César, Marisol and others, she tries in vain to get into discussion with the students. In the autumn of the same year Sedgley and Riley establish S.P.A.C.E., an organisation which provides artists with low-cost studios in large warehouse buildings. The project gets under way successfully with the move into St Katherine's Dock in 1969 and continues, with the support of the Arts Council of England, up to the present day.

1970–1971 Large European retrospective. It covers the period 1961–70 (including some work prior to 1961) and shows the development from the black-and-white works to the new colour paintings based on the interplay of only two or three colours. The exhibition opens at the Kunstverein Hannover, and subsequently travels to Bern, Düsseldorf, Turin and London, where it is extended and presented at the Hayward Gallery. It attracts more than 40,000 visitors. Robert Melville, who had so far followed her development rather critically, begins his review in the *New Statesman* with: 'No painter, dead or alive, has ever made us more aware of our eyes than Bridget Riley.'

1971–1973 Beginning of a period of radical change. After a final showing of her retrospective in Prague, she takes stock. Her visits to museums and art galleries while accompanying the exhibition have made her more curious about the European tradition in painting. She undertakes numerous journeys with Robert Kudielka: to see Tiepolo and Riemenschneider in Würzburg; Grünewald in Colmar. She visits the Alte Pinakothek in Munich, where she is deeply impressed by Altdorfer and Rubens, and the Prado in Madrid for the great Spanish painters and, above all, Titian. In such remote places as the Baroque churches of Upper Swabia in Germany she unexpectedly finds echoes of the luminous colours she is using at the time. All paths lead irresistibly and recurrently back to the vexing question occupying her in the studio: how to approach colour? At first she tries to extend her means through formal changes, but with *Pæan* 1973 she changes the formal organisation altogether, a move that anticipates the freer, more open structure of her work in the 1980s. In the spring of 1973, while looking at Altdorfer's cycle of the Passion in the convent of St Florian near Linz, news reaches her that her mother is suffering from an acute form of myeloma.

1974–1977 During the next two years she divides her time between London and Cornwall, where her parents have retired. She begins to read Proust, who influences her on many levels. She has her property in Vaucluse renovated, but does not use the newly-built studio until the beginning of the 1980s. With the 'curve' paintings, on which she worked exclusively between 1974 and 1978, her work takes a lyrical turn quite at odds with prevailing taste. Following the death of her mother in 1976 she concentrates on the preparation of another retrospective, and in connection with this she travels to Japan for three weeks at the end of March 1977, with a stopover in India where she visits the cave temples of Elephanta, Ellora and Ajanta. Her attraction to classical Japanese culture is spontaneous and ranges from painting and formal gardens through to Nô-theatre and the hospitality of the Ryokans. Kusuo Shimizu, the director of the Minami Gallery, Tokyo, gains her entrance to almost all the important sites in and around Kyoto and Nara. In the Osaka Museum she is given permission to examine Ogata Korin's famous sketchbook with his studies of waves.

1978–1980 A second retrospective exhibition, with just under a hundred paintings covering the years from 1959 to 1978, means that Riley travels extensively again. Opening in Buffalo, New York (September 1978), it continues with two further stops in the USA, two in Australia, and reaches its final destination in Tokyo (January 1980). In December 1977 she sees the exhibition *Cézanne: The Late Work* at The Museum of Modern Art, New York, visiting the show again in Paris the following year. In 1978 the exhibition *Monet's Years at Giverny: Beyond Impressionism* at the Metropolitan Museum, New York, engages her to such an extent that she goes to see it a second time in the autumn in St Louis. En route to the Sydney showing of her own exhibition she visits Tahiti. While in Australia she makes expeditions to the Barrier Reef, Alice Springs and Ayers Rock. She returns home via Indonesia: in Bali she enjoys the rich greens of the country and the extravagant colours of its festivals, especially the Barong theatre; and in Java she is particularly impressed by the pure, cool abstraction of the great temple of Borobudur in the middle of the jungle. Her artistic development takes an unexpected turn in the winter of 1979–80, when she travels, mainly on her sister's initiative, to Egypt. There she is taken by the contrast between the cultivation in the Nile Valley and the monumental works of art on the edge of the desert. In the Cairo Museum she is surprised by the consistent use of a certain group of colours in the arts and crafts of ancient Egypt; the tomb paintings on the West Bank of Luxor show her the full extent to which these colours could be developed. But it is only much later, after her return to London, that she recalls the particular palette and begins considering its potential for her own work.

1980–1985 The free reconstruction of the 'Egyptian palette' gives her for the first time a basic range of strong colours which, however, because of their intensity, demand a return to the simpler form of stripes. She begins to work regularly in her studio in Vaucluse and studies the use of colour by the French painters of classical Modernism. In 1981 she is appointed a trustee of the National Gallery in London. In the winter of 1981–2 she travels to Southern India where she visits the major Hindu and Buddhist monuments. In 1983, for the first time in fifteen years, she visits Venice to look at the paintings that form the basis of European colourism. She begins to give lectures on her work and accepts two commissions: in 1983 her wall paintings for the Royal Liverpool Hospital are completed, and in the same year, the Ballet Rambert gives a first performance at the Edinburgh Festival of the ballet *Colour Moves*, created by the American choreographer Robert North in response to her designs. During the planning of the extension of the National Gallery in London her role as a trustee becomes controversial. Almost single-handedly, she brings about the rejection of a commercial project for the new building and clears the way for the present Sainsbury Wing. In 1984 she gradually begins to prepare for a radical revision of her work in her Vaucluse studio, and in the spring of 1986 her painting takes a new direction.

1986–1991 In 1986, on the occasion of an exhibition in New York, she meets two postmodern 'appropriation' painters, Philip Taaffe and Ross Bleckner, who have made extensive use of her earlier work. She herself is moving into a new area. The breaking up of the vertical register of her paintings through the introduction of a dynamic diagonal disrupts the balance of her pictorial space and results in larger and smaller units in lozenge form. In order to be able to concentrate fully on the new work she sets up an additional studio in the East End of London. At the invitation of Wieland Schmied she runs a colour workshop at the 1987 Salzburg Summer Academy. In 1989 the National Gallery asks Riley to select the latest in the series of *The Artist's Eye* exhibitions. She chooses seven large figure compositions by Titian, Veronese, El Greco, Rubens, Poussin and Cézanne from the Gallery's collection. They all have in common an organisation shaped by diagonals and are characterised, if in varying degrees, by complex colour orchestrations.

1992–1995 In spring 1992 a retrospective, *Paintings 1982–1992*, opens at the Kunsthalle Nürnberg and travels to the Josef Albers Museum, Bottrop; the Hayward Gallery, London, with the sub-title *According to Sensation*; and the Ikon Gallery, Birmingham. It consists of paintings that cover the transition from the stripe formations to the dynamism of the lozenge structures. The success of the show coincides, particularly in England, with a series of exhibitions focusing on the art of the 1960s. Riley emerges as one of the few artists who were able subsequently to develop their work. The Tate Gallery in London puts on a Riley display, *Six Paintings 1963–1993*, drawn from its collection. As a result of the renewed interest in Riley's work BBC Radio 3 produces a series of five programmes in which Riley is in conversation with Neil MacGregor, E.H. Gombrich, Michael Craig-Martin, Andrew Graham-Dixon and Bryan Robertson. Broadcast in 1992, they are repeated the following year and published in book form in 1995. In 1993 she delivers her lecture, 'Colour for the Painter', at Darwin College in Cambridge. Riley is made Honorary Doctor of the Universities of Oxford (1993) and Cambridge (1995).

1995–1998 Her painting *From Here* 1984 lends its title to an exhibition of three generations of British abstract painters organised by Karsten Schubert and Waddington Galleries in 1995. After more than a thirty-year absence from teaching, Riley accepts an invitation to join the staff of De Montfort University, Leicester, as Visiting Professor. In 1996 she gives the 23rd William Townsend Memorial Lecture at the Slade School of Fine Art, choosing 'Painting Now' as the subject. Visits to the Mondrian retrospective at the Gemeentemuseum in The Hague in the winter of 1994–5 lead to an intense re-engagement with the work and writings of Mondrian. In November 1995 she contributes a paper to a Mondrian symposium at the Museum of Modern Art, New York. The following year she is asked by the Tate Gallery to select a Mondrian exhibition from the collection of the Gemeentemuseum. Installed by Riley and her co-curator, Sean Rainbird, the exhibition is the first comprehensive Mondrian show in England in forty years. Meanwhile her own work is showing signs of further change. Having slowly introduced colour harmonies equal to the prevailing contrast structure, she is now working with a new sensation of 'depth'. In spring 1997 she also begins to introduce circular or curvilinear forms into her developed rhomboid structures, to more easily facilitate the looping arc-like movements of the colour organisation. The renewed preoccupation with curves, and her interest in deep but not illusionistic pictorial space, lead to a large temporary wall drawing carried out for the *White Noise* exhibition at the Kunsthalle Bern in May 1998. The sensation of layered planes, previously achieved through complex colour relationships, is here the result of simple black-and-white drawing. The wall drawing has a major effect on her colour work. First results of this development are included in the exhibition *Bridget Riley: Works 1961–1998* shown at the Abbot Hall Art Gallery, Kendal (Cumbria), in winter 1998–9.

1999–2000 In the 1999 New Year's Honours, Riley is appointed a Companion of Honour. In June the exhibition *Bridget Riley: Paintings from the 1960s and 70s* opens at the Serpentine Gallery, London; on this occasion a collection of her writings and interviews, *The Eye's Mind: Bridget Riley, Collected Writings 1965–1999*, is published. In October the exhibition *Ausgewählte Bilder/Selected Paintings 1961–1999* is shown in the Kunstverein in Düsseldorf. It makes a connection between the early black-and-white painting *Kiss* 1961 and *Rêve* 1999, the first fully achieved painting using the new curvilinear rhythm. In spring 2000 her biggest architectural commission to date is completed: a hanging, curtain-like installation in the atrium of Citibank's European headquarters in London designed by Norman Foster and Partners. Extending over eighteen floors it consists of three planes of coloured aluminium plates suspended by steel cables. Although related to her rhomboid paintings, this open construction changes according to the viewpoint from which it is seen and the conditions of light in the office tower. In the summer a group of her new curve paintings and related works on paper is shown in London for the first time at Waddington Galleries, an exhibition organised by Karsten Schubert. In the autumn the Dia Center for the Arts in New York mounts a survey of her work under the title *Bridget Riley: Reconnaissance*. The exhibition is complemented by a show of recent paintings at PaceWildenstein. Both shows mark a major re-evaluation of her work in America. At the end of November she takes part in the international symposium *Das Bild: Image, Picture, Painting* at the Akademie der Künste in Berlin.

2001–2002 Much of Riley's time in 2000–1 is taken up with the preparation of a Paul Klee exhibition for the Hayward Gallery in London (co-curated with Robert Kudielka). Riley participates in the Santa Fe biennial, *Beau Monde: Toward a Redeemed Cosmopolitanism* 2001–2, curated by Dave Hickey, with the painting *Evoë 1* 2000. The exhibition *Paul Klee: The Nature of Creation* is shown at the Hayward Gallery, London, in the spring of 2002. In March, *Bridget Riley: New Work* opens at the Museum Haus Esters and the Kaiser Wilhelm Museum, Krefeld, the first museum show dedicated exclusively to the new curvilinear paintings.

2003 The year 2003 is dominated by the preparation and installation of Riley's retrospective exhibition at Tate Britain (June 26–September 28). Together with curator Paul Moorhouse, she selects fifty-six paintings from all periods since 1961 and a group of preparatory studies which give an insight into her working methods. In the first room, she makes a special wall drawing of circles that link the early black-and-white work with her most recent paintings. The exhibition is received to universal critical acclaim and draws 95,000 visitors. One week after the opening, it is announced that Bridget Riley has been awarded the Praemium Imperiale, the prestigious international prize of the Japan Art Association, for her achievement as a painter. In October, she travels to Tokyo to attend the ceremony and delivers the message of thanks on behalf of the other laureates (Mario Merz, Ken Loach, Claudio Abbado and Rem Koolhaas). During this trip, she renews her acquaintance with some of the masterpieces of Japanese art. Also in 2003, Riley revisits the great museums of Munich and sees the big Titian exhibition at the Prado in Madrid.

2004–2005 In 2004 Riley is involved in preparing a retrospective exhibition for venues in Australia, New Zealand and Switzerland. The show opens in December at the Museum of Contemporary Art in Sydney, travels the following year to the City Art Gallery in Wellington and finishes in the Aargauer Kunsthaus (Aarau) in September 2005. Despite these public commitments Riley steadily develops her work in the studio. In Autumn 2004 new paintings and gouaches are shown at PaceWildenstein's in New York, including *Painting with Two Verticals* 2004 in which the dynamism of the curves is pitched against vertical divisions. For the new building of the Akademie der Künste in Berlin (which in 2004 elects her as a member) she creates another temporary wall drawing (*Composition with Circles 5* 2005) that is shown in Spring 2005 in the exhibition *Prologue*. She works on the re-construction of her environment *Continuum* 1963 for 'L'oeil moteur', a survey of Optical and Kinetic Art at the musée d'Art moderne et contemporain in Strasbourg in May 2005. In April 2005 she delivers the Seamus Heaney lecture at St Patrick's College at the University of Dublin – her subject: 'Working'.

Exhibition History

Compiled by Robert Kudielka

Selected One-person Exhibitions

1962 Gallery One, London

1963 Gallery One, London

1965 Richard Feigen Gallery, New York
Feigen-Palmer Gallery, Los Angeles

1966 *Drawings*, Richard Feigen Gallery, New York
Bridget Riley: Preparatory Drawings and Studies, Robert Fraser Gallery, London

1966–7 *Bridget Riley: Drawings*, The Museum of Modern Art, New York; touring to venues in the United States

1967 Richard Feigen Gallery, New York
Robert Fraser Gallery, London

1968 Richard Feigen Gallery, New York
34th Venice Biennale, British Pavilion (with Phillip King); touring to Städtische Kunstgalerie, Bochum; Museum Boijmans Van Beuningen, Rotterdam

1969 Rowan Gallery, London
Drawings, Bear Lane Gallery, Oxford; Arnolfini Gallery, Bristol; Midland Group Gallery, Nottingham

1970–1 *Bridget Riley: Paintings and Drawings 1951–71*, Arts Council of Great Britain retrospective exhibition, Kunstverein Hannover; Kunsthalle Bern; Kunsthalle Düsseldorf; Galleria Civica d'Arte Moderna, Turin; Hayward Gallery, London; National Gallery, Prague

1971 *Drawings*, Rowan Gallery, London

1972 Kunstverein Göttingen

Drawings, Rowan Gallery, London

1973 *Bridget Riley: Paintings and Drawings 1961–1973*, Arts Council of Great Britain exhibition, Whitworth Art Gallery, University of Manchester; Mappin Art Gallery, Sheffield; D.L.I. Museum and Arts Centre, Durham; Scottish National Gallery of Modern Art, Edinburgh; City Museum and Art Gallery, Birmingham; Museum and Art Gallery, Letchworth; City Art Gallery and Arnolfini Gallery, Bristol

1975 Galerie Beyeler, Basel

Sidney Janis Gallery, New York

1976 Rowan Gallery, London

Coventry Gallery, Sydney

1977 Minami Gallery, Tokyo

1978 Sidney Janis Gallery, New York

1978–80 *Bridget Riley: Works 1959–78*, British Council retrospective exhibition, Albright-Knox Art Gallery, Buffalo; Dallas Museum of Fine Art; Neuberger Museum, Purchase, New York; Art Gallery of New South Wales, Sydney; Art Gallery of Western Australia, Perth; National Museum of Modern Art, Tokyo

1979 *Drawings*, Australian Galleries, Melbourne; Bonython Gallery, Adelaide

1980 Fruitmarket Gallery, Edinburgh; touring to venues in the United Kingdom

Artline, The Hague

1980–2 *Bridget Riley: Silkscreen Prints 1965–78*, Preston Hall Museum, Stockton-On-Tees; touring to venues in the United Kingdom

1981 *Recent Paintings and Gouaches*, Rowan Gallery and Warwick Arts Trust, London

1982 *Gouaches*, Juda Rowan Gallery, London

1983 *Bridget Riley: Paintings and Drawings 1981–83*, Nishimura Gallery, Tokyo

1984 *Bridget Riley: Project for the Royal Liverpool Hospital*, Royal Institute of British Architects, London

1984–5 Galerie Reckermann, Cologne

Working with Colour: Recent Paintings and Studies by Bridget Riley, Arts Council of Great Britain exhibition, D.L.I. Museum and Arts Centre, Durham; Huddersfield Art Gallery, Durham; Ferens Art Gallery, Hull; City Museum and Art Gallery, Stoke-on-Trent; Usher Gallery, Lincoln; City of Bristol Museum and Art Gallery; Towner Art Gallery, Eastbourne; Castle Museum, Norwich; Harris Museum and Art Gallery, Preston; York City Art Gallery; Mappin Art Gallery, Sheffield

1985 *Bridget Riley: An Australian Context*, Queensland Art Gallery, Brisbane

1986 Jeffrey Hoffeld Gallery, New York

1986–7 South Western Art Galleries Association in Scotland exhibition, Maclaurin Art Gallery, Ayr

1987 Galerie Konstructiv Tendens, Stockholm

Galerie und Edition Schlégl, Zürich
Bridget Riley: New Work, Mayor Rowan Gallery, London

1988 Galerie Teufel, Cologne

1989 Galerie und Edition Schlégl, Zürich
Bridget Riley: Works on Paper, Mayor Rowan Gallery, London

1990 Sidney Janis Gallery, New York
Nishimura Gallery, Tokyo

1992 *Bridget Riley: Works on Paper 1982–1992*, Karsten Schubert, London
Bridget Riley: Paintings, Galerie Ascan Crone, Hamburg

1992–3 *Bridget Riley: Paintings 1982–1992*, Kunsthalle Nürnberg; Josef Albers Museum, Bottrop; Hayward Gallery, London; Ikon Gallery, Birmingham

1993 *Bridget Riley: Colour Studies*, Karsten Schubert, London

1994 *Bridget Riley: Six Paintings 1963–1993, from the Collection*, Tate Gallery, London

1995 *Bridget Riley: Recent Paintings and Gouaches*, Kettle's Yard, Cambridge University
Bridget Riley: Recent Works – Paintings and Gouaches 1981–1995, Spacex Gallery, Exeter
Bridget Riley: Gouaches 1980–1995, Aberdeen Art Gallery, Aberdeen

1996 *Bridget Riley: Recent Paintings and Gouaches*, Waddington Galleries and Karsten Schubert, London
Bridget Riley: Gouaches 1980–1995, British School in Rome
Bridget Riley: Paintings and Gouaches 1980–1995, Leeds City Art Gallery
Bridget Riley, Museum für moderne Kunst des Landkreises Cuxhaven, Otterndorf

1997 *Bridget Riley: Paintings, Gouaches and Prints 1981–1986*, Green on Red Gallery Dublin

1998 *Bridget Riley*, Galerie Michael Sturm, Stuttgart
Bridget Riley, Galerie Aurel Scheibler, Cologne
Bridget Riley: Works 1961–1998, Abbot Hall Art Gallery, Kendal, Cumbria

1999 *Bridget Riley: Paintings from the 1960s and 1970s*, Serpentine Gallery, London
Bridget Riley: Ausgewählte Bilder/Selected Paintings 1961–1999, Kunstverein für die Rheinlande und Westfalen, Düsseldorf

2000 *Bridget Riley: New Paintings and Gouaches*, Waddington Galleries, London (in collaboration with Karsten Schubert)
Bridget Riley: Paintings 1982–2000 and Early Works on Paper, PaceWildenstein, New York
Bridget Riley: Reconnaissance, Dia Center for the Arts, New York

2001 *Bridget Riley: Complete Prints 1962–2001*, Hayward Gallery, London; toured to venues in the United Kingdom through 2003

2002 *Bridget Riley: New Work*, Museum Haus Esters and Kaiser Wilhelm Museum, Krefeld
Bridget Riley: Recent Paintings and Gouaches, Galerie Michael Sturm, Stuttgart

2003 *Bridget Riley*, Galerie Beyeler, Basel
Bridget Riley, retrospective exhibition, Tate Britain, London

2004 *Bridget Riley: Recent Paintings*, PaceWildenstein, New York
Bridget Riley: Complete Prints 1962–2003, British Council (toured through Eastern Europe until 2005)
Bridget Riley: Gouaches and Prints, Nishimura Gallery, Tokyo
Bridget Riley: Bilden und Gouachen 1981–2004, Galerie Aurel Scheibler, Cologne

Bridget Riley: Paintings and Drawings 1961–2004, Museum of Contemporary Art Sydney, Australia

2005 *Bridget Riley: Paintings and Drawings 1961–2004*, City Gallery Wellington, New Zealand

Bridget Riley. Bilder und Zeichnungen 1959–2005, Aargauer Kunsthaus, Aarau

Bridget Riley: Complete Prints 1981–2005, Galerie Schlégl, Zürich

Bridget Riley: Paintings and Studies, Cranbrook Art Museum, Bloomfield Hills, Michigan, USA

Selected Group Exhibitions

1955 *Young Contemporaries*, RBA Galleries, London

1958 *Diversion*, South London Art Gallery, London

Some Contemporary British Painters, Wildenstein Galleries, London

1962 *Towards Art?*, Arts Council of Great Britain exhibition, Royal College of Art; touring to venues in the United Kingdom

1963 *1962, One Year of British Art*, Tooths Gallery, London

John Moores Exhibition, Walker Art Gallery, Liverpool

Ten Years, Gallery One, London

1964 *The New Generation*, Whitechapel Art Gallery, London

Six Young Artists, Arts Council of Great Britain exhibition; touring to venues in the United Kingdom

Nouvelle Tendance, Musée des Arts Décoratifs, Paris

Marzotto Prize Exhibition, Italy; touring to venues in Europe

Painting and Sculpture of a Decade, 1954–1964, Tate Gallery, London

Carnegie International, Carnegie Institute, Pittsburgh

Young Artists Biennale, Tokyo

1964–5 *Contemporary British Painting and Sculpture*, Albright-Knox Art Gallery, Buffalo

Motion and Movement, Contemporary Arts Center, Cincinnati

1965 *The Responsive Eye*, The Museum of Modern Art, New York; touring to City Art Museum of St Louis; Seattle Art Museum; Pasadena Art Museum; Baltimore Museum of Art

John Moores Exhibition, Walker Art Gallery, Liverpool

The Great Society: A Sampling of Its Imagery, Arts Forum, Inc., Haverfort

A New York Collector Selects (Mrs Burton Tremaine), San Francisco Museum of Modern Art

Pop and Op, Sidney Janis Gallery, New York

4th Biennale des Jeunes Artistes, Paris

Tel Aviv Museum

1965–6 *London: The New Scene*, Walker Art Center, Minneapolis; touring to venues in Washington DC, Boston, Seattle, Vancouver, Toronto and Ottawa

1966 *Multiplicity*, Institute of Contemporary Art, Boston

Aspects of New British Art, Auckland; touring to venues in New Zealand and Australia

London under Forty, Galleria Milano, Milan

English Graphic Art, Galerie Der Spiegel, Cologne

Painting and Sculpture 1966, Fireside Lounge Gallery, University of Wisconsin, Milwaukee

1967 *Drawing Towards Painting 2*, Arts Council, London; touring to venues in the United Kingdom

Op Art, Londonderry, Dublin and Belfast

British Drawings, The Museum of Modern Art, New York; touring to venues in the United States

Carnegie International, Carnegie Institute, Pittsburgh

Premio International Escultura, Instituto di Tella, Buenos Aires

Acquisitions of the Sixties, The Museum of Modern Art, New York

Recent British Painting from the Collection of Peter Stuyvesant Foundation, New York, Tate Gallery, London

English and American Graphics '67 (from The Museum of Modern Art, New York), Belgrade; touring to venues in Yugoslavia

Jeunes Peintres Anglais, Palais des Beaux-Arts, Brussels

1968 *The New Generation: Interim Exhibition*, Whitechapel Art Gallery, London

Britische Kunst Heute, Hamburger Kunstverein

European Painters of Today, Musée des Arts Décoratifs, Paris; touring to venues in the United States

20th Century Art, Fondation Maeght, Saint Paul de Vence

New British Painting and Sculpture, organized by Whitechapel Art Gallery, London; touring to venues in the United States and Canada

Plus by Minus: Today's Half Century, Albright-Knox Art Gallery, Buffalo

Junge Generation Großbritannien, Akademie der Künste, Berlin

Leicestershire Education Authority Collection Part 2, Whitechapel Art Gallery, London

Graphics Exhibition, Museum of Modern Art, Oxford

Documenta IV, Kassel

British Artists: 6 Painters, 6 Sculptors, The Museum of Modern Art, New York; touring to venues in the United States

1969 *Phillip King: Beelden. Bridget Riley: Schilderijen en tekeningen*, Museum Boijmans Van Beuningen, Rotterdam

Contemporary Art: Dialogue between East and West, National Museum of Modern Art, Tokyo

Marks on Canvas, Museum am Ostwall, Dortmund, and Kunstverein Hannover

Black White, Smithsonian Institution, Washington DC; touring to venues in the United States

1970 *Contemporary Paintings from the Sebastian de Ferranti Collection*, Whitworth Art Gallery, Manchester

1971 ROSC '71, Royal Dublin Society, Dublin

1972 8th International Print Biennial, National Museum of Modern Art, Tokyo, and the National Museum of Modern Art, Kyoto

1973 *La peinture anglaise aujourd'hui*, Musée d'Art Moderne de la Ville de Paris

Henry Moore to Gilbert and George: Modern British Art from the Tate Gallery, Palais des Beaux-Arts, Brussels

1974 *British Painting '74*, Hayward Gallery, London

Graveurs Anglais Contemporains, Musée d'Art et d'Histoire, Cabinet des Estampes, Geneva

1975 *Contemporary British Drawings*, 12th Biennale de São Paulo

From Britain '75, Taidehalli, Helsinki

1976 *Art as Thought Process*, 11th Biennale International d'Art, Palais de l'Europe, Menton

Contemporary British Art, Galleries of Cleveland Institute of Art

Arte inglese oggi, Palazzo Reale, Milan

1977 Documenta VI, Kassel

Biennale de Paris, une anthologie: 1959–1967, Paris

British Artists of the '60s, Tate Gallery, London

Less is More, Sidney Janis Gallery, New York

12th International Exhibition of Graphic Art, Ljubljana

Contemporary Drawing, Art Gallery of Western Australia, Perth

1977–8 *Recent British Art*, British Council exhibition; touring to venues in Yugoslavia, Greece, Austria, Poland, Sweden, Norway and Finland

1978 *The Mechanised Image*, Arts Council of Great Britain exhibition, City Museum and Art Gallery, Portsmouth; touring to venues in the United Kingdom

Recent British Art, Nordjyllands Kunstmuseum, Aalborg

1979 *British Drawings since 1945 in the Whitworth Art Gallery*, Whitworth Art Gallery, Manchester

1979–80 *Peter Moores Liverpool Project 5: The Craft of Art*, Walker Art Gallery, Liverpool

1982 *Aspects of British Art Today*, Arts Council of Great Britain exhibition touring Japan; Tokyo Metropolitan Museum; Tochigi Prefectural Museum; National Museum of Modern Art, Osaka;

Fukuoka Art Museum; Hokkaido Museum of Modern Art, Sapporo

1984 *A Different Climate*, Kunsthalle Düsseldorf

Artists Design for Dance 1909–1984, Arnolfini Gallery, Bristol

1985 *Hayward Annual: 25 Years – Three Decades of Contemporary Art: The Sixties, the Seventies and the Eighties*, Annely Juda Fine Art, London

1986 *The Heroic Sublime*, Charles Cowles Gallery, New York

42nd Venice Biennale

1987 *British Art in the 20th Century*, Royal Academy, London; Staatsgalerie, Stuttgart

1988 *Exhibition Road: Painters at the Royal College of Art*, Royal College of Art, London

1988–9 *Viewpoints: Postwar Painting and Sculpture from the Guggenheim Museum Collection and Major Loans*, Guggenheim Museum, New York; touring to venues in the United States

The Presence of Painting: Aspects of British Abstraction 1957–1988, South Bank Centre, London;

Mappin Art Gallery, Sheffield; Hatton Gallery, Newcastle; Ikon Gallery, Birmingham

1989 *The Experience of Painting: Eight Modern Artists*, South Bank Centre, London; Laing Art Gallery,

Newcastle upon Tyne; Mappin Art Gallery, Sheffield; City Art Gallery, Stoke-on-Trent

1990 *Künstlerinnen des 20. Jahrhunderts*, Museum Wiesbaden

1992–3 *Ready Steady Go: Paintings of the Sixties from the Arts Council Collection*, South Bank Centre, London; touring to venues in the United Kingdom

1993 *New Realities 1945–1968*, Tate Gallery, Liverpool
1994 *Group Show*, Karsten Schubert Gallery, London
British Abstract Art Part 1: Painting, Flowers East, London
1995 *Drawing the Line*, South Bank Centre, London; toured venues in the United Kingdom
From Here, Waddington Galleries and Karsten Schubert, London
Patrick Heron, Bridget Riley: Colour and Nature, Castle Museum, Norwich
Karo Dame, Aargauer Kunsthaus, Aarau
Artist's Choice: Elizabeth Murray – Modern Women, The Museum of Modern Art, New York
1996 *British Abstract Art Part III: Works on Paper*, Flowers East, London
1997 *Treasure Island*, Centro de Arte Moderna José de Azeredo Perdigiao, Lisbon
A Quality of Light, Tate Gallery, St. Ives
1998 *White Noise*, Kunsthalle Bern
1999 *'45 – '49*, Kettle's Yard, Cambridge University; toured to venues in the United Kingdom
Sublime: The Darkness and the Light – Works from the Arts Council Collection, John Hansard Gallery, Southampton; toured to venues in the United Kingdom
2000 *Collection 2000*, Tate Modern, London
Blue, New Art Gallery, Walsall
Beau Monde: Toward a Redeemed Cosmopolitan,
4th International Biennial, Site Santa Fe
2002 *Good Vibrations: The Legacy of Op Art in Australia*, Heide Art Museum, Victoria
From Blast to Freeze: British Art in the 20th Century, Kunstmuseum Wolfsburg
2003 *Biennale d'Art Contemporain*, La Sucrière, Lyon
Painting from Rauschenberg to Murakami 1964–2003, Venice Biennale, Musée Correr, Venice
2004 *Art and the Sixties*, Tate Britain, London
2005 *L'œil moteur. Art Optique et Cinétique 1950–1975*, Musée d'art moderne et contemporain, Strasbourg

Other Activities

1965 Design of the background projection for T.S. Eliot's *Sweeney Agonistes* at the Eliot Memorial Performance
1974 Mural for Morley College, London
1980–3 Royal Liverpool Hospital project
1983 Design for the backcloth for *Colour Moves*, performed by the Ballet Rambert at the Edinburgh Festival
1986–7 St Mary's Hospital project, London
1988 Commission for ICI, Millbank, London
1989 *The Artist's Eye: Bridget Riley*, National Gallery, London
1996 *Mondrian: Nature to Abstraction*, Tate Gallery, London, co-curated with Sean Rainbird
1998–2000 Commission for Foster & Partners' Citibank Building, Canary Wharf, London
2002 *Paul Klee: The Nature of Creation*, Hayward Gallery, London, co-curated with Robert Kudielka

Bibliography

Compiled by Robert Kudielka

Writings and Interviews by the Artist

The Eye's Mind: Bridget Riley. Collected Writings 1965–1999, ed. Robert Kudielka, London: Thames and Hudson, in association with Serpentine Gallery, London, and De Montfort University, Leicester, 1999

German translation: *Malen um zu sehen: Bridget Riley. Gesammelte Schriften 1965–2001*, ed. Robert Kudielka, Krefelder Kunstmuseen and Hatje Cantz Verlag, 2002 (extended by German translations of 'Conversation with Isabel Carlisle', 1998, and 'Supposed to be Abstract', 2002)

The Eye's Mind includes all important writings and authorized interviews since 1965 except the following:

'Jenseits von Op-Art: Bridget Riley im Gespräch', interview by Robert Kudielka, *Das Kunstwerk*, vol. 22, nos. 3–4, December 1968–January 1969, pp. 15–25

'On Travelling Paintings', *Art Monthly*, vol. 5, no. 39, September 1980, pp. 5–9

'Bridget Riley interviewed', by Andrew Smith, *Arts Review*, vol. 33, no. 11, 5 June 1981, p. 228

'Hospital treatment', interview by Douglas Stephen, *Building Design*, 7 September 1984

'Henri Matisse, The Dance', *Daily Telegraph* magazine, 27 October 1990

'Bridget Riley: Visual Fabric', interview by James Roberts, *Frieze*, no. 6, September–October 1992, pp. 20–3

'Bridget Riley – Some things near and some far', conversation with Andrew Renton, *Flash Art*, vol. 26, no. 168, January–February 1993, pp. 59–61
'On Picasso', part of a collection of statements titled 'Artists on Picasso', ed. Helen Hague, *The Sunday Times*, 20 February 1994
'Bridget Riley on The Snail', *Daily Telegraph* magazine, 20 December 1997
Bridget Riley: Dialogues on Art. With Michael Craig-Martin, Andrew Graham-Dixon, Ernst H. Gombrich, Neil MacGregor and Bryan Robertson, ed. Robert Kudielka. Introduction by Richard Shone, London: Zwemmer, 1995 (reprinted London: Thames and Hudson, 2003)
'Bridget Riley – Musing on Poussin', *Independent*, 20 January 1995
'Colour for the Painter', *Colour: Art and Science*, ed. Trevor Lamb and Janine Bourriau, Cambridge: Cambridge University Press, 1995, pp. 31–64
'Conversation with Bridget Riley', by Isabel Carlisle, *Bridget Riley: Works 1961–1989*, Kendal, Cumbria: Abbot Hall Art Gallery and Museum, 1998, pp. 7–10
'She's a dedicated follower of abstraction', interview with David Thompson, *Independent on Sunday*, 15 November 1998
'Supposed to be abstract – Bridget Riley in conversation with Robert Kudielka' (English–German), *Parkett*, no. 61, May 2001, pp. 20–51
'Making Visible', *Paul Klee: The Nature of Creation*, London: Hayward Gallery in association with Lund Humphries, 2002, pp. 15–19

Selected Quotations

'Selected Quotations', ed. by STB, *Artlink*, vol. 24, no. 4, December 2004, pp. 6–9.
Bridget Riley in conversation with Jenny Harper, *Bridget Riley: Paintings and Drawings 1961–2004*, London: Ridinghouse, 2004, pp. 95–99
'Bridget Riley on Bridget Riley. Ausgewählte Zitate', ed. by Stephanie Britton, *Artlink*, vol. 24, No. 4, December 2004, pp. 6–9.

Catalogues and Books

Bridget Riley, London: Gallery One, 1962. Text by Maurice de Sausmarez
Bridget Riley, London: Gallery One, 1963. Texts by Anton Ehrenzweig and David Sylvester
The New Generation, London: Whitechapel Gallery, 1964. Text by David Thompson
Bryan Robertson, John Russell and Lord Snowdon, *Private View*, London: Thomas Nelson and Sons, 1965
London: The New Scene, Minneapolis: Walker Art Center in association with the Calouste Gulbenkian Foundation and The British Council, 1965. Texts by Martin Friedman and Alan Bowness
The English Eye, New York: Marlborough-Gerson Gallery, 1965. Texts by Bryan Robertson and Robert Melville
The Responsive Eye, New York: The Museum of Modern Art, 1965. Text by William Seitz
Poor Old Tired Horse 18, Gledfield Farmhouse, Ardgay: Wild Hawthorn Press (Ian Hamilton Finlay), 1966. Drawings and layout by Bridget Riley, writings and script by Ad Reinhardt
Bridget Riley: Drawings, New York: The Museum of Modern Art, 1966. Text by Jennifer Licht
Michael Compton, *Optical and Kinetic Art*, London: Tate Gallery Publications, 1967
Bridget Riley. The 34th Venice Biennale, London: The British Council, 1968. Text by David Thompson
A Dialogue: New British Painting and Sculpture, Los Angeles: UCLA Galleries, 1968. Texts by Herbert Read and Bryan Robertson
Op Art und Kinetik, Kassel: Documenta IV, 1968. Text by Werner Spies
Bridget Riley: Working Drawings, Oxford: Bear Lane Gallery, 1969. Text by Maurice de Sausmarez
Marks on Canvas, Dortmund: Museum am Ostwall, 1969. Text by Anne Seymour
Cyril Barrett, *Op Art*, London: Studio Vista, 1970
Maurice de Sausmarez, *Bridget Riley*, London: Studio Vista, 1970
Bridget Riley, Kunstverein Hannover, 1970. Texts by Manfred de la Motte and Bryan Robertson. Catalogue of the retrospective exhibition, reprinted with different layouts and additional texts at the following venues:

Kunsthalle Bern, 1970. Texts by Carlo Huber and Bryan Robertson
Kunsthalle Düsseldorf, 1970. Texts by Carl Ruhrberg, Wieland Schmied and Bryan Robertson
Galleria Civica d'Arte Moderna Turin, 1971. Text by Bryan Robertson

Bridget Riley: Paintings and Drawings 1951–71, London: Hayward Gallery, in association with Arts Council of Great Britain 1971. Text by Bryan Robertson. Extended version and catalogue of the 1970–1 European retrospective

British Painting '74, London: Arts Council of Great Britain and Hayward Gallery, 1974

Bridget Riley, New York: Sidney Janis Gallery, 1975. Text by David Thompson

Bridget Riley, Basel: Galerie Beyeler, 1975. Text by Bryan Robertson

Arte inglese oggi 1960–76, Milan: Electa Editrice, 1976, 2 vols. Texts by Norbert Lynton and David Thompson

Recent British Art, London: The British Council, 1977. Text by David Thompson

Bridget Riley: Works 1959–1978, London: The British Council, 1978. Text by Robert Kudielka. Catalogue of the retrospective exhibition shown in Albright-Knox Art Gallery, Buffalo; Dallas Museum of Fine Art; Art Gallery of New South Wales, Sydney; Art Gallery of Western Australia, Perth; Neuberger Museum, Purchase, New York; and National Museum of Modern Art, Tokyo (1980), where a Japanese version was published

Bridget Riley: Silkscreen Prints 1965–1978, London: Arts Council of Great Britain, 1980. Text by Robert Kudielka

Working with Colour: Recent Paintings and Studies by Bridget Riley, London: Arts Council of Great Britain, 1984. Text by Robert Cumming

Bridget Riley: Ölbilder und Gouachen, Cologne: Galerie Reckermann, 1984. Text by Robert Kudielka

Bridget Riley: An Australian Context, Brisbane: Queensland Art Gallery, 1985. Text by Jenny Harper

Karina Türr, *Op Art. Stil, Ornament oder Experiment?*, Berlin: Gebr. Mann Verlag, 1986

'Bridget Riley', *The Great Artists: Their Lives, Works and Inspiration*, vol. 4, part 86, London: Marshall Cavendish Ltd., Twentieth Century Series, 1986

British Art in the 20th Century. The Modern Movement, ed. Susan Compton, London: Royal Academy of Art, in association with Prestel-Verlag, Munich, 1986 (German edition 1987)

Bridget Riley, New York: Sidney Janis Gallery, 1990. Conversation with Robert Kudielka

Künstlerinnen des 20. Jahrhunderts, Museum Wiesbaden, 1990. Text by Karl Ruhrberg

Bridget Riley: Paintings 1982–1992, London: The Hayward Gallery, in association with Verlag für Moderne Kunst, Nürnberg, 1992. Texts by Lucius Grisebach and Robert Kudielka (German and English edition)

Bridget Riley: Works on Paper 1980–1992, London: Karsten Schubert, 1992

The Sixties Art Scene in London, London: Phaidon Press, in association with Barbican Art Gallery, 1993. Text by David Mellor

Colour and Nature: Patrick Heron and Bridget Riley, Norwich Castle Museum, 1995. Text by Andrew Moore

Bridget Riley: Recent Paintings and Gouaches 1981–1995, London: Waddington Galleries and Karsten Schubert, in association with Spacex Gallery, Exeter, 1996. Text by Richard Shone. Conversation with Alex Farquharson

Bridget Riley: Works 1961–1998, Kendal, Cumbria: Abbot Hall Art Gallery, 1998. Conversation with Isabel Carlisle

Bridget Riley: Selected Paintings 1961–1999, Ostfildern: Hatje Cantz, in association with Kunstverein für die Rheinlande und Westfalen, Düsseldorf, 1999. Texts by Michael Krajewski, Robert Kudielka and Raimund Stecker. German translation of the artist's conversations with Ernst H. Gombrich and Michael Craig-Martin from *Bridget Riley: Dialogues on Art*

Bridget Riley: Paintings from the 1960s and 70s, London: Serpentine Gallery, 1999. Texts by Lisa Corrin, Robert Kudielka and Frances Spalding

Bridget Riley: New Paintings and Gouaches, London: Waddington Galleries, in association with Karsten Schubert, 2000. Text by Lynn MacRitchie

Bridget Riley: Reconnaissance, New York: Dia Center for the Arts, 2000. Texts by Lynne Cooke and John Elderfield

Bridget Riley: Paintings 1982–2000 and Early Works on Paper, New York: PaceWildenstein, 2000. Text by Dave Hickey

Beau Monde: Toward a Redeemed Cosmopolitanism, Site Santa Fe, 2002. Curated by Dave Hickey. Texts by Louis Grachos and Dave Hickey
Bridget Riley. New Work, Stuttgart: Hatje Cantz, 2002. Texts by Martin Hentschel and Lynn MacRitchie
Bridget Riley: Complete Prints 1962–2001, London: Ridinghouse, 2002. Catalogue raisonné by Karsten Schubert. Texts by Craig Hartley and Lynn MacRitchie
Blast to Freeze: British Art in the 20th Century, ed. Henry Meyric Hughes and Gijs van Tuyl, Ostfildern: Hatje Cantz, in association with Kunstmuseum Wolfsburg, 2002
Bridget Riley, Basel: Galerie Beyeler, 2003. Conversation with Isabel Carlisle (English and German edition)
Bridget Riley, London: Tate Publishing, 2003. Texts by Paul Moorhouse, Richard Shiff and Robert Kudielka
Bridget Riley: Recent Paintings, PaceWildenstein, New York, 2004. Text by Richard Shiff.
Frances Follin: *Embodied Visions. Bridget Riley, Op Art and the Sixties*, London: Thames & Hudson, 2004
Bridget Riley: Paintings and Drawings 1961–2004, Museum of Contemporary Art, Sidney; City Gallery Wellington, London: Ridinghouse, 2004. Texts by Paul Moorhouse and Lynne Cooke, interview with Jenny Harper.
Modern Painting and Sculpture – 1880 to the Present – at the Museum of Modern Art, ed. by John Elderfield, New York: Museum of Modern Art, 2004
Bridget Riley: Bilder und Zeichnungen 1959–2005, Argauer Kunsthaus Aarau. Kunsthaus Aarau 2005. Texts by Lynne Cooke, Paul Moorhouse, Richard Shiff and Beat Wismer, interview with Jenny Harper (German–English)

Articles and Reviews

Michael Shepherd, 'Bridget Riley', *Arts Review*, vol. 14, no. 8, 5–19 May 1962, p. 19
David Sylvester, 'Bridget Riley', *New Statesman*, 25 May 1962
Norbert Lynton, 'London Letter, Bridget Riley', *Art International*, Lugano, vol. 6, no. 7, September 1962, p. 47
Edward Lucie-Smith, 'Round the Galleries, Assemblages', *Listener*, 7 February 1963, p. 254
Jasia Reichardt, 'Bridget Riley', *Architectural Design*, vol. 8, no. 354, August 1963
Norbert Lynton, 'London Letter, Riley', *Art International*, Lugano, vol. 7, no. 8, October 1963, p. 84
John Russell, 'Art News from London, Riley', *Artnews*, vol. 62, no. 7, November 1963, p. 47
'Bridget Riley', *Time Magazine*, 1 May 1964 (Atlantic Edition), p. 75
Robert Melville, 'The New Generation', *Architectural Review*, vol. 135, no. 808, June 1964, pp. 447–9
Ion Borgzinner, 'Op Art. Pictures that attack the Eye', *Time Magazine*, 23 October 1964, pp. 78–86
'Op Art', *Life Magazine*, 11 December 1964 (only illustrations)
'Op Art', *Life International*, 28 December 1964 (Warren R.Young, 'Bringing Chaos out of Order', pp. 60–2).
Anton Ehrenzweig, 'The Pictorial Space of Bridget Riley', *Art International*, Lugano, vol. 9, no. 1, February 1965, pp. 20–4
John Canaday, 'The Responsive Eye. Three Cheers and High Hopes', *New York Times*, 28 February 1965
John Canaday, 'That's Right It's Wrong', *New York Times*, 14 March 1965
Thomas B. Hess, 'You can hang it in the hall', *Artnews*, vol. 64, no. 2, April 1965, pp. 41–3
Anne Ryan, 'Top Op Artist', *Women's Wear Daily*, 11 May 1965
Rosalind Krauss, 'Afterthoughts on "Op"', *Art International*, Lugano, vol. 9, no. 5, June 1965, pp. 75–6
Elwyn Lynn, 'Op', *Vogue Australia*, vol. 9, no. 6, 1965, pp. 78–9
Prudence Fay, 'Op-position', *Queen*, 5 January 1966
Rosalind Krauss, 'Exhibition at Feigen Gallery, New York', *Artforum*, vol. 4, no. 10, June 1966, pp. 51–2

Gene Baro, 'Bridget Riley: Drawing for Painting', *Studio International*, vol. 172, no. 879, July 1966, pp. 12–13
Jack W. Burnham, 'The Art of Bridget Riley', *Triquarterly* 5, Evanston, Illinois, 1966
John Russell, 'Double Portrait: Bridget Riley and Phillip King', *Art in America*, vol. 55, no. 3, May–June 1967, pp. 98–102
Anthony Tucker, 'Something in Common', *Shell Magazine*, June 1967
Michel Claura, 'La Jeune peinture en Grande-Bretagne', *Lettres Françaises*, 17 January 1968
Norbert Lynton, 'The British Representation at the 34th Venice Biennale', *Art International*, Lugano, vol. 12, no. 6, Summer 1968, pp. 74–5
David Thompson, 'British Artists at Venice I: The Paintings of Bridget Riley', *Studio International*, vol. 175, no. 901, June 1968, pp. 295–9
John Russell, 'Venice is a Battlefield: Art the Loser', *The Sunday Times*, 23 June 1968
Edward Lucie-Smith, 'Bridget Riley's Venice Success', *The Times*, 29 October 1968
Gene Baro, 'Bridget Riley's Nineteen Greys', *Studio International*, vol. 176, no. 906, December 1968, pp. 280–1
David Thompson, 'Bridget Riley and Her Safe Roller Coaster', *New York Times*, 29 December 1968
Maurice de Sausmarez, 'Bridget Riley: working drawings', *Art and Artists*, vol. 4, no. 2, May 1969, p. 29
Pat Gilmour, 'Bridget Riley', *Arts Review*, vol. 21, no. 14, 19 July 1969, p. 465
Edwin Mullins, 'Riley in Colour', *Sunday Telegraph*, 20 July 1969
Ian Dunlop, 'Colour and Size make Riley's Art Different', *Evening Standard*, 21 July 1969
Guy Brett, 'Optical Energy Subtly Used', *The Times*, 25 July 1969
Norbert Lynton, 'Bridget Riley Turns to Colour', *Guardian*, 29 July 1969
Robert Hughes, 'Perilous Equilibrium', *Time Magazine*, 16 November 1970, p. 82
Peter Winter, 'Der fluktuierende Raum. Bridget Rileys grosse Retrospektive in Hannover', *Frankfurter Allgemeine Zeitung*, 7 December 1970
Robert Kudielka, 'Bridget Riley', *Das Kunstwerk*, vol. 24, no. 2, March 1971, pp. 114–15
Andrew Forge, 'On looking at paintings by Bridget Riley', *Art International*, Lugano, vol. 15, no. 3, March 1971, pp. 16–21
Helga Meister, 'Ein Fest der Farben. Die englische Op-Künstlerin Bridget Riley in Düsseldorf', *Düsseldorfer Nachrichten*, 13 March 1971
Yvonne Friedrichs, 'Die visuelle Zeit. Bridget Riley in der Düsseldorfer Kunsthalle – Vitalität in geometrischen Rastern', *Rheinische Post*, 15 March 1971
Günter Pfeiffer, 'Farbe vibriert wie gezupfte Saiten. Die Op-Art stammt vom Impressionismus ab: Zur grossen Retrospektive der englischen Malerin Bridget Riley in Düsseldorf', *Kölner Stadtanzeiger*, 6 April 1971
Luigi Carluccio, 'Con Bridget Riley arriva la magia dell'arte "op"', *Gazetta del Popolo*, Turin, 27 May 1971
Hilary Spurling, 'Bridget Riley's Colour Explosion', *The Times*, 21 July 1971
Robert Melville, 'An Art Without Accidents', *New Statesman*, 23 July 1971, p. 121
Nigel Gosling, 'Fearless on the Frontier', *Observer*, 25 July 1971
John Russell, 'Riley's Line', *The Sunday Times*, 25 July 1971
Peter Fuller, 'Bridget Riley', *Arts Review*, vol. 23, no. 15, 31 July 1971, p. 459
David Thompson, 'Bridget Riley', *Studio International*, vol. 182, no. 935, July–August 1971, pp. 16–21.
Michael Shepherd, 'Writing on Riley', *Sunday Telegraph*, 1 August 1971
Richard Cork, 'What has happened to this Woman's Eye-Bullying Art', *Evening Standard*, 5 August 1971
Pierre Rouve, 'Bridget Riley Drawings', *Arts Review*, vol. 24, no. 12, 17 June 1972, p. 356
Daniel Marchesseau, 'La Révélation de Bridget Riley', *Les Gullivériens*, March 1973
Bryan Robertson, 'Colour as Image', *Art in America*, vol. 63, no. 2, March–April 1975, pp. 69–71
Tom Wolfe, 'The Painted Word', *Harpers Magazine*, April 1975
Robert Hughes, 'Making waves', *Time Magazine*, 12 May 1975, pp. 52–3
Roberta Smith, 'Reviews (Bridget Riley exhibition at Sidney Janis)', *Artforum*, vol. 14, no. 1, September 1975, p. 71

John Spurling, 'Mind's Eye', *New Statesman*, 16 July 1976
Itsuo Sakane, 'Op Art', *Asahi Shimbun*, 25 July 1976
Sandra McGrath, 'Art', *The Australian*, 23 November 1976
Elwyn Lynn, 'Henry Moore, Francis Bacon and Bridget Riley', *Art in Australia*, vol. 14, nos. 3–4, January–April 1977, pp. 302–7
John Russell , 'Bridget Riley's show in Buffalo', *The Times*, 15 November 1978
'Bridget Riley', interview by John Gruen (1978), reprinted in John Gruen, *The Artist Observed. 28 Interviews with Contemporary Artists*, Chicago: capella books and Chicago Review Press, 1991, pp. 150–9
John Russell, 'The Cogency of Riley', *New York Times*, 28 January 1979
Lois Hunter, 'Imitation does not flatter', POL, Australia, September 1979
Barbara Thoren, 'The Week in Art: Bridget Riley', *Japan Times*, 6 February 1980
Robert Hughes, 'The Shock of the New VIII: The Age of the New has entered history', *Listener*, 13 November 1980
Edward Lucie Smith, 'The World of Bridget Riley', *Illustrated London News*, June 1981
John Russell Taylor, 'Consistent organic growth from optical illusion', *The Times*, 16 June 1981
Stephen Gardiner, 'An electric array of stripes', *Observer*, 17 July 1983
Roger Berthoud, 'Shining visions of an abstract future', *The Times*, 31 August 1983
David Dougill, 'Dancing down Riley's rainbow', *The Sunday Times*, 4 September 1983
William Packer, 'Putting across the message', *Financial Times*, 6 March 1984
Hans Peter Riese, 'Bridget Riley', *Die Zeit*, Hamburg, 30 November 1984
Carlo McCormick, 'poptometry, *Artforum*, vol. 24, no. 3, November 1985, pp. 87–91
John Russell, 'Bridget Riley', *New York Times*, 10 October 1986
Calvin Tomkins, 'Between Neo- and Post-', *New Yorker*, 24 November 1986
Karina Türr, 'Jenseits von Op Art? Überlegungen zu den Farbstreifen Bridget Rileys', *Pantheon, International Annual Art Journal*, vol. 44, 1986, pp. 157–63
Ludmilla Vachtova, 'Ruhe in feinster Bewegung', *Tages-Anzeiger*, Zürich, 30 January 1987
Larry Berryman, 'Bridget Riley', *Arts Review*, vol. 39, no. 13, 3 July 1987, p. 456
'Op Art. Special Feature on Bridget Riley', *art & man* (Scholastic under the direction of the National Gallery of Art, Washington DC), vol. 18, no. 5, March 1988
Andrew Graham-Dixon, 'Between the lines', *Independent*, 13 May 1989
Larry Berryman, 'Bridget Riley: Works on Paper 1978–1980 (Mayor Rowan Gallery) and The Artist's Eye (National Gallery)', *Arts Review*, vol. 41, no. 15, July 1989, pp. 572–3
Laurence Marks, 'The Life of Riley', *Observer* magazine, 2 July 1989
Richard Dorment, 'The colour of greatness', *Daily Telegraph*, 7 July 1989
Brian Sewell, 'Eye for Figures', *Evening Standard*, 20 July 1989
William Packer, 'Form passive, colour active', *Financial Times*, 25 July 1989
John Cunningham, 'A new optical nerve', *Guardian*, 28 July 1989
Peter Fuller, 'Hysteria as a hole in the head', *Sunday Telegraph*, 6 May 1990
Terry R. Myers, 'Bridget Riley at Sidney Janis', *Art in America*, vol. 78, no. 9, September 1990, pp. 199–200
Frank Whitford, 'Still groovy after all these years', *The Sunday Times*, 26 January 1992
Hans Pietsch, 'Meine Bilder sollen in sich selber ruhen', ART, Hamburg, April 1992
Walter Fenn, 'Die Tektonik farbiger Rauten', *Nürnberger Nachrichten*, 8 April 1992
Thomas Kliemann, 'Nürnberg: Bridget Riley mit Bildern von 1982–1992 in der Kunsthalle', *Das Kunst-Bulletin*, nos. 7–8, July–August 1992, pp. 53–4
John Whitley, 'The Art of Riley', *Sunday Telegraph* magazine, 22 August 1992
Andrew Graham-Dixon, 'Earning her stripes', *Independent*, 8 September 1992
Tim Hilton, 'Strokes of originality', *Guardian*, 17 September 1992
Louisa Buck, 'Orderly passion along colour lines', *The Sunday Times*, 20 September 1992
Richard Cork, 'Colour lights up the life of Riley', *The Times*, 29 September 1992

William Packer, 'Op Art thirty years on', *Financial Times*, 29 September 1992
Brian Sewell, 'A new slant on diagonal landscapes', *Evening Standard*, 8 October 1992
Larry Berryman, 'Bridget Riley (According to Sensation)', *Arts Review*, vol. 44, October 1992, pp. 480–1
Frances Spalding, 'London, Hayward Gallery: Bridget Riley – Paintings 1982–1992', *Burlington Magazine*, vol. 134, no. 1076, November 1992, p. 939
Tim Hilton, 'New pattern to the ever-changing life of Riley', *Independent on Sunday*, 27 December 1992
Judith Bumpus, 'Bridget Riley', *Contemporary Art*, vol. 1, no. 2, Winter 1992–3, pp. 33–6
Bryan Robertson, 'Bridget Riley: Work in Progress', *Modern Painters*, vol. 5, no. 3, Autumn 1992, pp. 32–3
Richard Cork, 'High hopes between the hard edges', *The Times*, 12 March 1993
Tim Hilton, 'That was the decade that wasn't', *Independent on Sunday*, 14 March 1993
Charles Harrison, 'Gossip monumentalised', *The Times Literary Supplement*, 30 April 1993
Ginny Dougary, 'Between the lines', *The Times*, 5 March 1994
Michael Bracewell, 'Psychedelic symmetries', *Observer*, 11 September 1994
Margaret Garlake, 'Bridget Riley (Tate Gallery, August 20 to October 9)', *Art Monthly*, vol. 28, no. 181, November 1994, pp. 28–9
Richard Cork, 'Regiments of colour in close combat', *The Times*, 6 February 1996
Clare Henry, 'Dizzy spells and good vibrations', *Glasgow Herald*, 17 June 1996
Michael Bracewell, 'A plea for painting', *Guardian Weekend Magazine*, 15 March 1997
Gwen McGarthy, 'Reclaiming the final word on her work', *Irish Times*, 7 May 1997
Hans-Peter von Däniken, 'Das Geheimnis des weissen Flimmerns', *Tages-Anzeiger*, Zürich, 28 May 1998
Laura Cumming, 'Riley, ace of stripes', *Observer*, 15 November 1998
Andrew Hickling, 'The life of Riley', *Guardian*, 17 November 1998
Tom Lubbock, 'Here's one in your eye', *Independent*, 17 November 1998
Lynn MacRitchie, 'Intimate display of dazzling talent', *Financial Times*, 28 November 1998
Marin Gayford, 'Puzzled by the life of Riley', *Daily Telegraph*, 23 December 1998
Stuart Wavell, 'An old master on the real artists (E.H. Gombrich at 90)', *The Sunday Times*, 4 April 1999
Richard Cork, 'Her brilliant career', *The Times magazine*, 12 June 1999
Adrian Searle, 'Eyes wide open', *Guardian*, 22 June 1999
Richard Dorment, 'It all depends on how you look at it', *Daily Telegraph*, 23 June 1999
Richard Cork, 'Dazzled by the life of Riley', *The Times*, 23 June 1999
Waldemar Januszczak, 'Is there more than meets the eye?', *The Sunday Times*, 27 June 1999
Brian Sewell, 'A persistent case of stripes before the eyes', *Evening Standard*, 1 July 1999
Andrew Lambirth, 'Optical dazzle', *Spectator*, 10 July 1999
Simon Morley, 'London: Bridget Riley', *Burlington Magazine*, vol. 141, no. 1158, September 1999, pp. 561–3
Hans-Peter von Däniken, 'Ein Erdbeben im Wahrnehmungskanal', *Tages-Anzeiger*, Zürich, 6 September 1999
John Spurling, 'In My Own Way: The paintings and writings of Bridget Riley', *Modern Painters*, vol. 12, no. 3, Autumn 1999, pp. 34–8
Georg Imdahl, 'Wille zur Welle', *Frankfurter Allgemeine Zeitung*, 8 December 1999
Michael Kimmelman, 'Modern Op', *New York Times magazine*, 27 August 2000
William Feaver, 'Dangerous Curves', *Artnews*, vol. 99, no. 8, September 2000, pp. 116–18
Michael Kimmelman, 'Not so square after all', *Guardian*, 28 September 2000
Roberta Smith, 'Saluting a Pure Form of Abstraction, Long May It Wave', *New York Times*, 29 September 2000
Alex Coles, 'Bridget Riley at Waddington', *Art in America*, vol. 88, no. 10, October 2000, p. 179
Lynn MacRitchie, 'Bridget Riley', *Elle Decor*, October 2000
Peter Schjeldahl, 'British Flash', *New Yorker*, 6 November 2000
Christopher Knight, 'Seeing the Top of the Op Artists', *Los Angeles Times*, 25 November 2000
Patrick Bahners, 'Sie ist die wahre Erbin Elstirs', *Frankfurter Allgemeine Zeitung*, 21 April 2001

Carol Kino, 'Bridget Riley: The Pleasure of Pure Seeing', *Art in America*, vol. 89, no. 4, April 2001, pp. 112–19
Christiane Fricke, 'Das Auge tanzt quer und gerade', *Süddeutsche Zeitung*, Krefeld, 8 April 2002
Michael Kohler, 'Die Intuition der Farbe', *Frankfurter Rundschau*, 11 April 2002
Janneke Wesseling, 'Gestuwd door de wind', *NRC Handelsblad*, 26 April 2002
Martin Gayford, 'Ripple effect', *Telegraph Magazine*, 31 May 2003, pp. 38–42
Lynne MacRitchie, 'Artist still living the life of Riley', *Financial Times*, 23 June 2003, p.15
Adrian Searle, 'Do not adjust you eyes', *Guardian*, 24 June 2003, pp. 12–14
Tom Lubbock, 'In the eye of the storm', *Independent*, 25 June 2003, p.14–15
Brian Sewell, 'Grand dame of jabberwocky', *Evening Standard*, 27 June 2003, p. 32–33
Richard Cork, 'The talented Ms Riley', *The Times*, 25 June 2003, p. 15.
Waldemar Januszczak, 'Behind Bridget Riley's rigid geometry...', *The Sunday Times Culture*, 29 June 2003, pp. 14–15
Laura Cumming, 'Enigmatic variations', *Observer*, 29 June 2003, p. 10
Richard Dorment, 'The dizzy heights', *Daily Telegraph*, 2 July 2003
Richard Cork, 'Moving with the Times", *Arts Review*, July 2003, pp. 58–61
William Packer, 'Artist has earned her stripes', *Financial Times*, 2 July 2003
Marion Löhndorf, 'Methode und Effekt', *Die Tageszeitung*, 29 July 2003, p. 12
Michael Carlson, 'Moved by a circular argument, *The Times Literary Supplement*, 15 August 2003
Lynne Cooke, 'Bridget Riley', *Burlington Magazine*, September 2003, pp. 659–660
Patrick Bahners, 'Hier stehe ich, ich darf jetzt anders', *Frankfurter Allgemeine Zeitung*, 5 September 2003, p. 33
Ken Johnson, 'Art in Review: Bridget Riley', *New York Times*, 15 October 2004
Peter Hill, 'The eyes have it', *The Sydney Morning Herald*, 1–2 January 2005
Sebastian Smee, 'Bridget Riley melds the retinal with the conceptual', *The Weekend Australian*, 1–2 January 2005
Peter Hill, 'An artist of a different stripe: the life of Riley and the nature of her abstraction', *The Age*, 1 March 2005

Illustrations

in chronological order

Paintings

Copy after Le Pont de Courbevoie by Georges Seurat 1959
Oil on canvas
28 × 36 in
71.1 × 91.1 cm
Private collection
page 10

Pink Landscape 1960
Oil on canvas
40 × 40 in
101.5 × 101.5 cm
Private collection
page 154

Hidden Squares 1961
Tempera on hardboard
36 × 36 in
91.4 × 91.4 cm
Private collection
page 153

Kiss 1961
Acrylic on linen
48 × 48 in
122 × 122 cm
Private collection
page 168

Movement in Squares 1961
Tempera on board
48½ in × 47¾ in
123.2 × 121.3 cm
Arts Council Collection,
Hayward Gallery, London
page 102

Blaze 1 1962
Emulsion on board
43 × 43 in
109 × 109 cm
Private collection
page 38

Fall 1963
Emulsion on board
55½ × 55¼ in
141 × 140.5 cm
Tate. Purchased 1963
page 107

Burn 1964
Emulsion on board
22 × 22 in
56 × 56 cm
Private collection
page 179

Current 1964
Emulsion on hardboard
58⅜ × 58⅞ in
148.1 × 149.1 cm
The Museum of Modern Art,
New York, Philip Johnson Fund, 1964
page 170

Pause 1964
Emulsion on hardboard
44 × 42 in
112.2 × 106.6 cm
Private collection
page 177

Shiver 1964
Emulsion on board
27⅛ × 27⅛ in
69 × 69 cm
Private collection
page 43

Turn 1964
Emulsion on hardboard
19½ × 19½ in
50 × 50 cm
Private collection
page 110

White Discs 2 1964
Emulsion on board
41 × 39 in
104 × 99 cm
Private collection
page 183

Arrest 2 1965
Acrylic on linen
76⅝ × 75 in
194 × 191 cm
Nelson-Atkins Museum of Art,
Kansas City, Missouri.
(Purchase: acquired through the
generosity of the William T Kemper
Foundation – Commerce Bank,
Trustee) 2001
page 200

Descending 1965
Emulsion on board
36 × 36 in
91.5 cm × 91.5 cm
Private collection
page 18

Breathe 1966
Emulsion on canvas
117 × 82 in
297 × 208 cm
Museum Boijmans Van Beuningen,
Rotterdam
page 184

Cataract 3 1967
PVA on canvas
87 × 87¾ in
221 × 222.9 cm
British Council Collection
page 66

Chant 2 1967
Emulsion on canvas
91 × 90 in
231.1 × 228.6 cm
Hoh Collection, Fürth
page 115

Deny 2 1967
PVA on canvas
85½ × 85½ in
217.2 × 217.2 cm
Tate. Purchased 1976
page 69

Late Morning 1967-8
PVA emulsion on canvas
88⅞ × 141⅝ in
226.1 × 359.4 cm
Tate. Purchased 1968
page 50

Byzantium 1969
Acrylic on canvas
65 × 146 in
165 × 371 cm
Westfalen AG
pages 33, 34

Orient 4 1970
Acrylic on canvas
88 × 127 in
223.5 × 322.6 cm
Berardo Collection, Sintra Museum
of Modern Art, Lisbon
pages 189, 190–191

Zing 1 1971
Acrylic on canvas
40 × 35 in
100.6 × 88.9 cm
Private collection
page 109

Entice 2 1974
Acrylic on linen
60¾ × 54⅛ in
154.3 × 137.5 cm
Camille Oliver-Hoffmann, Chicago
page 195

Aurulum 1978
Acrylic on linen
52 × 48 in
132.1 × 121.9 cm
Private collection
page 116

Song of Orpheus 5 1978
Acrylic on linen
77 × 102¼ in
195.6 × 259.7 cm
Museum of Fine Arts, Boston. Museum purchase with funds donated by the Catherine and Paul Buttenweiser Fund, Mr and Mrs Martin M Hale, gift of the Linde Family Foundation, and Eloise and Arthur Hodges
pages 55, 56–57

Andante 1 1980
Acrylic on linen
72 × 66½ in
182.8 × 169 cm
Private collection
page 77

To a Summer's Day 2 1980
Acrylic on linen
45⅝ × 110⅝ in
115.5 × 281 cm
Tate. Purchased 1982
page 16

Après Midi 1981
Oil on linen
91 × 77¾ in
231 × 197.5 cm
Private collection
pages 83, 84–85

Luxor 1982
Oil on canvas
87¾ × 77½ in
223 × 197 cm
Kelvingrove Art Gallery and Museum, Glasgow
page 119

Cherry Autumn 1983
Oil on linen
85½ × 71⅞ in
216.6 × 120.6 cm
Birmingham Museums & Art Gallery
page 159

Saraband 1985
Oil on linen
65½ × 53¾ in
166.5 × 136.5 cm
Private collection
page 120

Bloom 1987
Oil on canvas
64⅞ × 62¾ in
165 × 160 cm
Private collection
page 90

Justinian 1988
Oil on linen
65 × 89 in
165 × 226 cm
Private collection
page 123

Gaillard 1989
Oil on linen
65 × 89 in
165 × 226 cm
Private collection
page 112

Cool Place 1990
Oil on linen
65 × 89⅝ in
165 × 227.6 cm
Private collection
page 124

Close By 1992
Oil on linen
65¼ × 89⅞ in
165 × 227.5 cm
Private collection
pages 96, 98–99

High Sky 2 1992
Oil on linen
65 × 89¾ in
165 × 228 cm
Neues Museum, Nürnberg.
Gift of Dr Karl Gerhard Schmidt to the Museumsinitiative e.V.1992
page 146

Reflection 1 1994
Oil on linen
65 × 89⅞ in
165 × 228.3 cm
Private collection, Germany
page 162

Lagoon 1 1997
Oil on linen
58 × 76 in
147 × 193 cm
Private collection
page 203

Composition with Circles 1 1998
Graphite, acrylic paint and permanent marker on plaster wall
204 × 366 in
500 × 900 cm
Installation at Kunsthalle Bern
page 205

Rêve 1999
Oil on linen
89⅞ × 93¾ in
228.3 × 238.1 cm
Private collection
page 210

Two Reds 2000
Oil on linen
51 × 120 in
129.5 × 305.5 cm
Private collection
Courtesy PaceWildenstein, New York
page 227

Paired Colours 2001
Oil on linen
39 × 119⅝ in
99 × 304 cm
Private collection
page 218

Parade 2 2002
Oil on linen, two panels
89¼ × 207⅝ in
226.7 × 527.4 cm
Private collection
page 207

Evoë 3 2003
Oil on linen, two panels
76⅛ × 228⅛ in
193.4 × 579.8 cm
Tate. Presented by Tate Members 2003
page 207

Enchant 2004
Oil on linen
179⅜ × 76¾ in
456.5 × 194 cm
Dia Art Foundation, New York; Gift of Louise and Leonard Riggio
pages 231, 234–235

Painting with Two Verticals 2004
Oil on linen
75¾ × 103 in
192.4 × 261.6 cm
Collection James M. Allwin. Promised gift to the Dia Art Foundation, New York. Courtesy Dia Art Foundation
Page 228

Works on Paper

Tonal Landscape Study 1959
Pastel on paper
15½ × 16 in
39.4 × 40.7 cm
Private collection, Germany
page 8

Study for Broken Circle 1963
Ink, pencil, collage on paper
23½ × 21½ in
57.7 × 54.6 cm
Private collection
page 174

Untitled study related to Disturbance 1964
Pencil and gouache on graph paper
9½ × 15½ in
24.1 cm × 39.4 cm
Private collectior
page 21

Angle movement for Deny 4 and Static 3 1966
Pencil on tracing paper
13½ × 19¾ in
34.4 × 50.3 cm
Private collection
page 186

Study for Late Morning 1967
Gouache on paper
40 × 40 in
101.6 × 101.6 cm
Private collection
page 52

Firebird 1971
Screenprint on paper
30¼ × 40¼ in (sheet)
76.4 × 101.8 cm (sheet)
Edition of 45
Printed by Kelpra Studio, London
Donated to the Hayward Gallery, London
page 24

Study '72: Three Colours in Different Orders with Black 1972
Gouache on paper
18 × 28¾ in
45.7 × 73.2 cm
Private collection
page 71

Six colour studies for Pæan 1973
Gouache on paper
each 12 × 18½ in
30.5 × 47 cm
Private collection
page 73

Untitled (Rothko Portfolio) 1973
Screenprint on paper
Edition of 75
28 × 36 in (sheet)
71.1 × 91.5 cm (sheet)
Printed by Kelpra Studio, London
front cover, top

1st Cartoon for one of *Ka* Series 1980
Gouache on paper
29¾ × 26¾ in
75.6 × 68 cm
Collection of the artist
page 80

Study for painting, Four colours: black & white Colour cancellation = visual grey. Interrupted by blue'd passages 1981
Gouache on paper
34 × 25½ in
86.4 × 64.8 cm
Private collection
page 88

Rough study. July 2nd 1991
Gouache and pencil on paper
26⅝ × 35½ in
68.5 × 91.3 cm
Private collection
page 94

Rough study. July 4th 1991
Gouache and pencil on paper
26 × 35⅝ in
66.6 × 91.5 cm
Private collection
page 95

Final study for Curvilinear Grid 1998
Pencil on graph paper
28¼ × 17½ in
71.8 × 44.4 cm
Private collection
page 215

Collage studies for painting (in four stages) 2004
Gouache and collage on paper
11 × 33 in
27.5 × 82.5 cm
Collection of the artist
pages 222–223

Works by Other Artists

Claude Monet
The Magpie (*La Pie*) 1868–69
Oil on canvas
35 × 51⅛ in
89 × 130 cm
Musée d'Orsay, Paris
page 14

Piet Mondrian
Broadway Boogie Woogie 1942–43
Oil on canvas
50 × 50 in
127 × 127 cm
© 2005 Mondrian / Holtzman Trust
c/o HCR International, Warrenton,
VA, USA
page 93

Jackson Pollock
Autumn Rhythm 1950
Enamel on canvas
105 × 207 in
266.7 × 525.8 cm
The Metropolitan Museum of Art,
George A. Hearn Fund, 1957 (57.92)
page 100